Tony,

With best regards,

Dvd Mul

Portfolio Design

Founded in 1807, John Wiley & Sons is the oldest independent publishing company in the United States. With offices in North America, Europe, Australia, and Asia, Wiley is globally committed to developing and marketing print and electronic products and services for our customers' professional and personal knowledge and understanding.

The Wiley Finance series contains books written specifically for finance and investment professionals as well as sophisticated individual investors and their financial advisors. Book topics range from portfolio management to e-commerce, risk management, financial engineering, valuation, and financial instrument analysis, as well as much more.

For a list of available titles, visit our Web site at www.WileyFinance.com.

Portfolio Design

*A Modern Approach to
Asset Allocation*

RICHARD C. MARSTON

WILEY

John Wiley & Sons, Inc.

Published by John Wiley & Sons, Inc., Hoboken, New Jersey.
Published simultaneously in Canada.

Library of Congress Cataloging-in-Publication Data:

Marston, Richard C.
    Portfolio design : a modern approach to asset allocation / Richard C. Marston.
        p. cm. – (Wiley finance ; 641)
    Includes index.
    ISBN 978-0-470-93123-3 (hardback); ISBN 978-111-8-00705-1 (ebk);
    ISBN 978-111-8-00703-7 (ebk); ISBN 978-111-8-007044 (ebk)
    1. Asset allocation.   2. Portfolio management.   I. Title.
    HG4529.5.M374 2011
    332.6–dc22

                                                           2010051229

Printed in the United States of America

10 9 8 7 6 5 4 3

To Jerrilyn Greene Marston

Contents

Preface

I t is my belief that portfolio design—choosing the right mix of assets appropriate to a particular investor—is the key to successful investing. Choosing managers for individual asset classes is certainly important, but it's care in designing the asset allocation that can make or break a portfolio. Such care cannot protect an investor from losses in an economic downturn, but it can cushion the blow. Careful portfolio design will never make an investor rich, but it will help that investor accumulate wealth systematically.

It's possible to grow wealth much faster by investing in individual assets. After all, that's how family fortunes are made. Entrepreneurs bet everything on a single idea and, in at least a fraction of cases, the entrepreneur becomes wealthy enough to worry about how to invest that wealth more broadly. But most investors are not trying to make fortunes from their investments. They are trying to generate higher wealth, no doubt, but they are also trying to keep risks under control. That's true whether the investor is a foundation trying to carry out its mission or a family trying to accumulate enough wealth for retirement.

Since the early 1970s when pension law became better established under ERISA, investment advisors have become more sophisticated about their approaches to investing. Gone are the days when most advisors did their own stock selection. Investment managers are hired to do that. Advisors today worry about how to balance risk against return for the portfolio as a whole and they use sophisticated measures of performance to track portfolios. In the 1970s and 1980s, advisors who catered to institutional investors led changes in the industry, but more recently advisors to high net worth investors have applied the same methods to managing the portfolios of private clients. As a result, investors can find a variety of highly qualified investment advisors who can design portfolios that reflect all of the advances in investment theory and practice over the last 40 years.

Twenty years ago, I began teaching asset allocation in a program at the Wharton School established to train financial advisors in modern portfolio management. The program was established jointly by Wharton and the Investment Management Consulting Association (IMCA). Upon successful completion of this program, financial advisors are given the Certified

Investment Management Analyst (CIMA) designation. Today, there are more than 6,000 CIMAs in the United States and abroad, including many of the leading financial advisors at investment firms in this country. I had the privilege of training many of these advisors.

This book is based on the sessions that I developed for the CIMA program. The book is designed for investment advisors who want to provide diversified portfolios for their clients, whether they are high net worth private clients or institutional investors. The book examines all of the major asset classes that go into modern portfolios and asks how much they add to portfolio diversification.

Besides my participation in the CIMA program, I have taught in many other investment programs at the Wharton School. I have also given investment presentations on behalf of banks, brokerage firms, and insurance companies in more than a dozen countries as well as in conferences and meetings throughout this country.

My experience in asset allocation includes not only teaching the subject to professionals, but also designing portfolios for investors. For 10 years, I was a member of the asset allocation committee of one of the leading brokerage firms. We met monthly to discuss how to design portfolios for different types of clients. Today I advise a committee that has the fiduciary responsibility over portfolio design for a large number of clients, both institutions and individuals.

For the last dozen years, I have been academic director of a unique program at Wharton for ultra-high net worth investors, the Private Wealth Management Program. In this program, which Charlotte Beyer of the Institute for Private Investors and I founded in 1999, the investors themselves come to Wharton for a week to learn about how to invest their wealth. As of 2010, almost 600 ultra-high net worth investors have taken part in this program. This program has given me perspective from the investor's side of the advisor-investor relationship. I have also had extensive experience as an advisor to the family offices of ultra-high net worth investors and as a consultant to pension funds and endowments.

What I have learned is that investing isn't easy. But as shown in this book, thoughtful asset allocation provides discipline to the investment process and gives the best chance of building and safeguarding wealth. The purpose of this book then is to help guide the investment advisor through all of the major decisions in designing a portfolio.

RICHARD MARSTON
Philadelphia
May 2010

Acknowledgments

This book has been in the making since I started teaching asset allocation in the CIMA program at Wharton more than 20 years ago. More than 6,000 advisors have been through the program including many of the top institutional and high net worth consultants at the leading brokerage firms. I have had the privilege of teaching most of them, along with my colleagues in the program, Jeffrey Jaffe and Craig MacKinlay.

I want to thank the many financial advisors that I have met through the years, both in the CIMA program and in other programs at Wharton and throughout the country. Their insights have helped me to shape many of the ideas in this book about investing. A thoughtful advisor can make so much difference to the financial well-being of a family or institution. I like to think that the CIMA program has contributed to the increasing professionalism of the investment advisory business in this country.

I would like to thank two of my colleagues, Richard Herring of Wharton and Gordon Bodnar of SAIS at Johns Hopkins, for providing me with helpful comments on this book as well as on the teaching materials I use in the CIMA program. Other colleagues have been particularly helpful with specific topics in the book, including Joseph Gyourko on the topic of real estate, Andrew Metrick and Ayako Yasuda on venture capital, and Christopher Geczy on hedge funds.

One of the great pleasures of teaching at the Wharton School is to work with talented research assistants. Wharton students are best described as "scary smart", and I have known some of the best of these. I would like to thank Caroline Baniqued, Mark Klebanov, and Allyson White for their assistance with research on this book. Alex Feldman, then a student at the University of Michigan, also provided excellent research assistance.

The production of this book was immeasurably helped by assistance from Christopher Trollen, the Administrative Coordinator of the Weiss Center. To my two editors at Wiley, William Falloon and Jennifer Mac-Donald, I owe special thanks. Bill Falloon began to encourage me to write this book five years ago. I also want to thank my agent, John Wright, whose wise counsel is much appreciated.

The decision to join Wharton's faculty was one of the most important ones in my career. Its research environment has always been so supportive. What a splendid institution it is.

Finally, I would like to thank my spouse, Jerrilyn Greene Marston, for her lifelong support. There is nothing like having a brilliant wife to inspire you in all of your work, so I am dedicating this book to her.

About the Author

Richard C. Marston is the James R.F. Guy Professor of Finance at the Wharton School of the University of Pennsylvania. He is also Director of the George Weiss Center for International Financial Research at Wharton. He holds a BA from Yale University, a B Phil from Oxford University where he was a Rhodes Scholar, and a PhD from MIT. Marston has written or co-edited four previous books on finance, including his award-winning *International Financial Integration* (Cambridge, 1995).

Marston has taught asset allocation in the CIMA investment management certificate program at Wharton since the program was founded in 1988. He has also given investment presentations throughout this country as well as in more than a dozen countries in Europe, Latin America, and Asia. Since 1999, he has directed the Private Wealth Management Program at Wharton, a program for ultra-high net worth investors. He also serves as an advisor to several family offices and investment companies.

About the Book

This is a book designed to be read by investment advisors. The book is rich in information about individual asset classes, including both traditional assets like stocks and bonds as well as alternative investments such as hedge funds, private equity, real estate, and commodities. So it should appeal to all sophisticated advisors whether or not they are trying to qualify for one of the major investment designations. In fact, the book is designed to be read by any advisor who is as fascinated as I am by the investment process.

Disclaimers

Data from the 2010 SBBI Classic Yearbook is provided by ©2010 Morningstar. All rights reserved. Used with permission. Data is referred to below as ©Morningstar.

Russell Investment Group is the source and owner of the trademarks, service marks, and copyrights related to the Russell Indexes. Russell® is a trademark of Russell Investment Group.

Source of NACUBO data: National Association of College and University Business Officers, NACUBO Endowment Study, Various Years. Referred to as NACUBO.

The Dow Jones-UBS Commodity Indexes^{SM} are a joint product of Dow Jones Indexes, the marketing name of and a licensed trademark of CME Group Index Services LLC ("CME Indexes"), and UBS Securities LLC ("UBS Securities"), and have been licensed for use. "Dow Jones®", "DJ", "Dow Jones Indexes", "UBS" and "Dow Jones-UBS Commodity Index^{SM}" are service marks of Dow Jones Trademark Holdings, LLC ("Dow Jones") and UBS AG ("UBS AG"), as the case may be. All content of the Dow Jones-UBS Commodity Indexes ©CME Group Index Services, LLC and UBS Securities, LLC 2010. Referred to below as Dow Jones-UBS Commodity Indexes ©.

FTSE International Limited ("FTSE") ©FTSE 2010. All rights in the FTSE NAREIT indices vest in FTSE and the National Association of Real Estate Investment Trusts ("NAREIT"). Neither FTSE nor its NAREIT accept any liability for any errors or omissions in the FTSE NAREIT indices. Data is referred to below as ©FTSE.

Copyright ©2008, Credit Suisse/Tremont Index LLC. All rights reserved. This book, Portfolio Design, (the "Work") is provided by Richard C Marston, which takes full responsibility for providing it. Neither Credit Suisse/Tremont Index LLC nor its affiliates, subsidiaries, members, or parents (collectively, "Credit Suisse") have undertaken any review of this Work or any recommendations contained herein, or of the suitability of this information for anyone accessing this Work, and neither the Work nor the information contained in the Work is sponsored, endorsed, or approved by Credit Suisse. The Credit Suisse/Tremont Hedge Fund Index and the corresponding Sub-Indices, the Blue Chip Investable Hedge Fund Index and the corresponding Sub-Indices, the Credit Suisse/Tremont Sector Invest Indices, the Credit Suisse/Tremont AllHedge Index and any information in the Work relating thereto (collectively, the "Information") is made available to you for your own internal use and may not be reproduced or disseminated in any form, nor may it be used to create, offer, or sell any security, financial instrument, or index. The Information is provided "as is" and any use is at your entire risk. Credit Suisse disclaims any and all representations and warranties, whether express, implied, or statutory, regarding the information, including without limitation, any warranty regarding merchantability, fitness for a particular purpose, quality, or non-infringement, and any warranty regarding the accuracy, timeliness, suitability, availability, or completeness of the information, or the results obtained from the use thereof. Under no circumstances and under no theory of law, tort, contract, strict liability, or otherwise, will Credit Suisse have any liability in connection with the information or the use, whether direct or indirect, including special, incidental, consequential, exemplary, or punitive damages, and including, without limitation, any damages based on loss of profits, loss of use, business interruption, or loss of data, even if Credit Suisse has been advised of the possibility of such damages or was negligent. The source of the indexes is hereafter referred to as Credit Suisse/Tremont.

Portfolio
Design

CHAPTER 1

Asset Allocation

An Introduction

Asset allocation has different aims depending on the investor. A younger investor may want to build wealth over time, taking risks that would not be sensible for an older investor. Investors in retirement often want to hunker down to make sure that no unreasonable losses occur. The assets these two investors choose may not differ overall, but the relative weights given to each asset in the portfolio will surely differ a lot. For example, a younger investor will hold a higher proportion of equities than an investor nearing retirement. Institutional investors also differ in their investment strategies. One endowment, perhaps a family foundation, may want to preserve wealth if there are few opportunities to raise more funds in the future. Another endowment, perhaps a university endowment, may follow more aggressive investment policies knowing that there is a steady flow of additional funds from future donors.

This tradeoff between return and risk is central to all asset allocation. It's a genuine tradeoff even though some investors believe they can achieve returns without taking on risk. Asset allocation aims to find ways to make the tradeoff as attractive as possible. One key concept is the correlation between one asset and another. Almost every portfolio has substantial investments in both stocks and bonds because they tend to be low in correlation with one another. Many portfolios include both foreign and domestic assets for the same reason. Similarly, many portfolios include alternative investments such as real estate or commodities because they tend to have relatively low correlations with equities and bonds.

Investors should aim to form portfolios so that if one set of assets suffers low returns in a given period, perhaps another set of assets will provide higher returns. When the economy is booming, for example, equities tend to thrive as do other investments with equity-like characteristics. When the economy turns down, bonds tend to shine. Or perhaps there are equities from other parts of the world that do well.

Since Markowitz's studies in the 1950s, portfolio management has focused on ways to maximize returns for any given level of risk.[1] Investors should try to form portfolios that have the highest returns possible for that level of risk. But it's just as important to minimize risk for a given target return. There may be several types of assets that would provide the target return, but there is usually a portfolio mixture of these assets that will minimize risk.

To develop such portfolios, it's important for investors to have well-formulated estimates of asset returns. And perhaps more important are the estimates of risk and correlation. To obtain these, it's not enough to just take long-run averages of each asset class. It's important to study each type of asset in detail to understand why it has earned those returns and in what circumstances.

To show what this means, consider the two most basic assets, stocks and bonds. Investors need to ask how much equities or bonds can earn in the long run. We can certainly calculate long-run average returns for each asset class. But these long-run averages would be very misleading if inflation has varied over the sample period. If inflation is running over 10 percent per year, should an investor be pleased with a 12 percent return? So long-run estimates of returns should be done in real, not nominal, terms. But what period should we study?

If we were to examine bond returns in the 1980s to present, we would be enamored with bonds. They are terrific assets with high real returns and relatively little risk. In the long run, by which we mean periods stretching back through the post-war period or back to 1926 (when the Ibbotson SBBI dataset begins) or stretching back to the late nineteenth century, real bond returns are much lower.[2] In those longer periods, real bond returns typically average only 2 percent to 2.5 percent per year. Should we base our estimates of future bond returns on the recent past or on longer periods of history? As explained in Chapter 2, the answer is that the last 30 years have seen a one-time capital gain on bonds as inflation has fallen from double-digits to current levels. Basing future estimates of bond returns on the recent past would be foolhardy.

What about stock returns? Again, the time period chosen is important. In Chapter 2, we will show that post-war stock returns are higher than they have been in the long run. And more importantly, stock returns have been inflated by a rise in price-earnings ratios that may not be sustainable in the long run. Asset allocation requires that the investor understand these assets enough to assess how well they will perform in the future.

INGREDIENTS OF ASSET ALLOCATION

Investing has evolved over the last few decades. First, there is the shift away from individual stock selection toward diversification of stock holdings. Instead of choosing the 10 or 20 best stocks for the portfolio, an investment advisor is more likely to make sure the portfolio is properly diversified between different types of stocks. More specifically, the advisor deliberately balances different styles of stocks, choosing both growth and value stocks and large-cap and small-cap stocks. One reason for this shift in the approach to investing is the realization that investment styles go in and out of favor. For several years or more, growth stocks may outperform value stocks and investors become enthusiastic about new technologies (as they did in the early 1970s and late 1990s). But then value stocks thrive, and investors must switch their allegiances. This shift toward style investing was also driven by the discovery that value stocks provide a value premium over growth stocks and that small-capitalization stocks provide a small-cap premium over large-cap stocks. These premiums will be analyzed in detail in Chapters 3 and 4. Chapter 3 will show how small-cap stocks fit into the overall stock market and will present evidence about whether there is a premium for small-caps. Chapter 4 will examine value and growth stocks and present evidence on the value premium.

In the 1980s, investment in foreign equities gained favor. Capital controls had been lifted making it possible for investors in the industrial countries to spread their investments to other industrial countries. In doing so, investors were able to invest in a wider variety of firms and industries than would have been possible by sticking to U.S. stocks alone. And, because correlations between U.S. and foreign stocks were relatively low, investors were able to reduce risks in the overall portfolio. By the 1990s, interest in emerging stock markets also increased. Chapters 5 and 6 will examine these investments and will show how they help to diversify U.S. portfolios.

Fixed income investments have evolved even more than stock investments. Forty years ago, Treasury and corporate bonds were dominant in fixed income portfolios (along with municipals for taxable investors). There were high yield bonds, but those were typically "fallen angels" rather than newly issued bonds. Mortgage-backed bonds didn't exist because securitization of mortgages was just beginning. Today, Treasuries represent less than 16 percent of the U.S. bond market and corporate bonds another 20 percent. Chapter 7 examines this modern fixed income market in detail.

In Chapter 8, all of these traditional assets are combined in what we call a *strategic asset allocation*, a long-run portfolio allocation based on long-run returns. Modern portfolio theory has given us optimization methods that allow us to mix assets together in a portfolio in an optimum way. Many investors need to be able to estimate the expected return on a portfolio. For example, foundations need to estimate expected returns in order to formulate spending plans. And estimates are needed by individuals in developing their plans for saving for retirement and for spending during retirement years. This chapter will outline methods for estimating long-run returns for a diversified portfolio.

One of the themes of this book is that future capital markets are unlikely to provide investors with the high returns of the 1980s and 1990s. Bonds are likely to earn their long-run average (real) returns rather than the high returns experienced since the early 1980s, and stocks may not even reach their post-war average returns. So it's natural for investors to look to alternative investments for salvation. There are many alternative investments that might entice investors. But four have gained most attention. These are hedge funds, private equity, real estate, and commodities. Chapters 9 through 12 will study each of these asset classes.

In the last 15 years, hedge funds have become very popular among wealthier individuals as well as many institutional investors. We don't have much data on hedge fund returns and the data that we have available is not of high quality. Yet the asset class itself is fascinating to study because so many different investment strategies are represented. This is the ultimate investment for those who believe in *alpha*, the excess return attributable to investment expertise rather than systematic returns in the market or investment style. Chapter 9 will examine hedge funds.

Investors in private equity have privileged access to ownership in firms not available to the general public. By private equity, we usually mean investments in venture capital and buyout firms. Venture capital provides access to young firms with promising futures. These firms are typically in the technology or bio-technology sectors, but they can be in any industry and any part of the country. Buyout firms are partnerships that invest in older firms that have been taken private. Typically, the buyout firms take total control of the firm in contrast to the venture capital firms that take partial stakes. Chapter 10 will study both types of investments.

Real estate is the alternative investment for the ordinary investor. After all, most investors own their own homes. And many investors also own commercial real estate or other types of investable real estate either directly or indirectly through REITS. This is not to imply that residential real estate and commercial real estate are equivalent investments. In fact, it's important to contrast the returns on each of these investments. Chapter 11 will examine REIT returns as well as the returns earned by institutional investors on commercial real estate investments. But the chapter will also try to determine whether a home is a good investment.

The last 10 years have seen a tremendous commodities boom. So naturally, investors have discovered this asset class, since there is nothing like a burst of good returns to attract attention. Around 2000 in the midst of the tech boom, very few investors included commodities in their asset allocations. After all, the decade of the 1990s had seen very disappointing returns on commodities. That has all changed as oil prices quadruple and the world discovers that it is "running out of resources". Chapter 12 will study the resulting returns.

How much difference do alternatives make to asset allocation? Chapter 13 examines two approaches to alternatives. In one approach, investors confine their alternatives to real estate alone. This is the approach recommended by David Swensen, the director of the Yale endowment, in a book he wrote for ordinary investors.[3] Swensen has been so successful in shifting the Yale endowment away from conventional assets that he became concerned that ordinary investors would try to follow Yale's lead. So he wrote a book showing how conventional investments can provide unconventional success. In the second approach, the assets that Yale and other well-endowed investors prefer are added to the mix. Chapter 13 tries to assess the gains from adding alternatives to the portfolio. And it tries to determine the relative influence of asset allocation and manager performance in those gains.

The book continues with two chapters on spending. After all, investing has an important long-run aim, to provide enough wealth to sustain spending. That's true of a foundation or pension plan trying to grow wealth for current and future spending. And it's certainly true of an individual trying to save enough to sustain spending in retirement. It's even true of a philanthropist who intends to give wealth away because the ultimate aim is to fund spending by the charitable recipient. To study feasible spending rules, it's necessary to introduce simulation methods because the historical record itself will not allow us to anticipate all good and bad future scenarios. The simulation analysis will have to rely on sensible estimates of expected returns and risks, but it's important to consider scenarios where the bad returns occur early and often.

Chapter 14 examines feasible spending rules for foundations. How much can a foundation safely spend out of its portfolio? The answer to that question naturally depends on expected returns, but the first lesson will be that it's real, not nominal returns that matter. Also important will be the correlations and standard deviations of the assets in the portfolio. And included in the analysis will be cases where returns like those in 2008 occur soon after the portfolio is invested. Chapter 15 then turns to the harder case of an individual facing retirement. Why is it harder? A retiree faces mortality risk as well as investment risk. The fact that this investor will die in the future actually allows him or her to spend more than a foundation. But, the consequences of spending too much may be judged by many as being more severe. For a retiree, running out of money means not just shutting down some spending programs, but running out of food.

The book ends with a short chapter on rebalancing. The theme of the chapter is that asset allocation is hard. It requires that investors sell assets when they are soaring in value and buy assets after they have collapsed. The past decade gives us dramatic examples of such booms and busts.

So this book is about long-run investing and spending. But hasn't this theme been trumped by recent events? After all, how well did even smart investors like the Yale endowment fare in the current downturn? This nagging question may bother investors so much that the lessons of this book might fall on deaf ears. So in the first chapter I would like to address the issue of what good portfolio management can and cannot do.

LESSONS OF THE RECENT DOWNTURN

When the economy hits a downturn, businesses suffer. So it is not surprising that stock markets also suffer. Sometimes the drop in the stock market is severe, so portfolios are devastated. Investors inevitably wish that they had not taken chances in the stock market. Bonds are the place to be.

Since 1951, there have been nine recessions in the United States including the recession that began in December 2007.[4] The recessions themselves will be timed using the NBER's dating scheme. The National Bureau of Economic Research (NBER), a non-partisan research organization based in Cambridge, Massachusetts, has been dating recessions since the 1940s. In every one of these recessions, there has been a sizable fall in the U.S. stock market. The stock market typically begins its fall before the start of the recession, perhaps because investors anticipate the recession and the subsequent fall in corporate profits. Table 1.1 gives the dates of each recession as well as the dates when the S&P 500 index reached its peak and trough. These peaks and troughs are measured using monthly averages of the daily S&P 500 index.

The returns reported in Table 1.1 extend back to the early 1950s. Ibbotson SBBI Yearbooks (©Morningstar) report monthly stock and bond returns extending back to 1926.[5] These returns will be used in many of the tables to follow, so it is important to describe them at the outset. SBBI Yearbooks have two stock indexes. SBBI's Large Company stock index is based on the Standard & Poor's Composite Index. The Composite Index consists of 500 stocks from 1957 onward and 100 large-cap stocks prior to 1957. The specific methodology for computing the return on this index is described in Ibbotson SBBI (2010, p. 43). Unless noted otherwise, the SBBI large-cap series is used only through 1973. After that, the S&P 500 series provided

TABLE 1.1 Stocks and Bonds in Recessions, 1951–2009

Recession (NBER dating)	S&P 500 Peak-Trough	Large-Cap U.S. Stocks	Long-Term Treasury Return
Jul 53–May 54	Jan 53–Sept 53	−8.0%	1.2%
Aug 57–Apr 58	Jul 56–Dec 57	−14.3%	2.9%
Apr 60–Feb 61	Jul 59–Oct 60	−8.0%	8.9%
Dec 69–Nov 70	Dec 68–Jun 70	−26.3%	−4.6%
Nov 73–Mar 75	Jan 73–Dec 74	−36.2%	6.6%
Jul 81–Nov 82	Nov 80–Jul 82	−16.6%	17.8%
Jul 90–Mar 91	Jun 90–Oct 90	−14.1%	0.1%
Mar 01–Nov 01	Aug 00–Feb 03	−42.5%	32.3%
Dec 07–Jun 09	Oct 07–Mar 09	−46.6%	23.4%

The market peak and trough are determined by the monthly average of daily prices for the S&P 500 index. The S&P data is from Robert Shiller's web site, http://www.econ.yale.edu/~shiller/data.htm. The returns for large-cap U.S. stocks and Treasury bonds are from the 2010 SBBI Classic Yearbook (©Morningstar). The large-cap stock returns include dividends.

by Standard & Poor's (via the Zephyr StyleADVISOR database) is used instead. For this reason, the large-cap U.S. stock index will be referred to as the "S&P 500 index" even though it is the SBBI Large-Company Stock series from 1957 to 1973 and a narrower index prior to 1957. SBBI Yearbooks also report a small-cap index that will be described in detail in Chapter 3. There are four fixed income series in the SBBI yearbooks. In this chapter, the long-term Treasury return will be reported. This is the return on the 20-year Treasury bond. Other bond returns will be described in Chapter 7.

Table 1.1 shows the total return on the S&P index (capital gain plus dividends) in each recession since 1951. The returns are monthly returns measured from the peak to trough of the S&P index. Also reported are the returns on the long-term Treasury bond (capital gain plus income) over the same period. As Table 1.1 shows, the negative return on stocks is usually accompanied by a positive return on the Treasury bond. Only in the recession beginning in 1969 did the Treasury bond earn a negative (nominal) return, no doubt because inflation was beginning to rise in the United States. The impact of inflation on bond returns in the 1970s will be discussed in the next section. Otherwise, the Treasury bond fared relatively well during the recessions. In some recessions, in fact, the Treasury bond thrived. This is certainly true of three of the last four recessions when returns were in double digits. So a clear lesson from Table 1.1 is that stocks fare badly and bonds thrive in recessions.

TABLE 1.2   Does Diversification Pay? Returns in the Recent Crisis, October 2007 to March 2009

Asset	Index	Allocation	Return
U.S. bonds	Barclays Aggregate	30%	+7.6%
U.S. stocks	Russell 3000	40%	−46.9%
Foreign Stocks	MSCI EAFE	15%	−53.6%
Emerging M Stocks	MSCI EM	5%	−55.9%
REITS	FTSE-NAREIT	10%	−63.4 %
Portfolio			−37.3%

Data Sources: Barclays Capital, Russell®, MSCI, and ©FTSE.

Sophisticated investors hope that diversification of their portfolios will cushion any downturns. It goes without saying that such investors avoid excessive concentration in particular stocks or even investment in the stocks of particular industries. In the late 1990s, some investors forgot basic principles of diversification and concentrated their investments in the tech sector, much to their regret. Presumably few sophisticated investors have since repeated these mistakes. But suppose that investors have diversified their portfolios with different types of stocks, both foreign and domestic? And perhaps there is diversification beyond equities into real estate? The current downturn raises questions about how effective such diversification really is.

Consider Table 1.2 where a diversified portfolio of stocks and bonds is shown. The portfolio consists of 30 percent in bonds, 40 percent in U.S. stocks, 15 percent in foreign (industrial country) stocks, 5 percent in emerging markets, and 10 percent in REITS. Most observers would consider this portfolio to be pretty well diversified.

Each asset in the portfolio is represented by a well-known index. For example, U.S. bonds are represented by the Barclays Capital Aggregate bond index (formerly the Lehman Aggregate index), an index of investment grade U.S. bonds. Similarly, U.S. stocks are represented by the Russell 3000 stock index which includes both small-cap and large-cap U.S. stocks. Foreign stocks are represented by the MSCI EAFE index of foreign developed-country stocks and the MSCI Emerging Market stock index. Real estate is represented by the National Association of Real Estate Investment Trust's FTSE-NAREIT Reit index.

Portfolio returns are measured from the peak of the U.S. stock market in October 2007 through March 2009.[6] Over this period, U.S. stocks were down 46.9 percent and the portfolio as a whole was down by 37.3 percent. So diversification did not help very much! The reason is that there was virtually no place to hide. Foreign developed country stocks and emerging market stocks did worse than U.S. stocks, and REITS did worse still. Only bonds offered a refuge.

Is all of this a surprise? The answer is that it should not be. In every downturn, equity and equity-like investments suffer. It's true that the downturn in markets beginning in 2000 did offer shelter in real estate. The S&P 500 fell 42.5 percent in the 30 months from August 2000 until February 2003.[7] REITS, in contrast, rose by 24.9 percent over this same period. So in that downturn, diversification beyond U.S. stocks did help somewhat. But foreign stocks represented by the EAFE index fell 42.3 percent over this same period. And the 70/30 portfolio shown in Table 1.2 fell 18.8 percent.

The 2001 downturn, however, is the exception rather than the rule. Normally, portfolios heavily weighted to stocks have similar losses regardless of how well diversified the stock portfolios are. Table 1.3 presents the returns on different portfolios for the five recessions since the REIT and foreign stock indexes began in the early 1970s. Both portfolios have 30 percent invested in U.S. bonds (in the Barclays Aggregate Bond Index).[8] But one portfolio invests 70 percent in the S&P 500 only, while the other portfolio broadens stock investments to include midcap and small-cap stocks (by investing in the Russell 3000 rather than the S&P 500 index).[9] And this second portfolio has 20 percent in foreign stocks and 10 percent in REITS. So the second portfolio can be described as well diversified as far as equity is concerned.

TABLE 1.3 Does Diversification Pay? Returns on Portfolios in Past Recessions

S&P 500 Peak-Trough	70 % S&P 500/ 30 % Bonds	Diversified Stock-Bond Portfolio*
Jan 73–Dec 74	−24.9%	−24.2%
Nov 80–Jul 82	−6.3%	−4.9%
Jun 90–Oct 90	−9.4%	−9.7%
Aug 00–Feb 03	−26.1%	−18.8%
Oct 07–Mar 09	−33.5%	−37.3%

*The diversified portfolio is the same shown in Table 1.2 consisting of 30 percent in the Barclays Aggregate bond index, 40 percent in the Russell 3000, 20 percent in EAFE (15 percent in EAFE and 5 percent in MSCI Emerging Markets in 1990 recession and after), and 10 percent in the FTSE-NAREIT index. Because the Barclays index begins only in 1976, the Ibbotson Long Term Treasury bond index is used for the first recession. Prior to 1979 when the Russell series began, the Russell 3000 is replaced by a 35 percent allocation to the S&P 500 and 5 percent allocation to the Ibbotson Small-cap index.
Data Sources: Barclays Capital, Russell®, MSCI, ©FTSE, and ©Morningstar.

Does diversification of the stock investments help to mitigate the downturns? The answer is that it often does a poor job when the economy suffers a downturn. Bonds are supreme. It doesn't really matter whether an investor has a simple stock-bond mix or a sophisticated mix of different types of bonds, stocks, and real estate. The investor still suffers losses in the downturn. In the recession of the mid-1970s and the Gulf War recession of 1990, for example, the losses on the simple S&P 500/bond portfolio and the diversified portfolio are almost identical. It's true that either portfolio does better than the S&P 500 alone. But that just shows that bonds are the only refuge in a recession. Even in the downturn of the early 2000s discussed above, diversification of stocks had limited effect. The portfolio that included foreign stocks and REITS fell 18.8 percent. That's better than the 26.1 percent decline of the S&P/bond portfolio, but it's still a big loss. In a downturn, bonds are the one sure place to be.

SO ARE BONDS THE PLACE TO INVEST?

If bonds are such a savior in the current crisis, how good an investment have they been in the long run? Let's focus on the long stock market cycles over the past 60 years that include booms and busts. We might identify four cycles: the post-war expansion, the inflation decade of the 1970s, the boom period of the 1980s and 1990s, and the bust period through March 2009. The timing of these four cycles is arbitrary, but some basis for the timing can be seen in Figures 1.1 and 1.2 where the real return on the S&P 500 is displayed. It's important to examine long market cycles in real (inflation-adjusted) terms because it's the real return that matters to the investor. (For the short periods surrounding economic downturns, it usually doesn't matter whether real or nominal returns are examined). Besides, the inflation decade of the 1970s doesn't look that bad in nominal terms. It's only in real terms that we see the devastation caused by inflation during that decade.

Figure 1.1 suggests that the post-war expansion ended either in late 1968 or late 1972 (when returns were only marginally higher). During that period, the S&P 500 real return was 659.1 percent in cumulative terms or 12.0 percent per year. The subsequent period was a different story. The figure breaks up the period in two phases, Dec 1968 to September 1974 when the cumulative real return was −50.1 percent and October 1974 to July 1982 when the return was +28.6 percent. Over the whole period from Dec 1968 to July 1982, the cumulative return on the S&P 500 was −35.8 percent (in real terms) or −3.2 percent per annum. No wonder stocks fell out of favor during this period.

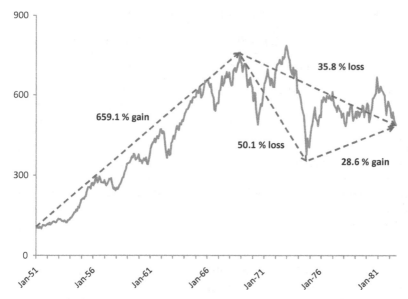

FIGURE 1.1   Real Return on S&P 500, Jan 1951 to July 1982
Data Source: ©Morningstar.

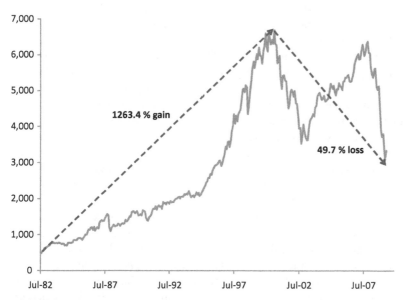

FIGURE 1.2   Real Return on S&P 500, Jul 1982 to Mar 2009
Data Source: ©Morningstar.

TABLE 1.4 Real Returns in Four Market Phases, 1951–2009

| | S&P 500 | | Long Term Treasury | |
Dates	Cumulative	Per Annum	Cumulative	Per Annum
Dec 50–Nov 68	659.1%	12.0%	−11.6%	−0.7%
Nov 68–Jul 82	−35.8%	−3.2%	−37.8%	−3.4%
Jul 82–Mar 00	1263.4%	15.9%	328.7%	8.6%
Mar 00–Mar 09	−49.7%	−7.4%	72.7%	6.2%
Whole Period				
Dec 50–Mar 09	3242.0%	6.2%	306.3%	2.4%

The S&P 500 and long-term Treasury bond returns are deflated by the consumer price index.
Data Sources: ©Morningstar and S&P.

Figure 1.2 traces stocks over the subsequent boom period of the 1980s and 1990s. The S&P 500 earned an astounding 1263.4 percent compound real return over the 18 years from August 1982 to March 2000. That's equivalent to a 15.9 percent per annum real return. Since 2000, however, stocks on balance have lost almost 50 percent in cumulative terms, at least through the bottom of the latest bear market in March 2009.

Now let's see just how well bonds would have fared over these same periods. Table 1.4 compares the real returns on the S&P 500 with those on the long-term (20 year) Treasury bond. The Treasury bond had negative real returns during the post-war boom period and during both of the inflation-ridden periods of the 1970s. In the post-war boom period ending in 1968 when stocks averaged a 12.0 percent real return, the Treasury bond had a small negative real return. And in the period from November 1968 to July 1982 when stocks were losing ground to inflation, Treasuries earned a cumulative real return of −37.8 percent for an annual return of −3.4 percent! Stocks and bonds, in fact, were equally miserable investments. The S&P 500 had an average annual real return of −3.2 percent. But bonds are supposed to be the safe haven for investors!

Then in the 1980s and 1990s, Treasuries came alive. As explained in the next chapter, Treasuries did so well because the Federal Reserve gained control over the runaway inflation of the late 1960s and 1970s. Inflation came down, and so did interest rates. There was a *once-in-a-lifetime* capital gain on Treasuries (as well as most other bonds). But Treasury returns paled in comparison with stock returns during this period. Stocks earned an average real return of 15.9 percent per year. Then when the stock market fell astray, Treasuries really started to shine. In contrast with a −49.7 percent return on the S&P 500, Treasuries have earned over 70 percent over the period beginning in 2000.

The longer historical record, however, certainly raises questions about whether Treasuries should be the primary foundation of a long-term portfolio. Consider the average real return on Treasuries over the full sample period. From 1951 through March 2009, the long-term Treasury bond had a compound return of 2.4 percent/year adjusted for inflation. During the same time period, U.S. large-cap stocks had a compound real return of 6.2 percent. The difference between these two returns is often called the "equity premium". Chapter 2 will discuss this equity premium in detail. The period prior to 1951 was no better. The real return on bonds between 1926 and 1950 was 2.7 percent, while the real return on stocks was 6.3 percent. And this period included the Great Depression! Investors who are currently enamored with bonds had better know the truth about the long-run return on bonds. It's terribly low. And it is not the basis for long-run wealth accumulation.

SO WHAT HAPPENS WHEN THE ECONOMY TURNS UP?

In the middle of a downturn in the U.S. economy, a substantial fraction of investors abandon stocks for good. That's a sensible strategy if the investors are so rich that they can afford to hide out in Treasuries or other types of bonds. With a real return of 2.4 percent, they had better be rich! A $ 1 million dollar portfolio earns only $24,000 in real terms (pre-tax). Try living on that in retirement. But spending 2.4 percent would be imprudent unless the investor was sure that inflation would not rise during retirement. As Chapter 15 will show, an investor needs to keep spending considerably below the expected real return on investments. So an all-bond investor would have to make sure that spending was substantially lower than 2.4 percent. That's a depressing prospect.

But there is another reason why investors need to keep their faith in equities, especially after they have been clobbered with a market downturn. Equities always rise as the economy recovers. Let's study past recessions. In every recession, equities will be traced from their trough during the recession over the 12 months succeeding the trough. Table 1.5 lists dates for the nine recessions since 1951 including the second half of the double-dip recession(s) of 1980–82.

The market trough is determined by the lowest monthly average of daily prices for the S&P 500 price index from Robert Shiller's web site, http://www.econ.yale.edu/~shiller/data.htm. The S&P 500 gain is based on

TABLE 1.5 S&P 500 Rallies After Recessions, 1951–2010

Recession months (NBER dating)	Market Bottom	Gain in first 12 months
Jul 53–May 54	Sept 53	46.0%
Aug 57–Apr 58	Dec 57	43.4%
Apr 60–Feb 61	Oct 60	32.6%
Dec 69–Nov 70	Jun 70	41.9%
Nov 73–Mar 75	Dec 74	37.3%
Jul 81–Nov 82	Jul 82	59.3%
Jul 90–Mar 91	Oct 90	33.5%
Mar 01–Nov 01	Feb 03	38.5%
Dec 07–Jun 09	Mar 09	49.8%

the total return on the S&P (including dividends) from the 2010 SBBI Classic Yearbook (©Morningstar). For every recession, Table 1.5 identifies the month when the S&P 500 reaches its trough for that cycle.[10] Then the table reports the return on the S&P 500 over the next 12 months. In all nine downturns, the S&P 500 shoots up like a rocket once it reaches its bottom. The return on the S&P ranges from 32 percent to 59 percent over the first 12 months. In all but one recession, the recession in 2001, the S&P reaches bottom *before the end of the recession*. So the investor cannot wait for clear signs that the recession has ended. For one thing, it takes the NBER business cycle committee months to decide that a recession has ended. In addition, the S&P usually rises earlier than that date. So market timers have to have unusual foresight!

Let's consider how easy it would be to bob and weave in these market cycles. We know that (a) bonds are supreme during market downturns and (b) stocks are supreme in upturns. So all we have to do is shift portfolios to bonds in time for recessions (or perhaps prior to the start of the recessions). Then we have to shift portfolios back to stocks *just in time*. It's plausible that Japanese automakers can run their production lines successfully with "just-in-time" inventory management. But it may be a trifle more difficult for investors to do the same.

So what should investors do in a downturn? The answer is that they should sit tight. David Swensen of the Yale endowment perhaps said it most clearly. When asked in January 2009 whether poor investment performance in 2008 would induce him to tinker with his asset allocation, he replied "I don't think it makes sense ... to structure a portfolio to perform well in a period of financial crisis. That would require moving away from equity-oriented investments that have served institutions with long time horizons well."[11]

Actually, investors have to do more than sit tight. If they believe that they have chosen a portfolio appropriate for their circumstances, they will have work to do to keep that portfolio allocation intact. In a boom, portfolios drift up toward assets with higher returns. And in a bust, portfolios drift away from assets with negative returns. So the investor has to sell high-flying assets in a boom and buy poor performing assets in a bust. This is called rebalancing the portfolio. That's a bit counterintuitive.

If an investor is relying on the portfolio for current spending needs, then there is one other thing to do—cut back spending in a downturn. That decision will be discussed in Chapters 14 and 15. It's not a cheery subject, but it's an important one.

That's enough focus on downturns and busts. The investor has to realize that busts do not last forever. Most of the postwar period, for example, has been a time of economic prosperity and positive investment returns. Investors have accumulated wealth. This book will be about how to choose a portfolio that will ensure that wealth accumulation proceeds as smoothly as possible.

SOME NECESSARY TOOLS FOR ANALYSIS

Investments involve returns and risks. So it's necessary to have a few tools to analyze each. This book will try to keep the mechanics as simple as possible. But an investment advisor has to have a few tools to do an effective job for a client. This section will list the tools briefly. An appendix will provide a description of each tool. Most of the tools are standard for any professional in the investment industry. But there is one measure, *alpha**, which may be new to many readers.

First, the advisor needs measures of returns, of which three are important: the *compound* (or geometric) *average*, the *arithmetic average*, and the average *real return*. The real return is obtained by adjusting the nominal return for the inflation rate. The compound average should be used to measure long-run returns, while the arithmetic average is the best estimate of next year's return and is used in many applications of modern portfolio management. Formulas for these averages are given in the appendix.

Second, the advisor needs measures of risk, two of which are the most important. The *standard deviation* is the standard measure of risk for financial assets. It reflects the total variability of an asset return. *Beta* measures only the variability that is systematically related to the market benchmark.

Third, the advisor needs measures of risk-adjusted returns. The *Sharpe ratio* measures the excess return on an asset (above the risk-free return) relative to the standard deviation. So the Sharpe ratio is appropriate for measuring the risk-adjusted return if the total risk of the asset is being considered. *Alpha* is a risk-adjusted return based on only the systematic risk of the asset. That is, alpha is the excess return earned on an asset above that explained by the beta of that asset. Alpha is often used to measure the risk-adjusted contribution of a mutual fund manager. It can also be used to measure the marginal contribution of an individual asset to a market-based portfolio.

The concept that may be new to many readers is alpha*. This is a measure of the excess return on the portfolio itself. Suppose that an investment advisor has measured the return on a portfolio in terms of its Sharpe ratio and wants to compare it with some benchmark. (In a later chapter, the performance of the Yale portfolio is compared with the benchmark of university portfolios as a whole). The advisor could simply compare the Sharpe ratios of the portfolio and benchmark. Sharpe ratios rather than alphas are appropriate because it is the total return and total risk that is being assessed. Alpha* provides a way of comparing the Sharpe ratios by measuring the excess return earned by the portfolio relative to its benchmark. To measure alpha*, the risk level of the benchmark has to be reduced to that of the portfolio. This measure is explained further in the appendix.[12]

With these tools, we can begin studying the assets that will be included in the portfolio. Chapter 2 starts off with the most basic assets, stocks and bonds. How much can we earn on these assets in the long run?

APPENDIX: DESCRIPTION OF THE STATISTICAL TOOLS

There are three measures of returns that will be used throughout the book:

(a) **compound (geometric) average** (R)—the best measure of the long-term return on an asset or portfolio. If r_j is the return in any given period, the compound average is defined by

$$(1 + R) = [(1 + r_1)(1 + r_2) \ldots (1 + r_T)]^{1/T}$$

where T is the number of periods in the sample.

(b) **arithmetic average** (r)—the best estimate of next period's return

$$r = \Sigma_j r_j / T$$

(c) average **real return**. The real return is defined using a compound formula as

$$\text{Real return} = (1 + R)/(1 + \pi) - 1,$$

where π is the compound average inflation rate.[13]

There are two measures of risk which will be used extensively in later chapters.

(a) <u>Standard deviation</u> (σ)—measures the total variability of the asset or the portfolio. It is the square root of the variance, σ^2, defined as

$$\sigma^2 = (1/T)\Sigma_j(r_j - r)^2$$

(b) <u>Beta</u> (β)—measures the systematic risk of an asset relative to a market benchmark. If r_A is the return on asset A and r_M is the return on the market benchmark, then

$$\beta = \text{Cov}(r_A, r_M)/\sigma_M^2,$$

where Cov (r_A, r_M) is the covariance between the asset and the market. Corresponding to these two measures of risk are two measures of risk-adjusted returns.

The **Sharpe ratio**—measures the ratio of a portfolio return to its standard deviation. This ratio is best defined using arithmetic averages because the standard deviation is measured relative to the arithmetic average rather than the compound average. If r_F is the average return on the risk-free asset, then the Sharpe ratio is defined as

$$(r_P - r_F)/\sigma_P,$$

where σ_P is the standard deviation of the portfolio.

Alpha (α)—measures the excess return on an asset relative to its market benchmark.

$$\alpha = r_A - [r_F + \beta_A(r_M - r_F)]$$

The expression in square brackets is the return on the market benchmark adjusted for the beta of asset A.[14] So α is the return above (or below) the security market line at the same level of risk as asset A.

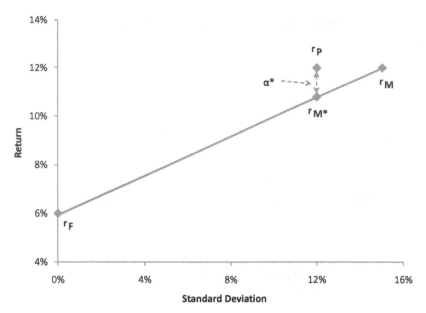

FIGURE 1.3   Evaluation of the Return on a Portfolio using Alpha-Star

If an investor is assessing the performance of an overall portfolio rather than an individual manager or an individual asset in the portfolio, a different excess return measure is called for. That excess return must be measured in the standard deviation space rather than beta space because it's the overall portfolio that is being evaluated, not an individual manager or individual asset. In Figure 1.3, the return on portfolio P, r_P, is compared with a market benchmark, r_M.[15] Most portfolios have less risk than the market as a whole, so it's important to compare returns at a common level of risk. Alpha* brings the risk level of the market down to that of the portfolio to be evaluated.[16] The expression for alpha* (α^*) shows how this is done:

$$\alpha^* = r_P - [r_F + (\sigma_P/\sigma_M)(r_M - r_F)]$$

Thus the portfolio return is compared with the risk-adjusted return on the market where risk is adjusted downward by the ratio of σ_P to σ_M. Alpha* doesn't give any more information about risk-adjusted returns than that which is provided by Sharpe ratios, but alpha* translates differences in Sharpe ratios into excess returns.[17] And excess returns can be understood easily by all investors. Alpha* will be used repeatedly in the book to show how well one portfolio is doing relative to another.

NOTES

1. Markowitz (1952) introduced the efficient frontier, the combination of portfolio returns and risks that maximize return for a given risk. The efficient frontier is discussed in Chapter 8.
2. Ibbotson SBBI returns are reported in SBBI Yearbooks (©2010 Morningstar). See Note 5.
3. David Swensen has written two books of interest to investors. Swenson (2005) is written for ordinary investors while Swensen (2009, 2nd edition) describes investment strategies for institutional investors (or family offices).
4. Technically, there have been ten recessions since 1951 because the recession in the early 1980s was actually a double dip downturn with a recession from January 1980 to July 1980 followed by a second recession from July 1981 to November 1982. In Table 1.1, only the second deeper recession is examined.
5. Ibbotson® SBBI® 2010 Classic Yearbook, ©2010 Morningstar. All rights reserved. Used with permission. (The SBBI series are cited hereafter as "©Morningstar").
6. The S&P 500 reached its low for this cycle on March 9, 2009.
7. The market trough is determined by the lowest monthly average of daily prices for the S&P 500 index. If daily prices for the S&P 500 are used, the trough occurs on October 9, 2002.
8. For the first recession in 1973–74, the Barclays Aggregate index is replaced by the Ibbotson long-term Treasury bond index.
9. The Russell series begins in 1979, so for the 1973–74 recession, the Russell 3000 is replaced with a 35 percent allocation to the S&P 500 and a 5 percent allocation to Ibbotson's Small-cap Index.
10. The trough is measured using the monthly average of the daily levels of the S&P 500 index.
11. Wall Street Journal, January 13, 2009, page C3.
12. Alpha* is explained at great length in Marston (2004).
13. The real return would be almost the same if the inflation rate is simply subtracted from the nominal return, at least in periods when inflation is low.
14. This return is obtained by moving up or down the security market line to the level of risk (β) of asset A.
15. Alternatively, a portfolio return can be compared with other portfolios. In Chapter 13, we compare the Yale portfolio with the average portfolio held by colleges and universities in the United States.
16. Alpha* compares the return on a portfolio with that of the market at the level of risk of the portfolio. Another possible approach is to compare the portfolio with the market at the level of risk of the market. This is what is done by Modigliani and Modigliani (1997) in their M^2 measure. M^2 rather than α^* is more appropriate if a whole group of portfolios is being compared.
17. In fact, alpha* can be expressed in terms of Sharpe ratios. If SP and SM are the Sharpe ratios of the portfolio and market, respectively, then $\alpha^* = (SP - SM)^*\sigma_P$.

CHAPTER 2

Long-Run Returns on Stocks and Bonds

Investors have a variety of assets in which they can invest, from private equity to mortgages to real estate. Yet it's best to begin a study of investments by focusing on the simplest of assets, stocks and bonds. The history of stock and bond returns extends much further back than any other assets. And the quality of the return data for stocks and bonds, at least government bonds, far exceeds the quality of return data for many alternative assets.

Most studies of U.S. markets rely on the well-known SBBI data set ((©)Morningstar) originally developed by Ibbotson Associates. The data set begins in 1926 when the University of Chicago's CRSP data set, on which it is based, also begins. The SBBI data set consists of six assets, large company and small company U.S. stocks, long-term and medium-term U.S. government bonds, U.S. corporate bonds, and U.S. Treasury bills. An inflation series based on the consumer price index is also reported. SBBI publishes an annual yearbook, Ibbotson SBBI, *Classic Yearbook—Market Results for Stocks, Bonds, Bills and Inflation*, that contains valuable analyses of these six markets.

This chapter will use the SBBI data set, but will focus on the post-war period beginning in 1951 rather than the entire period extending back to 1926. Choosing an historical period over which to study returns involves a trade off between two factors. On the one hand, the longer the data set, the more robust are any statistical inferences drawn from the data. On the other hand, the longer the data set, the more likely it is that structural changes will occur in the economy and in the investment markets. The early years of the SBBI data set from 1926 to 1950 includes a depression and a world war, two events that are unlikely to occur in the future.[1] Beginning in 1951 avoids the period after World War II when the U.S. Treasury followed a policy of pegging long-term interest rates. With the Treasury-Fed Accord of March 1951, interest rates could once again reflect market forces.

The period beginning in 1951 does include a variety of economic conditions. There are nine recessions during this period, so investment behavior over the business cycle can be studied in detail.[2] There is also a period of high inflation, in the 1970s, as well as two periods of relatively low inflation, in the 1950s and in the current decade. There are periods of rising interest rates and falling interest rates, so bond returns have fluctuated widely. And there are bull markets and bear markets for stocks.

Some observers might prefer to look at a much shorter sample period to make sure that any observations of past returns are relevant for today's markets. So, according to this reasoning, the last decade or last two decades might seem a better period to study. As will be shown below, the period since the early 1980s has been a very unusual one for both stocks and bonds. One of the biggest pitfalls for investors is to rely on this period to project future returns. Stocks and bonds do not always earn double-digit returns as they did in the 1980s and 1990s.

STOCKS AND BONDS SINCE 1951

To study stock and bond returns, we will begin by focusing on two series, large company stocks and Treasury bonds. The large-cap series is from SBBI prior to 1974 and from Standard & Poor's from 1974 to present.[3] Both series measure returns on the S&P Composite Index. The S&P Composite Index consists of 500 stocks from 1957 to present and a 90-stock S&P series prior to 1957. The Treasury bond is a 20-year Treasury bond also from SBBI.

Table 2.1 reports the average returns for these two assets. Also included is the one-month Treasury bill, the closest we can come to the risk-free

TABLE 2.1 Returns on Stocks and Bonds, 1951–2009

Asset	Geometric Average	Arithmetic Average	Standard Deviation	Sharpe Ratio
S&P 500	10.7%	11.3%	14.6%	0.45
Treasury bond	6.0%	6.3%	9.5%	0.17
Treasury bill	4.8%	4.7%	0.8%	

Prior to 1974, the SBBI Large Company Index (©Morningstar) is substituted for the S&P 500. The Treasury bond is the Long-Term Government Bond Index. It has an average maturity of 20 years. The Treasury bill is a one-month bill. Both are from 2010 SBBI Classic Yearbook.
Data Sources: ©Morningstar and S&P.

rate of modern portfolio theory. Two averages are reported. The geometric (or compound) average return is the best estimate of the average return earned over this entire period. The arithmetic average is the best (i.e., least unbiased) estimate of next year's return. Also included in the table is the standard deviation. The averages and standard deviations are both expressed in annualized terms.

There are several notable features of these returns that should be emphasized. First, consider the Treasury bill and bond returns. There is a relatively small gap between the returns on these two series. As a reward for investing in a 20-year bond rather than a one-month Treasury bill, the investor earns an extra 1.2 percent. The 20-year bond has a large standard deviation of 9.5 percent. A one standard deviation band around the average return includes negative returns. Indeed, in 1999, there was a return of −9.0 percent on this series. And in 1994, following the Federal Reserve's dramatic reversal of interest rate policy, the return on this series was −7.8 percent.[4]

The return on the S&P 500 is 4.7 percent higher than the return on long-term Treasury bonds, and it is 5.9 percent higher than the risk-free return. The excess return of stocks over the risk-free return has been given a specific name, the *equity premium*. Using geometric averages, the equity premium is defined as

$$\text{Equity premium} = (1 + r_{S\&P})/(1 + r_F) - 1$$
$$= (1 + 0.107)/(1 + 0.048) - 1 = 5.6\%$$

where $r_{S\&P}$ is the return on the S&P 500 and r_F is the risk-free Treasury bill return.[5] Sometimes the equity premium is defined by using the long-term bond rather than the risk-free return in which case the premium would be 4.4 percent rather than 5.6 percent. If the entire period from 1926 to present is studied, a period that includes the depression of the 1930s, the equity premium (defined relative to the risk-free return) is 5.9 percent. However it is defined, the equity premium is remarkably large.

This premium has provided equity investors with a rich reward for bearing the extra risk of owning equities. In a landmark study more than two decades ago, Mehra and Prescott (1985) showed that the equity premium is inconsistent with reasonable levels of risk aversion. They called the premium a puzzle. Since then, scores of finance researchers have set out to develop theoretical models of investor behavior that could explain the size of the premium.[6] Researchers have also studied the equity premium in other countries. A book by Dimson, Marsh, and Staunton (2002) estimates the equity premium for 16 industrial countries from 1900 to 2000 as ranging from 1.8 percent for Denmark to 7.4 percent for France, with an average equity premium of 4.9 percent. Wise investors don't spend too much time agonizing over the source of the premium. They simply take advantage of it by focusing on equities in their portfolios.

HOW MUCH MORE ATTRACTIVE ARE STOCKS THAN BONDS?

Many investors, though, see the equity premium as a necessary price for the extra risk of investing in stocks. After all, the standard deviation of the S&P 500 series is 14.6 percent in Table 2.1. But that explanation needs to be examined more closely because, as reported in Table 2.1, the standard deviation of the bond return is also quite high at 9.5 percent. To compare stocks and bonds, it's useful to ask the following question: If an investor were to choose between these two assets, which would be more attractive in risk-adjusted terms?[7]

To assess the return on stocks versus the return on bonds, the first step is to adjust each return for risk. The Sharpe ratio adjusts each return by first subtracting the risk-free rate, r_F, then dividing by the standard deviation. If r_j is the return on asset j and σ_j is its standard deviation, then the Sharpe ratio for asset j is

$$[r_j - r_F]/s_j$$

To calculate the Sharpe ratio, we use the arithmetic returns and standard deviations in Table 2.1. It's possible to define a Sharpe ratio using geometric returns, but only if the standard deviation is defined over a similar long horizon.[8] Using the returns in Table 1, the Sharpe ratios are defined by

$$Stocks : [0.113 - 0.047]/0.146 = 0.45$$
$$Bonds : [0.063 - 0.047]/0.095 = 0.17$$

The Sharpe ratio for stocks is more than twice the size of the ratio for bonds. So, after adjusting for the higher risk of stocks, the (excess) return on stocks is much larger than bonds.

One way to view the relative returns on equity and bonds is to conduct an experiment. If an investor were to choose a portfolio consisting of the S&P 500 and the risk-free return with the same standard deviation as that of bonds, how much of an excess return would be earned on bonds? Figure 2.1 calculates the excess return on bonds as *negative* 2.7 percent. That is, the gap in Sharpe ratios shown above can be translated into an excess return of

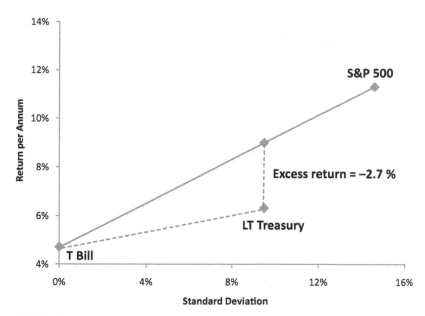

FIGURE 2.1   Comparing Stocks and Bonds, 1951–2009
Data Sources: ©Morningstar and S&P.

−2.7 percent at the level of risk of the bond. Viewed from this perspective, bonds are not very attractive.

How much difference does it make if we invest in medium-term bonds or if we study a longer period of time? If the medium-term bond is used instead of the long-term bond, the Sharpe ratio is 0.29 for the period since 1951, still much less than the Sharpe ratio for stocks. If stocks and bonds are compared over the entire period since 1926, the Sharpe ratio for stocks is 0.40, while that of long-term bonds is 0.22 and medium-term bonds is 0.32. So in both cases, the *risk-adjusted* return on stocks is substantially higher than that of bonds. Of course, no investor must choose between stocks and bonds. Later chapters will consider portfolios of stocks and bonds that will be more attractive than holdings of either asset alone.

REAL RETURNS

Until this point, average returns have been measured without taking into account inflation. For a long-run investor, however, inflation can substantially reduce the real gain on a portfolio. Even modest inflation does a lot of damage. If inflation averages 2.5 percent per year, the cost of living rises by 28 percent in 10 years and by almost 64 percent in 20 years. Over time, moreover, inflation varies a great deal, so comparing nominal returns over different periods can be very misleading. In the 1970s, nominal stock returns (8.4 percent) were as high as in the 1960s (8.2 percent), but real returns were much lower in the 1970s (0.4 percent in the 1970s versus 5.1 percent in the 1960s).

To obtain real, or inflation-adjusted, returns, it's important to use a compound formula. If π is the inflation rate, then the real return on asset j can be written as

$$\text{Real return} = (1 + r_j)/(1 + \pi) - 1.$$

Over the period from 1951 to 2009, the inflation rate has averaged 3.78 percent. So the real return on stocks and bonds is calculated as follows (using the geometric averages from Table 2.1).[9]

$$\text{Real return on stocks} = (1 + 0.1072)/(1 + 0.0378) - 1 = 0.067$$
$$\text{Real return on bonds} = (1 + 0.0602)/(1 + 0.0378) - 1 = 0.022$$

Inflation reduces bond returns proportionally much more than stock returns. A 2.2 percent real return on bonds seems small when earned by an asset with a 9.5 percent standard deviation.

The equity premium is seen in a new light once real returns are analyzed. Consider the following alternative investment strategies followed by a younger investor saving for retirement. If we assume that the investor has access to tax-deferred saving, the returns on the portfolio can be determined by simply calculating the accumulation of wealth based on real returns. The results are shown in Figure 2.2.

An investor who allocates all of a portfolio to bonds earns a real return of 2.2 percent over time. Over a 20-year period, for example, $100,000 turns into $154,000. It's important to note that this calculation has already taken inflation into account, so the investor can buy just as much with a dollar 20 years later. But a 54 percent cumulative return is not going to do much for retirement.

Contrast the bond return with the stock return. The same $100,000 invested at the 6.7 percent compound real return on stocks earned since 1951 increases to $366,000, or a 266 percent compound return. The equity premium may provide the extra return for a more comfortable retirement. Figure 2.2 shows the accumulation of (tax-deferred) wealth under the two alternative strategies.

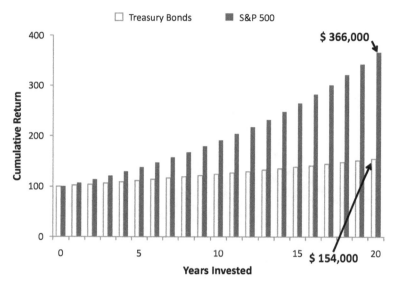

FIGURE 2.2 $100,000 Invested for 20 Years in Bonds versus Stocks (in 2009 Dollars)

Real returns are not just important to wealth accumulation. They are also vitally important to *spending*. Investors during their retirement years must base their spending plans on real returns, not nominal returns. So also must foundations, at least those that are unable to accumulate new funds to replace current spending.

RECONSIDERING BOND RETURNS

But what real returns can we expect in the future? As stated above, real compound returns on bonds since 1951 have averaged 2.2 percent. But many investors recall much higher returns over the last few decades. Huge capital gains enabled bond investors to earn equity-like returns. In fact, during the 1980s, bonds and stocks earned almost identical real returns of about 9 percent.

Bonds had splendid returns in the 1980s and early 1990s for a very simple reason. Inflation and bond returns fell over this period. Soon after Paul Volcker was first named to lead the Federal Reserve in 1979, the inflation rate started to recede from historic highs. That's because Volcker and the Fed instituted a tough monetary regime aimed at sharply lowering the double-digit inflation that the country was experiencing.

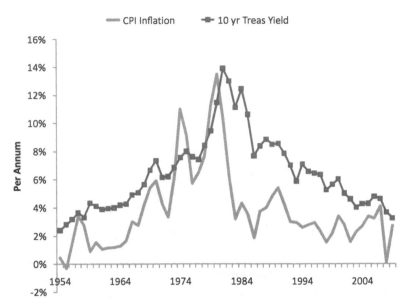

FIGURE 2.3 Inflation and Bond Yields, 1954–2009
Data Source: IMF, International Financial Statistics.

Figure 2.3 shows the inflation rate and 10-year Treasury bond yield over the period since the early 1950s. After Volcker succeeded in driving inflation to low single digits, the bond yield stayed stubbornly high for a time. But eventually the bond market adjusted as inflationary expectations fell. As a result, bond returns soared. Investors in this market benefited whether they bought and held high coupon-paying bonds or sold out their bond positions after registering large capital gains.

Some investors are waiting patiently for high bond returns to resume. But the driving force for these record real returns was the reversal of the same inflation that had undermined the bond market in the late 1960s and 1970s. For the decade of the 1970s as a whole, in fact, the real average return on 20-year bonds was –3.8 percent! This was at a time when the stock market was at least breaking even in real terms. With bond yields in the 4 percent to 5 percent range (and recently even lower), we are clearly in a very different market setting than in the early 1980s. In this setting, bond returns may not be far different than they have been in the longer run.

Consider Table 2.2 which reports bond returns over five periods extending back to 1926. All of these returns have been adjusted for inflation, so they can be compared directly with one another. The period from 1981 to 2000 saw unusually high real returns on both medium-term and long-term

TABLE 2.2 Real Returns on Medium-Term and Long-Term Treasury Bonds and Large-Cap Stock Index

Period	Medium-term Treasury Bond	Long-term Treasury Bond	S&P 500 Stock Index
1981–2000	6.2%	8.1%	11.7%
1951–1980	−0.2%	−2.0%	6.4%
1951–2009	2.4%	2.2%	6.7%
1926–1950	1.9%	2.7%	6.3%
1926–2009	2.3%	2.3%	6.6%

The real returns are compound averages based on the CPI inflation rate. The medium-term bond is a five-year Treasury bond and the long-term bond is a 20-year Treasury bond. The stock index is described in the text.
Data Sources: ©Morningstar and S&P.

bonds. An inflation-adjusted return of 8.1 percent per annum on a fixed income asset must be regarded as unusual! Investors in the 1980s and 1990s were blessed with high bond returns as well as stock returns. The longer period starting in 1951 witnessed much lower returns on bonds.[10] That's because long-term bonds suffered such large losses in the high inflation period of the 1970s. As Table 2.2 indicates, these losses lowered overall returns to −2.0 percent for the 30-year period ending in 1980.

Extending the bond series back to 1926 gives us returns that are very similar to those over the whole period from 1951 to present, 2.3 percent returns for the five-year medium-term bond and 2.3 percent for the 20-year long-term bond. The table also reports real returns over the period prior to 1951, which are also much lower than in the period from 1981 to 2000.

A reasonable way to interpret this historical record is that, in the long run, bonds earn real returns in the neighborhood of 2 percent to 2.5 percent. Recall that bond returns consist of a coupon plus a capital gain. In periods of rising inflation, there will be sustained capital losses on bonds as yields rise to reflect inflation. This is what we experienced in the 1970s. In periods of falling inflation, such as in the 1980s and 1990s, there will be sustained capital gains on bonds as yields fall. But unless inflation has a long-run trend to it, the capital gain element of the bond return should be close to zero in the long run. Indeed, since 1951, the capital gain component of the long-run bond return has been slightly negative at −0.4 percent.

On the basis of this historical record, how might we form expectations of future bond returns? Forecasts of bond returns in the short run are best left to Wall Street experts. They have about a 50 percent chance of being right in forecasting whether interest rates will rise or fall. Forecasts for the longer run ought to be informed by this long historical record. If real bond returns since 1926 have averaged around 2 percent to 2.5 percent, this seems like a prudent forecast for the future. The last 25 years were a great period to be an investor in bonds. But remember that these returns simply reversed the disastrous losses of the preceding decades.

RECONSIDERING STOCK RETURNS

The collapse of equity prices beginning in 2000 has led many investors to revise their estimates of long-run equity returns. In place of the optimistic estimates of high double-digit returns so characteristic of the late 1990s, some investors now envisage returns on equity equal to or even below those on fixed income.[11] If equity returns are this low in the future, there will have to be major revisions of long-run investment plans. Endowments and foundations will have to adopt significantly lower spending rules, and corporate pension funds will face increased funding costs. Individual investors will have to scale back their retirement plans.

As in the case of bond returns, it's instructive to look at historical returns, especially in periods prior to the bull market of the 1980s and 1990s. Table 2.2 reports average real compound returns over several past periods. The two-decade period from 1981 to 2000 saw unusually high real compound returns of 11.7 percent. No wonder that by the late 1990s, the expectations of investors had become so inflated.

Table 2.2 reports two sets of returns prior to the bull market. The first set of returns begins in 1951, like many estimates in this chapter, and ends in 1980. The second set of estimates begins in 1926 and ends in 1950. The two sets of estimates are remarkably similar, at least as far as the real returns are concerned. Without the bull market of the post-1980 period, the real return on stocks is 6.3 percent or 6.4 percent. An investor making plans in 1981 using historical averages to date would have assumed a much lower equity return than 20 years later.

The five years ending in 1999 saw the most incredible returns of the two decades. The real return on the S&P 500 index for these five years averaged 25.6 percent per year! These five years, moreover, had a dramatic effect on longer-term average returns even when returns are measured over a 50-year period. The average real return on the S&P 500 from 1951 to 1994 was only 7.2 percent. By the end of 1999, the average real return beginning in 1951 had risen to 8.9 percent. Figure 2.4 provides a graph of average real returns measured from 1951 to each year indicated on the graph starting with 1975. An investor measuring the real return on equity from 1951 to 1975 would have obtained a 6.8 percent average, but an investor measuring

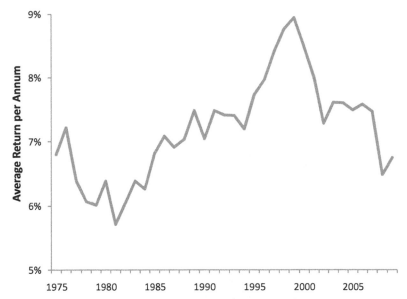

FIGURE 2.4 Estimates of Average Real Returns to Equity (Estimates from 1951 to Dates Shown)
Data Source: ©Morningstar

the return from 1951 to 1999 would have found an average 2.1 percent higher. The dramatic effects of 1995–1999 are evident in this figure.

Too many investors were misled by this bull market into believing that stock returns are always high. The most inflated expectations of future equity returns were adopted by investors who made the mistake of basing their estimates on the 1980s and 1990s only. But even investors who had the good judgment to look at longer spans of history ended up with inflated expectations because of the way that returns in the late 1990s temporarily inflated long-run averages. As Figure 2.4 shows, expectations based on data from 1951 to 1999 were inevitably inflated beyond what would have been reasonable just a few years earlier. The period since then has been one of retrenchment, culminating in the sharp downturn in stock prices during the financial crisis of 2007 and 2008. Figure 2.4 shows how even long-run averages vary widely depending on whether we have just experienced a dot-com boom or a financial crisis bust.

One reason why we might believe that average returns were being distorted by the 1980s and 1990s is that price-earnings (P-E) ratios rose so much over this period. Figure 2.5 shows the variation in P-E ratios for the S&P 500 index since 1951 as measured using the same methodology as

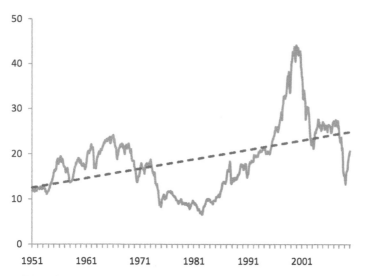

FIGURE 2.5   Price-Earnings Ratios for S&P 500, 1951–2009 (Current
Real Price Relative to 10-Year Average Real Earnings)
Data Source: www.econ.yale.edu/~Shiller described in Shiller (2000).

Robert Shiller in his book, *Irrational Exuberance* (2000).[12] Shiller compares
the S&P 500 index for a given year with the average reported earnings of
the S&P companies over the previous 10 years. Both series are expressed in
real terms using the CPI. The rise in P-Es during the 1990s, in particular, introduced an upward trend into the average real return on equity. Since P-Es
remained relatively high (at least prior to the financial crisis), average historical returns that include the recent period may overestimate future returns.
For that reason, several recent studies have adopted alternative approaches
to estimating equity returns that rely on corporate fundamentals instead of
market returns.

ALTERNATIVE ESTIMATES OF LONG-RUN STOCK RETURNS

Returns on equity are based on two components, the dividend yield and the
capital gain on the stock price. Rising valuations might inflate the capital
gain component, so average historical returns on stocks may give an inflated
estimate of future returns. For that reason, some experts have proposed
basing estimates of stock returns on corporate earnings or dividends rather
than market returns.

Fama and French's (2002) study of the equity premium provides alternatives estimates of stock returns based on these corporate fundamentals. According to Fama and French, the average return on equity can be estimated in three alternative ways. The first measure simply calculates stock returns as we have already done using average dividend yields plus the average capital gains on the S&P 500 index. The second and third measures replace the capital gain on stocks with either the rate of growth of dividends or the rate of growth of earnings of the same firms in the S&P 500 index. (These measures are discussed at greater length in the appendix). The idea behind these measures is that capital gains cannot indefinitely outpace corporate fundamentals, so let's base long-run estimates of stock returns on corporate fundamentals themselves.

Investors in equities are ultimately interested in receiving a stream of dividends on their ownership shares. So it would seem that a measure of equity returns based on the growth of dividends should be preferred to a measure based on earnings. But as Figure 2.6 demonstrates, there has been a long-term decline in dividend yields in the United States, particularly in the last 20 years.[13] As a result, the growth rate of dividends is much lower than that of earnings. The decline in dividend yields may be due to tax policy

FIGURE 2.6 Dividend Yield for S&P 500, 1951–2009
Data Source: www.econ.yale.edu/~Shiller and Bloomberg.

TABLE 2.3 Average Real Returns on the S&P 500, Arithmetic Averages, 1951–2007

Averages based on	Real Arithmetic Averages
Actual capital gain	8.6%
Dividend growth	5.0%
Earnings growth	6.9%

Note: Average returns are obtained by adding the average real dividend yield to the real capital gain as measured by the actual rise in stock prices, by the rate of growth of dividends, or the rate of growth of earnings of the S&P 500 firms.
Data Sources: The dividend and earnings data are from www.econ.yale.edu/~Shiller and the stock price data from Bloomberg.

which favors retained over distributed earnings, but it may also be due to the belief by corporations that internal investment will give stockholders higher returns than their dividends can earn.[14] A measure which is free of variations in corporate dividend policy is one based on earnings growth rather than dividend growth. This third measure replaces the capital gain on the S&P index with the rate of growth of earnings for the firms in that same index.

Table 2.3 reports alternative estimates of average real returns for the S&P 500 based on the three methods for estimating the equity capital gain. Each estimate is obtained by adding to the real dividend yield some measure of the real capital gain on equity. The alternative estimates use actual capital gains, the growth of dividends replacing capital gains, and the growth of earnings replacing capital gains. All three measures are expressed in real terms using the consumer price index. Arithmetic averages rather than geometric averages are reported since the Fama-French methodology calculates arithmetic averages (as shown in the appendix). The sample period used in Table 2.3 ends in 2007 rather than 2009 because reported earnings fluctuated so wildly during 2008 and 2009.[15]

Substituting dividend growth or earnings growth for the capital gain on stocks makes a huge difference. The substitution of dividend growth for the actual capital gains on stocks lowers the real arithmetic average return from 8.6 percent to 5.0 percent. Using earnings growth instead lowers the return to 6.9 percent. These alternative measures of average equity returns avoid reliance on the higher market valuations of the past two decades. But if they more accurately reflect future returns in the equity market, investors' expectations will have a large adjustment ahead.

UPPER AND LOWER BOUNDS FOR EQUITY RETURNS

Investors making decisions about saving rates for retirement need to form estimates of future equity and bond returns. Investors already beginning retirement need to form such estimates in order to set spending rates in retirement. With such a wide variation between estimated returns, how are investors going to make informed decisions about future returns on their portfolio? Perhaps it is most sensible to use the estimates of real returns discussed above to set upper and lower bounds for expected equity returns.

Investment plans should be based on compound real returns, not arithmetic averages. That's because these plans are designed to last for decades or more. So the averages reported in Table 2.3 must be converted into compound long-term equivalents. Fama and French develop what they call long-term estimates of real stock returns derived from arithmetic averages. (Their methodology is explained in the appendix). Table 2.4 reports long-term estimates using the same methodology for the period from 1951 to 2007. Two estimates are provided, one based on actual capital gains and the other based on earnings growth.

Actual capital gains on stocks provide an upper bound for our estimates of future expected equity returns. In Table 2.4, that estimate is 7.3 percent. Figure 2.4 shows that a similar average real return would have been calculated if the sample period ended in the later 1980s or early 1990s. If it had ended in 2000, the real return estimate would have been quite a bit higher, but that would have reflected the high market valuations of the late 1990s.

The lower bound for an estimate of future returns could be based on the rate of growth of dividends or earnings rather than actual capital gains.

TABLE 2.4 Alternative Estimates of Long-Run Real and Nominal Stock Returns (Based on 2.5 percent Inflation Rate), 1951–2007

Averages based on	Real Compound Averages	Nominal Compound Averages (based on 2.5% inflation)
Estimate based on actual capital gain	7.3%	10.0%
Alternative estimate based on earnings growth	5.3%	7.9%

The real compound averages are obtained from the real arithmetic averages in Table 2.3 by using the same methodology as in the Fama-French (2002) study (see text).

Data Sources: The dividend and earnings data are from www.econ.yale.edu/~Shiller and the stock price data from Bloomberg.

Because dividend yields have fallen so much in the last two decades, it's probably better to focus on the earnings-based measures of stock returns. In that case, the real return would be estimated as in Table 2.4 at 5.3 percent using reported earnings. The lower bound would be preferred by investors who are wary of current market valuations.

How much difference does this alternative estimate of equity returns make? Consider a spending rule for a 50/50 portfolio split between stocks and bonds.[16] If stock returns are lowered by 2 percent as in Table 2.4, spending must be lowered by about 1 percent. This is a substantial reduction in spending whether the investor is a foundation (with an unlimited horizon) or a retiree (whose goal is to have the portfolio last through retirement).

To translate estimates into the nominal averages that most investors focus on, we must adopt an explicit forecast for inflation. Table 2.4 calculates the implied nominal stock returns based on a forecast of 2.5 percent for inflation. The estimates of nominal compound returns range from 7.9 percent to 10.0 percent. Some observers might regard even the lower bound as overly optimistic. With the lower bound estimates being based on corporate fundamentals, such observers have to explain why U.S. corporations should be expected to perform significantly worse than they have for the last 50-plus years.

In any case, if investors lower their expectations to these levels from the lofty returns of the 1980s and 1990s, they will have better prospects for reaching their long-run investment goals. Later chapters will use these long-run estimates as the basis for formulating wealth accumulation strategies and for setting spending rules for institutions and families.

APPENDIX: ALTERNATIVE ESTIMATES OF STOCK RETURNS

To understand alternative approaches to estimating equity returns, we need to begin with the basic components of a stock return. The stock return in any given year is equal to the dividend yield plus the capital gain:

$$R_t = D_t/P_{t-1} + (P_t - P_{t-1})/P_{t-1},$$

where P_t is the stock price at the end of year t and D_t is the dividend paid in year t. Estimates of future expected returns based on past historical data implicitly assume that capital gains in the past will repeat themselves. If past capital gains have been inflated as P-Es have risen, however, then past data may not be a good basis for future expectations. For that reason, some experts reject the use of past returns to predict future returns, and turn instead to more fundamental measures of corporate performance.

According to Fama and French (2002), the average return on equity can be estimated in three alternative ways. The first method simply measures the arithmetic average return over the sample period.

$$(1) \quad A(R_t) = A(D_t/P_{t-1}) + A(GP_t),$$

where $GP_t = (P_t - P_{t-1}) / P_{t-1}$, the capital gain on the stock. If there is a rise in P-Es during the sample period, then the average capital gain will reflect this rise in P-Es, thereby inflating the estimate of future equity returns.

According to finance theory, the value of a stock should be based on expected future dividends. So an alternative measure of stock returns replaces the average capital gain by the average growth rate of dividends:

$$(2) \quad A(RD_t) = A(D_t/P_{t-1}) + A(GD_t),$$

where GD_t is the growth rate of dividends. Fama and French call this the *dividend growth* model of returns.

Finally, the third approach replaces the growth rate of dividends with the growth rate of earnings, GY_t:

$$(3) \quad A(RY_t) = A(D_t/P_{t-1}) + A(GY_t).$$

Fama and French call this model the *earnings growth* model.

In their study, Fama and French provided estimates of equity returns extending back into the nineteenth century. They report estimates of real equity returns for three periods, 1872 to 1950, 1951 to 2000, and 1872 to 2000. Their thesis is that the real return on equities over the last five decades is abnormally high not only when measured against either dividend or earnings growth (as discussed above), but also when compared with real returns in the earlier period, 1872–1950. The estimate of the real equity return using actual gains (equation 1) is only 6.4 percent for the 1872 to 1950 period, in contrast to their estimate of 7.9 percent for the 1951 to 2000 period.[17] On the other hand, the estimates of real equity returns based on real dividend growth (equation 2) are not much different in the earlier and later periods. Fama and French do not provide estimates of real equity returns based on earnings growth (as in equation 3) prior to 1951 because of the dubious quality of the earnings data. Fama and French conclude that it is the average real return using (1) measured over the last 50 years that is out of line.

Table 2.3 reports equity returns estimated for the 1951 to 2007 period using the Fama-French methodology. Arithmetic averages, expressed in real terms, are reported following the methodology in the Fama and French study. The equity returns reported in Table 2.3 are based on average annual returns for the S&P 500 generated as follows:

a. The data set consists of end-of-year price indexes (for the S&P 500) and annual totals (for dividends and earnings). The stock prices are from Bloomberg. The dividend and earnings series are provided by Robert Shiller on his web site, www.econ.yale.edu/~shiller. Both series are updated using the Standard and Poor's web site.
b. Real returns are calculated using the consumer price index from the IMF, International Financial Statistics

Equations 1 through 3 refer to arithmetic averages. Fama and French obtain long-term compound averages after adjusting for biases due to the higher volatility of earnings growth or stock price gains relative to dividend growth. Their procedure adjusts the arithmetic average of the RY_t series by subtracting 0.5 times the difference in the variances of the RY_t and RD_t series. They use a similar adjustment for the R_t series based on the actual capital gains on the stock index. When this procedure is applied to the arithmetic estimates of Table 2.3, we obtain the real compound averages reported in Table 2.4. These adjustments produce a long-term real return of 5.3 percent based on earnings growth compared with a long-term real return of 7.3 percent based on actual capital gains. The estimate of stock returns based on actual capital gains reported in Table 2.4 is about 1 percent lower than the estimate reported by Fama and French.[18] Their estimates ended in 2000 near the peak of the market. This underscores again the role of the stock market boom of the late 1990s in inflating long-term returns.

The estimates in Table 2.4 based on actual capital gains and earnings growth provide upper and lower bounds for stock market returns. With a gap of 2 percent, it makes a lot of difference whether long-run plans are based on the upper or lower estimates. In later chapters we will explore some of the implications of using these different estimates.

NOTES

1. Unlikely is not the same as inconceivable. It doesn't make much sense to base future estimates of asset returns on a period that includes such unusual events. In any case, as will be shown below, the inclusion of years 1926 through 1950 does not change conclusions regarding long-term real returns or the equity premium.
2. Nine recessions is admittedly not a large statistical sample, but it is certainly a larger sample than can be found when we study emerging markets or alternative investments where data sets begin in the 1980s or later.

3. See the discussion of the large-cap series in Chapter 1.
4. In February 1994, the Fed unexpectedly raised interest rates by 50 basis points. George Soros's hedge fund is said to have lost $600 million during this period, while Steinhardt Partners lost even more. (*New York Times*, March 4, 1994).
5. When compound averages are involved, geometric differences between two asset classes are calculated using division rather than arithmetic subtraction. See the discussion in Chapter 4 of Ibbotson SBBI (2008).
6. A good survey of this research is provided by Kocherlakota (1996).
7. That is, the investor is choosing between these assets in an either-or framework. Later we will discuss how the investor would choose an optimal portfolio of stocks and bonds.
8. As explained in Chapter 1, the arithmetic average is the least unbiased estimate of the return over a one-year horizon and the standard deviation is measured relative to the arithmetic average.
9. To avoid rounding errors, the returns are stated with more precision in this calculation.
10. Strangely enough, the real return on the medium-term series is actually higher than that of the long-term series. The arithmetic average for long-term bonds is higher than that of medium-term bonds.
11. Arnott and Bernstein (2002), for example, conclude that the equity premium over the risk-free rate is zero and that a sensible expectation for future real returns on stocks and bonds is 2 to 4 percent.
12. The stock price and earnings data are from www.econ.yale.edu/~shiller which updates series reported in Shiller (2000).
13. The dividend data are also from www.econ.yale.edu/~shiller. The dividend yield is calculated by dividing the dividend for a given year by the S&P price on the last day of the preceding year. The S&P price is from Bloomberg.
14. The 2003 tax legislation lowering taxes on dividends significantly reduced these tax disadvantages.
15. Average reported earnings fluctuated from 66.2 in 2007 to 14.9 in 2007 and 51.0 in 2009. The real rate of growth of earnings was −77 percent in 2008 and +233 percent in 2009. Even though the estimates in Table 2.3 are based on almost 60 years of data, the arithmetic averages for the earnings measure fluctuate widely over the 2008 to 2009 period.
16. As explained in Chapter 15 on retirement portfolios, a 50/50 portfolio might be chosen by an investor early in retirement.
17. This is the compound real return based on equation (1). The arithmetic average real return is 8.3 percent for 1872–1950.
18. Their estimate in Table IV of their paper is for the real equity premium, not the real equity return. But once the long-term equity premium is converted into a return, the estimate is about 8.3 percent for the real equity return based on actual capital gains.

CHAPTER 3

Small-Cap Stocks

The SBBI 2010 Yearbook displays a graph showing the cumulative returns of different kinds of stocks and bonds since 1926. A dollar invested in the SBBI small-cap index in 1926 grows to $12,231 by the end of 2009. In contrast, a dollar invested in the large-cap index grows to $2,592 and a dollar invested in long-term Treasury bonds grows to $84.[1] In assessing returns for any asset class, the natural question to ask is whether higher returns are offset by higher risks. So this chapter will compare the risk-adjusted performance of small-cap and large-cap stocks.

In the late 1970s, several researchers built a case that there is a small-cap premium even when small caps are adjusted for their greater risk. Banz (1981) was the first author to document the relationship between the size of a firm and its return. According to Banz, not only are returns on small-cap stocks higher than those on large-cap stocks, but there is an abnormal excess return when measured against the capital asset pricing model (CAPM) security market line. In a series of widely-cited studies, Fama and French show that the size effect (together with the book value effect to be discussed in the next chapter) is important in explaining stock market returns.[2]

Researchers established that small-cap stocks had another intriguing feature. Most of the small-cap premium occurs in one month, January. Keim (1983) was among the first studies to document this anomaly.[3] Using daily data for the period from 1969 to 1979, Keim showed that more than 50 percent of any small-cap premium is due to January returns and that 50 percent of this January premium is achieved in the first week of trading. No wonder investors (and researchers) were intrigued by small caps!

One of the themes of this chapter is that the small-cap premium seems to have diminished ever since research on small caps peaked in the early 1980s. It's as if researchers jinxed small caps. To show how much things have changed, consider average returns on small and large caps using the SBBI series as described in Table 3.1. (The SBBI small-cap series will be defined in greater detail in the next section). From 1951 to 1980, the average

TABLE 3.1   Evidence on Small-Cap Premiums: SBBI Small-Cap and Large-Cap Indexes

Arithmetic Averages in Percent per month	1951–1980	1981–2009
Small cap Premium over Large caps	0.375%	0.138%
Small cap Premium in January alone	5.27%	1.74%
Small cap January Return over Average for Rest of Year	5.90%	1.88%

First row shows premium of small caps over large caps in percent per month for the period indicated. Second row shows same premium for month of January alone. Third row shows the January return relative to the average return for the rest of the year.
Data Source: ©Morningstar.

excess return on small caps was 0.375 percent per month or 4.50 percent annualized. From 1981 to 2009, this excess return falls to 0.138 percent per month or 1.65 percent annualized. As we will see later in this chapter, the evidence for a small-cap premium is even weaker when the Russell 2000 small-cap index is analyzed.

The January premium is defined as the excess return of January relative to the *average* monthly return of the other 11 months of that year. The average excess return is a surprisingly large 5.90 percent per month over the 30-year period ending in 1980. The January return on small caps is also much larger than the large-cap return for the same month. In Table 3.1, the excess return for January for the SBBI small-cap index over the SBBI large-cap index is 5.27 percent per month (for the same 30-year period). This compares with an excess return for the year as a whole of 0.375 percent per month. So it is the month of January which is the key to the small-cap premium. This January effect has also seemed to diminish more recently. Since 1981, the small cap premium in January has diminished from 5.27 percent per month to 1.74 percent per month. That's still a hefty premium for a one month return, though transaction costs in the small-cap space may be large enough to prevent abnormal returns for investors seeking to exploit this premium.

This chapter will not focus on the January effect per se since this is not a book about short-term trading strategies. Instead, we will ask whether the small-cap premium continues to exist and, if so, how this should influence portfolio allocations. This chapter will investigate small-cap returns using several different databases. The Russell indexes are often used as benchmarks to measure portfolio performance for large-cap and small-cap managers. So the Russell indexes will be discussed first. Then several other indexes will be examined for a longer sample period. The chapter begins by describing the makeup of the U.S. stock market by size.

WHAT DO WE MEAN BY SMALL-CAP STOCKS?

Stocks in the United States range in value from a few million dollars to more than $340 billion. U.S. stocks are traded on a number of exchanges across the United States. But most stocks are listed on three exchanges: the New York Stock Exchange (NYSE), NASDAQ, and the American Stock Exchange (AMEX). The Ibbotson SBBI *2010 Yearbook* provides a breakdown of the stocks on these three exchanges into 10 deciles.[4] The deciles are defined by using NYSE stocks alone, but stocks from all three exchanges are included in each decile so the number of stocks varies from decile to decile.[5] The lowest decile (10) includes more than 1,300 stocks because many of the stocks listed on the NASDAQ and AMEX are much smaller than the average stock on the NYSE.

The largest U.S. stocks dominate the overall market capitalization of the U.S. stock market. The top decile includes only 168 firms, but these firms represent more than 63 percent of the total market capitalization of the three stock exchanges. The top three deciles include only 518 firms, but represent more than 83 percent of the total capitalization. On the other hand, the lowest two deciles contain more than 1,900 stocks, but represent less than 2.5 percent of the market capitalization!

The longest small-cap series available is the small-cap index reported in the SBBI Yearbooks, the index cited in Table 3.1. For most of the sample period, prior to 1982, the small-cap series consisted of the stocks in the lowest two deciles of the NYSE alone. Starting in 1982, the index became identical to the return series of Dimensional Fund Advisors Small Company Fund which is a fund that (until recently) invested in only the lowest two deciles of the NYSE and other exchanges. According to the Ibbotson SBBI *2010 Yearbook*, the Fund contains approximately 2,400 stocks with a median capitalization of $157 million.[6] So this small-cap index includes many micro-cap stocks that are too small to be included in other small-cap indexes (see below).

Perhaps the best-known small-cap index is the Russell 2000, an index that begins in 1979. This index is often used in benchmarking small-cap managers. The Russell 2000 is one component of the all-cap Russell

TABLE 3.2 Market Capitalization of the Russell Indexes

In $billions	Median	Largest Firm	Smallest Firm	Percent of Russell 3000
R 1000	$3.3	$341.0	$2.3	92%
R 2000	$0.3	$ 2.3	$0.08	8%
R 2500	$0.4	$ 4.2	$0.08	18%

Source: 2009 Capitalizations from Russell.com.

3000 consisting of the top 3000 stocks in the U.S. stock market. The Russell 2000 index, representing small-cap stocks, consists of the smallest 2000 of the stocks in the Russell 3000.

The Russell series are described in more detail in Table 3.2. There are three series of interest: the Russell 1000 index of large-cap stocks, the Russell 2000 index of small-cap stocks, and the Russell 2500 index of small-cap and mid-cap stocks. The latter consists of all stocks in the Russell 3000 index except the top 500. Table 3.2 provides information about the capitalizations of the median-, maximum-, and minimum-size firms in each index. Notice that the smallest firm in the Russell 2000 index has a capitalization of $80 million, while the smallest firm in the Russell 1000 index has a capitalization of $2.3 billion.

What types of firms do we find in the Russell 2000 small-cap index? Table 3.3 presents a breakdown of the industries represented in this index (as of August 2009). Financial services, a category that ranges from banks to insurance companies to real estate investment trusts, represent 20.8 percent of the index, while technology, consumer discretionary, health care, and producer durables represent more than 10 percent each. The top ten firms in this small-cap index, listed in the same table, are hardly household names. But each of these has capitalizations approaching $2 billion. The manager of a small-cap fund has to be knowledgeable about a host of smaller companies. On the other hand, with so little analyst coverage of these firms, active managers may be able to exploit market inefficiencies that are difficult to find in the large-cap space.

The most interesting information in Table 3.2 concerns the relative size of the total capitalization of the three indexes. The Russell 2000 index represents only 8 percent of the total capitalization of the Russell 3000 index. If an investor were using market capitalization to decide on asset allocation between large-cap and small-cap stocks, then that investor would assign only 8 percent of the U.S. stock allocation to small-cap stocks. Since many portfolios include substantially higher proportions allocated to

TABLE 3.3 Russell 200 Small-Cap Index

Industries	Market Cap	Top Firms	Market Cap
Financial Services	20.8%	Human Genome	0.27%
Technology	16.6%	Tupperware	0.27%
Consumer Discretionary	14.7%	Bally Technologies	0.25%
Health Care	14.3%	Medarex	0.24%
Producer Durables	13.8%	Highwoods	0.24%
Materials	7.5%	Skyworks	0.24%
Utilities	4.6%	Polycom	0.23%
Other Energy	4.0%	Jack Henry	0.23%
Consumer Staples	2.5%	Rock-Tenn	0.22%
Autos & Transport	0.5%	Tetra Tech	0.22%

Source: 2009 Capitalizations from ishares.com.

small-cap stocks, there must be significant evidence justifying what we might term over-weights to small-cap stocks. We will consider such evidence in the sections to follow.

Before introducing this evidence, consider the relative capitalization of small- and mid-cap stocks together as represented in the Russell 2500 index. This index constitutes 18 percent or almost one-fifth of the U.S. stock universe. Some investors have chosen to use the Russell 2500 index as a benchmark for two reasons. First, the market capitalization of this benchmark makes it easier to justify a separately managed account for this part of the portfolio.[7] Second, the mid-cap stocks included in this index have had unusually strong performance since the Russell indexes began. We will consider the relative performance of the small-mid cap index below.

RELATIVE PERFORMANCE OF LARGE-CAP AND SMALL-CAP STOCKS—RUSSELL SERIES

Over the 30 years since the Russell indexes began, small- and large-cap stocks have fluctuated widely relative to one another. Figure 3.1 compares the returns on the Russell 1000 and 2000 indexes by showing the yearly excess return on small caps (defined as the Russell 2000 return minus the Russell 1000 return). In some years, small caps outperform large caps by 10 percent or more. In other years, large caps shine. In 1998, large caps outperformed small caps by almost 30 percent. Overall, however, there seems no clear winner. So there doesn't appear to be a small-cap premium.

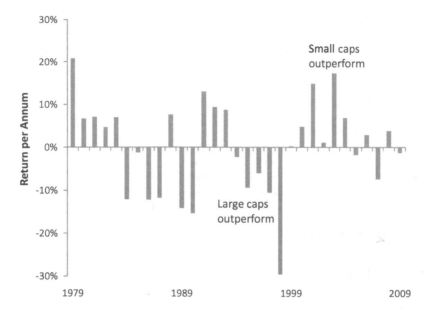

FIGURE 3.1 Excess Returns: Russell 2000 minus Russell 1000 Index
Data Source: Russell®.

This impression is confirmed in Table 3.4 where we summarize the long-run performance over the 30 years as a whole. Both geometric (compound) averages and arithmetic averages are reported for the period from 1979 through December 2009. The compound geometric return on large caps is actually higher than that on small caps, 11.5 percent versus 11.3 percent. Using arithmetic averages, small caps have the higher average return, but the two returns are still very close to one another.[8]

Table 3.4 also reports the (annualized) standard deviations for the two asset classes. The standard deviation for small-cap stocks, 19.9 percent, is

TABLE 3.4 Returns for Russell Large-Cap, Small-Cap, and Small-/Mid-Cap Stocks, 1979–2009

	Geometric Average	Arithmetic Average	Standard Deviation	Sharpe Ratio
Russell 1000	11.5%	12.2%	15.6%	0.43
Russell 2000	11.3%	12.8%	19.9%	0.37
Russell 2500	12.7%	13.7%	18.5%	0.44

Data Source: Russell®.

much larger than that for large-cap stocks, 15.6 percent. In the last column of the table, the Sharpe ratios are calculated using the arithmetic averages over the sample period. The arithmetic average is used rather than the geometric average because risk-adjusted performance is most easily calculated using the arithmetic average.[9] With the standard deviation being so much larger for small-cap stocks, the Sharpe ratio is much smaller for this asset class.

Table 3.4 also gives summary statistics for the Russell 2500, the combined small- and mid-cap index (which is often referred to as the SMID index). The R 2500 index has a much higher average return than either the R 1000 or R 2000 index. It also has a higher Sharpe ratio than the small-cap index since the standard deviation of the R 2500 index is smaller than that of the small-cap index. The Sharpe ratio of the R 2500 is even as large as that of the Russell 1000. Thus the R 2500 small- and mid-cap index provides an attractive alternative to the R 2000 small-cap index as a way of broadening the portfolio beyond large-cap stocks.

There is a potential pitfall in broadening the portfolio to include mid-cap stocks. Mid-cap stocks are already included in a large-cap allocation, since allocations to the Russell 2500 index overlap with allocations to the Russell 1000 index. That is, the bottom 500 stocks in the R 1000 are included in both the R 1000 and R 2500 indexes. An alternative approach to allocation is to break the R 1000 into two mutually exclusive sub-indexes. Russell offers two additional indexes, the Russell 200 and the Russell 800, with the latter comprising the 800 smallest stocks of the Russell 1000. The latter is called the mid-cap index. It's not clear why Russell chose to define mid caps differently in its stand-alone mid-cap index (R 800) and its SMID index (R 2500). In any case, there are few managers that track the R 200, so pursuing this strategy of dividing stocks between the R 200 and R 800 does not seem viable at this time. An easier alternative is for the large-cap manager to be benchmarked against the S&P 500 and the small/mid-cap manager to be benchmark against the Russell 2500.[10]

The Sharpe ratio provides a comparison between small-cap and large-cap stocks that adjusts for the total risk of each index, both systematic and unsystematic risk. Table 3.5 adjusts the risk of each index for systematic risk alone using the capital asset pricing model. This table reports the betas of each index measured relative to the Russell 3000 all-cap index. Both the Russell 1000 and 2000 indexes have near-zero alphas relative to the Russell 3000. This isn't surprising in the case of the Russell 1000 index because it represents 92 percent of the Russell 3000 index. But it is surprising that the Russell 2000 has no positive alpha. That is, the Russell 2000 index provides *no small-cap premium* once it is adjusted for systematic risk.

Table 3.5 also reports the beta of the Russell 2500 SMID index relative to the market as a whole. This index has a beta of 1.08 and an alpha of

TABLE 3.5   Russell Returns Relative to Security Market Line, 1979–2009

	Average Return	Beta	CAPM Return	Size Premium (Alpha)
Russell 1000	12.2%	0.99	12.1%	+ 0.1%
Russell 2000	12.8%	1.11	12.9%	−0.1%
Russell 2500	13.7%	1.08	12.7%	+ 1.0%

Data Source: Russell®.

1.0 percent. So in this sample period, a small-cap premium is found only when the small-cap index is augmented with mid caps.

RELATIVE PERFORMANCE OF LARGE-CAP AND SMALL-CAP STOCKS—SBBI SERIES

It is important to investigate whether the relative performance of small-cap stocks is due to the particular sample period selected. The Russell data provide 31 years of evidence beginning in 1979. For most of the sample period beginning in 1979, the U.S. economy was booming and U.S. stocks were in a sustained rally from the lows of the 1970s. Interest rates, after hitting a peak in 1981, fell for most of the next 30 years. So perhaps there is something unusual about the recent period that limits the small-cap premium.

To investigate this possibility, we turn to the SBBI series to study returns for the longer period. The SBBI small-cap series begins in 1926, but as in the previous chapter we will begin the analysis in 1951. Table 3.6 reports the basic statistics for the SBBI small-cap series (previously described) and the SBBI large-cap series for 1951 to 2009. The results are quite different than those reported for the Russell series. The SBBI small-cap index has a return that is 2.4 percent above that of the large-cap index. As discussed above, this small-cap premium inspired research studies in the early 1980s which were among the first to criticize the standard capital asset pricing model.

TABLE 3.6   SBBI Large-Cap and Small-Cap Returns, 1951–2009

	Geometric Average	Arithmetic Average	Standard Deviation	Sharpe Ratio
Large-Cap Index	10.7%	11.3%	14.6%	0.45
Small-Cap Index	13.1%	14.4%	20.1%	0.48

Data Source: ©Morningstar.

Two studies, by Banz (1981) and Reinganum (1981) are especially notable, the latter describing the small-cap premium as an anomaly.

Figure 3.2 shows the yearly excess returns for small caps over large caps. It is evident from this figure that small caps did particularly well in the late 1960s and in the period from 1975 to 1983. In 1969, for example, small caps had an excess return of almost 60 percent. Over the period from 1975 to 1983, moreover, small-cap returns exceeded large-cap returns by more than 19 percent per year on average.[11] It's this extended period of small-cap dominance that explains the higher average returns found over the period beginning in 1951. It's interesting that studies of the small-cap premium emerged near the end of this period of small-cap dominance.

It is useful to ask to what extent is the long-run small-cap premium, as measured using the SBBI series, a reward for risk. Table 3.6 reports Sharpe ratios for the SBBI small-cap and large-cap series. If the large-cap and small-cap returns are adjusted for risk using Sharpe ratios, there is only a minor difference between the two series (with the Sharpe ratio of small caps being 0.48 versus a ratio of 0.45 for large caps). If the systematic risk of small caps is measured instead of the total risk, however, the advantages of small-cap stocks are more evident. For measuring systematic risk, we use the total market index from the Fama-French database. The total market index is

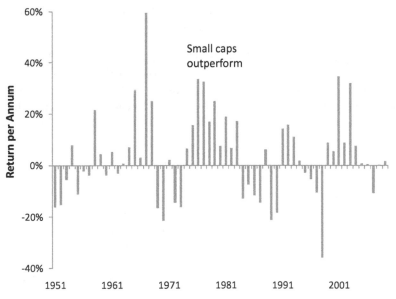

FIGURE 3.2 Excess Returns: SBBI Small-Cap minus Large-Cap Index
Data Source: ©Morningstar.

a value-weighted index of all of the stocks in the Center for Research in Security Prices (CRSP) data set used by Fama and French in their studies.[12] Since there are more than 4000 stocks in their database (as of December 2009), the index is broader than that of the Russell 3000.[13] Using the value-weighted total market index as the measure of the market, the beta of the SBBI small-cap index is 1.13. With a return on the market of 11.2 percent, small caps should have a return of 12.1 percent.[14] Instead, the return on small caps is 14.4 percent. So the alpha for small caps, the excess return relative to the security market line, is an impressive 2.3 percent. Evidently it's possible to diversify away at least some of the risk of small-cap stocks. If only systematic risk as measured by beta remains, the excess return provided by small-cap stocks as measured by alpha provides a substantial small-cap premium.

RELATIVE PERFORMANCE OF LARGE-CAP AND SMALL-CAP STOCKS—BROADER ANALYSIS

A broader analysis of small-cap stocks confirms that there is a sizable small-cap premium for the longer sample period. This broader analysis draws on a data set developed by Fama and French using CRSP data. As part of their study of size and style effects on stock returns, Fama and French developed a data set dividing U.S. stocks by size in deciles and in quintiles. This chapter will analyze the quintile data in detail.[15]

Table 3.7 summarizes this data set. The methodology to divide stocks into deciles and quintiles is similar to that reported in the SBBI Yearbook discussed above.[16] The quintiles are defined using NYSE stocks alone, then stocks from the NASDAQ and AMEX are added to each quintile. For that reason, Quintile 1 with the largest stocks has only 340 firms, but 77.2 percent

TABLE 3.7   Stock Market by Quintile, 1951–2009

Quintile	Number of Firms	Percent Capitalization	Average Return	Standard Deviation
Largest	340	77.2%	10.9%	14.4%
Quintile 2	372	12.3%	12.9%	16.8%
Quintile 3	454	5.6%	13.3%	17.7%
Quintile 4	712	3.1%	13.8%	19.3%
Smallest	2229	1.9%	13.7%	20.7%

Data Source: Fama-French Database.

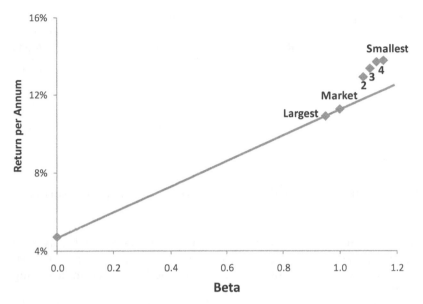

FIGURE 3.3   Stocks by Quintile, 1951–2009
Data Source: Fama-French Database.

of the market capitalization. In contrast, Quintile 5 with the smallest stocks has 2229 firms but only 1.9 percent of the capitalization.

Table 3.7 shows a systematic increase in returns as the average size of firms diminishes. The smallest firms have an average return that is 2.8 percent larger than the largest firms. But the firms in Quintiles 2, 3, and 4 also have sizable premiums over those of the largest firms. A similar set of findings is obtained if the stock market is broken up by deciles. In that case, all nine of the smaller deciles have substantial excess returns relative to Decile 1 which has the largest stocks.

The small-cap premium still prevails if the returns are adjusted for risk. Figure 3.3 shows a security market line defined by using the value-weighted total market index and the one-month Treasury bill return. The quintile indexes are then displayed relative to the security market line. As detailed in the accompanying Table 3.8, all four of the smaller quintiles have positive alphas. The alphas range from 1.1 percent for Quintile 2 to 1.6 percent for Quintile 5 (the latter with the smallest firms). There is a small-cap premium in this data set even after the stocks are adjusted for (systematic) risk. This is true whether Quintile 4 or Quintile 5 is chosen to represent small caps. There is also a mid-cap premium as evidenced by the alphas found for Quintiles 2 and 3.

TABLE 3.8 Beta and Alpha by Quintile, 1951–2009

Quintile	Return	Beta	Alpha
Largest	10.9%	0.95	0.0%
Quintile 2	12.9%	1.08	1.1%
Quintile 3	13.3%	1.11	1.4%
Quintile 4	13.8%	1.15	1.5%
Smallest	13.7%	1.13	1.6%

Data Source: Fama-French Database.

Let's summarize the findings about returns and risks for small-cap stocks.

1. Over the longer run, small-cap stocks appear to have a higher average return than large-cap stocks. This is not true of the period of the Russell data set from 1979 to 2009, but is true of the longer period beginning in 1951.
2. For both periods analyzed, the standard deviation of small-cap stocks exceeds that of large-cap stocks.
3. If the Russell data set is used in the 1979–2009 period, the risk-adjusted return on large caps is actually higher than that on small caps if Sharpe ratios are used. If only systematic risk is considered, the alpha for small caps is slightly negative. So there is no evidence of a small-cap premium once small caps are adjusted for risk.
4. For the period extending back to 1951, the small-cap premium is substantial. This premium is found both using the SBBI small-cap index as well as the quintile data provided by Fama and French.

So over the long period of capital market history favored in this study, the small-cap premium is an important phenomenon. How it should affect portfolio decisions will be considered in the last section.

LARGE-CAP AND SMALL-CAP STOCKS IN A PORTFOLIO CONTEXT

The analysis so far has not considered the role of small-cap stocks within a portfolio with both bonds and stocks. It's useful to consider the returns of small-cap stocks by themselves or relative to large-cap stocks. But most portfolios also have significant holdings of bonds, so the performance of small caps in a portfolio of stocks and bonds is therefore of interest. This

TABLE 3.9 Returns on U.S. Stocks and Bonds

Asset	Average Return	Standard Deviation	Correlation with R 1000	Correlation with R 2000
Russell 1000	12.2%	15.6%	1.00	
Russell 2000	12.8%	19.9%	0.85	1.00
Russell 2500	13.7%	18.5%	0.90	0.99
Barclays Aggregate	8.4%	5.9%	0.24	0.15

Data Sources: Barclays Capital and Russell®.

section will consider small-cap performance in portfolios that have 30 percent invested in bonds and 70 percent in stocks.

The first set of portfolios will be based on Russell data for small caps and large caps. Recall that small caps as represented by the Russell 2000 index did not outperform large caps either in terms of returns or risk-adjusted returns. Nonetheless, it's entirely possible that small-cap stocks could perform well in a portfolio consisting of bonds and stocks depending on the correlations among the asset classes. To examine this possibility, we will consider a three asset portfolio consisting of large and small-cap stocks, represented by the Russell 1000 and 2000 indexes, and bonds, represented by the Barclays Capital Aggregate Bond Index. As an alternative to this portfolio, the Russell 2500 small/mid-cap index will replace the Russell 2000 small-cap index.

Table 3.9 reports the returns and risks of each asset for the period from 1979 to 2009. The table also reports the correlations among the asset classes. The correlation between large-cap and small-cap stocks is high at 0.85. So there is limited diversification benefit from mixing these two types of U.S. stocks. The correlation between large caps and the Russell 2500 small/mid-cap index is even higher at 0.90. Small-cap stocks have a lower correlation with bonds than do large-cap stocks, but the correlations in both cases are quite low.

Table 3.10 examines the effects of diversification into small or mid caps. The top half of the table reports on diversification over the 1979 to 2009 period using Russell data. Three portfolios are reported. The first portfolio (large only) has 70 percent invested in the Russell 1000 and 30 percent in the Barclays Capital Aggregate bond index. The second and third portfolios reduce the large-cap allocation to 50 percent and substitute either the Russell 2000 small-cap index or the Russell 2500 small/mid-cap index. So 20 percent is allocated either to the R 2000 or R 2500. The results are quite disappointing. Substituting 20 percent into the Russell 2000 actually lowers the Sharpe ratio (though only marginally). That's because the standard

TABLE 3.10 Effects of Diversification into Small-Cap and Mid-Cap Stocks

	Average Return	Standard Deviation	Sharpe Ratio
Russell Data 1979–2009			
Large cap only	11.1%	11.5%	0.48
with Russell 2000	11.2%	11.9%	0.47
with Russell 2500	11.4%	11.8%	0.50
SBBI Data 1951–2009			
Large cap only	9.8%	10.5%	0.48
with small caps	10.4%	10.9%	0.52

Large only portfolio consists of 70 percent in large-cap stocks and 30 percent in bonds. Alternative portfolios consist of 50 percent in large caps, 30 percent in bonds, and 20 percent in either small caps or small/mid caps. The Barclays Aggregate series is used for 1979–2009 and the SBBI medium term Treasury for the longer period. *Data Sources:* Barclays Capital, ©Morningstar and Russell®.

deviation of the portfolio increases relative to that of the portfolio with only large caps. Substituting 20 percent into the Russell 2500 raises the Sharpe ratio, but again only marginally. So, at least during the Russell sample period from 1979 to 2009, diversification into small caps or small and mid caps makes little difference.

The bottom half of Table 3.10 examines the effects of diversification into small caps during the longer period beginning in 1951. This set of experiments uses SBBI data for large-cap and small-cap stocks and for medium-term Treasury bonds. The experiments are set up just as before. In the large-only portfolio, a 70 percent allocation to large caps is combined with a 30 percent allocation to medium-term bonds. In the portfolio with small caps, the allocation shifts to 50 percent in large caps, 20 percent in small caps, and 30 percent in bonds. The results are a little more encouraging for small caps. Shifting 20 percent of the portfolio into small caps raises the return on the portfolio by 0.6 percent and raises the Sharpe ratio from 0.48 to 0.52. Alpha* translates this difference in Sharpe ratios into an excess return. At the level of risk of the portfolio with small caps included, there is an excess return of 0.4 percent. That's not very impressive for a 20 percent allocation to an asset class. But at least there is an increase rather than decrease in risk-adjusted returns. Presumably we will be able to find more effective ways to diversify the portfolio as we introduce other assets later in this book.

What lessons can be drawn from this analysis? The most obvious lesson is the relative performance of small-cap stocks varies widely by sample period. The late 1960s and the late 1970s were terrific periods for small-cap stocks. But another lesson is equally important—that all U.S. stocks are highly correlated with one another. We will have to find more effective ways to diversify.

SUMMARY—KEY FEATURES OF SMALL-CAP STOCKS

Small-cap stocks represent less than 10 percent of the market capitalization of the U.S. stock market. Whether they should be allotted a higher proportion of the strategic portfolio depends on their risk and return characteristics. If one analyzes the Russell indexes for small and large-cap stocks, indexes that begin in 1979, it is difficult to build a case for overweighting small-cap stocks. Whether returns are analyzed using Sharpe ratios or beta and alpha, the results are the same. Small caps do not outperform large caps. The small-cap premium found in the academic literature published in the early 1980s does not seem to exist in the Russell sample period. Only when mid-cap stocks are added to small caps to form the Russell 2500 (or SMID) index is it possible to find a premium for the smaller stocks.

The picture changes significantly if the analysis is extended back through the 1950s. This is true if the SBBI small-cap index is adjusted for risk using standard deviations and Sharpe ratios or using beta and alpha from CAPM. Moreover, the same type of results are found favoring a small-cap premium if the analysis is extended to consider quintiles of stocks above the lowest quintile used in the SBBI small-cap index. For the 59 years beginning in 1951, the small-cap premium is alive and well.

The implications for asset allocation depend on which set of data and period the investor relies on. If the Russell data and the shorter sample period of this data are relied on, then the investor is probably better off confining the small-cap allocation to its weight in the market which is less than 10 percent. Or, alternatively, the investor could choose a manager that invests in both small and mid-cap stocks in which case the allocation could rise to 20 percent of stocks or more. If the full 59 years of evidence is considered, then the allocation to small caps could rise considerably. But even then the gain from diversification is limited.

NOTES

1. Ibbotson SBBI *2010 Yearbook*, p. 25.
2. See particularly Fama and French (1992) and (1993).

3. Reinganum (1983) investigated whether the January returns were related to tax-loss selling.
4. These deciles are defined by the Center for Research in Security Prices (CRSP) at the Graduate School of Business of the University of Chicago.
5. The deciles are defined by splitting NYSE stocks into 10 equal-sized groups of stocks in order of their capitalization, then stocks from the NASDAQ and AMEX are assigned to the deciles depending on their capitalization. The NYSE universe excludes closed end funds, preferred stocks, REITS, foreign stocks, ADRs, etc.
6. In April 2001, DFA changed the name of its fund to the DFA Micro Cap Fund and changed some of the criteria. The key change was that it began to target stocks in the bottom 4 percent of U.S. equities (including those on AMEX and NASDAQ). So now the SBBI index includes stocks that are in deciles above 9 and 10. See Ibbotson SBBI *2010 Yearbook*, p. 43.
7. Separately managed accounts (as opposed to mutual funds) often have minimum investments as large as $100,000. In a $1 million portfolio, it is difficult to justify a separate manager for 9 percent of the U.S. equity part of the portfolio and even more difficult to divide the small-cap allocation between value and growth managers. Mutual funds, as opposed to separately managed accounts, typically have very low minimums, so diversification of small-cap allocations along growth and value lines would not be limited.
8. The gap between geometric and arithmetic averages is proportional to the variance of the series. In the case of small-cap stocks, the relatively large variance leads to a particularly large gap between the geometric and arithmetic means.
9. See the discussion in Chapter 1.
10. The S&P 500 firms are not necessarily the same firms as in the top half of the Russell 1000, but there is a lot of overlap between these two sets of firms.
11. Siegel (2002) notes how much higher small cap stock returns were in the 1975 to 1983 period than over the longer run.
12. The index is reported on the web pages of Kenneth French at http://mba. tuck.dartmouth.edu/pages/faculty/ken.french/data_library.html
13. The capitalization of the Russell 3000, however, is more than 99 percent of the capitalization of the total market.
14. That is, a security with a beta of 1.13 should have an expected return of 12.1 percent on the security market line since the risk-free return is 4.7 percent and the market return is 11.2 percent.
15. The decile data leads to similar conclusions, but is more difficult to summarize.
16. Note that the numbering of the deciles and quintiles found in the database has been reversed in this chapter to make it comparable to the Ibbotson SBBI *2010 Yearbook* table.

CHAPTER 4

Value and Growth Investing

In the last chapter, we searched for a small-cap premium using a variety of data sets and time periods. There is a corresponding value premium that is said to reward investment in value stocks relative to growth stocks. Value stocks are usually identified as those with relatively low market prices to book values. This chapter will investigate whether value stocks do offer a premium over growth stocks.

For the past two decades, many investment advisors have divided their U.S. stock allocations along the value-growth dimension. Since portfolios are also typically divided by size, many of these same advisors divide portfolios into four quadrants called *style boxes*: large-cap value and growth and small-cap value and growth. Two influential papers by Eugene Fama and Kenneth French present evidence that book-to-market and size explain a large portion of the cross-section variation of stocks, so it makes sense to divide portfolios along these two dimensions.[1] We will examine the chief characteristics of value and growth indexes, beginning with a description of large-cap value and growth stocks.

DESCRIPTION OF THE RUSSELL 1000 INDEXES

Value and growth stocks will be compared using the Russell indexes which were developed in the 1980s with most indexes beginning in 1979. Stocks in the United States range in value from a few million dollars to more than $300 billion. As explained in Chapter 3, the 3000 largest firms in terms of capitalization are represented in the Russell 3000 index. The Russell 3000, in turn, is sub-divided by size into the Russell 1000 index of the largest stocks and Russell 2000 small-cap index of the next largest 2000 stocks. The Russell 1000 represents 92 percent of the market capitalization of the Russell 3000 index even though it includes only 1000 of its 3000 stocks.[2]

TABLE 4.1   Russell 1000 Growth

Industries	Market Cap	Top Firms	Market Cap
Technology	28.4%	Microsoft	3.6%
Health Care	16.6%	IBM	3.2%
Consumer Durables	15.1%	Apple	2.9%
Consumer Staples	12.4%	Johnson & Johnson	2.6%
Financial Services	6.7%	Cisco	2.6%
Producer Durables	6.2%	Wal-Mart	2.2%
Materials	5.3%	Google	2.2%
Other Energy	2.8%	Proctor & Gamble	2.1%
Autos	2.6%	Philip Morris	1.8%
Integrated Oils	1.8%	Pepsico	1.8%

Source: July 2009 Capitalizations from ishares.com.

The Russell 1000 index, in turn, is divided into two indexes for value and growth. Russell uses two criteria to assign firms to the value and growth indexes: (a) price-to-book ratio and (b) estimates of the long-run growth of earnings as provided by Institutional Brokers Estimate System (IBES). Every June, the indexes are reconstituted using current market capitalization weights. The firms are arrayed in order according to the two criteria (using an algorithm which is proprietary). Seventy percent of the firms at the two ends of the array are assigned to the value or growth indexes, respectively, depending on the two criteria. The remaining 30 percent of firms in the middle of the array are then divided proportionally into value and growth depending upon the same two criteria. So these are included in both indexes, but with different weights. IBM, for example, is assigned weights in both indexes, but with a greater weight in the growth index.

Table 4.1 gives the breakdown of the Russell 1000 Growth Index by industry after the June 2009 reconstitution. Technology is the largest sector with more than 28 percent of the market weight. The next two industries, consumer discretionary and health care, were roughly the same size as technology three years earlier, but have fallen in relative value. Prior to the collapse of the NASDAQ in 2000, however, technology dominated this index even more dramatically. As of October 2000, technology was 50.5 percent of the index as compared with a weight of only 16.2 percent for health care. So the nature of the growth index has changed significantly since the height of the tech market. Table 4.1 lists the top 10 firms in the index listed by market capitalization. Technology firms such as Microsoft, Apple, and Cisco Systems are included on the list, but there are also other non-tech firms (like Wal-Mart) in the index.

TABLE 4.2 Russell 1000 Value

Industries	Market Cap	Top Firms	Market Cap
Financial Services	24.3%	Exxon Mobil	5.2%
Utilities	13.0%	AT&T	3.1%
Integrated Oils	10.6%	JP Morgan	3.1%
Health Care	9.5%	General Electric	2.9%
Consumer Durables	8.8%	Chevron	2.8%
Other Energy	8.0%	Bank of America	2.7%
Producer Durables	5.8%	Pfizer	2.2%
Consumer Staples	5.1%	Wells Fargo	2.2%
Materials	4.9%	Verizon	1.8%
Technology	3.5%	Goldman Sachs	1.6%

Source: July 2009 Capitalizations from ishares.com.

Table 4.2 gives the industry breakdown for the Russell 1000 Value Index. The stocks of financial services firms dominate this index with utility stocks, health care stocks, and integrated oil stocks far behind. But the financial crisis in 2007 and 2008 has reduced the share of financial services from more than 35 percent to 24 percent, though four banks, JP Morgan, Bank of America, Wells Fargo, and Goldman Sachs are among the top 10 value stocks. The largest firm in the index is an energy firm (Exxon Mobil) and Chevron is also large enough to make the top 10.

RELATIVE PERFORMANCE OF GROWTH AND VALUE INDEXES

The relative performance of these two indexes might be measured in three different ways:

1. Average returns
2. Returns adjusted for risk using standard deviations
3. Returns adjusted for systematic risk using beta

It would be normal for the index with the higher average return to also have the higher risk. The last two measures help us to assess whether the higher return is offset with higher risk.

Table 4.3 presents summary statistics for the Russell 1000 indexes over the period from 1979, when the Russell indexes begin, through 2009. The Russell 1000 value index gives a substantially higher average return than

TABLE 4.3 Returns for Russell 1000 Growth and Value Stocks, 1979–2009

	Geometric Average	Arithmetic Average	Standard Deviation	Sharpe Ratio
Russell 1000 Growth	10.5%	11.6%	17.8%	0.34
Russell 1000 Value	12.1%	12.6%	14.9%	0.47

Data Source: Russell®.

the growth index over this period. This is true whether geometric (compound) averages or arithmetic averages are used. Table 4.3 also reports the (annualized) standard deviations for the two asset classes. The standard deviation for large-cap growth stocks, 17.8 percent, is much larger than that for large-cap value stocks, 14.9 percent. Normally, an asset with higher risk would be expected to have a higher return to compensate for that risk. This is not the case for growth stocks, at least over this sample period of the last 31 years. With the average return lower for growth stocks, there is no compensation at all for the higher risk of this asset class.

To be more precise about the extent to which higher risk is compensated with higher return, Table 4.3 reports the Sharpe ratios for both indexes. The arithmetic average is used rather than the geometric average because risk-adjusted performance is most easily calculated using the arithmetic average.[3] With the standard deviation being so much larger for large-cap growth stocks, the Sharpe ratio is much smaller for this asset class. The higher Sharpe ratio for value stocks suggests that investors are not being sufficiently compensated for the higher risk of growth stocks.

How sensitive is this result to the time period studied? The answer to this question will be sought by examining a shorter period of time using the Russell data and by using another data set for value versus growth over a longer period.

The relative performance of growth and value stocks has varied widely over the 31-year period since the Russell series began. Figure 4.1 shows the *ratio* of the cumulative return of Russell 1000 growth stocks over that of Russell 1000 value stocks from the start of the index in December 1978. For most of the 1980s and early 1990s, the cumulative return on value exceeded that of growth so the ratio of growth to value was below 1.0. During that period, the geometric average return on value stocks, measured from 1979 on, exceeded that of growth. Then in the late 1990s, growth stocks soared so the ratio rose almost to 1.4. The collapse of tech stocks beginning in 2000 drove the ratio far below 1.0 to a level at the end of 2009 below 0.65.

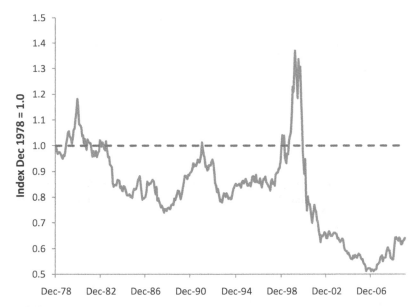

FIGURE 4.1 Ratio of Russell 1000 Growth Stocks to Russell 1000 Value Stocks, 1979–2009
Data Source: Russell®.

To assess the long-run performance of growth versus value, it's instructive to examine cumulative returns as of the peak of growth performance. After all, many observers in the late 1990s urged investors to concentrate on growth stocks (just as they had in the early 1970s when the "nifty fifty" were the rage). If returns are measured from January 1979 to February 2000, the peak month for cumulative performance of the growth index, the average return on value was 16.2 percent while that of growth was 17.9 percent. With the return on growth exceeding that of value by 1.7 percent, the Sharpe ratio is slightly higher for growth than for value (0.67 versus 0.66). But it took several years of spectacular returns in the growth sector in the late 1990s to achieve this result. It is apparent from Figure 4.1 that the excess cumulative return on growth soon collapsed as the bear market crushed growth stocks. It is also apparent from Figure 4.1 that over most of the period since 1979, value returns exceeded those of growth. And since the standard deviation is higher for the growth index than for the value index, the risk-adjusted returns on value stocks are clearly superior.

This conclusion is not altered by examining growth and value returns using S&P 500 indexes for value and growth. Until a few years ago, S&P teamed up with Barra to provide growth and value indexes for the

TABLE 4.4 Returns for S&P 500 Growth and Value Indexes

	Geometric Average	Arithmetic Average	Standard Deviation	Sharpe Ratio
1975–2009*				
Growth	10.7%	11.6%	17.0%	0.36
Value	12.4%	12.8%	14.8%	0.49
July 1995–December 2009**				
Growth	6.6%	8.1%	18.0%	0.26
Value	6.7%	7.8%	15.6%	0.28

*Combined S&P/Barra and S&P/Citigroup series consisting of the S&P/Citigroup indexes from 1975 until June 1995 and the S&P/Barra indexes from July 1995 through the end of 2009.
** S&P/Citigroup series.
Data Source: S&P.

S&P 500. These indexes, which use book-to-market data to separate the S&P 500 into growth and value subgroups, began in 1975. More recently, S&P has teamed up with Citigroup to develop a new set of growth and value indexes. Introduced in 2005, the S&P/Citigroup indexes extend back to July 1995. The methodology used to develop the S&P/Citigroup is more complex than that used for either the Russell or S&P/Barra indexes. The S&P 500/Citigroup indexes use seven criteria to divide stocks into value and growth: book value to price, cash flow to price, sales to price, dividend yield, five-year earnings per share growth, five-year sales per share growth, and five-year internal growth. Using these criteria, the S&P 500 is divided into three groups of stocks, one-third pure growth stocks, one-third pure value stocks, and one-third with weights in both indexes.

Table 4.4 reports the average returns for these indexes. In the top of the table, the two S&P 500 indexes are combined into one to measure value and growth over the 35-year period from 1975 to 2009.[4] In the bottom of the table, the S&P/Citigroup indexes are measured over the period from July 1995 through the end of 2009.

Consider first the results from combining the two indexes. These results are very similar to those obtained using the Russell indexes over the 1979 to 2009 period. Value has a higher return, a lower standard deviation, and a higher Sharpe ratio. The results are similar despite the fact that the two sets of indexes differ in three dimensions: the S&P indexes (a) begin four years earlier, (b) focus on 500 of the largest stocks rather than 1000 stocks, and (c) base their division between growth and value on different criteria.

The gap between growth and value is almost eliminated if only the S&P/Citigroup data are considered from July 1995 through December 2009

TABLE 4.5 Russell Returns Relative to Security Market Line, 1979–2009

	Average Return	Beta	CAPM Return	Style Premium (Alpha)
Russell 1000 Growth	11.6%	1.09	12.8%	− 1.2%
Russell 1000 Value	12.6%	0.89	11.4%	+ 1.2%

Data Source: Russell®.

as in the lower half of Table 4.4. The return on value is only 0.1 percent higher than the return on growth if geometric averages are used and is smaller than the return on growth for arithmetic averages. To see if this is simply due to the surge in growth stocks in the late 1990s, the Russell growth and value returns are examined over the same period. Over the common period starting in July 1995, the return on the Russell 1000 Growth index is 0.9 percent *lower* than that of the S&P 500/Citigroup Growth index and the return on the Russell 1000 Value index is 1.2 percent *higher* than that of the corresponding S&P 500/Citigroup index. So the value premium in the S&P 500/Citigroup data is smaller than in the Russell data not because of the shorter sample period. Instead, it must be because of the very different criteria used by the two vendors to select value and growth stocks. The differences between these two sets of indexes should be kept in mind if either set is used to judge manager performance. Everything else equal, it seems that growth (value) managers will look worse (better) judged against S&P/Citigroup indexes than when judged against the Russell indexes. The fact remains, however, that in both data sets value stocks have better risk-adjusted performance than growth stocks, at least when risk is measured with standard deviations and Sharpe ratios.

Standard deviation is a measure of risk that ignores how an asset fits within the portfolio. What if the systematic risk of growth were compared with that of value by focusing on beta? To measure beta, it's important to use a broad market index. The Russell 3000 index consisting of small- and large-cap stocks is therefore chosen. Table 4.5 reports the betas of the Russell 1000 value and growth indexes measured relative to the Russell 3000. As in the case of standard deviations, the value index emerges as the less risky of the two indexes, with a beta less than one. Table 4.5 also reports the excess return on each index relative to the security market line defined by the betas. The excess return, or alpha, is positive for the value index and negative for the growth index. An alpha of +1.1 percent for the Russell 1000 Value index reflects not only superior returns for value over growth, but also a lower portfolio risk (as measured by beta). Value looks even more impressive relative to growth when the two are compared in terms of beta and alpha.

As in the case of the equity risk premium, researchers have searched for reasons why value stocks outperform growth stocks on a risk-adjusted basis. An interesting approach is provided by a study by Campbell and Vuolteenaho (2004).[5] They distinguish between good beta, the volatility of stocks due to changes in the market's discount rates, and bad beta, the volatility of stocks due to changes in the market's cash flows. Only the latter is highly correlated with business cycle risks, hence the bad beta description. Campbell and Vuolteenaho show that value stocks have considerably higher cash-flow betas than do growth stocks. These higher betas, according to the authors, lead investors to require higher returns on value than growth stocks. So perhaps there is a reason why value stocks outperform growth stocks that has to do with the larger business cycle risks facing investors. But by conventional measures of risk, value stocks clearly outperform growth stocks, at least over the last few decades.

VALUE AND GROWTH INDEXES FOR EARLIER PERIODS

Stock market data collected by the University of Chicago's CRSP data set are available back through 1926. These market data form the basis for the SBBI data set of large and small cap stock returns. To develop value and growth indexes, however, it's necessary to obtain the book value of common equity from the balance sheets of the firms being studied. The Compustat data set provides this information, but this data set does not have book value data prior to 1963 (and is in any case biased by overweighting larger firms).[6]

Fama and French have developed indexes for value and growth extending all the way back to 1926. The division between small-cap and large-cap stocks is based on stocks in the NYSE only even though the indexes include stocks from the AMEX and NASDAQ (the latter after 1972). The median stock in the NYSE by size is used to split stocks into the two size categories. To extend value and growth indexes back prior to 1963, Fama and French use hand-collected data on book value to rank firms by their book-to-market ratios. Unlike the Russell indexes, therefore, the Fama-French indexes are based only on book value-to-market data. The results reported below are for the indexes defined using the 30 percent of firms with the highest book-to-market ratios as the value firms and the 30 percent of firms with the lowest book-to-market ratios as the growth firms. (The remaining 40 percent of the firms with median book-to-market ratios are omitted from either index).

Table 4.6 reports the statistics for these value and growth indexes as measured over two periods prior to 1979, 1927 to 1978 and 1951 to 1978. The shorter period is examined to make sure that the results were not unduly

TABLE 4.6 Comparison between Large-Cap Growth and Value, Fama-French Data

	Geometric Average	Arithmetic Average	Standard Deviation	Sharpe Ratio
1927–1978				
Growth	7.9%	9.6%	24.0%	0.30
Value	11.0%	14.6%	29.2%	0.41
1951–1978				
Growth	8.8%	9.5%	20.5%	0.27
Value	13.5%	13.9%	21.5%	0.47

Data Source: Fama-French Database.

influenced by the economic depression and world war. The table provides several interesting results.

1. First, unlike the period of the Russell indexes starting in 1979, the value index has the larger standard deviation. This is true of the period from 1927 to 1978 as well as for the shorter period.
2. The average return for value stocks is also higher to compensate for the higher risk. In the 1927 to 1978 period, the average return on value is more than 3 percent higher than that of growth. For the shorter period starting in 1951, the excess return of value over growth is a startlingly large 4.7 percent.
3. The value index should have a higher return if it is to compensate for a higher standard deviation. The Sharpe ratio measures whether that return is higher even after compensating for risk. In both periods, the Sharpe ratio is higher for value than for growth.

The conclusion that must be drawn from this earlier period is that value outperforms growth whether it is adjusted for risk or not. As in the later period of the Russell 1000 data, value outperforms growth on a risk-adjusted basis.

RELATIVE PERFORMANCE OF SMALL-CAP GROWTH AND VALUE STOCKS

The Russell 2000 small-cap index is divided into growth and value indexes using the same methodology as with the Russell 1000 index. That is, every June, the Russell 2000 index is divided between growth and value stocks.

TABLE 4.7 Industry Composition of Russell 2000

Growth Index	Market Cap	Value Index	Market Cap
Health Care	24.2%	Financial Services	33.9%
Technology	22.1%	Cons. Discretionary	13.0%
Consumer Discretionary	21.5%	Materials	11.5%
Financial Services	7.8%	Producer Durables	9.2%
Producer Durables	7.2%	Technology	8.3%
Materials	5.6%	Utilities	7.1%
Other Energy	3.5%	Health Care	4.8%
Autos & Transport	2.9%	Other Energy	4.5%
Consumer Staples	2.6%	Autos & Transport	4.0%
Utilities	2.0%	Consumer Staples	2.3%

Source: July 2009 capitalization from ishares.com.

The two indexes for growth and value are designed to have the same total capitalization. Table 4.7 shows the industry breakdowns following the latest reconstitution in June 2009. The relative importance of different industries is similar to that found in the large-cap indexes. The health care, technology, and consumer discretionary industries are the largest in the Russell 2000 growth index, while financial services dominate the Russell 2000 value index (with more than 33 percent of the total weight). Energy plays a much smaller role in the Russell 2000 value index than in the corresponding large-cap index.

Table 4.8 summarizes the long-run performance of growth and value stocks over the 31 years since the Russell series began. To provide a more complete analysis of small-cap performance, the statistics for large-cap growth and value stocks are also included in the table. Recall the four-

TABLE 4.8 Returns for Russell Growth and Value Indexes, 1979–2009

	Geometric Average	Arithmetic Average	Standard Deviation	Sharpe Ratio
Russell 1000				
Growth	10.5%	11.6%	17.8%	0.34
Value	12.1%	12.6%	14.9%	0.47
Russell 2000				
Growth	8.8%	11.3%	23.5%	0.25
Value	13.3%	14.2%	17.4%	0.50

Data Source: Russell®.

quadrant division of U.S. stocks along the large versus small dimension and the growth versus value dimension. This table compares all four asset classes.

The first column of the table reports the compound (geometric) average return for the period from January 1979 through December 2009. The returns for the four indexes range from 13.3 percent for small-cap value to 8.8 percent for small-cap growth. The return for small-cap value is 120 basis points above its next closest competitor, large-cap value. Compare these results with those of Table 3.4 above. It's clearly the case that the performance of the Russell 2000 as a whole was dragged down by the poor performance of the Russell 2000 growth index.

To what extent is the higher return for small-cap value stocks offset by higher risk for this asset class? Table 4.8 also reports the (annualized) standard deviations for the four asset classes. The standard deviation for small-cap value stocks is smaller than that for large-cap growth stocks and much smaller than that for small-cap growth stocks. Only large-cap value stocks have a smaller standard deviation. In contrast, the standard deviation of 23.5 percent for the Russell 2000 Growth Index rivals that of emerging market stocks. The last column of Table 4.8 reports the Sharpe ratios for the four asset classes. The Sharpe ratio for small-cap growth is much lower than for any other asset class. The low return on the Russell 2000 growth index together with the high standard deviation (23.5 percent) leads to a Sharpe ratio that is half the size of that of the Russell 2000 value index. It's puzzling how an asset class with a standard deviation more than 23 percent can have a compound return 4.5 percent below that of small-cap value over such a long period of time.

An even more dramatic difference between small-cap value and growth is found when the two are compared in terms of systematic risk using CAPM. Figure 4.2 shows the performance of all four Russell growth and value indexes relative to the security market line defined using the total market index, the Russell 3000. With the standard deviation of the small-cap growth index being so high, it should not be surprising that the beta is also high at 1.28. The small-cap growth index return is so low that the alpha of this index is –2.7 percent. In contrast, the alpha for the small-cap value index is +2.4 percent. Viewed in terms of its marginal contribution to a portfolio, the small-cap growth index looks even worse than when viewed as an independent asset class.

These decidedly negative results for small-cap growth could be a fluke of the sample period. So it's important to look at periods prior to the Russell data (which begin in 1979). The Fama and French database comes to the rescue again. Their database extends back to the later months of 1926. Table 4.9 presents the statistics for small-cap growth and value over two periods ending in 1978 (when the Russell data begin). From 1927 until 1978,

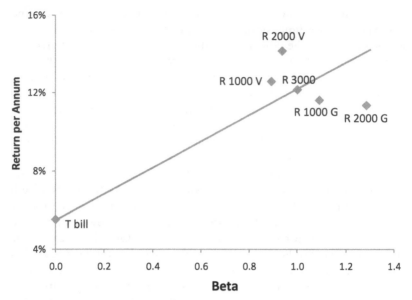

FIGURE 4.2 Russell Style Indexes Relative to Security Market Line, 1979–2009
Data Source: Russell®.

the geometric return on growth falls short of the value return by 3.8 percent. From 1951 to 1978, the shortfall is a surprisingly large 5.5 percent. So the results based on Russell data are only confirmed using the longer data set from Fama and French. The only difference between the two data sets is that the standard deviations for value stocks are higher than those of growth

TABLE 4.9 Comparison between Small-Cap Growth and Value, Fama-French Data

	Geometric Average	Arithmetic Average	Standard Deviation	Sharpe Ratio
1927–1978				
Growth	9.3%	12.8%	28.9%	0.36
Value	13.1%	17.5%	31.0%	0.48
1951–1978				
Growth	9.5%	11.2%	24.3%	0.30
Value	15.0%	15.7%	23.2%	0.51

Data Source: Fama-French Database.

stocks in the period from 1927 to 1979. The Sharpe ratios for value stocks remain higher. The conclusion that must be drawn from this earlier period is that value out-performs growth whether it is adjusted for risk or not. As in the later period of the Russell 2000 data, the relative strength of small-cap value as an asset class is evident.

PORTFOLIOS WITH GROWTH AND VALUE

Since growth stocks underperform value stocks in the small-cap as well as large-cap spaces, it's natural to ask the question whether growth stocks belong at all in a portfolio. Or, at the very least, whether growth stocks should be underweighted in a portfolio. To try to answer this question, let's consider the following experiment. Build a portfolio of stocks and bonds with and without growth stocks and evaluate the difference in performance.

Table 4.10 reports on this experiment. There are two portfolios described in the table with 30 percent invested in bonds (in the Barclays Aggregate index) and 70 percent in stocks. In the top of the table is a portfolio with an equal allocation to the Russell 1000 Growth and Value indexes (30 percent each) and with an equal allocation to the Russell 2000 Growth and Value indexes (5 percent each).[7] In the bottom of the table is a portfolio where all of the large-cap allocation is given to the Russell 1000 Value index and all of the small-cap allocation is given to the Russell 2000 Value index. The results are interesting. The return on the value-only portfolio is

TABLE 4.10 Portfolios with and without Growth Stocks, 1979–2009

	Average Return	Standard Deviation	Sharpe Ratio
Growth and Value Portfolio	11.1%	11.7%	0.48
30% R 1000 Value			
30% R 1000 Growth			
5% R 2000 Value			
5% R 2000 Growth			
30% Barclays Aggregate			
Value-only Portfolio	11.5%	11.0%	0.54
60% R 1000 Value			
10% R 2000 Value			
30% Barclays Aggregate			

Data Source: Barclays Aggregate and Russell®.

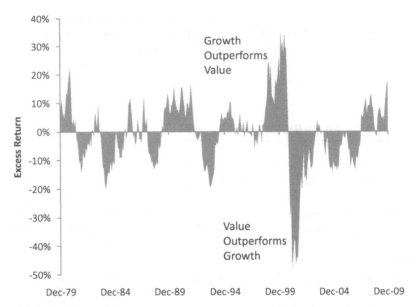

FIGURE 4.3 Excess Returns on Large-Cap Growth Stocks: Rolling One-Year Average Returns, 1980–2009
Data Source: Russell®.

0.4 percent higher, while the standard deviation is 0.7 percent lower. As a result, the Sharpe ratio is 0.54 for the value-only portfolio compared with a Sharpe ratio of 0.48 for the diversified value and growth portfolio. Translated into an excess return at the level of risk of the diversified portfolio, the investor gives up 0.7 percent return by diversifying into growth stocks.[8] In this case, diversification clearly does not pay.

So why don't portfolios focus on value stocks alone? One reason is suggested in Figure 4.3 where the excess return on large-cap growth stocks is traced out over time. The figure shows excess returns measured over one-year rolling periods since December 1979. Despite the fact that large-cap growth returns trail large-cap value returns by an average of 1.6 percent over the 31 years, there are long stretches of months (and years) when growth exceeds value. And the excess returns often exceed 10 percent. Indeed, the excess return on growth exceeded 30 percent in the late 1990s followed by a stretch of time when value returns exceeded growth returns by 30 percent. How many investors would keep long-run excess returns in mind when the short run fluctuations of growth versus value are this large?

The sharp fluctuations in growth and value returns exhibited in Figure 4.3 also suggest how important it is to measure the performance of investment managers relative to their style benchmarks. In 1999, the Russell 1000 Growth index had a return of 33.1 percent while the Russell 1000 Value index had a return of 7.3 percent. To judge how well a large-cap manager did that year, it would be imperative to identify the manager's style first. Value managers who earned 10 percent returns that year actually performed quite well, while growth managers with 25 percent returns underperformed. With fluctuations as wide as these, no wonder portfolio managers retain growth as well as value stocks.

SUMMARY—KEY FEATURES OF GROWTH AND VALUE STOCKS

This chapter has provided a wide range of evidence on the long-run performance of growth and value stocks. The evidence is based on the Russell and S&P 500 indexes for the recent period and the Fama-French indexes for the earlier periods.

The long-run performance of large-cap value stocks is quite impressive. In all of the data sets reported, value stocks give higher average returns than growth stocks. In the more recent period covered by the Russell and S&P indexes, value stocks have lower standard deviations than growth stocks. So the risk-adjusted performance of value stocks, as measured by Sharpe ratios, is clearly superior to that of growth stocks. Because of the high correlation between growth and value stocks, moreover, the superiority of value stocks is also found in a portfolio context. The beta for value stocks is below one, while that of growth exceeds one. The alpha for value, moreover, is positive and the alpha for growth negative. In the earlier period covered by the Fama-French data, value also outperforms growth. In this earlier period, value has a higher standard deviation than growth, but its risk-adjusted performance is still superior. There is no doubt that there is a value premium in the U.S. stock market.

NOTES

1. Eugene F. Fama and Kenneth R. French (1992) and (1993).
2. The capitalization figures are for June 2009 and are taken from the web site, www.russell.com.
3. See the discussion in Chapter 1.
4. The S&P/Barra index is used through June 1995 and the S&P/Citigroup index is used beginning in July 1995.

5. Earlier papers that documented differences between value and growth stocks include Basu (1977) and Rosenberg et al. (1985).
6. See the discussion in Fama and French (1992, page 429).
7. Notice that this allocation gives a modest overweight to small-cap stocks since 14 percent (10/70) of the stock allocation is devoted to small caps compared with their market weight of 8 percent.
8. As explained in Chapter 1, alpha* translates the difference in Sharpe ratios into an excess return. In this case, $\alpha^* = (0.48 - 0.54) * 0.117 = -0.7\%$.

CHAPTER 5

Foreign Stocks

The world stock market had a capitalization of $35.0 trillion in 2008. Of that total, the U.S. stock market had a share of only 33.6 percent.[1] Another 39.9 percent consisted of stocks from the other industrial countries, with the remaining 26.5 percent being stocks of the so-called emerging markets. Many of the larger firms in these foreign markets are household names in the United States. In fact, many Americans may not even know that Nestle, Unilever, and Philips are foreign firms. Yet American investors have only small proportions of foreign stocks in their portfolios. They often regard foreign stocks as too risky.

It's actually more complicated than that. International investing goes in and out of favor in the United States. In the 1980s and early 1990s, international stock returns were quite impressive, so U.S. investors flocked to international stock funds. Diversifying portfolios made sense to investors when returns were higher abroad. Then throughout the late 1990s, foreign stock returns lagged those in the high-flying U.S. markets. Arguments for international diversification fell on deaf ears when investors became caught up with the excitement of the fabulous returns on U.S. stocks in the late 1990s, particularly those in the technology industry. Why invest in London or Tokyo when Silicon Valley offers such superior returns? Then from 2002 to 2007, interest in foreign stocks picked up again. Why? A cynic would say that it was because foreign stock returns were surging ahead of U.S. stocks, propelled by the rebound of the Euro from its lows in early 2002.

There is a longer trend in international investing that is worth noting. International diversification has gone through three phases in the last 100 years or so. In the decades prior to the Depression of the 1930s and the Second World War, capital flowed freely around the world. London and Paris were the dominant financial centers for most of this period.[2] Bonds were issued in London and Paris to finance companies and projects around the world. For example, much of the financing for the building of the American railways originated in London. Other countries like South Africa, Australia, and Argentina benefitted from ready access to European financial markets. Equity issues were less frequent than bond issues. But foreign investors had sizable stakes in many American companies.

The second phase began in the Great Depression of the 1930s when capital controls were imposed by most countries and when many previously issued foreign securities went into default. Private international investing almost ceased for three decades thereafter.[3] Many of the capital controls were left in place throughout the 1950s and 1960s, severely inhibiting international investing. During this period, financing was available primarily through loans from national governments and (in the postwar period) international agencies such as the World Bank. Even banks were wary of foreign lending.

The third phase began in the early 1970s when capital controls began to be lifted. It was in this period that the so-called Bretton Woods system of fixed exchange rates came to an end. In 1971, the Nixon Administration ended the dollar's tie to gold. Over the next few years, many industrial countries allowed their currencies to float vis-à-vis the dollar. With less need to defend their currencies, governments began to relax their capital controls. Some countries lagged behind in this process. Investors in Britain, for example, had to contend with controls until the late 1970s when the Thatcher government finally removed them. In the meantime, British residents were not allowed to take more than £50 out of the country! The French government had similar control limiting outflows by French residents.[4] By the late 1980s, however, there were virtually no limitations on foreign investing in any of the industrial countries.

The third phase of international investing saw the development of international stock indexes to track the performance of stocks around the world. In particular, beginning in 1970 the Morgan Stanley Capital International (MSCI) indexes provided a common methodology for measuring stocks in all of the industrial countries. Of course, it is possible to trace stock markets much earlier than 1970. Indeed, Dimson et al (2002) reports on the stock returns of many industrial countries for the century from 1900 to 2000. But the quality of national indexes varies widely during earlier periods. For example, how reliable do you think German stock indexes were during the hyperinflation of the 1920s or during the period of the second World War? Hardly any emerging stock markets have data prior to the mid-1970s. Global emerging market stock market indexes begin in the mid to late 1980s.

This chapter will focus on the last four decades of stock market performance in the industrial countries using the MSCI indexes. The next chapter will address the emerging stock markets.

RETURNS ON FOREIGN AND U.S. STOCKS

Figure 5.1 shows the stock market capitalization of the major regions of the world as reported in 2009 in the annual *S&P Global Stock Markets Factbook.*[5] As stated above, foreign industrial countries represent 39.9 percent of the world total, while emerging markets represent another 26.5 percent. Emerging markets are defined by S&P as countries with low per capita income.[6] The stocks of industrial countries other than the United States are often referred to as core foreign stocks.

The Morgan Stanley EAFE (Europe, Australasia, and the Far East) index is normally used to describe returns in these core countries even though this index excludes the Canadian market. The makeup of this index (as of 2009) is shown in Table 5.1. 64.4 percent of EAFE's market capitalization is in the European sub-index consisting of 16 countries and the rest is in the five markets of the Pacific region. Japan's market is the largest in the index with a 25.1 percent weight. In the late 1980s, this market was even larger than that of the United States.

Figure 5.2 tracks the cumulative returns on the EAFE index compared with those of the S&P 500.[7] It's evident that after 40 years the two indexes have ended up very close to one another. EAFE's returns exceeded those of the United States throughout most of the 1970s and 1980s. The S&P 500

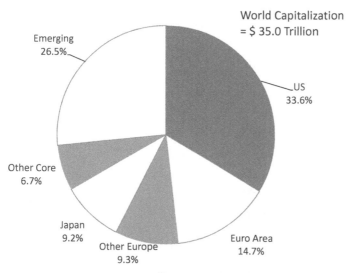

FIGURE 5.1   World Stock Market Capitalization
Source: S&P Global Stock Markets Factbook, 2009.

TABLE 5.1 Country Composition of MSCI EAFE Index

Europe Index	64.4%	Pacific Index	35.6%
Austria	0.6%	Australia	5.3%
Belgium	1.3%	Hong Kong	3.6%
Denmark	1.0%	Japan	25.1%
Finland	1.2%	New Zealand	0.2%
France	11.6%	Singapore	1.4%
Germany	8.6%		
Greece	0.7%		
Ireland	0.4%		
Italy	4.1%		
Netherlands	3.0%		
Norway	1.0%		
Portugal	0.5%		
Spain	7.4%		
Sweden	2.0%		
Switzerland	6.7%		
United Kingdom	14.4%		

Source for market capitalization: S&P Global Stock Market Factbook, 2009.

FIGURE 5.2 S&P 500 and EAFE Cumulative Returns, 1970–2009
Data Sources: MSCI, ©Morningstar, and S&P.

TABLE 5.2 World Stock Returns, 1970–2009

	Geometric Average	Arithmetic Average	Standard Deviation	Sharpe Ratio
S&P 500	9.9%	10.7%	15.6%	0.33
EAFE	10.2%	11.2%	17.2%	0.33
Europe	10.8%	11.9%	17.4%	0.36
Pacific	9.8%	11.5%	20.7%	0.29

Data Sources: ©Morningstar, MSCI, and S&P.

surged ahead in the 1990s with the huge boom in U.S. stocks. Then more recently EAFE has overtaken the lead. That it's a close horse race should not be surprising. After all, most industrial countries are at the same level of development. Individual countries may excel in one industry or another. The Japanese, for example, lead in autos and electronics, the Germans in machine tools, the French in luxury goods and nuclear technology, and the Americans in software and finance. But overall no country or region has a clear advantage in firm profitability and stock market performance.

Table 5.2 reports returns on the stocks of the industrial countries, measured in U.S. dollars, from 1970 (when the Morgan Stanley data set begins) to 2009. Three MSCI-developed country indexes are reported: the EAFE index, the European index (made up of the European component of the EAFE index), and the Pacific index (the Pacific component of that index). Two averages are presented, the compound (or geometric) average and the arithmetic average. All of the returns in this table are clustered near one another. The geometric return for the U.S. market is 0.1 percent above that of the Pacific market, but below those of the EAFE and European indexes. The arithmetic returns for the foreign markets are all somewhat higher than those of the United States. Table 5.2 also reports the Sharpe ratios for each index. The Sharpe ratios are also clustered around one another with ratios for the EAFE and S&P indexes exactly the same. So for the 40-year period as a whole, the returns on foreign and U.S. stock markets are remarkably similar.[8]

Over shorter periods, however, there are wide variations in returns. It's instructive to look at returns by region from decade to decade. Figure 5.3 reports returns in dollars for four markets (with the emerging markets data beginning only in the 1990s). In the 1970s, 20 percent returns from the Pacific stock markets led the other markets, with the United States trailing Europe by 2.7 percent per year on average. In the 1980s, markets in the Pacific and Europe again outperformed the U.S. market with the gap between Europe and the United States averaging 2.6 percent. No wonder that

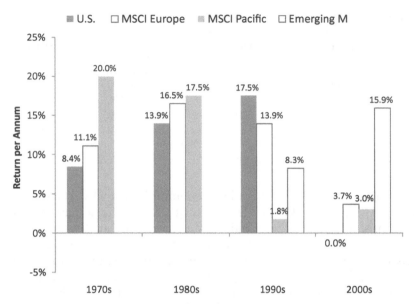

FIGURE 5.3 U.S. and Foreign Stock Returns by Decade, 1971–2009
Data Sources: MSCI, ©Morningstar, and S&P.

American investors became enthusiastic about foreign stocks as these first two decades evolved. In the 1990s, tables were turned as the U.S. market outshone all the others. So far in the current decade, U.S. markets have lagged behind the others.

An investor examining this record of returns must focus on the following question. Which markets will outperform in coming decades? The sensible response is that investors do not know the answer to this question. That is the most cogent argument for diversifying abroad. Ignore correlations for the moment and focus on Figure 5.3. Should investors be concentrated in U.S. stocks if we could plausibly face decades more similar to the 1970s and 1980s than the 1990s?

To see to what extent markets can vary relative to one another, consider the EAFE and the S&P indexes over the 20-year period beginning in 1990. The gap in returns is an astonishingly large 3.8 percent per year. The main reason for EAFE's underperformance was the collapse of the Japanese market which peaked in December 1989 before falling more than 75 percent. At its peak when the Nikkei index reached 38,900, the Japanese stock market was the largest in the world. In late 2009, it was still below 11,000. This helps to explain why the Pacific region did so well in the 1970s and 1980s, but then faltered so badly in the 1990s. An index of EAFE stocks *excluding*

Japan outperforms the EAFE index as a whole by 4.0 percent per year! How much better off would Japanese investors have been if they had chosen a global rather than national portfolio?

CURRENCY CAPITAL GAINS AND FOREIGN STOCK RETURNS

The returns reported in Table 5.2 and the accompanying figures are all measured in U.S. dollars in order to make them comparable to one another. Foreign stocks are denominated in their local currencies, but it's the return measured in dollars that matters to American investors. The return in dollars reflects both the return in local currency and the capital gain on the foreign currency.

Let R_L be the return on foreign stocks in local currency and R_X the capital gain on the foreign currency (measured in dollars per foreign currency). Then the return on foreign stocks measured in dollars, $R_\$$, is obtained as follows:

$$R_\$ = (1 + R_L)(1 + R_X) - 1.$$

In 2003, for example, the return on Japanese stocks was 23.0 percent measured in yen, but the yen appreciated by 10.7 percent. So the return on Japanese stocks measured in dollars for the American investor was 36.2 percent:

$$R_\$ = (1 + 0.230)(1 + 0.107) - 1 = 0.362 \quad \text{or} \quad 36.2\%.$$

The Japanese investor received the 23.0 percent return measured in yen, while the American investor received the higher 36.2 percent return that reflects the capital gain on the yen in 2003.

Figure 5.4 shows the average compound returns on foreign stocks measured in local currency and in dollars. In the case of the EAFE index as a whole, for example, the return in local currency from 1970 to 2009 was only 8.3 percent, but the return in dollars was 10.2 percent. The much higher return in dollars was due to an appreciation of 1.8 percent per year in the dollar value of foreign currencies (weighted by the size of each stock market in the EAFE index). The role of currency gains is particularly important in the case of the Japanese market. The average dollar return on Japanese stocks since 1970 is 9.7 percent per year, while the local currency return (in yen as viewed by a Japanese investor) is only 6.0 percent. The appreciation of the yen by an average of 3.5 percent accounted for the rest.[9] The country

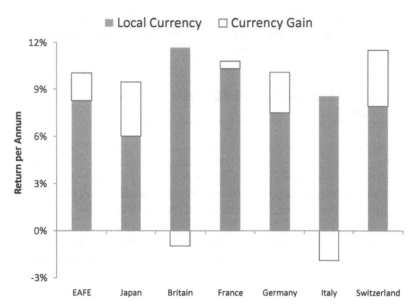

FIGURE 5.4 Foreign Stock Returns in Local Currency and Currency Gains, 1970–2009
Data Source: MSCI.

with the lowest return by far is Italy. Its return in local currency was a respectable 8.6 percent, but the depreciation of the lira lowered the return measured in dollars to 6.5 percent. The country with the highest return in dollars is Switzerland. Its relatively low return in Swiss francs was offset by a large appreciation of its currency relative to the dollar. The United Kingdom would have had as large of a return as Switzerland if the pound had not depreciated against the dollar over this 35-year period.

In the short run, exchange rate movements can lead to much larger variations in stock returns measured in dollars. Consider the period of Ronald Reagan's presidency, 1981 to 1988. During Reagan's first term, the dollar rose sharply against the other major currencies. For example, the French franc price of the dollar rose from less than five FF per dollar in January 1981 to more than 10 FF per dollar in February 1985. As a result, the dollar returns on French stocks were severely depressed. As shown in Table 5.3, the return on French stocks in local currency was 19.4 percent per annum during the four-year period from 1981 to 1984, whereas the return on these same stocks measured in dollars was a negative 1.1 percent. The gap between these returns was due to an average depreciation of the French franc of 17.2 percent from 1981 to 1984. During the same four years, the pound

TABLE 5.3 Average Returns on Group of Five Country Stocks during First and Second Reagan Administrations

	1981–1984		1985–1988	
Country	In local currency	In U.S. dollars	In local currency	In U.S. dollars
United States		10.9%		17.1%
Britain	25.7%	5.0%	15.6%	29.1%
France	19.4%	−1.1%	25.5%	40.9%
Germany	16.9%	5.0%	13.6%	31.1%
Japan	20.1%	14.0%	29.0%	53.5%

Data Source: MSCI.

depreciated by 16.5 percent, the deutschmark by 10.2 percent, and the yen by 5.1 percent.

The Group of Five industrial countries are studied in Table 5.3 because they were the five countries taking part in the famous Plaza Accord meetings in September 1985. This meeting, held at the Plaza Hotel in New York City, was hosted by Secretary of the Treasury James Baker and included finance ministers and central bankers from the United States, Britain, France, Germany, and Japan. The Plaza Accord introduced a joint policy to drive the dollar down to more competitive levels. The Accord met with almost immediate success. The dollar had already fallen from its peak in March 1985 even before the Plaza meeting, but its fall accelerated after the meeting and kept falling until it had reached pre-Reagan levels against most major currencies.

The right side of Table 5.3 shows the effects of the dollar's fall (or the rise in foreign currencies) on stock returns. The right side of the table measures returns during the second Reagan administration from 1985 to 1988. While foreign stock returns in local currency were impressive during this four-year period, the returns in dollars were from 13.5 percent to 24.5 percent higher than the local currency returns.

The period of the Reagan administration is not the only time that the dollar has varied sharply relative to other major currencies. A similar rise and fall in the dollar occurred soon after the new European currency, the Euro, replaced the currencies of 12 European countries. As shown in Figure 5.5, the Euro was introduced in 1999 at a price of $1.18 per Euro and proceeded to fall all the way to $0.83 per Euro in October 2000. Over the three years from January 1999 through December 2001, the fall in the Euro (and other European currencies) dragged down European stock returns

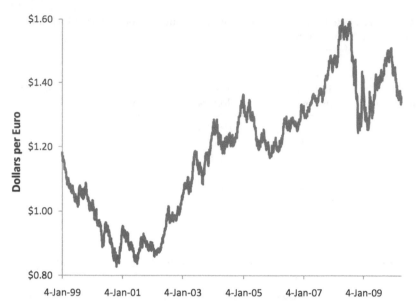

FIGURE 5.5 Exchange Rate for the Euro since 1999
Data Source: Federal Reserve Board.

by 7.2 percent. The Euro didn't reach its $1.18 price again until May 2003, but it kept soaring after that.

Figure 5.6 decomposes the dollar return on the MSCI European stock index into its two components. In the three years from 1999 to 2001, the dollar return on the European index averaged −5.0 percent per year because the currency loss of 7.2 percent more than offset the 2.3 percent stock return in local currency. The period after 2001 was very different. As shown in Figure 5.6, currency gains contributed 4.5 percent per year to European stock returns from 2002 through 2009. As a result, European stocks measured in dollars had positive returns of 7.0 percent per year, much higher than the 2.5 percent return in local currency during this period.

If currencies move this sharply, two natural questions arise. First, can such currency movements be forecasted? Second, if accurate forecasts are difficult, does currency hedging pay? Currency forecasting is too extensive a topic to cover adequately here. But investors should be skeptical if they see claims that forecasting is easy, particularly short-term forecasting. And they should also be skeptical if fund managers claim to know when to hedge and when not to.

What can be established is that in the long run a policy of hedging currencies has not had a major effect on overall returns, at least as far

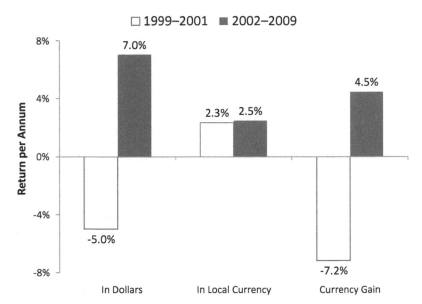

□ 1999–2001 ■ 2002–2009

FIGURE 5.6 European Stock Returns since Euro was Introduced
Data Source: MSCI.

as the currencies of the major industrial countries are concerned. That's because currency futures contracts are fairly priced. In the long run, there is little profit or loss from selling currencies in the forward market (which an investor would do in order to hedge the currency risk). A policy of selling French francs to hedge the currency exposure on French stock investments, for example, made an average profit of minus 0.7 percent per year between 1979 and June 2009 ignoring transactions costs. The same policy applied to Deutschemarks made an average profit of only +0.5 percent per year.[10] It should not be surprising that returns are so small, since consistently high profits would be soon eliminated by additional speculators joining in the game.

A more surprising result is shown in Table 5.4. Currency hedging does not have much impact on risk. Table 5.4 compares the standard deviations of the country indexes when the stock returns are hedged and when they are left un-hedged. In the case of the British stock index, hedging reduces the standard deviation from 19.9 percent to 17.1 percent, but in the case of the German stock index, the standard deviation of the hedged return is virtually identical to that of the un-hedged return. More importantly, in no case does hedging make much of a difference. Why is that the case? Hedging has a marginal impact on risk because currency gains have a low correlation with

TABLE 5.4 Standard Deviations of Un-Hedged and Hedged Quarterly Returns on Stock Markets, Jan 1979–June 2009

Stock market	Unhedged dollar return	Hedged dollar return
Britain	19.9%	17.1%
France	24.0%	23.1%
Germany	24.6%	24.5%
Japan	25.3%	22.0%
Switzerland	20.3%	20.4%

Data Sources: IMF, International Financial Statistics, and MSCI.

foreign stock returns. This is in contrast to the case of foreign bonds studied in Chapter 7 where hedging makes a big difference. Because hedging has little effect on stock market risk, few investment managers choose to hedge their foreign stock portfolios.

A far more effective way to reduce the risk of foreign stock investments is to diversify the country risk. Figure 5.7 shows the standard deviations of MSCI country index returns measured in dollars and compares these with

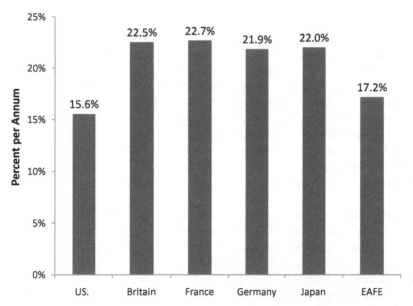

FIGURE 5.7 Standard Deviations of Stock Market Returns in Dollars, 1970–2009
Data Sources: MSCI, ©Morningstar, and S&P.

the standard deviation of the EAFE index as a whole. By diversifying across country stock markets, an investment manager can reduce the standard deviation of foreign stocks from an average of about 22 percent per market to 17.2 percent for the EAFE index as a whole. Most active foreign stock managers do diversify country risk. That's true even of the bottom-up managers who base their portfolio choices on the performance of individual firms, not the markets in which they are listed.[11]

To summarize, currency effects add an extra dimension to investing in foreign stock markets. In the long run, returns on foreign stocks include a currency component that can either raise or lower the total return on these stocks as measured by an American investor. In the case of the EAFE index, for example, the return in dollars averaged 1.9 percent above the local currency return from 1970 through 2009. The higher return in dollars reflected the depreciation of the dollar that occurred over this period. At times, currency gains or losses can be a dominant factor, as in the first and second terms of Ronald Reagan's presidency. But there is little evidence that such currency gains or losses can be easily forecasted. An American investor must decide whether the total return on foreign stocks, including the currency component, is sufficiently attractive to warrant investment. As with all assets, returns have to be evaluated on a risk-adjusted basis, and the risk of foreign stocks is best evaluated in a portfolio context where their diversification benefits can be assessed.

DIVERSIFICATION BENEFITS OF FOREIGN STOCK INVESTING

A traditional argument in favor of diversification into foreign stocks was the relatively low correlation between foreign and domestic stocks. This low correlation meant that the risk of an internationally diversified portfolio could be lower than that of an all-U.S. portfolio. Over the period from 1970 (when the EAFE index begins) and 2009, for example, the correlation between EAFE and the S&P 500 index is only 0.60. The effects of this low correlation have often been illustrated using a horseshoe diagram like that found in Figure 5.8. The horseshoe shows various portfolios of U.S. and foreign stocks ranging from an all-S&P 500 portfolio (at the lower right end) to an all EAFE portfolio (at the higher right end). The powerful message of this chart is that diversified portfolios of foreign and domestic stocks have the dual benefit of *lower risk* and *higher return*. The horseshoe diagram was often used in the marketing materials of foreign stock mutual fund managers during the mid-1990s. Then for about 10 years, the horseshoe disappeared as a marketing device because EAFE was being outperformed so badly by the

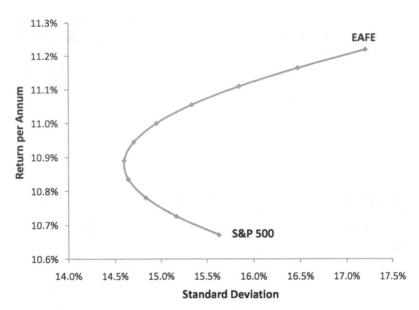

FIGURE 5.8   Portfolios of U.S. and Foreign Stocks, 1970–2009
Data Sources: MSCI, ©Morningstar, and S&P.

S&P that the horseshoe inverted. Diversified portfolios still lowered risk, but portfolios with high proportions of foreign stocks had lower returns than U.S.-only portfolios. With the surge in foreign stock returns since 2002, the horseshoe has become viable again. But notice that in Figure 5.8, the gap in returns between EAFE and the S&P 500 is only about 0.5 percent. It's the reduction in risk that matters for foreign diversification, not the increase in return.

To see how foreign diversification can improve the performance of a portfolio, consider Table 5.5 which compares portfolios with and without the EAFE index. The first comparisons are for the period starting in 1970 when the EAFE index was introduced. There is an all-American portfolio consisting of 75 percent invested in the S&P 500 and 25 percent in the medium-term Treasury bond. The diversified portfolio replaces one third of the stock allocation, 25 percent of the whole portfolio, with foreign stocks. The portfolio containing EAFE has a higher return and lower standard deviation. So the Sharpe ratio is also higher at 0.41 as opposed to 0.37 for the all-American portfolio. That is not much of a difference, but it translates into 0.4 percent excess return for the diversified portfolio.[12]

The second set of portfolios is for a shorter period beginning in 1979. This set of portfolios replaces the S&P 500 with the Russell 3000 all-cap

TABLE 5.5 Performance of Portfolio with EAFE Added

	Geometric Average	Arithmetic Average	Standard Deviation	Sharpe Ratio
Portfolio A (1970–2009)				
Without EAFE	9.7%	10.0%	12.0%	0.37
25% EAFE	9.9%	10.1%	11.2%	0.41
Portfolio B (1979–2009)				
Without EAFE	11.0%	11.2%	12.2%	0.47
25% EAFE	10.8%	11.0%	11.6%	0.47

Portfolio A: Portfolio without EAFE consists of 25 percent in medium-term U.S. Treasuries and 75 percent in the S&P 500. When a 25 percent EAFE position is added, the S&P is reduced by 25 percent.

Portfolio B: Portfolio without EAFE consists of 25 percent in the Barclays Capital Aggregate, and 75 percent in the Russell 3000 all-cap stock index. The portfolio with EAFE has 25 percent in EAFE and 50 percent in the Russell 3000.

Data Sources: MSCI, ©Morningstar, S&P, Barclays Capital, and Russell®.

U.S. stock index and it replaces the medium-term Treasury with the Barclays Capital Aggregate Index (formerly the Lehman Aggregate index). Over the period beginning in 1979 (when the Russell indexes begin), the portfolio with 25 percent invested in EAFE has a lower return, but also has a lower risk. The Sharpe ratio of this diversified portfolio is exactly the same as that of the all-U.S. portfolio. So the benefits of international diversification disappear in this later period.[13]

One reason that the foreign diversification is less effective in more recent years is that the correlation between foreign and domestic stocks has increased markedly, so foreign diversification reduces risk less than it did in the past. Consider Table 5.6 where the correlations between the S&P 500 index and various foreign stock indexes are reported. For the full period beginning in 1970, EAFE has a correlation with the S&P 500 of only 0.60

TABLE 5.6 Correlations between U.S. and Foreign Stocks

	Correlation with S&P 1970–2009	Correlation with S&P 2000–2009
EAFE	0.60	0.87
MSCI Europe	0.67	0.86
MSCI Pacific	0.43	0.72

Data Sources: MSCI, ©Morningstar, and S&P.

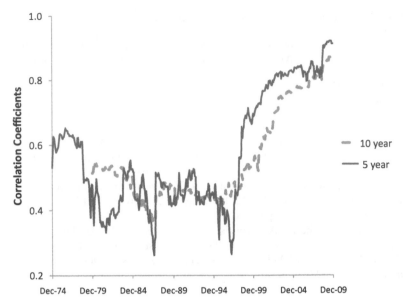

FIGURE 5.9 Correlations between S&P 500 and EAFE Measured over Five and Ten Year Periods, 1970–2009
Data Sources: MSCI, ©Morningstar, and S&P.

and MSCI Pacific has an even lower correlation of 0.43. But for the last 10 years alone ending in 2009, the correlation between EAFE and the S&P rises to 0.87. There are correspondingly large increases in correlations between the S&P and the regional MSCI indexes.

When did this increase in correlations occur? Consider Figure 5.9 which shows five- and 10-year correlation coefficients between the EAFE and S&P 500 indexes. Since the EAFE index starts only in 1970, the graph begins in 1975 for the five-year correlation and in 1980 for the 10-year correlation. The figure is noteworthy in several respects. First, the correlations vary widely over time whether they are measured over five- or ten-year intervals. The five-year correlation begins above 60 percent and at times falls below 30 percent. The 10-year correlation shows less variability over time. But as late as 1997, the 10-year correlation is below 45 percent. Second, the sharp rise in correlation occurs relatively late in the sample period, in 1998 for five-year correlations and 2001 for 10-year correlations.

Most experts explain the recent rise of correlations on *increased integration of the world economy*. Over the last 20 or 30 years, international trade and international capital flows have both increased at rapid paces. There is such a contrast between the capital control world of the 1960s and today's

TABLE 5.7 Standard Deviations of Diversified Portfolios of EAFE and S&P 500

Portfolio	Standard Deviation 1970–2009	Standard Deviation 2000–2009
EAFE alone	17.2%	18.1%
S&P 500 alone	15.6%	16.1%
20% EAFE	14.8%	16.2%
40% EAFE	14.6%	16.4%

20 percent (40 percent) portfolio consists of 20 percent (40 percent) EAFE and the remainder in the S&P 500.

Data Sources: MSCI, ©Morningstar, and S&P.

world of free-flowing capital. There has also been a marked improvement in information flows. Information has always been transmitted almost instantly between countries, at least since the establishment of the world-wide telegraph system in the 1860s. But now there is much more information readily available about markets and companies than there was as recently as the 1970s. Databases of corporate performances, for example, are available for many foreign companies. And the web has provided instant access to annual reports and other corporate records.

Nonetheless, it's hard to explain why this trend in integration should lead to an abrupt increase in correlations in the late 1990s. There is no evidence of an abrupt increase in international trade or capital flows around that time. Nor did instant communications become even more instantly available in the late 1990s.[14] However, without an alternative explanation of this phenomenon, all we can do is observe the change in correlations and study their impact on portfolios.

How much difference does the rise in correlations make to the case for international diversification? In Table 5.7, we compare the standard deviations of various portfolios for the full sample period of the EAFE index and for the last 10 years alone. For portfolios measured since 1970, a 20 percent allocation to EAFE lowers the risk of a stock portfolio by 0.8 percent. But for portfolios measured only over the past 10 years, a 20 percent allocation to EAFE actually raises risk marginally. So the gains from international diversification have disappeared.

So why should American investors go to the trouble of investing abroad? Those investors skeptical of international investing ought to think about turning the question around. Why should I keep all of my equity investments at home? Recall Figure 5.3 which shows the decade-by-decade performance of U.S. and foreign stocks. Returns vary a lot across regions over periods as long as a decade. Why would an American investor want to put all of his or her chips on one country? Betting on America alone paid off in the 1990s, but it wasn't as smart a strategy in the 1970s and 1980s. So far in this decade, no markets have done well except those of the emerging markets, but American markets have performed the worst of all.

ARE THERE SHORTCUTS TO OWNING FOREIGN STOCKS?

Investors have considered two shortcuts to owning foreign stocks that allow them to keep their money at home. The first shortcut involves investing in American Depository Receipts (or ADRs) instead of stocks of the same companies listed on foreign stock exchanges (foreign stocks). The second shortcut involves investing in the stocks of U.S. multinational firms that have extensive sales or production in foreign countries. The first shortcut represents a legitimate and convenient way to invest in foreign companies. The second shortcut fails to provide the foreign diversification that investors are seeking.

Consider first the ADR market. First developed in the 1920s, ADRs are negotiable certificates issued by a U.S. bank with rights to the underlying shares of stock held in trust at a custodian bank. These ADRs are sold, registered, and transferred within the United States like any share of stock in a U.S. company. Dividends are paid in foreign currency to the custodian bank that converts them to dollars. American investors find investing in ADRs very convenient compared with investing in shares in foreign stock markets. Investors do not have to worry about foreign currency transactions and custody remains in the United States.

To what extent is the American investor getting true foreign diversification by investing in ADRs? First, it's important to recognize that arbitrage will ensure that the returns on ADRs and on the underlying foreign stocks are identical except for transactions costs. Second, there are now almost 3000 ADRs available in the U.S. market for firms from virtually every country that has an active stock market, so it's possible to invest in a wide variety of foreign stocks through ADRs.

To examine pricing of ADRs, consider first the case of liquid stocks that are widely traded by investors. If traders notice price discrepancies between the prices of ADRs and the underlying stocks, they will immediately jump on the opportunity to make an arbitrage (or riskless) profit. They will buy in the cheaper market and sell in the higher-priced market. Some investors believe that ADRs allow investors to avoid exchange risk because they are priced in dollars whereas foreign shares are priced in local currency. Arbitrage, however, will ensure that all gains and losses in currencies are reflected in ADR prices so that the return on the ADR (R_{ADR}) is aligned with the return on the underlying stock in the local market (R_{LStock}) as follows:

$$R_{ADR} = (1 + R_{L\,Stock})(1 + R_X) - 1,$$

where R_X is the capital gain or loss on the local currency. ADRs and the shares of the same companies listed on their home exchanges should have the same prices and the same returns (when expressed in dollars) unless governments impose restrictions on the purchase and sale of the latter by foreigners.

Figure 5.10 illustrates how closely aligned are the prices of Toyota stock in Tokyo and Toyota's ADR in New York. Of course, the former is quoted in yen in the Japanese market, so Toyota's stock price must first be expressed in dollars to provide a meaningful comparison. In Figure 5.10, it's difficult to make out two distinct lines representing the ADR and Tokyo stock prices. The two lines will not be perfectly aligned because there are transactions costs in each market and, more importantly, because the two

FIGURE 5.10 Toyota Tokyo Stock Price in Dollars and Toyota New York ADR Price in Dollars.
Data Source: Datastream.

TABLE 5.8   Characteristics of ADRs, 2008

Region	Number of Stocks
Europe	1194
Asia	1296
Latin America	284
Africa	104
Other	56

Exchange where Traded	Number of Stocks
NYSE	295
NASDAQ	114
AMEX	3
OTC	1434
Other	1088

Source: Bank of NY/Mellon.

prices are recorded at the end of the trading day in each market (and there are 13 hours between the closing times of the Tokyo and New York markets).

Not all stocks are as liquid as Toyota. As with all financial assets, if trading is infrequent, price discrepancies may at times develop between the prices of the underlying foreign shares and those of the ADRs. In addition, some governments like Singapore put restrictions on foreign ownership of the underlying shares in the local market, so discrepancies between ADR prices and the prices of the underlying shares may remain persistently large. But that's because governments prevent arbitrage from working.

Table 5.8 gives a breakdown of ADRs by region and by the exchange on which they are traded in the United States. There are 1200 or so ADRs available from both Europe and Asia, and almost 300 from Latin America. So it is evident that an investor can build a diversified portfolio of foreign stocks with ADRs alone. Indeed, some money managers offering foreign stock mutual funds only invest in ADRs. Some ADRs are listed on organized exchanges like the NYSE or NASDAQ, while others are sold only over the counter. Some ADRs are sponsored by the company involved, while others are offered to the American public without any formal sponsorship. ADRs are clearly an attractive alternative to the ownership of shares abroad.

While ADRs provide an effective way to diversify American portfolios, the stocks of American multinational firms do not. Many American multinational firms have extensive operations abroad. Their sales are multinational and, in many cases, so also is their production. Johnson and Johnson, for example, derives about 40 percent of its sales from foreign markets. And it has production facilities all over the world. Many investors believe that they can diversify their portfolios by investing in such American multinational companies.

In order for the stocks of these multinationals to provide effective foreign diversification, they must be correlated with the foreign stocks they are meant to replace in the portfolio. However, research has shown that the stocks of U.S. multinationals are much more highly correlated with the U.S. stock market than with foreign stock markets.[15] So replacing Nestle with Hershey or Coca-cola will lead to a portfolio that is not internationally diversified. There is no clear evidence why this is the case. Perhaps it's because U.S. multinational stocks are held predominantly by Americans, whereas European stocks are held predominantly by Europeans. It could also be because there is much more trading of foreign stocks on foreign exchanges than on U.S. exchanges.[16] Whatever the reason, the stocks of these multinationals can in no way substitute for the stocks of foreign firms represented in the foreign stock index.

SUMMARY—KEY FEATURES OF FOREIGN STOCKS

In the long run, foreign stocks deliver comparable returns to those of U.S. stocks. From year to year and decade to decade, however, there are wide variations in performance across regions of the world. This provides a strong argument for diversification.

It has long been recognized that the relatively low correlation between foreign and U.S. stocks provides a portfolio diversification benefit. That correlation, however, has risen sharply since 1998. Most observers believe that the rising correlation is due to the increased integration of the world economy. There should be some doubts about this explanation if only because the rise in correlation occurred abruptly beginning in 1998 rather than in a continuous process over last 20 years as integration occurred.

Currency movements influence stocks, particularly in the short run. The most dramatic example is found during the first and second terms of the Reagan administration when the dollar first soared, then fell back to earth. More recently, the dollar rose sharply against the Euro in the first three years of the latter's life only to fall back sharply since then. There is little evidence, however, that short-term currency movements can be accurately forecasted on a consistent basis.

Investors like to find shortcuts to investing in stocks listed on foreign exchanges. Buying ADRs instead of foreign stocks provides an effective way to diversify internationally because arbitrage keeps returns on ADRs closely aligned with those of the underlying stocks. Investing in

U.S. multinational stocks, however, does not provide an effective means of diversification.

Perhaps the strongest argument for foreign stocks is that there is no reason to restrict a portfolio to the stocks of companies that happen to be headquartered in the United States. There is no way of knowing whether foreign stocks will outperform U.S. stocks in the decades ahead, so there is no reason to restrict investment to U.S. stocks.

NOTES

1. These figures are derived from market capitalization statistics in the S&P Global Stock Market Factbook, 2009 edition.
2. Only in the 1920s did New York emerge as a major competitor.
3. That is, cross-border investments in stocks and bonds fell sharply. Multinational firms still found ways to expand across borders.
4. Successive French governments relaxed these controls during the 1970s, but the election of Francois Mitterand as French president in 1981 brought the re-imposition of controls on outward flows of capital by French residents. These controls were finally lifted in the late 1980s.
5. The Global Stock Markets Factbook was developed by the International Finance Corporation, an arm of the World Bank. The division between industrial countries and emerging markets was determined by the IFC. Recently, the Factbook and the database for emerging markets stocks were sold by the IFC to the Standard & Poor's Corporation.
6. According to the S&P Factbook, any country with per capita income below Korea's is classified as an emerging market.
7. The EAFE index is from the MSCI database at www.mscibarra.com. The S&P index is from the SBBI database until 1973 and thereafter from the Zephyr database.
8. This is less the case for individual foreign countries (as will be seen in the following text), but it is true of the broad regional returns reported in Table 5.2.
9. The yen began the 1970s at its fixed rate of 360 ¥ per dollar (or $0.28 per hundred yen), while recently the yen has traded below 100 ¥ per dollar. Most of the appreciation of the yen occurred in the first 20 years.
10. The hedging policy consists of selling the French franc at the three-month forward rate quoted at the end of the preceding quarter, then closing the contract using the spot rate quoted at the end of the quarter. Beginning in 1999, the Euro exchange rate replaces the French franc and Deutschmark in these calculations.
11. Of course, managers must pay attention to the economies where the firms operate and must worry about overconcentration in any one economy or region.
12. That is, alpha* = 0.4 percent at the level of risk of the U.S.-foreign diversified portfolio.

13. If the S&P and MT Treasury bond is substituted for the R3000 and Barclays Aggregate bond index, the results are similar. So it is the shorter time period that leads to less gain from international diversification.
14. The internet became important in the late 1990s, but just a little bit earlier, 1869 to be exact, a telegraph cable across the Atlantic linked New York markets with those in London and Paris.
15. If the returns on U.S. multinationals are regressed on both U.S. and foreign stock indexes (instead of just U.S. stock indexes as in a standard beta regression), the betas with respect to the foreign stock indexes are generally close to zero and statistically insignificant. See the discussion in Bodnar et al (2004).
16. There are exceptions to this pattern. Royal Dutch Shell, for example, has large trading on three exchanges, London, Amsterdam, and New York.

CHAPTER 6

Emerging Markets

Emerging markets—it may be one of the best marketing phrases ever devised. The phrase seems to describe markets that hold a lot of potential for future economic growth and the promise of future returns for investors. Since this phrase is usually attached to national markets where income is relatively low, a more accurate description would be the markets of less developed countries. Some countries will have great potential for growth and may actually be growing quite rapidly. Other countries, however, may have either little growth or actually be stumbling backwards. Naturally, few investors would want to invest in submerging markets, so all are labeled emerging.[1]

The World Bank champions the use of the term emerging markets through its affiliate, the International Finance Corporation (IFC). The IFC was created to foster private investment in developing countries. The IFC was the first organization to establish a database of stock market returns for the less developed countries, and it also started publishing an annual yearbook with extensive statistics describing the world's stock markets. (As discussed later, MSCI also has an extensive data set of emerging market stock returns). In 2000, Standard & Poor's purchased the database and yearbook from the IFC, so the yearbook is now entitled the Standard & Poor's *Global Stock Markets Factbook*.

This chapter will show that emerging markets have provided handsome returns for international investors—at least over the last two decades since stock and bond returns first became available. Risks of investing in emerging markets, however, have also been quite sizable. Returns on emerging market stocks will be studied first. Then, because the bonds of emerging market countries are so closely related to the stocks of these countries, emerging market bonds will be studied in this chapter rather than in the fixed income chapter to follow.

WHAT IS AN EMERGING MARKET?

How is an emerging market defined? The International Finance Corporation traditionally used one criterion, gross national income per capita.[2] Any country that was classified by the World Bank as a low income or middle income country was also classified as an emerging market. In 2008, China had a total gross national income of $3,899 billion, but a per capita income of only $2,940. Singapore, in contrast, had a gross national income of $168 billion, but a per capita income of $34,760.[3] So China is classified as an emerging market even though its total output was many times that of Singapore because its income per capita is so low.

The bulk of the world's income is earned by the high income countries. Figure 6.1 shows the division of the world's gross national income (GNI) in 2008. Only 27.2 percent of GNI is earned by the emerging market countries even though they represent 84 percent of the world's population. The developed countries dominate world output and world income. Western European countries (including the Euro area and other European industrial countries like the United Kingdom) produce almost 30 percent of world income and the United States another 25 percent, while the other developed countries of the world including Japan make up the rest.

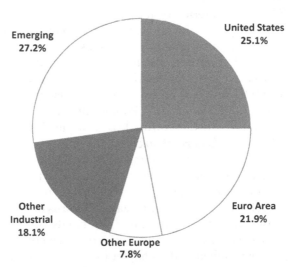

FIGURE 6.1 World Gross National Income in U.S. Dollars, 2008
Source: World Bank, World Development Indicators Database.

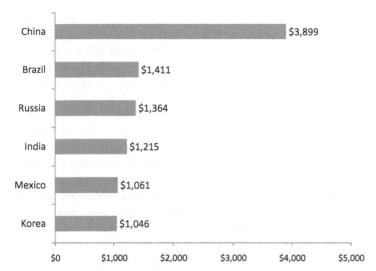

FIGURE 6.2 Gross National Income of Largest Emerging Market Countries, Billions of Dollars in 2008
Source: World Bank, World Development Indicators Database

Figure 6.2 breaks out the GNI of the six largest emerging market countries. China has the largest economy of any emerging market with a GNI larger than all but two of the developed countries (United States and Japan). With its rapid growth over the last two decades, China's economy is now larger than those of Germany, the United Kingdom, France, and Italy. China is one of the four BRIC countries highlighted in discussions of economic development, the others being Brazil, Russia, and India. All four of these countries are among the six economies shown in Figure 6.2. As shown later, the ranking of these six countries would be very different if adjusted for population size. China's huge GNI must be shared by a huge population.

When measuring national income, it's sensible to adjust for the cost of living. That is certainly true within a single country over time. If you want to measure the income of the average American today relative to decades ago, the only sensible way to measure income is to adjust for changes in the cost of living. So we might compare gross national income per capita in the year 1960 versus that of 2010 in terms of today's cost of living (2010 dollars). A similar approach might be used in comparing GNI per capita between countries at the same time since there might be substantial differences in the cost of living across countries. A basket of goods might be much less expensive in China than in Japan even if the basket itself were identical in both countries.

Irving Kravis and his colleagues at the University of Pennsylvania developed a methodology for measuring the cost of living across countries.[4] This methodology, which has since been adopted by the World Bank and other international agencies, deflated gross national income using the cost of a common market basket to produce GNI adjusted for purchasing power parity or PPP. The results follow a consistent pattern. Less developed countries have lower costs of living than industrial countries. So the GNI adjusted for PPP of the less developed countries tends to be larger than the unadjusted GNI. In the case of the industrialized countries, the reverse is true. The GNI adjusted for PPP of these countries tends to be smaller than unadjusted GNI.

Figure 6.3 presents the GNI per capita of the six largest emerging market economies using two measures of national income. One measure, labeled unadjusted, simply converts the GNI per capita of a country into dollars using recent exchange rates.[5] The second measure, labeled PPP, adjusts for the cost of living using the Kravis methodology. The results are quite striking. China's GNI per capita is only $2,940 when measured at current exchange rates. But when it is adjusted for the low cost of living in China, GNI per capital rises above $6,000. Similarly, Mexico's GNI per capita is only $9,980 when measured using current exchange rates, but it rises to $14,270 when measured using PPP. Korea (by which we mean South Korea since the World Bank doesn't even have economic statistics for North Korea) is the richest of all emerging markets with a GNI per capita above $28,000 when using PPP.

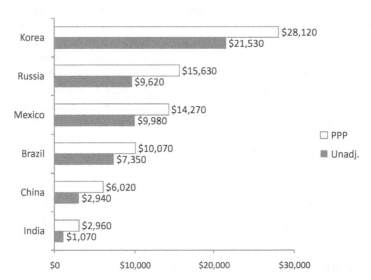

FIGURE 6.3 GNI Per Capita, Actual and PPP-Adjusted, 2008
Source: World Bank, World Development Indicators Database.

To give some perspective on these GNI figures, consider the GNI per capita of some of the major industrial countries. The United States has a GNI per capita of $47,580 using current exchange rates and $46,970 using PPP. France has a GNI per capita of $42,250 at current exchange rates and $34,400 using PPP. The gap between the incomes of emerging markets and industrial economies is wide indeed.

EMERGING STOCK MARKET INDEXES

Once definitions of emerging and developed countries are established, it's possible to divide the world's stock markets along the same lines. Emerging stock markets represent 26.5 percent of the world's stock markets of the total $35 trillion world stock market capitalization. So a block of countries with about 27 percent of the world's national income hosts about the same percentage of the world's stock market capitalization. The bulk of the market capitalization is found in the developed countries with the U.S. stock market representing almost 33.6 percent of the total (despite having only 25 percent of the world's gross national income).

The emerging stock markets are divided along regional lines in Figure 6.4. East Asia provides the largest block in terms of capitalization.

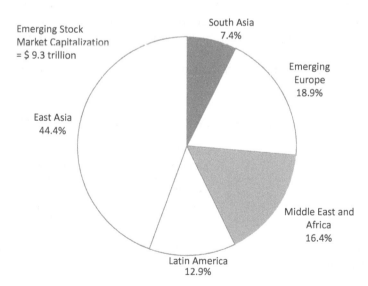

FIGURE 6.4 Stock Market Capitalization of the Emerging Markets
Source: S&P Global Stock Markets Factbook, 2009.

This region consists of all markets between Indonesia and Korea except for Japan, Singapore, and Hong Kong (the latter being measured independently of China). South Asia includes India which accounts for most of the region's market value. (East Asia and South Asia are combined in the Asia region in some of the statistics below). The Middle East and Africa region includes two of the largest emerging stock markets, South Africa and Saudi Arabia.

These measures of market capitalizations may be misleading if we are interested in stocks that are actually available to the international investor. Not all shares issued by a firm are available to ordinary investors of that country, and even fewer are available to residents of other countries. There are several issues to sort through. First, some shares may be owned by the government or closely held by other investors. For example, firms in the same industrial group can cross-hold each others' shares. Second, some or all shares of a firm may be off-limits to foreign investors. Most foreign investment restrictions have been removed by developed countries, but such restrictions are widespread in the emerging countries.

To illustrate how different emerging markets look if we consider only investable indexes, consider Table 6.1 which compares actual (total) market capitalization for the emerging markets with the weights of the same regions or countries adopted by MSCI in its investable indexes. China has a 37.7 percent weight in the total market capitalization of the emerging markets, but only a 15.9 percent weight in the MSCI investable index. In contrast, Korea and Taiwan represent only 11.2 percent of the total market capitalization, but they represent 24.2 percent of the MSCI investable index. China has many stocks which are off limits to foreigners or stocks that are only partially accessible to foreigners. Korea and Taiwan are much more open to foreign investors (even though their markets used to be subject to multiple restrictions).

TABLE 6.1 Emerging Market Capitalization Compared with MSCI Weights, 2007

Markets	Actual Market Capitalization	MSCI Weights
China	37.7%	15.9%
Korea and Taiwan	11.2%	24.2%
Rest of Asia	16.5%	14.5%
Brazil	8.3%	13.3%
Rest of Latin America	5.5%	7.0%
Europe, Middle East, and Africa	20.8%	25.1%

Sources: S&P Factbook (2008) for actual market capitalization, MSCI Barra (2008) for MSCI weights.

MSCI has strict criteria for dividing countries in its three stock market categories, Developed, Emerging, and Frontier.[6] The criteria measure economic development, the size and liquidity of stock markets, and market accessibility. Developed countries are those that have country GNI per capita that is 25 percent above the World Bank's high income threshold for three consecutive years and those that also satisfy high liquidity and accessibility requirements. (The GNI per capita threshold was $11,456, unadjusted for PPP, in 2007). Emerging Markets are distinguished from Frontier Markets by having significant openness to foreign ownership and ease of capital inflows and outflows as well as having sufficient size and liquidity of its markets. Some countries shift between categories over time. Thus Israel was scheduled to be elevated to developed status in the spring of 2010, while Argentina has fallen to frontier status.

Because the investable universe is so different from the total emerging market universe, it's imperative for investors to use proper benchmarks for evaluating emerging market managers. Performance should be judged relative to the MSCI indexes, not relative to the broad stock market indexes of a country or region. Shanghai's stock market may have soared 20 percent over a particular period, but that does not mean that the investable indexes tracked by American investors have soared that much. They may have risen more or less than the Shanghai index.

EMERGING STOCK MARKET RETURNS

Emerging markets tend to be volatile and crisis-prone. But before examining the risks of investing in emerging markets, let's consider the returns earned in the past. The data sets for emerging market stocks do not extend back as far as those of developed countries. There are indexes for individual countries that extend back into the 1970s, but the broad indexes begin in the late 1980s. As in the case of the stocks of industrial countries, MSCI provides stock market indexes for the emerging markets that are widely used as benchmarks for emerging market funds. These indexes start in 1989.[7] There is a composite index for the emerging markets consisting of 22 emerging markets including five from Latin America, eight from Asia, and nine from Europe, the Middle East, and Africa. There are also regional indexes. The Latin American Emerging Market consists of Brazil, Chile, Colombia, Mexico, and Peru. The Asian index consists of China, Indonesia, India, Korea, Malaysia, Philippines, Taiwan, and Thailand. The Europe and Middle East index consists of Czech Republic, Hungary, Israel, Poland, Russia, and Turkey.[8]

TABLE 6.2 Emerging Market and Developed Market Stock Returns, 1989–2009

	Geometric Average	Arithmetic Average	Standard Deviation	Sharpe Ratio
Emerging Markets				
MSCI Composite	12.7%	15.1%	24.7%	0.46
Asia	7.7%	10.9%	26.1%	0.27
Latin America	20.0%	23.7%	32.1%	0.62
Europe & Middle East	11.5%	15.3%	29.8%	0.39
Developed Markets				
S&P 500	9.2%	10.0%	14.9%	0.41
MSCI EAFE	4.7%	6.2%	17.5%	0.13

Data Sources: MSCI and S&P.

Table 6.2 examines returns on the composite index for the emerging markets as a whole as well as regional emerging market indexes. The table compares emerging market returns with those of the S&P 500 and the MSCI EAFE developed country indexes.

Let's summarize the broad patterns:

1. Emerging market stock returns as a whole exceed those of the S&P 500 and far exceed those of the MSCI EAFE index. Recall that the EAFE index suffered badly from the collapse of Japan beginning in 1990. So any comparison that begins in the late 1980s is bound to show EAFE in a bad light.
2. Emerging market Asia has been a disappointment to investors. Returns beginning in 1989 fall far short of the emerging market index as a whole. The reason for this poor performance will be examined later in this chapter.
3. The Latin America index earned extraordinary returns during this period. No doubt the period studied matters here. Latin America suffered a lost decade in the 1980s because of the Latin American debt crisis that began in 1982. From low levels Latin American stock markets (as a whole) have risen sharply.
4. Europe and the Middle East have lagged behind Latin America.

As shown in Table 6.2, returns for the Asian region are much lower than those for the other regions as well as emerging markets as a whole. This is a true puzzle because Asia has grown faster than any other region in the world. The largest emerging market economy, China's, has had double-digit

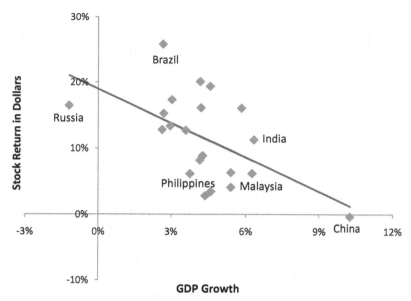

FIGURE 6.5   Growth and Stock Returns, 1990–2009
Sources: Data for GDP growth (1990–2005) from World Bank Development Indicators Database and for stock returns (1990–2009) from MSCI.

growth for much of the period. Shouldn't growth translate into high stock returns?

To answer this question, it is useful to correlate economic growth rates with stock returns. This is done in Figure 6.5 where the stock returns of 21 of the 25 largest emerging stock markets are regressed against the growth rates of these same economies.[9] The period studied is from 1990 to 2005 for economic growth and from 1990 to 2009 for stock market returns.[10] If economic growth is translated into stock returns, the regression line should be positively sloped. Higher economic growth should generate higher stock returns. Instead, the regression line has a negative slope (-0.55). A country like Russia has had (slightly) negative economic growth, on average, over this period, but its stock return has been huge. China, on the other hand, has had very fast economic growth averaging almost 10 percent per year. But its stock return has been a little below zero, on average, since 1990. Note that if these two countries are omitted from the analysis, the correlation between economic growth and stock returns is still negative at –0.43.

Economists do not have a good explanation for why there is no positive relationship between economic growth and stock returns. The economic causation should go from high economic growth to high firm profits to high stock returns. There could be a break in the chain if high expected profits have already priced stocks in that country relatively high. Think of Japan in the 1980s when future growth and future profits appeared to have no upper limit, so Price-Earning Ratios (P/E) were sky high. There could also be a break between high growth and high profits. Certainly Soviet Russia had high growth (at least in the 1950s and 1960s), but were profits in this state-controlled economy high? (By profits we mean economic profits since all large enterprises were state owned). In any case, the automatic assumption on Wall Street that a fast growing country or region will deliver high returns seems unwarranted at best.

To investigate the peculiar case of China in more detail, consider the returns on Chinese stocks beginning in December 1992 (when the MSCI China series begins) through 2009. The compound geometric return on China's investable index is −0.3 percent per year from 1993 through 2009 with a standard deviation of 38.5 percent. It is hard to believe that an economy growing as fast as China's could deliver such paltry returns. Figure 6.6 compares the return on the Chinese market with the return on the MSCI Asia index as a whole. The MSCI Asia index did not fare that well, but at least it had a positive return of 5.9 percent over the same period. It's important to note that the returns just cited are investable returns, so they record what

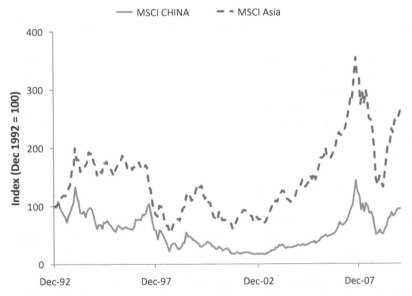

FIGURE 6.6   China and Emerging Asia Stock Markets Compared, 1992–2009
Data Source: MSCI.

an average foreign investor would earn in these markets. Growth evidently does not reward all investors.

China, however, did have a terrific run late in the period. For the two years prior to the peak of its market in October 2007, the MSCI China index had a return of 306.4 percent! No wonder investors were rushing into this market. From that peak, the Chinese index fell 64.8 percent through October 2008. Through December 2009, it has again risen spectacularly by 87.9 percent. It has been quite a roller coaster ride. The key question is whether China's recent stock market performance is more indicative of the future than the full record of returns since 1992. China will no doubt remain volatile. But will it deliver more than the paltry returns seen *on average* since December 1992?

RISKS OF INVESTING IN EMERGING STOCK MARKETS

Emerging markets are inherently risky. This is seen most simply by comparing the standard deviations of the emerging market indexes with those for the developed markets as in Table 6.2. But there are two features of emerging market risks that need to be explored in more detail. The first concerns the impact of emerging market stocks on portfolio risk. Emerging market stocks tend to be relatively low in correlation with developed country stocks, so their contribution to the overall risk of the portfolio may not be that great. The second feature concerns the volatility of emerging market stocks. The risks of emerging market stocks may be underestimated by conventional measures because they are prone to crises.

Table 6.3 reports correlations between emerging market stocks (MSCI Emerging Markets Composite Index) and the two developed country indexes, the S&P 500 and EAFE indexes. Two sets of correlations are shown, the first for the period beginning in 1989 when the investable indexes start and the second for the last 10 years alone, 2000 to 2009. For the period as a whole, the correlation between emerging market stocks and the S&P 500 is moderately lower than that found between the EAFE index and the S&P 500. A correlation of 0.66 is certainly lower than would be found between two types of U.S. stocks, like small-cap and large-cap stocks or value and growth stocks. So it shouldn't be surprising that diversification into emerging market stocks could lower the risk of an American stock portfolio. But, as shown in later chapters, emerging market stocks do not offer as much diversification as some alternative asset classes. This should not be that surprising given that many emerging market economies depend on exports to

TABLE 6.3 Correlations between Emerging Market Stocks and
Developed Market Stocks

	Correlation with S&P 500	Correlation with EAFE
1989-2009		
EAFE	0.71	
MSCI EM	0.66	0.68
2000-2009		
EAFE	0.88	
MSCI EM	0.79	0.88

Data Sources: MSCI and S&P.

the developed countries, so their stock markets tend to boom at times when developed economies are doing well.

The last chapter documented the rise in correlations between the EAFE index and U.S. stock market indexes in the last decade. A similar rise has occurred in the correlations between emerging market stocks and the developed country indexes. The correlation between the composite emerging market index and the S&P 500 has risen from 0.66 over the whole period to 0.79 over the last 10 years. No doubt the rise in correlation would have been even larger if the index had been available back through the 1970s and early 1980s. So whatever diversification benefits that were available over longer periods have been diminished, at least as long as correlations remain higher.

For American investors, the most important issue is how emerging markets fare within a portfolio because emerging markets are likely to be only a marginal asset within a portfolio dominated by American stocks and bonds. With the relatively low correlations reported in Table 6.3, it should not be surprising that a marginal allocation to emerging market stocks improves the performance of the portfolio.

Table 6.4 reports the results of two diversification experiments. In the first experiment, labeled Portfolio A in the table, an all-stock portfolio consisting of the S&P 500 index alone is diversified by adding a 10 percent allocation to emerging markets (using the MSCI EM index). In the second experiment, labeled Portfolio B in the table, a well-diversified portfolio of stocks and bonds is further diversified by adding 10 percent to emerging markets. This second portfolio consists of 25 percent in the Barclays Aggregate U.S. bond index, 50 percent in the S&P 500 index, and 25 percent in the EAFE index in the absence of emerging market stocks. When emerging market stocks are added to this portfolio, a 10 percent allocation to

TABLE 6.4 Impact of Emerging Market Stocks on Portfolio Performance, 1989–2009

	Geometric Average	Arithmetic Average	Standard Deviation	Sharpe Ratio
Portfolio A				
Without Emerging Markets	9.2%	10.0%	14.9%	0.40
With 10% Emerging Markets	9.7%	10.5%	15.2%	0.43
Portfolio B				
Without Emerging Markets	8.0%	8.3%	11.2%	0.38
With 10% Emerging Markets	8.5%	8.8%	11.7%	0.41

Portfolio A consists of the S&P 500 alone or 90 percent S&P 500 with 10 percent in the MSCI Emerging Markets composite index.
Portfolio B is a diversified portfolio with 25 percent in the Barclays Aggregate index for U.S. bonds, 50 percent S&P 500, and 25 percent EAFE. The 10 percent in emerging markets reduces the S&P 500 weight to 40 percent.
Data Sources: Barclays Capital, MSCI and S&P.

emerging market stocks reduces the S&P 500 allocation to 40 percent. The results are similar in both experiments. Emerging market stocks improve the risk-adjusted returns on both portfolios. The addition of a 10 percent allocation to emerging market stocks raises the return on the portfolio but also raises the standard deviation of that portfolio. But the net effect is positive in that the Sharpe ratios of the portfolios with emerging markets are higher than those without emerging markets. In the case of the all-stock portfolios (labeled A in Table 6.4) adding emerging markets raises portfolio returns by 0.5 percent after adjusting for risk. That is, the alpha* of the portfolio including emerging markets is 0.5 percent compared with the portfolio with the S&P 500 alone.[11] In the case of the stock/bond portfolios (labeled B in the table), the alpha* of the portfolio including emerging markets is 0.4 percent. Diversification into emerging markets seems to pay, at least over the sample period for emerging market stocks beginning in 1989.

Another way to assess the contribution of emerging markets to a portfolio is to examine its systematic risk. Suppose that the emerging market index is to be added to an existing portfolio of stocks represented by the MSCI World index. The beta of the emerging market investable index, measured over the period from January 1989 through the end of 2009, is 1.17. The reason why the beta is so high is that the standard deviation of the emerging market series is 24.7 percent. So the relatively low correlation between emerging market stocks and this portfolio, 0.724, is not enough to keep the beta low.[12] On the other hand, the returns on the emerging market series are high enough to provide an excess return (or alpha) relative to the security market line of 7.1 percent! That is, the return on the investable index, 15.1 percent, exceeds the corresponding return on the security market line, 8.0 percent, by more than 7.1 percent over the period from 1989 to 2009. Diversification into emerging market stocks still pays despite the standard deviation and relatively high beta of these stocks. Note that if the S&P 500 is used as the market benchmark, then the risk-adjusted excess return on the Emerging Market Index (or alpha) shrinks to 4.6 percent because the S&P 500 return is 2.6 percent higher than the World Index return over this period.[13]

The indexes available for emerging market stocks extend back only to the late 1980s at best. With such a short history available, it's difficult to form judgments about how high returns will be in the future. Perhaps Asia, and China in particular, will provide much larger returns in the longer run. But, even more importantly, it's difficult to assess how risky emerging markets really are. Emerging stock markets are highly volatile and they are vulnerable to economic and financial crises.

Consider an investor trying to make decisions about emerging market stocks in early 1997. At that time, there were only eight years of data from the MSCI database. As shown in Figure 6.7, over the eight years ending in 1996, the compound return on the Asian Emerging Market Index was 14.8 percent per annum and the return on the composite index for all emerging markets was 19.9 percent per annum. It's true that over the same period, the S&P 500 offered hefty returns of 16.4 percent per year. But the correlations between emerging markets and U.S. stocks were low enough to justify large allocations to emerging market stocks.

In early 1997, few investors realized that Asian markets were about to be hit by a financial tsunami that would drive many markets down by 75 percent or more. The crisis first hit the Bangkok foreign exchange market in early July 1997 when the Thai central bank was forced to float the Thai baht. Speculation against Thailand's currency had been building up in the late spring, but few observers realized the extent of the speculation because the Thai central bank was secretly intervening in the foreign exchange market to keep forward exchange rates steady.[14] After the Bank of Thailand had committed most of Thailand's foreign exchange reserves to these operations, the Thai Government was forced to float the Baht. The value of the baht was cut in half almost immediately (with the dollar initially rising against the Baht from Bt 25 per dollar to Bt 50 per dollar).

The collapse of the baht soon set off speculation against the Malaysian Ringgit, the Indonesian Rupiah, the Korean Won, and other Asian currencies. Why was there such widespread contagion? The most important reason is that firms in all of these countries had loaded up on dollar debt and other

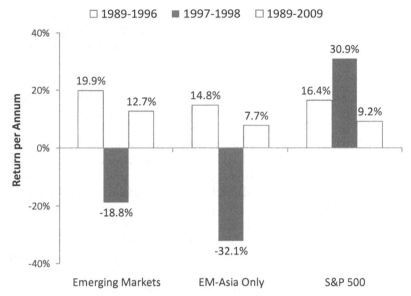

FIGURE 6.7 Emerging Market Stocks Before and After the Asian Crisis Years of 1997–1998
Data Source: MSCI.

foreign currency debt. Once rumors of depreciation spread in the market, these firms rushed to hedge their foreign currency liabilities. If a fire breaks out in a ballroom, every one heads to the exits at the same time.

Stock market investors suffered grievously. Figure 6.7 shows that the Asian markets as a whole returned –32.1 percent per annum in 1997 and 1998. The stock markets of Thailand, Malaysia, and Korea all fell by 60 percent or more (in dollar terms). The contagion even spread to Latin America where markets fell 12.9 percent over the two year period. Within a few years afterwards, emerging markets as a whole had recovered most of their lost ground. But in the case of the Asian stock markets, the index return per annum over the whole period from 1989 to 2009 is still more than 7 percent below what it was at the end of 1996!

The Asian crisis is not an isolated incident. Other markets have been prone to crisis. Consider three other important examples, Mexico in 1994, Russia in 1998, and Argentina in 2000 to 2002.

The Mexican crisis was precipitated by a currency collapse just as in the case of Thailand. In December 1994 following the inauguration of President Ernesto Zedillo, the peso depreciated from Ps 3.5 per dollar to Ps 7.0 per dollar. The depreciation led to widespread bankruptcies among Mexican firms (including major banks) because so much debt was denominated in dollars. The impact on the stock market was dramatic. The Mexican market fell by 60 percent (in dollar terms). It took several years for the Mexican economy to recover from this disaster.

The Russian crisis involved a default by the Russian government on its debt rather than currency depreciation. The Russian stock market began a dramatic decline a year before the actual default which occurred in July 1998. Between September 1997 and a year later, the Russian stock market declined (in U.S. dollar terms) by more than 80 percent. The bond default itself precipitated a fall in many bond markets worldwide. Bond markets worldwide are not supposed to be very highly correlated. If you invest in Russian bonds and Brazilian bonds and Chinese bonds, it would seem that your portfolio is diversified. But when Russia defaulted on its bonds, there was a reassessment of risk worldwide. Spreads on bonds widened sharply both in the emerging bond markets and in the high-yield U.S. bond market (for so-called junk bonds). The most dramatic effect of this reassessment of risks was the collapse of Long-term Capital Management, which had to be rescued by the major investment banks in September 1998.

The Argentine crisis began as early as 2000 when the long-established peg to the U.S. dollar began to be seriously questioned. In the early 1990s, the Argentine government had established a currency board to permanently fix the peso to the dollar.[15] Argentine inflation, which had soared more than 1000 percent in the late 1980s, almost completely disappeared with this peg. Dollars and pesos became interchangeable in ordinary transactions as well as in financial contracts. By the late 1990s, however, the economy had slumped because of an overvalued exchange rate, especially after Brazil let its own currency depreciate against the dollar. In January 2002, Argentina was forced to float its currency and put controls on financial outflows. By that time, the stock market had already plummeted. From February 2000 until June 2002, a few months after the crisis, the Argentine market fell more than 80 percent in dollar terms.

Even in the absence of specific crises, these markets tend to be highly volatile. Consider the example of China once again. With a standard deviation of 38.5 percent, China's stock market is like a roller coaster. In the two years starting in December 1993, China's market fell 61 percent. It recovered most of this ground by 1997, but in August 1997 it fell sharply again as the Asian crisis hit. Within a year, the Chinese market had fallen by 80 percent (measured in dollar terms). Investors must be prepared for volatility if they invest in these markets.

Prior to the 2008 crisis, emerging markets' returns soared more than 85 percent from December 2005 to December 2007. So it has been hard to convince investors of the risks of investing in emerging market stocks.

Of course, the plunge by 53 percent in 2008 may help.[16] It's even harder to remind investors that emerging market bonds have downside risk.

EMERGING MARKET BONDS—A BRIEF HISTORY

Emerging market bonds have been around for two centuries at least. But most investors consider them a new asset class. The reason is that they almost entirely disappeared for more than 50 years. From the 1930s to the late 1980s, very few emerging market bonds were issued because investors had suffered too grievously from defaults in the 1930s.

There is a long tradition of defaults on emerging market bonds. The expectation has always been that some bonds will go into default because they had done so often in the past. In the late nineteenth century, emerging economies like those of Argentina, Brazil, South Africa, and China regularly raised capital in London and Paris by issuing bonds. So did the emerging economy of the United States. Most of these bonds were denominated in pounds or French francs rather than in local currency. With fairly regular, but unpredictable frequency, these bonds would go into default. An example was the Argentina default that occurred during the Baring Brothers Crisis of 1890. The crisis began with a financial panic in Argentina, but soon affected the bond markets of other emerging economies such as the United States, and led to the collapse (and subsequent rescue by the Bank of England) of Barings Brothers itself, a long-established merchant bank in London.

When issuing bonds, most governments did not plan to default on their bonds. In fact, they often went to great lengths to avoid default. An example is the 1904 issue by the Chinese Imperial Railway, denominated in pounds and guaranteed by the Imperial Government of China. This bond continued to be serviced even after the Chinese revolution of 1911 under Sun Yat-sen for the simple reason that the revolutionary government wanted to retain access to the international capital markets. Only in the 1920s and 1930s did successor governments default on such bonds.[17] The 1930s saw many defaults by sovereign debtors. More than 70 percent of the foreign bonds issued in the U.S. market during the late 1920s (so-called Yankee bonds) went into default during the 1930s.[18]

After the Second World War, there was little eagerness to underwrite new bonds issued by the less developed countries. It was only in the 1970s that any sizable financing occurred outside of official channels such as the World Bank. But the new financing in the 1970s took the form of bank loans provided by the banks of the developed world rather than bonds. The innovation that occurred was that these loans were syndicated among a large group of banks so the originating bank or banks could place most of the loans and hence offload most of the default risk to other banks. Syndicated loans reached a peak in the early 1980s. It was then that the Latin American countries began to default on their loans. Technically, the loans were not in complete default, but the banks were eventually forced to reschedule the terms of these loans. Needless to say, syndicated loans ceased to be a major source of financing for emerging markets. With no sizable bond market financing available, emerging economies suffered from a lack of financing.

It was the American Treasury Secretary under President George H.W. Bush, Nicholas Brady, who resurrected the long-dormant international bond market. Brady did this by engineering the packaging of bank debt in the form of bonds that could be sold to non-bank investors. The resulting Brady bonds often contained Treasury bonds as partial collateral to make them more attractive to non-bank investors. The market for emerging market debt slowly revived.

RETURNS ON EMERGING MARKET BONDS

In the last decade, emerging market bonds have become an increasingly important source of finance for emerging economies and an attractive asset for investors seeking international diversification. Emerging economies have been able to expand financing through newly issued Eurobonds, bonds syndicated and sold internationally, and through bond issues in traditional national bond markets.[19] Most of these bonds are denominated in dollars, although bonds denominated in local currencies have become increasingly important.

The return series for emerging market bonds typically begin in the early 1990s after the Brady bonds were introduced. Table 6.5 reports the return on one such series, the Merrill Lynch Emerging Market Sovereign Plus index. This table compares emerging market bonds with U.S. dollar-denominated bonds, using the Barclays Capital Aggregate Bond Index (formerly the Lehman Aggregate Bond Index), and with two stock market indexes, the S&P 500 U.S. index and the MSCI emerging market stock index. The results are very surprising. Over this sample period, 1992 to 2009, emerging bonds deliver a 12.2 percent compound return. So these bonds deliver returns far above those of either stock index or the U.S. bond index. The standard deviation of 14.3 percent is very high for a bond index, but it appears that emerging market bonds deliver stock-like returns.

The surprising performance of emerging market bonds is explained by the reassessment of emerging market risks that has occurred since the early 1990s. Consider Figure 6.8 which shows the spread of emerging market bonds over U.S. Treasuries (of the same maturity). Since reaching a peak

TABLE 6.5 Emerging Market Bond Returns Compared with Other Returns,
1992–2009

	Geometric Average	Arithmetic Average	Standard Deviation	Sharpe Ratio
Bonds				
Emerging Market	12.2%	12.6%	14.3%	0.64
U.S.	6.4%	6.3%	3.8%	0.74
Stocks				
Emerging Market	9.6%	12.2%	24.2%	0.36
U.S.	7.7%	8.6%	14.8%	0.35

Emerging market bond index is the Merrill Lynch Emerging Market Sovereign Plus
index. Other indexes are the Barclays Capital Aggregate U.S. bond index, MSCI
Emerging Market stock index, and the S&P 500 U.S. stock index.
Data Sources: Barclays Capital, Merrill Lynch, MSCI, and S&P.

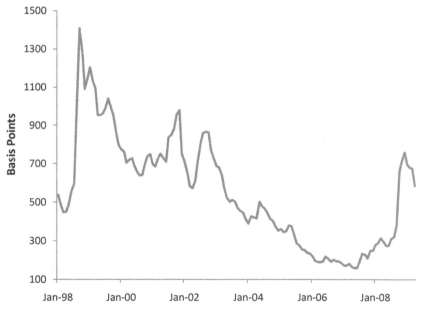

FIGURE 6.8 Emerging Market Bond Spread (in Basis Points above U.S.
Treasury Yield)
Data Source: Datastream.

of 1400 basis points following the Russian bond default, emerging market spreads fell to 200 basis points or less prior to the 2007 and 2008 crisis. During this period of falling spreads, these bonds were increasingly viewed as almost like U.S. investment grade corporate debt. When interest spreads fall from 1400 basis points to 200 basis points, investors thrive.

How should an investor interpret a spread of 200 basis points? A fair interpretation is that the market no longer foresees the possibility of Mexican-like devaluations or Russian-like defaults. The era of Argentine-like crises is forever behind us, or so it seems. For investors with a more skeptical attitude, the proper approach is to ask whether the returns shown in Table 6.5 are good indicators of future returns on emerging market bonds. The sensible answer is that there has been a once-for-all reassessment of emerging market risks. The reassessment may prove short-lived. But even if emerging market risks stay low, the investment gains from the reassessment have already been earned. The past returns on emerging market bonds should be viewed much like U.S. bonds were viewed in Chapter 2. Between the early 1980s and present, there has been a once-for-all reassessment of inflation risks in the U.S. market. This has led to a once-for-all reduction in U.S. bond yields and a temporary increase in U.S. bond returns. In the case of both types of bonds, the great returns are probably behind us.[20]

For the future, it's important to determine how emerging market bonds might fit in the portfolio. They are an odd bond series in that they are highly volatile, more like junk bonds in the United States than either U.S. or European conventional bonds. In Table 6.6, we report correlations between the emerging market bond index and the three other bond and stock indexes of Table 6.5. The highest correlation is not with other dollar bonds, but with the emerging market stock index. That's because both asset classes are subject to emerging market country risk.

TABLE 6.6 Correlations between Emerging Market Bonds and Other Assets, 1992–2009

	Merrill Lynch Emerging Market Bond Index	Barclays Aggregate Bond Index	MSCI Emerging Market Stock Index
EM Bonds	1.00		
Barclays Aggregate	0.32	1.00	
EM Stocks	0.66	−0.02	1.00
S&P 500	0.54	0.12	0.70

Data Sources: Emerging market bond index is the Merrill Lynch Emerging Market Sovereign Plus index. Other indexes are from Barclays Capital, MSCI, and S&P.

Why are emerging market stocks and bonds so highly correlated? There is a common thread, emerging market country risk, tying these two asset classes together. If there is a crisis in Russia or East Asia or Latin America, emerging market bonds and emerging market stocks will both be reassessed. As an example, consider the markets for Argentine stocks and Brady bonds between January 1997 and January 2002. The Argentine stock index (measured in dollars) gave a return of −15.0 percent over this period. Argentine Brady bonds provided an annualized compound return of −12.7 percent. The reassessment of Argentine risks hit both markets very hard. The early success of the Argentine stabilization plan was followed by an accelerating slide into crisis culminating in the abandonment of the dollar peg in January 2002. Emerging markets are risky. Emerging market stocks and bonds may still deserve a place in the portfolio. But the investor should be very aware of their volatility.

SUMMARY—KEY FEATURES OF EMERGING MARKET STOCKS AND BONDS

The world's stock and bond markets are divided into developed and emerging for a good reason—emerging markets are riskier. The dividing line between the countries themselves is somewhat arbitrary, but the division between the assets of these two sets of countries is a meaningful one. Standard deviations have been a step above those of developed stock markets. Consistent with higher risks, emerging market stocks have delivered stellar returns since the series began in the mid-1980s. And these stocks also provide diversification to a more traditional portfolio.

Unlike emerging market stocks, emerging market bonds seem too good to be true. The returns since the early 1990s have been better than stock returns with standard deviations below those of the S&P 500. This chapter has argued that the returns are due to a dramatic downward assessment of risks. This reassessment has provided once-for-all returns much like we have enjoyed from the reassessment of inflation in the U.S. bond market. Emerging market bonds, like their stock counterparts, are crisis-prone. But many investors will not believe this until the next crisis occurs. Caveat emptor.

NOTES

1. The term submerging markets is due to Goetzmann and Jorion (1999). These authors examine stock markets like those of Argentina and China that

re-emerged after decades of closure due to political instability. The term frontier market is given to a subset of emerging markets at lower stages of development.

2. More recently, the IFC (and Standard & Poor's after it took over the IFC database) refined the criteria used to distinguish emerging markets from developed markets. The criteria include the depth of the market, its lack of discriminatory controls on foreign investment, and its transparency.

3. All gross national income statistics are from the World Bank, World Development Indicators Database.

4. See Kravis et al (1975). The International Comparison Project that Kravis and his co-authors pursued was financed under grants from the World Bank and other international agencies.

5. The unadjusted figure is obtained by using a moving average of the past three year's exchange rates. The World Bank calls this the Atlas method for calculating GNI.

6. See MSCI/Barra MSCI Market Classification Framework, June 2009.

7. As mentioned above, S&P also provides emerging stock market indexes including investable indexes begun by the International Finance Corporation and later sold to S&P. Those indexes give roughly similar results to the MSCI indexes.

8. The remaining countries in the composite index are from Africa: Egypt, Morocco, and South Africa.

9. This is an analysis updated from a similar one reported by Jeremy Siegel in his study of long-run returns on stock markets (Siegel, 1998). The four countries omitted either do not have GDP data available (Qatar) or have stock market data for only a few years (Kuwait, Saudi Arabia, and UAE).

10. Some countries have stock returns beginning later than 1990. Returns for China, for example, begin in 1992. If the stock returns are measured from 1990 to 2005 only, the correlation between growth and stock returns is even more negative.

11. Deriving alpha* from the Sharpe ratios, $\alpha^* = (0.43 - 0.40) * 0.152 = 0.5\%$.

12. The high standard deviation of the emerging market series (relative to a standard deviation of 15.3 percent for the World Index) ensures that the beta is relatively large, $(0.724 * 0.247) / 0.153 = 1.17$.

13. The World Index performs badly for the same reason that EAFE does over this period, the collapse of the Japanese market. Note that it is more appropriate to use the World Index to measure the beta of Emerging Markets than to use a U.S. index alone.

14. The Central Bank of Thailand was keeping the spot exchange rate fixed against a basket of currencies with a weight of 80 percent on the U.S. dollar. This was well understood by the foreign exchange market. What was less well known is that the supposedly market-determined forward exchange rate was also being held fixed by secret intervention. The Central Bank knew that a depreciating forward rate would alert investors worldwide to the weakness of the currency.

15. A currency board takes away the discretion over monetary policy that a traditional central bank always retains. The finance minister of the time, Domingo

Cavallo, believed that only a currency board could establish credibility for an exchange rate peg.

16. That's compared with a 37 percent decline in the S&P 500 in 2008. In 2007 and 2008, the world learned that even industrial countries can suffer major financial crises!

17. Goetzmann et al (2007) reviews some of the history of Chinese government debt issues and their subsequent defaults.

18. The U.S. bond market had become the primary source of international funding for emerging economies in the 1920s. The 70 percent excludes issues by Canadian borrowers.

19. Eurobonds were first issued in the 1960s long before the European currency, the Euro, was introduced. The term Euro reflects the European origin of the market, although Eurobonds can be issued by borrowers from anywhere in the world and are often sold to non-European investors.

20. This is not to deny that returns can be sizable for a short period following a crisis. In the case of the 2007 and 2008 crisis, spreads rose more than 7 percent, thus creating a short-term opportunity for investors once the crisis passed.

CHAPTER 7

Bonds

S tocks and bonds are the most important assets in most portfolios. This book has focused so far on stocks because they provide the long-run appreciation necessary to sustain portfolios. Chapter 2 showed that long-run bond returns are so low that they hardly allow for any growth in wealth over time, at least after the returns have been adjusted for inflation. That chapter focused only on long-term Treasury bonds. This chapter will discuss three types of bonds, U.S. Treasury bonds, other bonds issued in the United States, and bonds issued in other industrial countries. The United States is the largest market for bonds in the world, but the bond markets of the other industrial countries are growing rapidly, particularly the markets in the Euro currency area. The returns on bonds have varied widely over the last few decades, so the chapter will investigate the main determinants of bond returns.

Bonds are often favored by investors because they provide fixed income in contrast to the variable returns offered by equities and by most other assets. A stream of fixed income payments is often viewed as essential to retirees as well as many institutional investors because of their need for continual income. Investors focusing only on yields, however, are too often disappointed by the overall performance of their investments. Bond yields represent part of the total return to fixed income assets, but the variation in yields over time leads to capital gains and losses that sometimes dominate the total return from holding bonds. That's especially true if the total return takes into account changes in the cost of living. In the 1970s, for example, bond yields were quite high relative to long-run averages. Yet bond returns were quite abysmal because of capital losses. As inflation and interest rates rose over the decade, existing bonds fell in value. So the total return on these bonds, including capital gains as well as coupons, was far lower than the coupons themselves. Returns on bonds in the 1970s were lower still when adjusted for inflation.

The fixed income of bond investments is illusory in countries with high inflation. It is also often illusory for securities with high default risk. So it's useful to begin with a discussion of what determines the interest rate on a bond. This discussion will help to explain why bond returns are so miserably low in some periods, particularly when adjusted for inflation, and why they are surprisingly high in other periods. Two important determinants of bond yields are (expected) inflation rates and (expected) default rates. The discussion of default risk will be postponed until later in this chapter by first focusing on U.S. government bonds with little if any default risk.

TREASURY BONDS

How does inflation affect interest rates? In the short run, central banks often play a critical role in setting short-term interest rates. For example, the Federal Reserve directly controls the Federal Funds interest rate, the rate at which banks borrow in the inter-bank market. And other short-term dollar interest rates, such as the commercial paper and Treasury bill interest rates in the United States or the LIBOR rate on dollar deposits in London, are loosely linked to the Fed Funds rate.[1] So if the Fed raises the Fed Funds rate by 25 basis points, or 0.25 percent, the commercial paper and Treasury bill rates and LIBOR are likely to rise by a similar amount (in normal times, at least). In the long-run, however, the role of the Federal Reserve is very different. In the long run, U.S. interest rates are primarily determined by inflation. And it is the Fed's role in helping to determine the inflation rate that matters.

Consider the history of U.S. interest rates since the late 1940s as shown in Figure 7.1. Except for a temporary bout of inflation during the Korean War, inflation remained low in the United States until the late 1960s and 1970s. Inflation peaked following two oil price shocks in 1973 and 1974 and 1979. Beginning in the late 1960s, interest rates slowly but surely responded to rising inflation as inflation expectations became imbedded in bond yields. The same inflation expectations led to rising wage demands and to downward pressure on the U.S. dollar. To lower interest yields from their highs in the late 1970s, it was necessary for the Federal Reserve to pursue a tight monetary policy. This shift in policy began with the appointment of Paul Volcker as Fed chair in 1979. The low interest rates that we experience today were made at the Fed. But in the long run, low interest rates result from low inflation, not from the Fed lowering the Fed Funds rate.

To provide further evidence of the link between inflation and interest rates, consider the bond *returns* earned on long-term Treasury bonds in each decade since 1950 as shown in Figure 7.2. This chart shows the

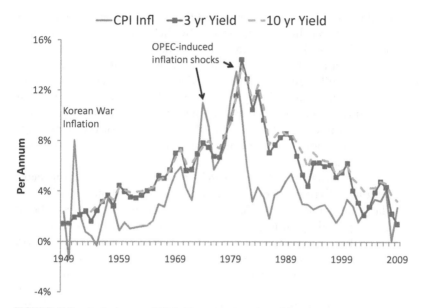

FIGURE 7.1 Inflation and U.S. Treasury Bond Yields, 1949–2009
Data Source: IMF, International Financial Statistics.

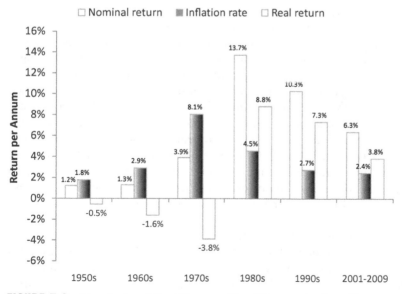

FIGURE 7.2 Nominal and Real Treasury Bond Returns by Decade
Data Source: ©Morningstar.

nominal bond return, the inflation rate, and the real bond return. The latter is obtained by deflating the nominal return by the inflation rate.[2] The low bond yields of the 1950s were matched by almost equally low inflation. The net result was a real bond return that was (slightly) negative. Over the next two decades, inflation expectations evidently lagged behind actual inflation so bond holders earned negative real bond returns of −1.6 percent and −3.8 percent, respectively! Fixed income earners were deceived by the steadiness of the coupons on their bonds. The real value of the bonds was being eroded by inflation, and the coupons themselves were being debased by rising price levels.

The terrific returns earned since 1981 are a direct result of the Fed's policy of fighting inflation. Over this period, bond yields and inflation expectations lagged behind actual inflation once again. But in this case, bond holders were surprised by falling inflation and they were rewarded with unusually large real returns on their bonds. In the decade from 1981 to 1990, the compound real return on the long-term (20-year) Treasury bond was 8.8 percent. That return was followed by a 7.3 percent compound return in the 1990s. Those returns are to be expected when inflation falls from 13.5 percent to its current level and when bond yields fall from almost 15 percent to less than 5 percent.

It's important for investors to realize how fundamental is the link between inflation and interest rates. Consider the experience of the major industrial countries over the last few decades. All of these countries have benefited from a decline in inflation and a decline in interest rates since 1980. So the triumph of the Federal Reserve over inflation was matched by similar victories in the other industrial countries. In Europe, the fight against inflation was spurred on by currency regimes that sought to limit exchange rate changes between European countries. In particular, the planned introduction of the Euro in 1999 forced countries to cut inflation in order to qualify for the currency union.[3] But despite these pressures, European countries differed widely in their inflation rates as did the other industrial countries. Between 1981 and 2008, inflation rates as measured by the consumer price index ranged from an average of 2.3 percent in Germany to 5.7 percent in Spain. Two countries outside the European Union, Japan and Switzerland, had even lower inflation rates than Germany, Japan's being only 1.0 percent.

The wide range of inflation rates was matched by an equally wide range of interest rates. Consider Figure 7.3 which shows the array of interest rates and inflation rates in 16 industrial countries between 1981 and 2008. If all of these countries maintained the same real interest rates throughout, they would all lie along a line. In practice, some countries have higher interest rates than their inflation rates justify, while others have lower interest rates.

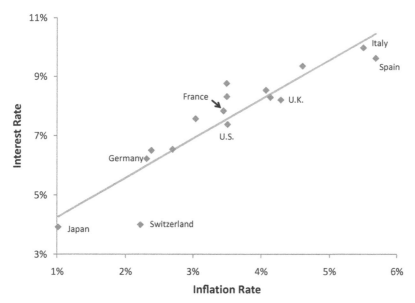

FIGURE 7.3 Interest Rates and Inflation Rates of the Major Industrial Countries, 1981–2008
Data Source: IMF, International Financial Statistics.

The extreme case is that of Switzerland which has an average inflation rate of 2.2 percent and an average interest rate of only 4.0 percent. The United States, in contrast, has an average inflation rate of 3.5 percent and an average interest rate of 7.4 percent. Despite these differences, Figure 7.3 shows a very clear link between inflation and interest rates in the long run. It's important to keep this in mind when considering bond returns earned over equally long periods.

Besides inflation, interest rates on Treasury bonds vary by maturity. In most periods, the term structure of interest rates is upward sloping. That is, longer maturity issues pay higher yields than those with shorter maturity. Consider Figure 7.4 which shows the term structure of yields on U.S. Treasury bonds in three different years, 1985, 1995, and 2005. In all three years the economy was growing, so the term structure of yields had its normal upward slope. (If a recession had occurred in one of these years, the term structure of yields could have been inverted temporarily). Over the two decades shown in the figure, inflation and interest rates were dropping. So the whole term structure of yields fell over time. Thus the figure illustrates two of the three determinants of bond yields, inflation and the maturity of the bond. The third factor, default risk, is negligible in the case of Treasuries.

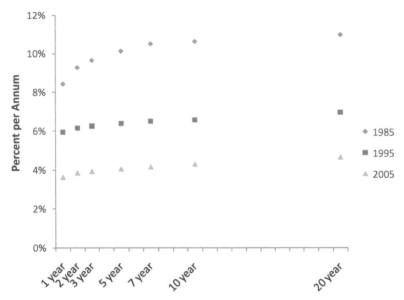

FIGURE 7.4 Term Structure of Treasury Bond Yields
Data Source: Federal Reserve Board.

Bond yields are only one component of bond returns. Bond *returns* reflect both the coupon paid and the capital gain over the holding period of the return. If C is the coupon on a Treasury bond and B_{t-1} is the price of the bond at the end of the previous period, then the bond return during period t, R_t, is given by:

$$R_t = C/B_{t-1} + (B_t/B_{t-1} - 1)$$

The first term is the coupon price ratio and the second term is the capital gain on the bond during period t. Table 7.1 reports bond returns for two maturities of U.S. Treasuries. The long-term bond is a 20-year Treasury bond, while the medium-term is a five-year Treasury. First consider returns over the whole period since 1951. The long-term bond has higher volatility with a standard deviation of 9.5 percent compared with one of 5.0 percent for the medium-term issue. Over this long period, however, investors were not compensated for this higher volatility since the return on the long-term bond was only marginally higher than on the medium-term bond.

In periods of falling interest rates, such as those in the 1980s until present, long-term bonds should outperform medium-term bonds. That is indeed the case if performance is measured only in terms of returns.

TABLE 7.1 Treasury Bonds by Maturity

Maturity	Coupon Yield	Capital Gain	Total Return	Standard Deviation	Sharpe Ratio
1951–2009					
Long-term	6.3%	0.0%	6.3%	9.5%	0.17
Medium-term	5.9%	0.3%	6.2%	5.0%	0.29
1981–2009					
Long-term	7.4%	3.0%	10.4%	11.1%	0.47
Medium-term	6.6%	1.8%	8.4%	5.3%	0.60

The Treasury returns reported are for long-term 20-year bonds, and medium-term five-year bonds.
Data Source: ©Morningstar

In Table 7.1, the return on the 20-year bond is 2.0 percent higher than on the 5-year bond during the period from 1981 to 2009. During this period, the capital gain component of the bond return contributed 3.0 percent to the total return. But the standard deviation of the 20-year bond is still substantially higher than that of the five-year bond, so the Sharpe ratio for the longer-term issue is still much lower than for the medium-term issue. So even in a period of falling interest rates, the 20-year bond seems to be dominated by the five-year bond. That's true at least if investors are focusing on one-year horizon returns. For investors with long-term liabilities, however, the 20-year bond may be the most attractive alternative. Such investors might be able to match long-term liabilities with long-term assets, thereby minimizing the volatility of their net asset positions.

THE WIDER U.S. BOND MARKET

At the end of 2008, the U.S. bond market encompassed securities with a total market value of $33.5 trillion (or $33,500 billion) according to the Securities Industry and Financial Markets Association.[4] Figure 7.5 shows the breakdown of fixed income securities as of the end of 2008. U.S. Treasury securities represent only 17.7 percent of the U.S. market. Municipal bonds (issued by local as well as state governments) represent 8.0 percent of the market, while corporate debt represents another 18.8 percent. Mortgage-related securities, 26.6 percent of the market, include those issued by the government agencies Fannie Mae and Freddie Mac as well as collateralized mortgage obligations (CMOs). Federal agency securities, 9.7 percent of the market, are non-mortgage obligations of agencies like the Federal Farm

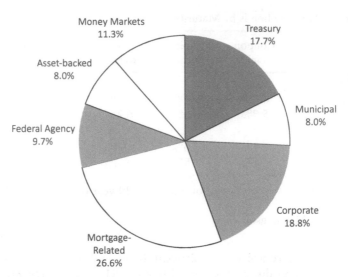

FIGURE 7.5   U.S. Bond Market in 2008
Source: Securities Industry and Financial Markets Association, 2009.

Loan Mortgage Corporation and the Student Loan Marketing Association. Money market securities and asset-backed bonds round out the rest.

The relative importance of Treasury bonds has declined over time because other bond markets have grown more rapidly. Part of this growth is due to financial innovation that has led to the securitization of assets that were previously held in bank balance sheets such as mortgages and commercial loans. Figure 7.6 shows how the bond market since 1985 has shifted away from Treasury securities toward other types of bonds that were relatively unimportant then. Thus Treasuries have shrunk from 31.3 percent of the U.S. bond market to only 17.7 percent as of 2008. Mortgage-related bonds have grown from 8.1 percent to 26.6 percent of the total. Asset-backed bonds, which didn't exist in 1985, are now 8.0 percent of the total.

Because most of the bonds shown in Figure 7.5 have higher default risk than U.S. Treasury bonds, their bond yields are correspondingly higher (adjusted for maturity). Consider the default premiums for investment grade corporate bonds. Both Standard & Poor's and Moody's rate the default risk on corporate bonds. According to the classification by Moody's, investment grade bonds are rated in four categories ranging from AAA to BAA. Over the period from 1980 to 2005, the 10-year Treasury bond had an average yield of 7.7 percent.[5] Over the same period, the yield on the highest rated of these corporate bonds, those with an AAA rating, averaged 8.8 percent for a premium of 1.1 percent over Treasuries.[6] The yields on the lowest-rated

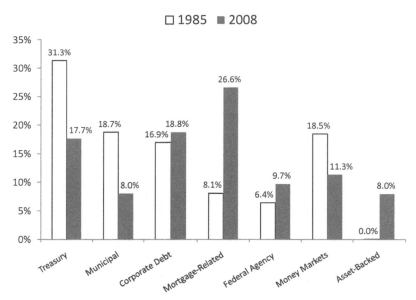

FIGURE 7.6 U.S. Bond Market in 1985 and 2008
Source: Securities Industry and Financial Markets Association, 2009.

investment grade bonds, those with a BAA rating, had an average yield of 9.9 percent, so the premium over Treasuries was 2.2 percent and the premium over the highest grade corporate bonds was 1.1 percent. These premiums give some indication of the importance of default risk in the pricing of non-Treasury bonds.

Default risk is of utmost importance in pricing so-called high-yield bonds. Until the 1980s, the high-yield market consisted primarily of fallen angels, bonds that were originally issued as investment grade, but that had fallen below investment grade because of poor financial performance. It was only in the 1980s that investment banks such as Drexel Burnham saw the potential for issuing non-investment grade (or junk) bonds to provide financing for firms with weaker credit standing. Since then, the high-yield market has become an important part of the overall corporate bond market in the United States. According to Altman and Karlin (2008), the high-yield market at the end of 2007 totaled $1,090 billion in outstanding issues. SIFMA reports that total corporate debt outstanding in 2007 was $6,281 billion, so high yield represents about 17 percent of total corporate debt.

Figure 7.7 displays the default rates for high-yield bonds. The average default rate between 1984 and 2009 was 4.1 percent. This default rate varies widely over time, however, since recessions force many firms into financial

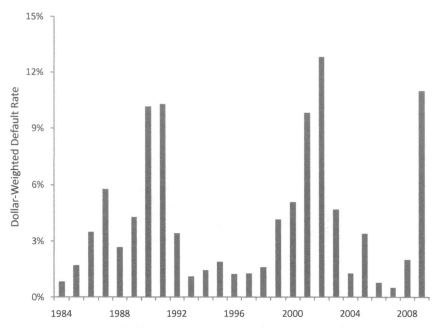

FIGURE 7.7 High-yield Default Rates, 1984–2009
Data Source: JP Morgan.

distress. The effects of the Gulf War recession of 1990 to 1991 and the 2001 recession are evident in the high default rates shown on the graph. Notice that the recession that began in December 2007 saw only a modest rise in default rates in 2008 but then defaults rose to more than 10 percent in 2009.

The spreads of high-yield bonds over Treasury bonds also vary over time, through booms and busts. Figure 7.8 shows these spreads from 1985 through early 2009. The effects of the three recessions during this period are evident in the figure. During the Gulf War recession of 1991 to 1992 and during the 2001 recession, the spread rose more than 10 percent. In the recession beginning in December 2007, the spread reached almost 20 percent in late 2008 despite seeing relatively few defaults in that year. Such a high spread probably reflects as much the illiquidity of the high-yield market during the financial crisis as it does the expectation of future defaults.

High-yield spreads reflect the *ex ante* default risk of a bond, but do not indicate the *ex post* returns that the investor receives from investing in that bond. These ex post returns are measured using the Barclays Capital High-yield index which begins in July 1983. The returns on some of the other types of bonds shown in Figure 7.5 can be measured using indexes extending back into the 1980s or earlier. Corporate bond returns are one of

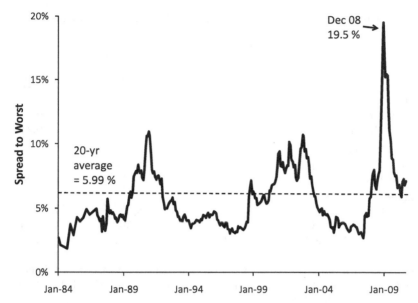

FIGURE 7.8 Spread of High-yield Bonds over Treasuries
Data Source: JP Morgan.

the series provided in the SBBI Yearbooks with returns beginning in 1926 like the rest of the Morningstar series. Mortgage-backed bonds have a return series from Merrill Lynch beginning in 1976. Finally, there is a widely used investment-grade bond index called the Barclays Capital Aggregate Index (formerly the Lehman Aggregate Index).[7] This series also begins in 1976.

RETURNS ON U.S. BONDS

The natural question to ask is: how well have non-Treasury bonds performed over time? Table 7.2 provides an analysis. Since bond returns begin at different times, each series is compared with the five-year medium term Treasury bond *over a common period*. In Table 7.2, there are three periods studied, each corresponding to the period over which a bond series is available:

1951–2009: Corporate Bond Index from Morningstar

1983–2009: Barclays Capital High Yield Bond Index

1976–2009: Barclays Capital Aggregate Bond Index and Merrill Lynch Mortgage-backed Bond Index

TABLE 7.2 Comparisons between Medium-Term U.S. Treasuries and Other Bonds

Period	Average Return	Standard Deviation	Sharpe Ratio
1951–2009			
Medium-Term Treasury	6.2%	5.1%	0.29
Corporate Bond	6.5%	8.6%	0.21
July 1983–December 2009			
Medium-Term Treasury	7.7%	5.0%	0.62
High-yield Bond	9.3%	8.8%	0.53
1976–2009			
Medium-Term Treasury	8.0%	5.8%	0.42
Mortgage-Backed Bond	8.6%	7.0%	0.44
Barclays Aggregate Bond	8.2%	5.7%	0.47

Data Sources: ©Morningstar for Medium-Term Treasuries and Corporate Bonds. Barclays Capital for the High-Yield and Aggregate Indexes and Merrill Lynch for the Mortgage-Backed Bond Index.

As shown in Table 7.2, non-Treasury bonds generally provide higher returns than Treasury bonds, at least over the long periods studied in the table. But risks (as measured by standard deviations) are also higher for these bonds. The last column of the table reports the Sharpe ratio for each series. The Sharpe ratios for corporate bonds and high-yield bonds are lower than that of the medium-term Treasury bond, while the Sharpe ratio for mortgage-backed bonds is a little higher.[8]

Bonds should also be evaluated in a portfolio setting just like any other asset. Table 7.3 reports the correlations between the major bond indexes and the medium-term Treasury bond. The last column of the table also reports the correlations with the S&P 500. Generally speaking, all of the U.S. bonds are highly correlated with Treasuries except for the high-yield series. The correlations are 0.70 or more for long-term Treasuries, (high-grade) corporate bonds, and mortgage-backed bonds. High-yield bonds have a near zero correlation of −0.02 with MT Treasuries because the high-yield market is so cyclically sensitive. (We will postpone discussion of the foreign government series until the last section of this chapter).

Bonds are often part of a larger portfolio with substantial allocations to stocks. So it's interesting to consider the correlations between the bond indexes and the S&P 500. It's clear from Table 7.3 that all of the bonds have relatively low correlation with stocks except for the high-yield series. The correlation between high-yield bonds and the S&P 500 is 0.56, so

TABLE 7.3 Correlations, 1985–2009

Bond Type	Correlation with Medium-Term Treasury Bond	Correlation with S&P 500
Medium-Term Treasuries	1.00	0.02
Long-Term Treasuries	0.84	0.11
Corporate Bonds	0.70	0.23
Mortgage-Backed	0.82	0.16
High-yield	−0.02	0.56
Barclays Aggregate	0.88	0.21
Foreign Bonds	0.42	0.01

The bond indexes used are the Medium-Term and Long-Term Treasury Bond and Corporate Bond indexes from ©Morningstar, the High-Yield and Aggregate Bond indexes from Barclays Capital, the Mortgage-Backed Bond index from Merrill Lynch, and the Citigroup non-dollar World Bond Index.

the diversification benefits of bonds in a portfolio heavily weighted toward stocks are certainly reduced when high-yield bonds are involved.

How much difference does it make if an investor diversifies a bond portfolio? This is an interesting question which an investment advisor often faces when the choice is between investing in a bond fund that is well diversified and investing in a narrow set of bonds directly. Consider the following experiment: An investor chooses between investment in the medium-term Treasury bond or the diversified Barclays Capital Aggregate Bond Index, the index described earlier that has only 23.9 percent in U.S. Treasuries. The Barclays Aggregate gives the investor exposure to corporate bonds (17.2 percent) as well as mortgage-backed bonds (44.8 percent) in addition to other investment-grade bonds. The comparison is shown in Table 7.2. Over the period from 1976 to 2009, the Barclays Aggregate has a return 0.2 percent higher than that of the medium-term U.S. Treasury bond, but the standard deviation is 0.1 percent lower. So the Sharpe ratio is higher. Alpha* allows us to compare the two bond investments after adjusting the Barclays Aggregate for the slightly higher level of risk associated with the Treasury bond. The investor gains an extra 0.3 percent excess return by investing in the Barclays Aggregate.[9] So the gains from diversification are evident even though most of these bonds are highly correlated.

BOND MARKETS OUTSIDE THE UNITED STATES

The world's bond markets have grown enormously in the last few decades. According to the Bank for International Settlements, the total value of all

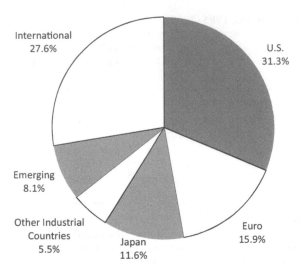

FIGURE 7.9   World Bond Markets, 2008 (Total Size
of the World Bond Market in 2008 = $82.5 trillion)
Source: Bank for International Settlements, 2009.

bonds outstanding as of September 2008 was $82.5 trillion.[10] This compares
with a market capitalization of $54.2 trillion for the world's stock markets
(at the end of 2007). The relative size of the world bond markets is shown
in Figure 7.9. The U.S. bond market represents 31.3 percent of this total
capitalization. But there are also major bond markets in the Euro area, Japan,
and other industrial countries. All together, these national bond markets
represent another 33.0 percent of the world market. The bond markets of
the developing (or emerging market) countries add another 8.1 percent to
the world's total. The remaining 27.6 percent are international bonds.

In addition to traditional national bond markets, there are parallel bond
markets called international bond markets where most investors are offshore
investors, but where borrowers can be from any country including the United
States. Take the example of a U.S. dollar international bond issued in London
by an American company with American and foreign underwriters and
investors who are predominantly foreign. Twenty years ago, this bond would
have been described as a Eurobond because it was underwritten in Europe,
but today it is less confusing to call this dollar bond an international bond.[11]
Since now there are no significant capital controls separating the U.S. bond
market from the international bond market, an international bond issued by
an American company will be almost identical in yield and price to a bond
issued by the same company in the United States (as long as both bonds

are denominated in dollars). The major difference between the two bonds is in ownership, since there are restrictions on sales of international bonds to U.S. residents. International bonds cannot be offered to Americans when they are first issued because these bonds have not been registered with the U.S. Securities and Exchange Commission. Some institutional investors buy these issues in the secondary market, but international bonds are primarily sold to foreign not American investors.[12]

This book is focused on investing, not borrowing, so the analysis to follow will ignore international bonds entirely. Instead, we will study investments in the national bond markets of foreign industrial countries.[13] These are the traditional national bond markets of countries like the United Kingdom and Japan. Many of these bonds are government bonds issued by the national governments of the countries involved, but there are also corporate bonds much like we find in the U.S. market. Almost all such national bonds are denominated in that country's currency. In Figure 7.9, these traditional national markets represent 33 percent of world bond markets or $27.2 trillion as of 2008.

The introduction of the Euro in 1999 led to consolidation of the bond markets of the 12 countries initially joining the European Union.[14] So instead of having separate bond markets (and separate trading centers) in countries like Germany and France, there was now a single market located in London with much-enhanced liquidity. As shown in Figure 7.9, the Euro area bond market is 15.9 percent of the world bond market, or roughly half the size of the U.S. national market.[15] Among foreign national bond markets, the Euro bond market is particularly attractive to Americans because it is the largest and most liquid foreign national bond market.

Interest rates on foreign bonds vary widely by country. First, interest rates are directly influenced by national inflation rates as shown earlier in Figure 7.3. These inflation rates vary widely by country depending upon the monetary policies of the central banks. Second, interest rates reflect the sovereign risk of the countries issuing the securities. For most of the sample period, the bonds of the industrial countries had little default risk. The government bonds of most of these countries carried AAA or AA ratings. That was true at least until the Greek crisis in 2010 when concerns about defaults in Europe led to default premiums for several national markets.

The returns on foreign bonds depend upon the currency in which they are measured. In their own local currencies, the returns are dependent on coupon yields and capital gains, just as in the case of U.S. bonds. But when measured in dollars, the returns on foreign bonds also depend on the capital gains or losses on the foreign currency itself. Thus the return on a foreign bond received by a U.S. domestic investor consists of two elements, the return expressed in foreign currency compounded by the capital gain on the

TABLE 7.4 Returns on Foreign and U.S. Government Bonds Measured in US Dollars, 1987–2009

Bond Market	Average Return	Standard Deviation	Sharpe Ratio
France	9.3%	11.0%	0.47
Germany	8.1%	11.4%	0.35
Japan	7.1%	12.8%	0.23
Switzerland	7.2%	12.2%	0.25
United Kingdom	9.3%	11.4%	0.45
Non-dollar World	8.1%	9.6%	0.41
U.S. Medium-Term	6.7%	4.8%	0.54
U.S. Long-Term	8.4%	9.9%	0.44

The foreign government bond series are all Citigroup indexes measured in dollars. The Non-Dollar World index is a 21-nation series. The U.S. government bond series are the Medium-Term (5-year) and Long-Term (20-year) indexes from Morningstar. *Data Sources:* Citigroup and ©Morningstar.

currency. If $R_\mathcal{\euro}$ is the return on a Euro-denominated bond *in Euros* and if R_X is the capital gain on the Euro, then the return on this bond as viewed by a dollar-based investor is given by

$$\text{Return in } \$ = (1 + R_\mathcal{\euro}) * (1 + R_X) - 1.$$

Returns on foreign bonds will be enhanced during periods when foreign currencies are rising against the dollar just as they benefit from rising bond prices within the Euro markets themselves.

Consider the returns on some of the major government bond markets as reported in Table 7.4. The bond indexes represented in the table are Citigroup indexes measured in dollars from 1987 through 2009. Also included in the table is a broader foreign bond index provided by Citigroup called the Non-U.S. Dollar World Government Bond Index. This index is a world-ex-U.S. government bond index representing the government bond markets of 21 industrial countries. All of the government bonds are denominated in domestic currency and each market represented has at least $20 billion in capitalization.[16] For comparison purposes, the returns on the two SBBI U.S. government bonds series, those for five-year medium-term bonds and 20-year long-term bonds, are also reported.

The first column of the table reports the average returns on each bond series, while the second column reports the standard deviations. All of the average returns for the foreign bond markets exceed those of the medium-term U.S. Treasury. The French and U.K. returns also exceed those of the long-term U.S. Treasury. But all of the standard deviations of the foreign bond indexes are much higher than those of medium-term U.S. bond and only the (non-dollar) World index has a lower standard deviation than the long-term U.S. Treasury. There is no doubt that the high volatility of the foreign bond returns is primarily caused by the volatility of the exchange rates used to translate local currency returns into dollars. Exchange rates are extremely volatile. In fact, the standard deviations for the foreign exchange gains and losses range from 10.0 percent for the dollar to pound exchange rate to 11.5 percent for the dollar to Swiss franc rate.[17] These foreign bonds may be too volatile to be attractive to an American investor as an *alternative* to U.S. Treasury bonds. That is even true of the diversified World Index which has a return of 8.1 percent and a standard deviation of 9.6 percent. The Sharpe ratio for the World Index is much lower than that of the medium-term U.S. Treasury bond.

Yet foreign bonds are unlikely to be viewed as an *alternative* to U.S. bonds by any American investor. Instead, they might be considered as a *complement* to U.S. bonds in a well-diversified bond portfolio. How well do foreign bonds fare in a portfolio context? Table 7.3 indicates that the foreign bond index, which is the Non-U.S. Dollar World Government Bond index from Citigroup, has a relatively low correlation of 0.42 with the U.S. Treasury bond and a correlation of 0.01 with the S&P 500. Both correlations are attractive enough to consider adding foreign bonds to a U.S. portfolio.

Table 7.5 reports the gains from diversifying a U.S. bond portfolio by adding a 20 percent allocation to foreign bonds. The second row of the table reports the returns on a portfolio that has 20 percent in the Citigroup non-dollar World Government Bond Index and 80 percent in the Barclays

TABLE 7.5 Effects of Diversifying a Bond Portfolio with Foreign Bonds, 1985–2009

	Average Return	Standard Deviation	Sharpe Ratio
Barclays Aggregate	7.9%	4.3%	0.81
Portfolio with Un-hedged Foreign Bonds	8.3%	4.7%	0.84
Portfolio with Hedged Foreign Bonds	7.7%	3.9%	0.86

Notes: The diversified portfolios with foreign bonds consist of 80 percent in the Barclays Aggregate and 20 percent in the Citigroup non-dollar World Government Bond Index. The second row has the un-hedged world index of foreign bonds and the third row has the hedged world index.
Data Sources: Barclays Capital and Citigroup.

Aggregate. The results are modest. The average return on the diversified U.S.-foreign bond portfolio is 0.4 percent higher than the portfolio based on the Barclays Aggregate Index alone, but the standard deviation is also higher. The net result is a Sharpe ratio of 0.84 for the diversified portfolio versus a Sharpe ratio of 0.81 for the Barclays Aggregate alone. This translates into an excess return, or alpha*, for the portfolio with foreign bonds of only 0.1 percent. A reasonable interpretation of this result is that investors have made most of their diversification gains by moving from U.S. Treasuries to the Barclays Aggregate mix of U.S. bonds. There is only a modest gain from diversifying further into foreign bonds.

If foreign currency capital gains and losses raise the standard deviation of the foreign bond return, perhaps there is a case for hedging the currency risk. As in the case of foreign stocks considered in Chapter 5, we will consider the simplest type of currency hedge where the foreign currency value of the bond investment at the beginning of the period is hedged using a forward contract. In that case, the hedged return consists of the return on the bond in local currency plus the forward premium on the hedge.

How much does the hedge reduce the risk of the foreign bond investment? Figure 7.10 compares the standard deviations of the Citigroup foreign

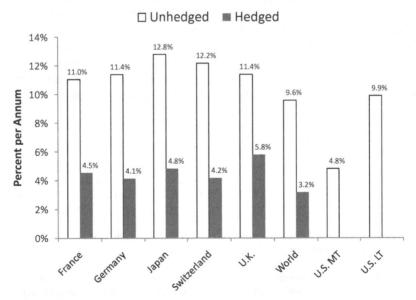

FIGURE 7.10 Standard Deviations of Government Bond Returns in Dollars, Hedged and Unhedged, 1987–2009
Data Sources: Citigroup, ©Morningstar, and IMF (for foreign exchange rates).

TABLE 7.6 Hedged Returns on Foreign and U.S. Government Bonds, 1987–2009

Bond Market	Average Return	Standard Deviation	Sharpe Ratio
France	6.7%	4.5%	0.56
Germany	6.3%	4.1%	0.52
Japan	7.0%	4.8%	0.59
Switzerland	6.2%	4.2%	0.50
United Kingdom	6.2%	5.8%	0.36
Non-dollar World	6.8%	3.2%	0.86
U.S. Medium-Term	6.7%	4.8%	0.54
U.S. Long-Term	8.4%	9.9%	0.44

Notes: The hedged return is obtained by selling an equivalent amount of foreign currency in the forward market at the beginning of each period. In the case of the Citigroup world index, the hedge adjusts for any cash flows expected during the period.
Data Sources: Citigroup, ©Morningstar, and IMF (for foreign exchange rates).

government bond indexes before and after hedging. Hedging has a dramatic effect on the risk of a foreign bond investment. In the case of French bonds, for example, the standard deviation falls from 11.1 percent to 4.5 percent. For the Citigroup non-dollar World Government Bond Index, the standard deviation is cut by two-thirds.[18] All but two of the standard deviations of the hedged foreign bond series are below that of even the U.S. medium-term bond. So, unlike in the case of foreign stocks, hedging foreign bonds greatly reduces the risk faced by an American investor. Since currencies are highly correlated with the returns on foreign bonds *expressed in dollars*, hedging the currency risk sharply reduces the risk of the foreign bond investment.

Table 7.6 reports the returns on the hedged investments in foreign bonds. For all foreign bonds studied, returns on the hedged investments are lower than those on the un-hedged investments because the dollar fell against many currencies over this time period. As explained in Chapter 5, hedge positions should not necessarily provide gains or losses in the long run (unless there are risk premiums on one currency or another). But over a particular sample period, a hedge may provide either gains or losses for an investor based in any particular currency. Over the 23 years ending in 2009, a dollar-based investor *selling* foreign currencies to hedge bond investments lost money on hedges involving the major currencies. The hedge for the world index lost 1.3 percent per year on average over this period.

Table 7.6 also reports the standard deviations and Sharpe ratios of the hedged investments. With standard deviations so low, the foreign bond returns generally have Sharpe ratios higher than that of the un-hedged foreign bond series. In some cases, these Sharpe ratios are also higher than those of the U.S. Treasury bond indexes. Consider the world index hedged for exchange risk. By hedging, the return falls from 8.1 percent to 6.8 percent, but the standard deviation falls from 9.6 percent to 3.2 percent. The Sharpe ratio rises sharply to 0.86, far above that of the U.S. bond indexes.

Hedging the currency risk does raise the correlation between the foreign bond and U.S. bonds and stocks. The correlation with the medium-term Treasury bond rises from 0.42 to 0.61. That should not be surprising since a lot of the advantage of the foreign bond as a diversifier stems from the foreign currency component of the bond return, and hedging all but eliminates this factor from the bond investment. Consider the portfolio experiment again reported in Table 7.5 where foreign bonds are mixed with the Barclays Aggregate. If the foreign bond index is hedged, the resulting portfolio has a smaller standard deviation (3.9 percent rather than 4.3 percent for the Barclays Aggregate alone). The Sharpe ratio of the portfolio containing hedged foreign bonds is 0.86 versus 0.81 for the Barclays portfolio alone. The diversified portfolio delivers an excess return, or alpha*, of only 0.2 percent compared with the Barclays Aggregate alone. That is a very modest gain for international diversification of the bond portfolio!

What is the conclusion of all of this evidence regarding foreign bonds? The answer has to be that it is probably worthwhile to include bonds from foreign industrial countries in a diversified bond portfolio. Foreign bonds won't dramatically alter the performance of such a portfolio, but there is a marginal improvement in risk-adjusted returns. There is a strong case for hedging the foreign bonds if the investor is concerned about the *volatility* of foreign bond investments, since hedging reduces that volatility quite dramatically. The case for hedging is less compelling if foreign bonds are viewed as a component of an otherwise well-diversified portfolio.

SUMMARY—KEY FEATURES OF BONDS

Above all else, bond returns depend upon inflation. In the long run, inflation affects the yield offered on bonds. This link can be illustrated by studying the variation over time of interest rates and inflation in the United States or by studying the close link between average interest rates and average inflation rates in the industrial countries. Inflation also profoundly affects the real returns on bonds, especially in periods when inflation is rising or falling significantly as in the 1970s and 1980s. Real bond returns were unusually low in the 1970s (and even earlier) because bond yields failed to keep pace with inflation expectations. Similarly, the sharp downturn in inflation since the early 1980s has led to unusually high real bond returns.

Bond returns in the United States vary by type of bond. Over the last few decades, the bond market has evolved extensively as new classes of securities have emerged. The introduction of mortgage-backed bonds in the 1970s, high-yield debt in the 1980s, and other securitized debt in the 1980s and 1990s has greatly expanded the scope of the U.S. bond market. The returns on these new classes of bonds have fallen in line with those of the existing Treasury and corporate issues, at least when measured on a risk-adjusted basis. But their introduction has allowed investors to further diversify their portfolios. The gains from diversification are reasonably large.

Diversification into foreign bonds also makes some sense. The bonds of foreign industrial countries share many of the same characteristics as U.S. bonds, but their returns vary widely because of their (foreign) currency denomination. When these bonds are left un-hedged, their standard deviations are very high (when measured in dollars for a U.S. investor). But hedging can reduce risk by almost two-thirds. And when these bonds are included in a diversified bond portfolio, even the un-hedged bonds help to reduce risk, although only modestly.

NOTES

1. LIBOR stands for the London Inter-bank Offer Rate in the dollar deposit market in London. The LIBOR market is one of the largest money markets in the world. The LIBOR rate serves as a benchmark for many interest rate contracts, including many floating rate mortgages in the United States.
2. As explained in Chapter 2, the real return is defined as (1 + nominal return)/(1 + inflation rate) − 1.
3. The European Monetary System (EMS), introduced in 1979, committed countries to maintaining their exchange rates within bands relative to fixed rates. But the EMS did not prevent countries from occasionally realigning their fixed rates by devaluing or revaluing their exchange rates with other partner countries, so inflation varied widely across the EMS countries. It was the Maastricht Treaty of 1991, setting Europe on a path toward monetary union in 1999, that spurred the high-inflation countries like Italy and Spain to reign in their monetary policies to qualify for the union.
4. SIFMA, Outstanding U.S. Bond Market Debt, SIFMA web site table, March 2009.
5. The yields are reported in the IMF, International Financial Statistics (CD data set), May 2007.
6. The annual data for corporate yields are reported by www.bondmarkets.com. It would be misleading to attribute all of this gap of corporate yields over

Treasury yields to default risk since U.S. Treasuries have a state income tax advantage not afforded to corporate bonds. According to the U.S. Constitution, U.S. Treasuries are exempt from state and local taxes. If the marginal investor in U.S. Treasuries is a taxable U.S. resident, then the interest yield on Treasuries reflects this tax advantage.

7. As of the end of October 2008, this index had 23.9 percent in Treasuries, 13.5 percent in government-related bonds, 17.2 percent in corporate bonds, 44.8 percent in mortgage-backed bonds, and less than 1 percent in ABS. 81.4 percent of this index represented AAA-rated bonds. Source: www.barcap .com/indices.

8. Recall that the Treasury bond is free of state and local taxes, so the relative returns may reflect tax factors as well as default risk.

9. Alpha* $= (0.47–0.42)^*0.057 = 0.3\%$.

10. This figure is obtained by aggregating the national bond markets and international bond markets as reported on the Bank for International Settlements web site (http://www.bis.org/statistics/secstats.htm).

11. The Eurobond or international bond market was initially developed to allow U.S. and foreign companies to raise debt financing in foreign markets to fund their foreign operations. Since many countries had capital controls inhibiting the flow of financing from their domestic markets, the international bond market offered a way to finance the multinational operations of these companies. Capital controls have largely been abolished in the industrial countries, so this market is now closely integrated with the national bond market in the same currency.

12. See Solnik and McLeavy (2004), Chapter 7.

13. Recall that Chapter 6 analyzed the bonds of emerging markets.

14. The countries adopting the Euro in 1999 included France, Germany, Belgium, Luxembourg, the Netherlands, Italy, Spain, Portugal, Ireland, Austria, and Finland. Greece joined in 2002. The 12 countries had only 11 bond markets because Belgium and Luxembourg shared a common currency even before the Union.

15. Both markets would be larger if international bonds issued in dollars and Euros, respectively, were included in the totals.

16. Most of the bonds have AAA or AA credit quality. The 21 countries represented in the index are Australia, Austria, Belgium, Canada, Denmark, Finland, France, Germany, Greece, Ireland, Italy, Japan, the Netherlands, Norway, Poland, Portugal, Singapore, Spain, Sweden, Switzerland, and the United Kingdom.

17. These standard deviations are measured for the capital gain/loss factor in the equation in the text, R_X.

18. Citigroup provides a hedged version of its 21-nation world (non-U.S.) government bond index. According to Citigroup (2006), the hedge is designed to offset not only the value of the investment at period t-1 but also any expected cash flows between t-1 and t.

CHAPTER 8

Strategic Asset Allocation

Mean-variance analysis has become so ingrained in investment management that it is difficult to conceive of a time when investments were guided by some other principles. Prior to the 1950s, investors naturally worried about risk at the same time that they strove to achieve returns. But there was little systematic thought about how the risk and return were related. It was Markowitz's achievement to show that there was a natural tradeoff between risk and return, and that correlations among assets affected the risk of the overall portfolio.[1]

Figure 8.1 summarizes some of the insights provided by Markowitz's work. Suppose that we consider a series of portfolios derived from a mixture of bonds and stocks. The portfolio with the lowest return on the left-hand chart consists of bonds alone. The portfolio with the highest return consists of stocks alone. All of the other portfolios are mixtures of the two assets. The risk itself is measured as the standard deviation of each portfolio.

One noteworthy result is illustrated in the left-hand chart: the portfolio with the lowest risk asset, bonds, is *dominated* by other portfolios consisting of a mixture of stocks and bonds. That's the case for portfolios consisting of U.S. bonds which are dominated by portfolios with mixtures of U.S. stocks and bonds (see below). As the chart illustrates, there are a range of bond-heavy portfolios that are dominated by other portfolios with higher proportions of stocks. So moving toward the riskier asset can actually reduce risk. The dominated portfolios form an inefficient segment of the frontier (every point below the horizontal bar).

The right hand chart focuses only on the efficient segment of the frontier (which we call the *efficient frontier*). Every portfolio that is represented on the frontier is the lowest risk portfolio for that given return. That is, the optimization process has minimized risk for a given return. Of course, this efficient frontier is based on stocks and bonds alone. This chapter will show how the efficient frontier shifts as the menu of assets is expanded.

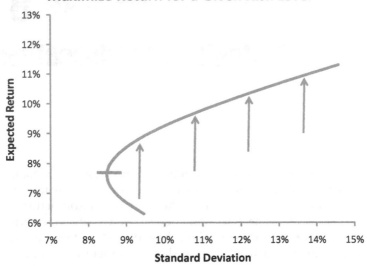

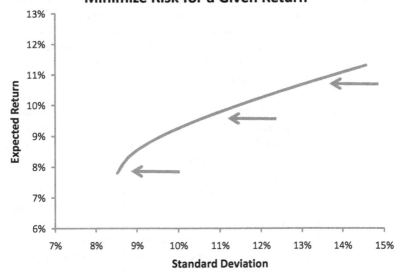

FIGURE 8.1 Portfolios of U.S. Stocks and Bonds Illustrating the Markowitz Efficient Frontier

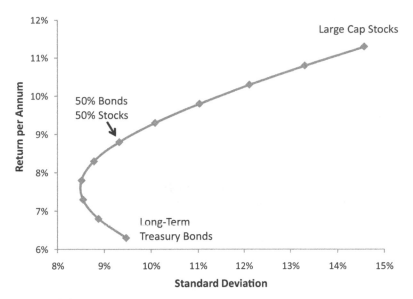

FIGURE 8.2 Portfolios of Stocks and Bonds, 1951–2009
Data Sources: ©Morningstar and S&P.

Figure 8.2 shows an array of actual portfolios of stocks and bonds measured over the period from 1951 through 2009.[2] In this figure, bonds are represented by the long-term (20-year) Treasury bond reported in the SBBI Yearbooks (©Morningstar). Stocks are represented by the S&P 500 (and prior to 1974, by the large-cap stock series from Morningstar). Notice that the all-bond portfolio is easily dominated by portfolios with stocks and bonds.

In Figure 8.2, the 50/50 stock/bond portfolio is highlighted. Note that this portfolio has about the same risk as the all-bond portfolio. But the return is 2.5 percent higher (over the sample period from January 1951 to December 2009). The equity premium is evidently at work here. To the right of this portfolio, higher returns must be accompanied by higher risk. Thus a portfolio with (say) 70 percent or 80 percent in stocks will naturally have a standard deviation considerably higher than that of the 50/50 portfolio.

EXPANDING THE PORTFOLIO TO INCLUDE OTHER BONDS AND STOCKS

What if the portfolio choice is expanded to include other U.S. stocks and bonds? One simple way to diversify the portfolio is to replace the

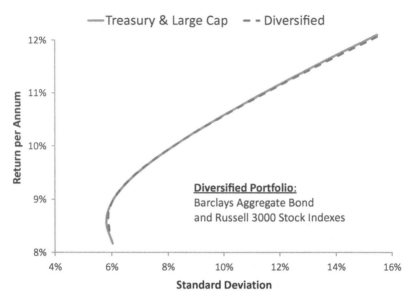

FIGURE 8.3   Comparison between Two Portfolios, 1979–2009
Data Sources: ©Morningstar, Barclays Capital, and Russell®.

Treasury bond and the large-cap index with broader aggregates. In place of the Treasury bond, the Barclays Capital Aggregate Bond Index (formerly the Lehman Aggregate Index) will be used. The Barclays Aggregate has less than a 25 percent weight for Treasury bonds with the rest concentrated on U.S. agency debt (including issues by Fannie Mae and Freddie Mac) and investment-grade corporate debt. Because the average maturity of the Barclays index is less than six years, the Treasury bond used in the comparison will be the five-year Treasury rather than the 20-year long-term Treasury bond used in the previous analysis. In place of the S&P 500, the Russell 3000 all-cap U.S. stock index is used. As explained in Chapter 3, the Russell 3000 has an 8 percent weight on small caps and a 10 percent weight on mid caps.

Figure 8.3 displays the two sets of portfolios. Since the Russell indexes begin only in January 1979, the comparisons are done from 1979 through 2009. The first set of portfolios consists of stock and bond combinations, ranging from all bond to all stocks, using the medium-term Treasury and the S&P 500. The second set consists of a similar range of portfolio combinations using the Barclays Aggregate index and the Russell 3000 index. It's not necessary to analyze these portfolios in depth. They are almost identical. Once the investor has chosen a portfolio consisting of Treasury bonds and large-cap stocks, there is only a marginal gain from diversifying further in the U.S. markets.

Is this result surprising? The answer is that it should not be. First consider the bond market. In terms of risk-adjusted performance, diversifying beyond Treasuries makes little difference in the long run. As shown in Chapter 7, the Sharpe ratios for different types of investment-grade bonds are very similar. Investment-grade bonds are highly correlated with one another. The correlation between Barclays Aggregate index and the Treasury return is 0.92. Shifting from the Treasury bond to the Barclays Aggregate raises risk-adjusted return, or alpha*, by only 0.3 percent. Similarly, the correlation between the S&P 500 and Russell 3000 all-cap index is very high at 0.99. The returns on these two indexes, moreover, are almost identical over the sample period since the Russell series was introduced in 1979. Diversifying beyond the S&P 500 into small- and mid-cap stocks has a negligible effect on the risk-adjusted return.

What these experiments suggest is that the investor is going to have to look beyond U.S. stocks and bonds for diversification gains.[3] But note how much the investor has already accomplished. By spreading out stock market investments across the entire S&P 500, the investor has already achieved substantial diversification. And by mixing stocks with bonds, the investor has combined two assets with very low correlation (0.24 in this sample period). It's important to realize that the investor who is choosing among the portfolios in Figures 8.2 and 8.3 is already very well diversified.

EXPANDING THE PORTFOLIO TO INCLUDE FOREIGN STOCKS

How does the efficient frontier shift if foreign equities are added to the portfolio? Figure 8.4 adds the MSCI EAFE index to the original mix of Treasury bonds and the SBBI Large Company index. The EAFE index begins only in January 1970, so the portfolio optimization is done only over the period since then. Figure 8.4 shows two alternative sets of portfolios. One is defined for the U.S. stocks and bonds alone. The second is defined for a mix that includes the EAFE index.

The results are encouraging. Expanding the menu of assets to include foreign stocks lowers risk at any given level of return. That's because the correlation between EAFE and the large-cap U.S. stock index is relatively low at 0.60 over this sample period.[4] Consider the portfolios on these two frontiers consisting of 70 percent in stocks and 30 percent in bonds. For the 70/30 portfolio on the original frontier, the return is equal to 10.1 percent with a standard deviation of 12.1 percent. For the 70/30 portfolio on the

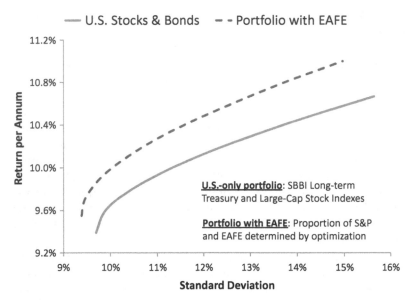

FIGURE 8.4 Addition of Foreign Stocks to U.S. Portfolio, 1970–2009
Data Sources: ©Morningstar, MSCI, and S&P.

enhanced frontier, the return rises to 10.4 percent with a standard deviation 0.7 percent lower at 11.4 percent. The Sharpe ratio of the 70/30 portfolio that includes EAFE is 0.42 compared with a Sharpe ratio for the U.S.-only portfolio (on the original frontier) of 0.38. That translates, using alpha*, into an excess return of almost 0.5 percent for the portfolio including EAFE. So the conclusion is that international diversification does pay, at least over this sample period. It should be noted that the optimization was done without any constraints being imposed on the proportion of equities invested outside the United States. In this optimization, the proportion of foreign stocks ranges from 58 percent of total stocks in the 50/50 stock/bond portfolio to 61 percent of stocks for the portfolio with only 10 percent in bonds.

What if foreign stocks were constrained in the internationally diversified portfolio? Suppose that foreign stocks are constrained to be only 40 percent of the total stock allocation so foreign stocks are 28 percent (i.e., 40 percent of 70 percent) of the overall portfolio allocation. The result is reported in the top half of Table 8.1. Investing 40 percent of the stocks in the EAFE index, the average return rises from 10.1 percent to 10.3 percent, while the standard deviation drops from 12.0 percent to 11.3 percent. The higher Sharpe ratio of the internationally diversified portfolio adds an extra 0.4 percent to the risk-adjusted return. So over the sample period from

TABLE 8.1 Diversification Gains from Adding International Stocks to U.S.-only Portfolios

	Average Return	Standard Deviation	Sharpe Ratio	Alpha*[1]
Period: Jan 70 to Dec 09[2]				
U.S.-only portfolio	10.1%	12.0%	0.38	
Portfolio with EAFE	10.3%	11.3%	0.42	0.4%
Period: Jan 79 to Dec 09[3]				
U.S.-only portfolio	11.0%	11.4%	0.48	
Portfolio with EAFE	10.8%	11.0%	0.48	0.0%
Portfolio with EAFE and EM	11.2%	11.2%	0.51	0.3%

Notes: All portfolios have 70 percent in stocks and 30 percent in bonds.
[1]Alpha* measures the excess return on the diversified portfolios (relative to United States only).
[2]U.S. only portfolio consists of SBBI Long-term Treasury bonds and SBBI Large-Cap U.S. stock index. Diversified portfolio also includes MSCI EAFE index
[3]U.S.-only portfolio consists of Barclays Capital Aggregate bond index and Russell 3000 all-cap U.S. stock index. Portfolio with EAFE has 40 percent of the stocks overseas (or 28 percent of the entire portfolio). Last portfolio in table has a two-thirds weight on EAFE and one-third weight on Emerging Markets. Prior to the beginning of the EM index in 1990, EAFE alone represents international stocks.
Data Sources: ©Morningstar, MSCI, Barclays Capital, and Russell®.

1970 to 2009, there is a clear case for international diversification even if the portfolio is constrained.

Does the gain from international diversification disappear in the more recent period? In Chapter 5 we learned that the correlation between foreign and domestic stocks has risen markedly in recent years. In that chapter we also learned that the EAFE index had much lower returns in the last 20 years because of the collapse of the Japanese market. So the short answer to the question is that international diversification is much less effective in the recent period if confined to the industrial country stocks represented by the EAFE index. Consider the following experiment. Compare a portfolio with the Barclays Aggregate Bond Index and the Russell 3000 all-cap U.S. stock index with one that also includes the MSCI EAFE Index (with 40 percent of the stocks overseas). The results are shown in the lower half of Table 8.1 in the row marked Portfolio with EAFE. If the sample period begins in 1979 when the Russell data begin, there is no gain from international diversification. That is, the Sharpe ratios of the U.S. only and internationally diversified portfolios are identical, so alpha* is zero.

But what if emerging market stocks are included in the analysis? The MSCI Emerging Markets Index begins only in January 1990. In Table 8.1, a portfolio with both MSCI indexes, EAFE and Emerging Markets, is compared with a U.S.-only portfolio. The internationally diversified portfolio consists of MSCI EAFE alone before 1990. Beginning in 1990, MSCI EM has a one-third weight in the international index with MSCI EAFE having a two-thirds weight. The results are a little more satisfactory. The risk-adjusted return on the internationally diversified portfolio is 0.3 percent above that of the U.S.-only portfolio. So international diversification helps in the more recent sample period only if the investor puts one-third of the foreign allocation in emerging market stocks.

The results above suggest that we will have to search more widely for assets to enhance portfolio performance. Diversifying into a range of investment-grade bonds does not add much to portfolio performance. Neither does diversifying the U.S. stock portfolio into small caps and mid caps. It's true that international stocks do enhance portfolio performance, but less than they did in earlier sample periods. We need alternative investments to improve portfolio performance.

Before studying alternative investments, we will consider two further topics in asset allocation. The first one concerns the optimization process itself. Does optimization result in sensible looking portfolios? We will investigate this question by looking at U.S. stock and bond portfolios. The second topic is about how to develop estimates of portfolio returns. Such estimates are needed for many practical applications including the formulation of spending rules for foundations and individuals. Then we will examine the performance of portfolios featured on MarketWatch.com, three so-called Lazy Portfolios.

THE DIRTY SECRET OF OPTIMIZATION

Since the early studies of Markowitz, researchers have used optimization methods to determine the ideal weights of stock and bond portfolios. Today there are excellent optimization software programs such as the Zephyr AllocationADVISOR software used in this study. But researchers have to use common sense in their applications.

Consider a simple optimization experiment. So far we have represented U.S. stock portfolios with a single index, either a large-cap index or an all-cap index. Suppose that the portfolio consists of different indexes for growth and value stocks and for small-cap stocks. As discussed in early chapters, many portfolios are divided along style and size dimensions. Often a portfolio will have separate allocations for large-cap growth and large-cap value as well as small-cap growth and small-cap value. Some portfolios go even further by adopting nine different allocations, with value and growth being augmented with an allocation to core and with small and large being augmented with an allocation to mid cap. It's interesting to investigate how optimization programs would allocate such portfolios.

For the experiment, a four asset portfolio will be compared with a two asset portfolio that contains a single U.S. stock index. The two asset portfolio consists of the Barclays Aggregate index and Russell 3000 all-cap index only. In the four asset portfolio, the U.S. stock allocation will be divided in three segments, large-cap growth and value stocks using the Russell 1000 growth and value indexes, and small-cap stocks using the Russell 2000 index. So there are four asset classes altogether including the Barclays Aggregate bond index. Since the Russell series began only in 1979, the optimization is carried out using monthly data from January 1979 through December 2009.[5]

The four asset portfolio is optimized without imposing any constraints on the optimization. For comparison purposes, the two-asset portfolio described above is used as a benchmark. The results are shown in Figure 8.5 where the two sets of portfolios are compared. The portfolios based on the four-asset optimization dominate those based on the two-asset optimization

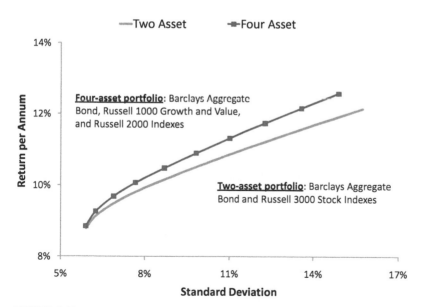

FIGURE 8.5 Two and Four Asset Portfolios, 1979–2009
Data Sources: Barclays Capital and Russell®.

at every risk level. This is not surprising since the four-asset portfolio allows
the optimizer to raise or lower allocations to the three U.S. stock indexes
without imposing any constraint on the optimization. In contrast, the Russell 3000 index imposes market capitalization weights on the U.S. stock
market indexes. That is, the Russell 3000 index weights the Russell 2000
relative to the Russell 1000 by market capitalization. In 2009 the Russell
2000 was 8 percent of the total U.S. stock allocation. And the Russell 3000
index equalizes the weights of the Russell 1000 large-cap value and growth
indexes.

How much better do the unconstrained portfolios perform? The four-
asset portfolios outperform the constrained two-asset portfolios by 0.2 percent to 0.5 percent depending on the proportion allocated to bonds.[6] This
gap is not very large, but investors should prefer the unconstrained portfolios
if those portfolios otherwise make sense.

Before we rush to adopt this superior set of portfolios, it's important
to examine the allocations that have been selected by the optimizer. Figure 8.6 shows the allocations for 10 portfolios ranging from the portfolio

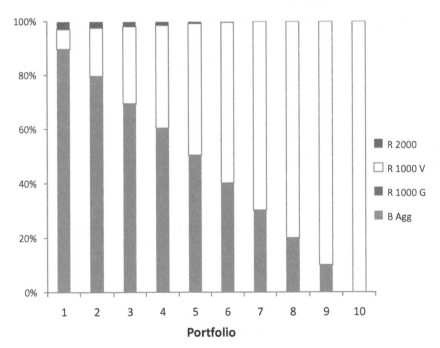

FIGURE 8.6 Asset Allocation in Four-Asset Portfolio
Data Sources: Barclays Capital and Russell®.

with the lowest allocation of 10 percent in stocks to the portfolio that is invested wholly in stocks.[7] Large-cap growth stocks, as represented by the Russell 1000 Growth Index, do not appear in any of the 10 portfolios. The Russell 1000 Growth Index is dominated by the Russell 1000 Value Index. This result should not be surprising given the analysis in Chapter 4. Russell 1000 Value has a higher return and a lower standard deviation than Russell 1000 Growth. What's more, the two indexes are highly correlated with a correlation coefficient of 0.82. The optimizer finds that one series is totally dominated by the other. So the optimizer rejects one whole asset class. The optimizer is also not fond of small-cap stocks. The Russell 2000 Index has a small weighting in the lowest risk portfolios, and its role disappears in portfolios with larger allocations to stocks.

The point of this experiment is not to show the inferiority of large-cap growth stocks or small-cap stocks. Indeed, small caps would fare better if we examined a different sample period like the late 1960s and 1970s when small caps far outperformed large caps. (See Chapter 3 for a discussion). The point is that the optimization process will go to corner solution where whole asset classes are rejected out of hand.

Let's extend the experiment by investigating what it would take to add large-cap growth to the portfolio. That is, how much of an increase in the return on large-cap growth is necessary to raise the allocation to market weight (as in the Russell 1000 large-cap index) and how much of an increase in the return on small caps is necessary to raise the allocation to market weight (as in the Russell 3000 all-cap index)? This experiment will be done while holding the bond allocation at 30 percent (so the portfolios examined will be 70/30 stock/bond portfolios). The four-asset optimization is repeated, but with the returns on large-cap growth and small caps being raised. The return on the Russell 1000 Growth Index must be raised by 2.0 percent to induce the optimizer to adopt market weights for this index. With this higher return, the Russell 1000 Growth and Value indexes assume (roughly) equal weights. This gap of 1.9 percent is one measure of how much the growth index has underperformed over the historical period since 1979. The return on the Russell 2000 small-cap index has to be raised only 0.9 percent to induce the optimizer to raise the small-cap allocation to 8 percent (its market weight).

The experiment just described was introduced for two reasons. First, it sheds light on how much the Russell 1000 Growth and Russell 2000 indexes have underperformed relative to the Russell 1000 Value index. But the experiments also provide an introduction to the next section of the chapter where the following issue is addressed: what returns would be required to make sure that the whole portfolio chosen in the optimization process matches market weights?

ALTERNATIVE APPROACHES TO OPTIMIZATION

In 1974, William Sharpe published an article that turned the portfolio optimization problem around. Usually portfolio optimization asks what portfolio weights would be chosen *given a set of expected returns*. Instead, Sharpe (1974) asked *what expected returns* would lead an investor to hold the set of assets that this investor has chosen. Sharpe used the portfolios of a large investment firm as an illustration.[8] He calculated the expected returns that were consistent with the portfolio chosen by this firm. These expected returns might prove to be surprisingly high or low to the firm. This would then give the firm a basis for modifying its initial portfolio choice.

Sharpe's insight later led to the Black and Litterman (1992) method for analyzing portfolios. Black and Litterman asked a different question than did Sharpe. They asked what expected returns would be necessary for investors to hold the *assets available in the market*. Instead of using historical returns for optimization, Black and Litterman generate *equilibrium expected returns* that are consistent with the weights of each asset in the market.

To see the intuition behind the Black-Litterman method, consider a simple example. Suppose that the only assets in the world were U.S. large-cap value and growth stocks. Russell defines the Russell 1000 Growth and Value Indexes so that they have equal market capitalization weights. But growth stocks have lower returns than value stocks. And, over the Russell sample period from 1979 to present, growth stocks have higher standard deviations than value stocks. So in order to entice investors to hold them in equal weights, there would have to be a higher expected return on growth than value stocks. The equilibrium-expected returns on growth stocks would have to exceed those on value stocks.

The Black-Litterman method provides a set of expected returns that will generate market portfolios. But the method may have limited applicability if the implied returns are so much at variance with past history. It's interesting to know how much growth returns would have to change to make them attractive enough to hold at equal weights with value stocks, but what is the investor to do with the information? The real strength of the method is in its extension to incorporate investors' expectations that future returns on some assets will be higher or lower than the equilibrium implied returns. Suppose that investors believed that in the near future, value stocks would outperform growth stocks by 4 percent per year rather than only 1.4 percent per year. Then the Black-Litterman method makes it easy to calculate how much the portfolio should be tilted toward value stocks. By starting out at a point of market equilibrium where the assets in the market would be willingly held by investors, Black and Litterman can then examine how much higher or lower expected returns would alter equilibrium holdings of assets. How this is done is beyond the scope of this chapter, but this issue is discussed in He and Litterman (1999).

ESTIMATING PORTFOLIO RETURNS—THE PREMIUM METHOD

As just explained, Black and Litterman (1999) ask what equilibrium returns are consistent with modern portfolio theory (MPT) and the capitalization weights found in the marketplace. Investors often want to address a different question: what return can be expected from a portfolio *chosen by the investor* (rather than a market-weighted portfolio)? And what is the standard deviation of that portfolio? To answer those questions, it's necessary to provide estimates of the expected returns on the individual assets in the portfolio. And it's necessary to provide estimates of the standard deviations and correlations for the assets in the portfolio. The investor could begin with the equilibrium returns estimated using Black-Litterman methods, but these returns might be at sharp variance with historical returns.

Consider first a portfolio consisting of the basic capital market assets, stocks and bonds. Earlier in the chapter, Figure 8.2 showed an efficient frontier defined by these two assets where SBBI's large-cap U.S. stocks and U.S. Treasury bonds represented stocks and bonds, respectively. Figure 8.2 was based on actual historical returns measured in nominal terms over the period from 1951 through 2009. Average stock returns exceeded 11 percent and average bond returns exceeded 6 percent over this period. In Chapter 2, however, we argued that real returns provided a firmer basis for calculating expected returns. The investor is ultimately interested in real returns, not nominal returns. That's true regardless of whether the investor is accumulating capital for long-run goals such as retirement or sustaining a spending rate out of an existing portfolio.

In Chapter 2, real returns were estimated over the period from 1951 through 2009. The average compound real return on the large-cap U.S. stocks was 6.7 percent while the average real return on the medium-term Treasury bond was 2.4 percent. Chapter 2 raised some doubts about whether stock returns will be as high in the future as in the post-war period because stock market valuations have risen so much in the last 25 years. So the historical estimates of real returns might have to be modified before proceeding further. Ignoring such considerations for the purposes of this discussion, consider how we would obtain estimates of expected nominal returns. There is a strong case for not using historical inflation rates because inflation has changed significantly over time. If investors believe that the low inflation policy experienced recently is likely to continue into the future, it makes more sense to adjust real returns by the expected inflation rate than by the historical inflation rate.[9] Suppose that the expected inflation rate is 2.5 percent. That then gives an estimate of the nominal compound return for U.S. stocks of 9.4 percent and for the medium-term Treasury bonds of 4.9 percent. There is an additional complication that optimizers use arithmetic averages rather than geometric averages. So it's necessary to convert the compound geometric averages we have cited to arithmetic averages before using them in an optimizer.[10] So instead of a 9.4 percent compound nominal return, the large-cap stock index has a 10.0 percent arithmetic average return.[11]

Most portfolios, however, consist of assets with much shorter historical records than the capital market assets in the SBBI data set. For example, the MSCI EAFE index begins in 1970, not 1951 or 1926. And the Russell indexes begin in 1979. If these series are chosen in an optimizer program, as they were in developing Figures 8.4 and 8.5 in this chapter, then the optimizer will *truncate* the data set so as to estimate portfolio returns over a common period. If hedge fund returns were also included in the optimization, then the data set would be truncated to start in whatever year in the 1990s the hedge fund data begins.[12] Clearly, this is not a sensible way to estimate returns for a portfolio. Beginning estimation in 1979, for example, ensures that both bond and equity returns are far above their long-run historical averages.

Rather than truncating all series to the lowest common denominator, the *premium method* makes use of the shorter data sets by tying their returns to the basic capital market returns (for the S&P 500 or Treasury bond) that are available for much longer periods. The premium method measures the excess return on an asset relative to its capital market counterpart over the common period for which both returns are available. Then it estimates the return on that asset by adding the excess return to the return on the basic capital market variable (measured over the period since 1951). So for the MSCI EAFE index, the premium of the EAFE index over the S&P 500 is measured over the period from 1970 to present. From 1970 through December 2009, the EAFE return was 10.2 percent, while the S&P 500 earned 9.9 percent over the same period. So the premium earned by the EAFE index was 0.3 percent.[13]

Table 8.2 reports the premiums for some of the major stock and bond indexes. The Russell 3000, for example, has no premium or discount relative to the S&P 500 over its common period from 1979 through 2009. The Russell Growth and Value Indexes, in contrast, have premiums of –0.9 percent and +0.5 percent, respectively, over that same period.

Table 8.3 then reports the estimated returns for each of these stock indexes based on the underlying estimate for large-cap stocks of 9.4 percent. Thus the Russell 1000 Growth Index is estimated to have a return of

TABLE 8.2 Premiums over the S&P 500 and Treasury Bond, Various Periods

Stock Index	Premium over S&P 500	Sample Period
Russell 3000	0.0%	Jan 1979–Dec 2009
Russell 1000 Growth	−0.9%	Jan 1979–Dec 2009
Russell 1000 Value	+0.5%	Jan 1979–Dec 2009
Russell 2000	−0.2%	Jan 1979–Dec 2009
MSCI EAFE	+0.3%	Jan 1970–Dec 2009
MSCI Europe	+0.9%	Jan 1970–Dec 2009
MSCI Pacific	−0.1%	Jan 1970–Dec 2009
MSCI Emerging Markets	+2.0%	Jan 1989–Dec 2009*
Bond Index	Premium over Medium-Term Treasury	Sample Period
Barclays Aggregate	+0.3%	Jan 1976–Dec 2009
Barclays TIPS	+0.5%	Mar 1997–Dec 2009

The premiums are measured in compound terms. *The actual premium for MSCI Emerging Market is 3.5 percent for the 1989-2009 period (see text).
Data Sources: ©Morningstar, S&P, MSCI, Barclays Capital, and Russell®.

TABLE 8.3 Estimated Returns Based on Premium Method

	Premium	Estimate
S&P 500		9.4%
Russell 3000	0.0%	9.4%
Russell 1000 Growth	−0.9%	8.4%
Russell 1000 Value	+0.5%	9.9%
Russell 2000	−0.2%	9.2%
MSCI EAFE	+0.3%	9.7%
MSCI Europe	+0.9%	10.3%
MSCI Pacific	−0.1%	9.3%
MSCI Emerging Markets	+2.0%	11.4%
Medium-term Treasury		4.9%
Barclays Aggregate	+0.3%	5.2%
Barclays TIPS	+0.5%	5.4%

All estimates are geometric averages in nominal terms. Estimates for the S&P 500 and MT Treasury bond are based on real compound returns from Jan 1951 through Dec 2009 converted to nominal estimates using a 2.5 percent inflation rate. Estimates for the other assets are obtained using the premiums in Table 8.2.
Data Sources: ©Morningstar, S&P, MSCI, Barclays Capital, and Russell®.

8.4 percent (i.e., $(1.094)*(1 - 0.009) - 1$). Similarly, the Russell 2000 small-cap index has an estimated return of 9.2 percent.

Emerging markets pose a problem for this methodology. Since 1989, the MSCI Emerging Market Index has outperformed the S&P 500 by 3.5 percent. That outperformance is due to the surge in emerging market stocks in the last five years. Indeed, the MSCI Emerging Market Index lagged behind the S&P 500 by 0.4 percent over the period from 1989 to 2004. Yet many observers believe that emerging market stocks will have higher returns in the future than the developed countries. No doubt some of this optimism is based on the questionable belief that higher growth necessarily translates into higher stock returns. (For evidence to the contrary, recall the discussion in Chapter 6.) Nonetheless, it's seems plausible that emerging markets will perform better than their developed counterparts because of the inherent dynamism in many of those economies. As an alternative to the historical premium for emerging market stocks, consider the premium estimated by the Yale Endowment in its annual reports. Each year, David Svensen and his endowment staff provide estimates of the returns they expect on the main asset classes over the next few decades. In the latest report (Yale, 2009), the real returns on U.S. and developed equity markets abroad are estimated to be 6.0 percent per year. So also are the returns on hedge funds as well as real assets. But emerging equity markets are expected to outperform developed equity markets by 2.0 percent per year. We will adopt this lower estimate of 2 percent for our premium calculations.

In the case of fixed income returns, premiums are measured relative to the medium-term Treasury bond. The premium for the Barclays Aggregate Bond Index is 0.3 percent for the period since 1976. Since the estimate of the return on the medium-term Treasury bond is 4.9 percent, the estimated return on the Barclays Aggregate is 5.2 percent.

With the new set of estimates for expected returns, we could perform optimization calculations similar to those reported above for Figures 8.5 and 8.6 But without constraints on the optimization, we would still find portfolios consisting of value stocks and excluding growth stocks (just as we did using historical returns for a shorter sample period). The new portfolios would have lower returns because they are based on a much longer data set beginning in 1951 rather than in the 1970s and are based on lower expected inflation rates than experienced on average since the decade of the 1970s.

Typically, however, the investor is not interested in the portfolios obtained from optimization (for the reasons cited above). Instead, the investor would like to find out what the expected returns and risks will be for a portfolio *that the investor has chosen*. The estimated return on this portfolio is to be based on the expected returns on individual assets reported in Table 8.3. But that still leaves a question of how to estimate the standard deviations and correlations of these assets. If we use the historical series since 1979 to estimate these risk parameters, then we have enough information to estimate the return on the portfolio as a whole.

What could an investor do with such an estimate? The most obvious answer is that the investor might be able to use it as a basis for planned investment or spending. A foundation, for example, could use the estimate to formulate its spending rule. An individual could use the estimate to formulate a plan for wealth accumulation during the working years or spending in retirement. For the reasons discussed in Chapters 14 and 15, the estimate needed for spending rules is the estimate of the compound real return on the portfolio.

Another application of the same methodology would be to estimate the expected returns and risks of a whole set of model portfolios tracing out a frontier looking something like the efficient frontiers in Figure 8.1. Investment firms often offer a set of model portfolios from which investors can choose (depending on their risk aversion and circumstances). More recently, target date retirement funds have offered a range of model portfolios that an investor can transition through as he or she gets closer to retirement (the target date).

To illustrate such a frontier using the three indexes introduced earlier, let's imagine holding the proportion of foreign stocks to total stocks constant at 40 percent. Thus all portfolios on our frontier will have 40 percent of stocks in the foreign market. The frontier will be traced out by varying the proportion of bonds to stocks from 10 percent to 100 percent. The frontier is illustrated in Figure 8.7. (As mentioned above, the optimizer requires arithmetic averages, so the geometric returns in Table 8.3 must first be converted to arithmetic returns). The returns on the frontier range from 5.7 percent to 9.9 percent. The standard deviations on the frontier range from 5.7 percent to 14.8 percent. The investor would still have to decide which portfolio is best given the investor's circumstances. Given that portfolio choice, the expected return and risk is given by the point on the frontier. So the optimization software has been used to determine the returns consistent with the original set of capital market assumptions. Of course, those returns are only as reliable as the capital market assumptions themselves.

PORTFOLIOS IN PRACTICE—EXAMPLE OF MARKETWATCH.COM'S LAZY PORTFOLIOS

The last section described in theory how we might analyze portfolios, but how does this work in practice? To illustrate how an investor might analyze a portfolio ex ante, let's examine three simple portfolios as described on Paul

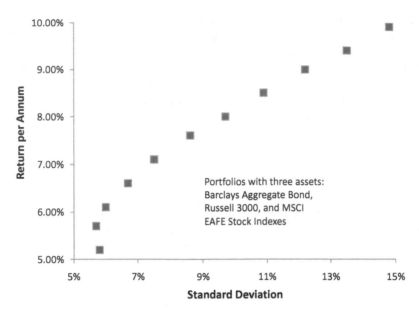

FIGURE 8.7 Model Portfolios Based on Table 8.3 Returns
Data Sources: Barclays Capital, MSCI, and Russell®.

B. Farrell's MarketWatch.com web site. Farrell labels them Lazy Portfolios because they can be implemented easily using index funds.[14] The three portfolios chosen are the three simplest of his eight portfolios. They are labeled A through C in Table 8.4, but on his web site they have the colorful names Margaritaville, Dr. Bernstein's No Brainer, and Second Grader's Starter.[15] The portfolios range from conservative to aggressive with investment in bonds ranging from 33 percent, 25 percent, to 10 percent, respectively. The portfolio returns are estimated by using the premium estimates reported in Tables 8.2 and 8.3. The standard deviations are measured over the 20-year period from 1990 through 2009.[16]

Table 8.4 analyzes the three MarketWatch.com portfolios as well as a simple U.S.-only bond/stock portfolio. The table reports the proportion invested in each asset as well as the returns and standard deviations of each portfolio. Portfolio A has 33 percent invested in bonds, while at the other extreme Portfolio C has only 10 percent. Portfolio A is a little unusual in that all of the bond allocation is invested in TIPS rather than conventional bonds. And half of the stock allocation is abroad. Portfolio B is also unusual in two respects: there is a large allocation (25 percent) to small caps and all of the international equity allocation is invested in Europe.

TABLE 8.4 *MarketWatch.com* Portfolios Compared

	Market Watch A	Market Watch B	Market Watch C	U.S.-Only Portfolio
Barclays Aggregate		25%	10%	33%
TIPS	33%			
S&P 500		25%		
Russell 3000	34%		60%	67%
Russell 2000		25%		
MSCI EAFE	22%		22%	
MSCI Europe		25%		
MSCI Emerging Markets	11%		10%	
Average Return	9.17%	9.37%	10.31%	8.57%
Standard Deviation	10.79%	12.10%	13.74%	10.58%
Sharpe Ratio	0.53	0.49	0.50	0.48

MarketWatch portfolios A, B, and C are the three simplest portfolios described by Paul B. Farrell of MarchWatch.com. The portfolios, labeled Margaritaville, Dr. Bernstein's No Brainer, and Second Grader's Starter on MarketWatch.com, vary the bond allocation from 33 percent to 10 percent. The U.S. only portfolio is shown for comparison purposes. The returns are based on the premium estimates in Table 8.3. The standard deviations are calculated over the period from 1990 to 2009.
Data Sources: ©Morningstar, S&P, MSCI, Barclays Capital, and Russell®.

Portfolio C is more conventional with one-third of the equity allocation overseas.

Because Portfolio A has a much larger bond allocation, the return on Portfolio C is much larger than that of Portfolio A. But so also is the risk as measured by the standard deviations. The three portfolios are illustrated in Figure 8.8 where all of them are compared with the capital market line defined relative to the Russell 3000 (the latter of which has a Sharpe ratio of 0.48). All three portfolios are at least marginally above the line, but Portfolio A appears to be substantially above the line. Sure enough, Portfolio A has the highest Sharpe ratio. In fact, the alpha* of Portfolio A, measured with the Russell 3000 as a benchmark, is an impressive 0.5 percent.

What accounts for the superior performance of Portfolio A? There are two possible candidates: the TIPS allocation and the heavy reliance on foreign stocks. If the Barclays Capital Aggregate Index replaces the Barclays TIPS Index, there is virtually no effect on portfolio performance. But if the international stock allocation is replaced with an all-U.S. stock allocation, then the performance of Portfolio A deteriorates substantially. This alternative portfolio, with 67 percent in the Russell 3000 and the rest in the Barclays

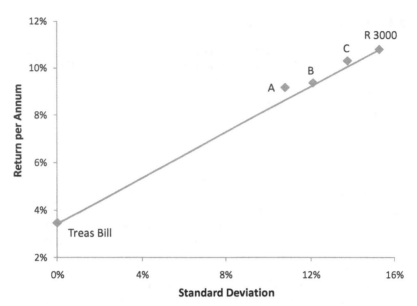

FIGURE 8.8 MarketWatch.com Portfolios Compared
Data Sources: ©Morningstar, S&P, MSCI, Barclays Capital, and Russell®.

Aggregate Index, is shown in the last column of Table 8.4. The Sharpe ratio of this portfolio, at 0.48, is identical to that of the Russell 3000 alone.

The reason why the international allocation makes such a difference was explained earlier in this chapter. EAFE has only a 0.3 percent premium over the S&P 500 (and a similar premium relative to the Russell 3000). But the MSCI Emerging Market Index has a premium of 2.0 percent in Table 8.2 even though that premium was reduced relative to the actual historical average premium of 3.2 percent. So the extra return earned in Portfolio A (designed by Scott Burns for the MarketWatch.com site) is due to its reliance on emerging markets. Whether such a portfolio would outperform other portfolios in practice is dependent on how well the emerging markets actually perform.

An investor could perform similar analyses for his or her own portfolio. Assign an index that most closely corresponds to each asset in the portfolio, then use the estimates in Table 8.3 (or alternative estimates chosen by the investor) to estimate the total return on the portfolio. By using indexes, the investor can also estimate the likely risk of that portfolio. It's true that the actual manager chosen for each asset class may have higher or lower risk than the index, but nonetheless the methodology should still provide a reasonably accurate estimate of the risk of the entire portfolio.

BEYOND THE TRADITIONAL EFFICIENT FRONTIER

What has been left out of this discussion of asset allocation? The main purpose of asset allocation is to diversify investment risks. Yet the menu of assets we have considered offers relatively little opportunity to diversify into low correlation assets. It's true that stocks and bonds have a very low correlation. But within the stock and bond categories, almost every asset is highly correlated. That's even true of foreign stocks which are relatively highly correlated with domestics stocks, especially over recent periods. Similarly, as shown in Chapter 7, most U.S. bonds are highly correlated with one another.

To truly achieve diversification, perhaps the investor has to move beyond ordinary capital market assets. That is certainly the lesson learned from the experience of the Yale University Endowment. In Chapter 13, we will review that experience in detail. At this point, let's just point out that the Yale University Endowment portfolio bears little resemblance to the portfolios discussed in this chapter. Less than 25 percent of the portfolio is invested in traditional capital market assets, bonds and stocks. Interestingly enough, the allocation to foreign stocks is larger than that to domestic stocks (10 percent versus 7.5 percent). The rest of the portfolio is allocated to three types of alternative investments:

1. Private equity (mostly venture capital and buyout funds)
2. Absolute return (mostly hedge funds with either event-driven or value-driven strategies)
3. Real assets (mostly real estate, oil and gas, and timberland)

Yale's allocation to alternatives is high even by the standards of the large university endowments.[17] But Yale's superior investment performance, to be described in Chapter 13, forces other investors to pay heed to Yale's allocation.

What lessons can be learned from Yale's experience? The most important one is that we should at least consider adding alternative investments to the portfolio. There may be very good reasons why even very wealthy investors should not try to emulate Yale. We shall discuss some of those reasons in the chapters ahead. But we should consider how some of these alternatives might improve performance on ordinary portfolios. The chapters ahead will consider these alternatives one by one. Then in Chapter 13, we will revisit the topic of asset allocation to see how alternatives can shift the efficient frontier.

NOTES

1. See Markowitz (1952).
2. The Zephyr optimizer program, Zephyr AllocationADVISOR, was used to calculate the returns and standard deviations of both sets of portfolios.
3. The investor could achieve greater diversification by investing in high-yield bonds. As Chapter 7 showed, this is the one U.S. bond class that is low in correlation with other U.S. bonds. But unless the investor had a relatively high allocation to this asset class, the efficient frontier is unlikely to be much different from that shown in Figure 8.3.
4. The sample period is from January 1970 to December 2009. As discussed in Chapter 5, this correlation has been much higher over the last five or 10 years.
5. Optimization programs typically truncate the data set to match the shortest series. This issue will be discussed at greater length later in the chapter.
6. That is, the alpha* of the unconstrained portfolio is from 0.2 percent to 0.5 percent compared with the constrained portfolio after adjusting for risk.
7. Any portfolio that has less than 10 percent in stocks is suboptimal, so it is not part of the efficient frontier.
8. Sharpe asked what set of returns would generate the portfolios recommended by Merrill Lynch, Pierce, Fenner & Smith in its so-called beta book.
9. The forecast horizon is measured in decades rather than years. So the inflation expectation is over a similar forecast period.
10. Estimates of expected returns in modern portfolio theory are based on arithmetic averages, not geometric averages. So optimization programs explicitly call for arithmetic averages as inputs. An approximate formula for conversion of geometric to arithmetic averages is $r_A = r_G + 1/2 \, \sigma^2$.
11. The compound nominal return on large-cap stocks is 9.4 percent per annum or 0.75 percent per month. Using a monthly standard deviation of 4.21 percent, the equivalent arithmetic average is 0.84 percent per month or 10.0 percent per annum.
12. The Tremont hedge fund data set, for example, begins in 1994, while the HFRI data set begins in 1990.
13. Since geometric averages are involved, the premium is measured using the compound formula, $(1.102)/(1.099) - 1 = 0.3\%$. And the estimate of the EAFE return based on the S&P 500's 9.4 percent return is calculated as $(1.094)*(1.003) - 1 = 9.7\%$.
14. These portfolios are all invested in Vanguard Index Funds. The analysis below substitutes the bond and stock indexes which most closely correspond to the Vanguard funds involved.
15. Margaritaville was developed by Scott Burns, a Dallas Morning News financial columnist. Dr. Bernstein is a financial advisor to high net worth individuals, and Second Grader is presumably a young investor with a long enough horizon to invest 90 percent in equity! After we introduce alternative investments, we will consider another MarketWatch portfolio, the *Unconventional Success* portfolio recommended by David Svensen of the Yale Endowment.

16. The Zephyr AllocationADVISOR software was used to calculate the standard deviations and correlations. Portfolio A invests in TIPS which were introduced only in 1997. So for that portfolio, the standard deviation and correlations of that series were estimated separately over the shorter period and entered manually in the Zephyr allocation program.
17. Harvard's endowment in 2008, for example, had 55 percent in alternative investments including 19 percent in absolute return funds. In a later chapter, Yale's portfolio will be compared with the average portfolios reported in surveys by the National Association of College and University Business Officers (NACUBO).

CHAPTER 9

Hedge Funds

Hedge funds are difficult to define if only because they have morphed into so many different shapes. The term *hedge* used to mean that the funds attempted to hedge one set of assets with another. This was certainly true of the first hedge fund formed in 1949 by A.W. Jones, and is still true of hedge funds following market-neutral strategies (as explained later). But many hedge funds have directional strategies that are anything but hedged.

Perhaps it's better to define hedge funds by the fees they charge. The Investment Company Act of 1940 insists that a Registered Investment Company (RIC) like a mutual fund charge *symmetrical* investment fees. So their fees remain fixed in percentage terms whether the fund rises or falls. Hedge fund managers insist on *asymmetrical* fees typically consisting of a management fee paid regardless of performance and an *incentive fee* charged as a percentage of the upside. A typical fee schedule would be to charge a 1 percent or 2 percent management fee on all of the assets under management and a 20 percent incentive fee.[1] To avoid having to register as an RIC, the hedge fund must be offered to investors only through a private placement.

Hedge funds are organized as partnerships with the general partners being the managers and the limited partners being the investors. The form of the partnership is similar to that used by private equity and venture capital firms. In fact, these firms also charge asymmetrical investment fees. So how are hedge funds different from private equity and venture capital firms? The answer is that their investment horizons and their investments are very different. Hedge funds have short-term strategies and typically invest in publicly available securities such as equities and bonds. Private equity and venture capital invest for extended periods in firms and they invest in projects not generally available to the general public. Of course, the lines between the hedge funds and private equity/venture capital are not always sharply drawn, but it helps to think of them as distinct types of investments.

Under the Investment Company Act of 1940, hedge funds (and other limited partnerships) have traditionally been exempt from many regulations including SEC registration. That's because they were intended only for wealthy private investors or wealthy institutions that could presumably take care of themselves. The Act specified that only 100 limited partners could invest in a fund. More recently, a distinction has been drawn between different types of investors. Accredited investors are those who have a net worth of $1 million *or* have income of $200,000 for the last two years ($300,000 for a married couple). Qualified purchasers are investors with at least $5 million in investment assets. Hedge funds that limit investors to qualified purchasers have less onerous regulations than those open to accredited investors.[2]

The hedge fund industry has grown rapidly over the last two decades. From less than $200 billion in assets under management in 1994, the industry grew to more than $400 billion in 2000 and then to almost $2 trillion in 2007 as interest in hedge funds increased dramatically (AIMA, 2008). As the AIMA study points out, it's actually difficult to pin down the size of this industry because there is no central reporting. Hedge Fund Research estimates that there was $1.9 trillion under management in June 2008, whereas HedgeFund.net puts the number much higher at $2.8 trillion.[3] The number of hedge funds has also grown exponentially in the last two decades. In 1994 there were less than 2,000 hedge funds, but by 2007 that number had grown to 7,600 before falling off to 6,800 by the end of 2009.[4]

The investors in hedge funds (the limited partners) can be individuals, companies, or institutions. Traditionally, individual investors have provided a majority of the funding. Table 9.1 shows that in 1997, 62 percent of the investments in hedge funds came from individuals directly investing in the funds. In addition, there were also individual investors who invested through fund of funds. By 2005, the share of individual investors had fallen to 44 percent. Endowments and foundations merely maintained their shares while pension funds fell in relative importance. In contrast, corporations and institutions, the latter including educational institutions, almost tripled their

TABLE 9.1 Investors in Hedge Funds

Investor	1997	2005
Individuals	62%	44%
Fund of Funds	16%	28%
Pension Funds (Public and Private)	10%	7%
Corporations and Institutions	5%	14%
Endowments and Foundations	7%	7%

Source: Hennessee Group LLC (2007).

share. We will discuss hedge fund investments by educational institutions in greater detail in Chapter 13.

INVESTMENT STRATEGIES

The investment strategies followed by hedge funds range from the absolute return strategies that aim to hedge away most market movements to directional strategies that aim to profit from directional bets in one market or another. Before getting into the terminology used to describe narrower types of strategies within the industry, let's consider strategies in terms of beta and alpha. A pure hedge or absolute return strategy would try to eliminate most of the systematic risk of the market by keeping beta close to zero. The hedge fund would then be judged by whether the manager could produce alpha. A directional strategy would earn part of its return from the market itself.[5] The manager would still try to produce additional return from the superiority of the manager's security selection, so the total return would be enhanced by alpha (much like a long-only mutual fund manager).

How would a hedge fund manage to keep its beta close to zero following an absolute return strategy? To do this, a fund might match each long position in a security with a short position in a second, highly correlated security. Suppose the fund manager is focusing on the stocks of utility companies. The manager knows that utility stocks are likely to rise and fall with the market and to be highly correlated with one another. So if the manager takes a matching long and short position in this industry, the market exposure of the position should be marginal. This matching of long and short positions results in what is called a *market-neutral* fund. The alpha of this manager depends on his or her ability to invest in utility stocks that will outperform other stocks in the industry and to choose utility stocks to short that will under-perform. Security analysis is important just as it is with a long-only manager.

Market-neutral strategies can take a variety of forms. It will be helpful to consider a real-life strategy that paid off handsomely for some hedge funds in the mid 1990s. This strategy was called the convergence play in the European bond market. Under the Maastricht Treaty of 1991, the Euro was to be introduced in 1999, but the countries to be admitted were to be chosen at the end of 1997. To join the new monetary union, countries had to satisfy certain conditions regarding their currencies, inflation rates, and budget deficits. Only those countries that had satisfied these conditions would be invited to join the union. Once in the union, all countries would see their interest rates converge to one level.

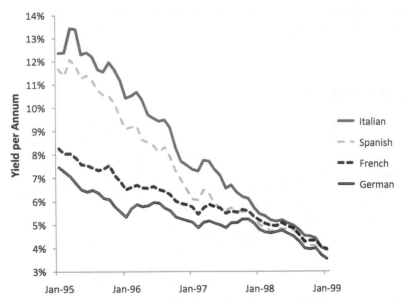

FIGURE 9.1 Convergence of Bond Yields in Europe, 1995–1998
Data Source: IMF, International Financial Statistics.

In 1995, the market as a whole had little faith that Italy or Spain would be able to join the union. The evidence for this is shown in Figure 9.1 where the interest rates on the government bonds of Italy, Spain, France, and Germany are displayed. The Italian government had to offer an interest rate on its bonds that was about 6 percent higher than German interest rates. The market simply did not believe that Italy could satisfy all of the conditions for the union, and therefore a huge interest rate premium was required to induce investors to buy Italian bonds.[6] In particular, there was skepticism that the Italian government could bring its fiscal deficit down from more than 9 percent of GDP in 1995 to 3 percent of GDP as required by the Treaty.

Some hedge funds, notably Long Term Capital Management (LTCM), believed otherwise. These funds trusted that Italy would do whatever was necessary to qualify for the union by the end of 1997. So these funds bought Italian bonds. To hedge their positions and ensure market neutrality, they simultaneously borrowed and sold short German bonds (or equivalent derivatives). With offsetting positions in two European bond markets, it did not matter whether or not European currencies rose or fell against the dollar. A rise in the dollar, for example, would lead to losses on the long Italian bond position and gains on the short German bond position. Similarly, it

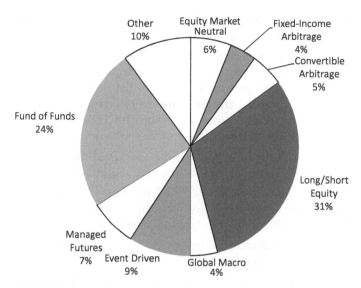

FIGURE 9.2 Hedge Funds by Strategy in TASS Database, 2004
Source: Getmansky, Lo, and Mei (2004b).

did not matter whether the general level of European interest rates rose or fell. All that mattered is that Italian bonds outperformed German bonds in the run-up to the end-1997 deadline. It is evident from Figure 9.1 that this convergence strategy paid off handsomely. This was particularly true for LTCM which made spectacular gains from the strategy.[7]

The hedge fund industry employs a variety of strategies and some of the names of the strategies vary from firm to firm. Generally, the databases accept whatever classification is used by the hedge fund itself. Figure 9.2 gives a breakdown of the strategies used by the funds in the TASS database as of August 2004.[8] The most important category of fund is the long/short equity fund representing 31 percent of the TASS database. The global fund category associated with George Soros and Julian Robertson, two famous managers from the 1990s, is only 4 percent of the total.

A brief description of some of these strategies might be useful:

Fixed income arbitrage: betting on mispricing of related interest rate securities.

Convertible arbitrage: betting on discrepancies in the prices of convertibles relative to the underlying stocks.

Equity market neutral: as its name implies, this strategy works with matching short and long positions that keep overall market risk low. The first three strategies are all normally market neutral and offer absolute returns.

Long/short equity: a variation on equity market-neutral where the manager has a larger long position than the short position that is hedging it. The manager may also make a bet on style (e.g., by favoring value over growth), size, or some other factor that makes the position more directional than a market-neutral fund. The beta of such funds could be much higher than that of market-neutral funds.

Equity hedge: this category is used by the HFRI database and encompasses both equity market-neutral and equity long-short strategies.

Relative value: also used by the HFRI database. This strategy attempts to take advantage of relative pricing discrepancies between instruments including equities, debt, options, and futures.

Global macro: big directional bets on currencies or interest rates or some other macro variable.

Event driven: bets on corporate events such as mergers and acquisitions, corporate restructurings, or share buybacks.

Managed futures: long or short bets on futures contracts for commodities or currencies.

Emerging markets: invests in the securities of companies or the sovereign debt of emerging countries

Fund of funds: a fund that invests in a number of hedge funds to diversify the manager risk.

The list of strategies will vary from one database to another. Naturally returns vary widely across strategies. But, as explained earlier, so do risks, particularly the systematic risks associated with beta. We will examine returns and risks in the next section.

HEDGE FUND RETURNS

All mutual funds in the United States must report their returns publicly each period. Databases such as that developed by Morningstar allow investors (and researchers) to examine returns earned on the universe of mutual funds just like they can examine returns on individual stocks. Because hedge funds are offered through private placement, they cannot advertise their returns publicly. Nor is there any requirement that they report returns to official agencies. So the collection of return data is haphazard and incomplete.

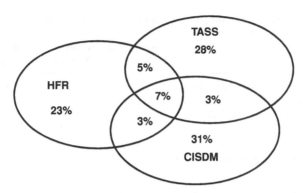

FIGURE 9.3 Overlap of Databases
Source: Agarwal, Daniel, and Naik (2009).

Consulting firms like TASS or HFR have developed databases of returns that they sell to the investment industry. The returns are provided by the hedge funds, but only on a voluntary basis. So these consulting firms will contact all of the hedge funds of which they are aware and ask for the funds to report their returns on a regular basis. Some funds do and some don't. Some do for a while, then don't. Some don't for a while, then provide backfilled returns.[9]

To see how incomplete these data collections can be, consider the overlap of three database providers, TASS, HFR, and CISDM as reported in Agarwal et al (2009).[10] Many of the hedge funds appear in two or more of these databases, so it is important to ask to what extent is any one database capturing the universe of hedge funds? The answer is revealed in Figure 9.3 where a Venn diagram shows the overlap among the three databases.[11] Only 7 percent of the funds appear in all three databases. On the other hand, 28 percent of the funds only appear in the TASS database, 31 percent only appear in the CISDM database, and 23 percent in the HFR database. This figure shows how limited is the coverage of any single database.

The biases that develop from using these databases will be analyzed in a later section of the chapter. Before doing so, let's consider the performance of the hedge fund indexes developed from these databases. That is, let's ignore any biases in the data and consider the return and risk characteristics of hedge funds using the same kinds of return data that the investment industry normally analyzes. We will find the case for investing in hedge funds very compelling whether viewed on a stand alone basis or as part of a broader portfolio strategy.

One of the most widely used set of indexes is that provided by Hedge Fund Research (HFR). Indexes have been developed for hedge funds as a

TABLE 9.2 Hedge Funds Compared with Other Assets, 1990–2009

	Geometric Average	Arithmetic Average	Standard Deviation	Sharpe Ratio
HFRI Fund Weight Hedge Fund Index	12.2%	11.8%	7.1%	1.13
Barclays Aggregate Bond Index	7.0%	6.9%	3.9%	0.80
Russell 3000 All-Cap Stock Index	8.4%	9.2%	15.2%	0.36
MSCI EAFE Stock Index	4.4%	5.9%	17.5%	0.12

Data Sources: HFRI, Barclays Capital, Russell®, and MSCI.

whole as well as for individual strategies. As with most indexes, the series begin in the early 1990s, 1990 in the case of the HFR indexes. Table 9.2 gives a standard set of statistics examining the average return, standard deviation, and Sharpe ratio of the HFR Fund-Weighted (total) Index. This index is an equally weighted average of all of the funds in the HFR database. The statistics are based on monthly returns from 1990 through 2009. The table compares hedge fund returns with stock and bond returns. The results are quite impressive. The HFR index gives a compound return of 12.2 percent over a sample period when the Russell 3000 could barely beat the Barclays Aggregate Bond Index. And the HFR index had half of the standard deviation of the Russell series. Foreign stocks as represented by the EAFE index performed even more miserably over this same period.[12]

In most portfolios, hedge funds will represent only a portion of the asset allocation. So it makes sense to view hedge funds in a portfolio context. Table 9.3 reports correlations between the HFRI Fund-Weighted hedge fund index and other stock and bond indexes. Hedge funds are low in correlation

TABLE 9.3 Correlations Between Hedge Funds and Other Assets, 1990–2009

	HFRI Fund-Weighted Hedge Fund Index	Barclays Aggregate Bond Index	Russell 3000 Stock Index
HFRI Fund-Weighted Hedge Fund Index	1.00		
Barclays Aggregate Bond Index	0.11	1.00	
Russell 3000 Stock Index	0.77	0.17	1.00
MSCI EAFE Stock Index	0.65	0.14	0.73

Data Sources: HFRI, Barclays Capital, Russell®, and MSCI.

TABLE 9.4   Betas and Alphas of HFRI Hedge Fund Indexes, 1990–2009

HFRI Hedge Fund Index	Correlation with R 3000	Standard Deviation	Beta	Alpha
Fund-Weighted (Aggregate)	0.77	7.1%	0.36	6.1%
Event Driven	0.73	7.0%	0.33	6.5%
Relative Value	0.51	4.5%	0.15	5.7%
Equity	0.75	9.2%	0.46	7.5%
Macro	0.36	7.8%	0.18	8.6%
Emerging Market	0.64	14.7%	0.62	7.2%

Note: Betas are calculated using the Russell 3000 index as the market benchmark.
Data Sources: HFRI and Russell®.

with U.S. bonds, but have sizable correlations with domestic and foreign stocks. The correlation between the HFRI Fund Weighted index and the Russell 3000 is 0.77, while the correlation between the hedge fund index and MSCI EAFE is 0.65. These correlations are lower than they would be between most U.S. stock indexes, but they are still relatively high.

Table 9.4 reports the betas and alphas of the HFRI Fund-Weighted (total) Index and HFRI-style hedge fund indexes. Consider first the beta of the HFRI Fund-Weighted Index. With a correlation of 0.77 with the Russell 3000 index, the beta is nonetheless only 0.36 because the standard deviation of the HFRI index is 7.1 percent compared with a standard deviation for the Russell 3000 index of 15.2 percent.[13] So it is the very low standard deviation of the hedge fund series, not its correlation with the market, which gives it a low beta. With such a low beta, the alpha is 6.1 percent.[14]

The beta is even lower for the relative value strategy reported in the table. This strategy has a relatively low correlation with respect to the Russell 3000 (0.51). The low beta is more due to its low standard deviation (4.5 percent) than to the low correlation. This strategy is not truly market neutral, but its low beta provides ample opportunity for managers to earn a high alpha (5.7 percent).

Somewhat less impressive results were obtained in Bernstein Wealth Management (2006) using the TASS database of individual hedge fund returns. To try to minimize some of the biases discussed below, the study included fund returns only after they started reporting returns to the database and kept all funds in the calculations even if they later stopped reporting returns to TASS. Bernstein created equal-weighted indexes for both the directional and market-neutral funds using fund returns from 1996 to 2005. The study found that market-neutral hedge funds had an alpha of 3.1 percent, while directional hedge funds had an alpha of 3.5 percent.

TABLE 9.5 Performance of Other Hedge Fund Indexes, 1994–2009

	HFRI	Tremont	Hennessee	MSCI
Correlation with HFRI	1.00	0.81	0.98	0.88
Average Return	9.7%	9.2%	9.1%	9.1%
Standard Deviation	7.3%	7.8%	7.1%	5.1%
Beta	0.36	0.28	0.35	0.20
Alpha	4.3%	4.3%	3.8%	4.6%

Note: the four indexes shown are those reported by Hedge Fund Research, CSFB/Tremont, Hennessee Group, and MSCI. Beta is measured with the Russell 3000 as the market benchmark.
Data Sources: HFRI, Credit Suisse/Tremont, Hennessee, MSCI, and Russell®.

It is also useful to compare the results for the HRFI Fund-Weighted Hedge Fund index with those of aggregate hedge fund indexes of three other index providers. As shown in Table 9.5, the three indexes have correlations with the HFRI index ranging from 0.81 to 0.98.[15] All of the indexes have similar returns. Average returns range from 9.1 percent to 9.7 percent, betas range from 0.20 to 0.36, and alphas range from 3.8 percent to 4.6 percent.

Beyond the standard statistics for hedge fund indexes, there should be interest in any unusual statistical properties of hedge fund returns. For example, are there reasons to believe that hedge fund returns follow a non-normal statistical distribution? Do the measured standard deviations properly account for the potential volatility of these investments?

Malkiel and Saha (2005) provide evidence on the distribution of the hedge fund returns in the TASS index. They find that the returns are characterized by high kurtosis, so the tails of the returns distribution are fatter than what you would find in a normal distribution. And these returns have a negative skewness, so returns are asymmetrical in the downward direction (not exactly what an investor desires). They can reject normality for all strategies except managed futures and global macro. Getmansky, Lo, and Makorov (2004a) show that hedge fund returns (for most strategies) have high serial correlation suggesting that hedge fund investments are relatively illiquid and/or the managers deliberately smooth their returns. The authors show that the serial correlation is higher for strategies where you would expect investments to be illiquid such as event-driven or emerging market investments.

A more difficult issue to address is whether hedge funds may perform worse in a crisis than the statistical measures indicate. Certainly the experience of hedge funds following the Russian bond default of July 1998 was not reassuring. There are two issues involved. First, in a crisis, does

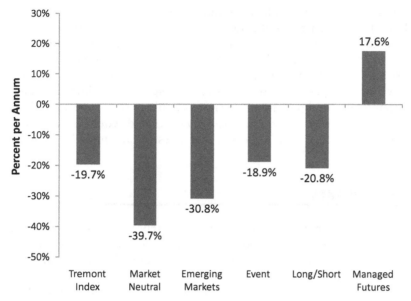

FIGURE 9.4   Hedge Fund Returns in the Crisis, October 2007 to December 2008
Data Source: Credit Suisse/Tremont.

the systematic factor drag down hedge fund returns to the extent that they are correlated with the market? Second, does the crisis itself pose a risk to hedge funds to the extent that they become more illiquid? Both issues were at work in the crisis beginning in 2007. First, the stock market itself fell more than 50 percent at one point dragging down hedge fund returns with significant beta exposure. Second, both bond and stock markets became increasingly illiquid, particularly after the failure of Lehman Brothers in September 2008.

In the crisis beginning in 2007, hedge funds faltered badly. Consider the returns on a range of hedge fund strategies as reported by Credit Suisse/Tremont from October 2007 (the peak of the U.S. stock market) through December 2008. Figure 9.4 reports the returns over this period. The hardest hit strategy was market neutral, down 39.7 percent. Illiquidity adversely affected this strategy, especially at the peak of the crisis after Lehman failed. The Tremont index as a whole was down almost 20 percent.[16] Only managed futures fared well with a positive 17.6 percent return. Evidently many of the managed futures managers were able to reverse their oil and other commodity bets in time for the sharp turnaround in oil prices in summer 2008.

What has this crisis taught us about hedge funds? First, hedge funds should not be referred to as absolute return investments as they so often are. Nonetheless, hedge funds did provide returns superior to virtually all equity investments. After all, the S&P 500 was down 40.1 percent over this same period, while the MSCI EAFE and MSCI Emerging Market Indexes were down by 46.2 percent and 56.3 percent, respectively. Third, investors learned that hedge fund positions were not as liquid as they expected. Many hedge funds slammed the gates on their investors and would not let them out of their investments. That's a lesson that investors are unlikely to forget.

HEDGE FUND BIASES

Because of the way that hedge fund returns are reported, biases inevitably develop that undermine the performance results reported by the investment industry. This section will describe the major biases and then will attempt to measure how large they are.

There are two major biases affecting hedge fund returns. One bias plagues all asset return data—survivorship bias—although usually it's relatively easy to correct for it if there is a full universe of data available. The other bias—backfill bias—is peculiar to hedge funds. We will begin by describing backfill bias because it affects data sets from the very beginning.

1. Backfill bias. This is the bias that arises when hedge funds first begin reporting to a database. If a hedge fund has been operating for a few years prior to its first reporting, it's natural for the managers to offer all of their return data including returns that occurred before database reporting began. Thus the database backfills the return data for that fund. The bias is important in the hedge fund industry because many hedge funds are incubated in their early stages. Families and friends of the manager may be the only investors in the fund at start-up. Or the manager may choose not to report returns at first because the fund is too small. Or the manager may want to see how the fund performs before providing data to an outside consultant. In some cases, hedge fund managers may start multiple funds at the same time and then see which funds perform well. In any case, the result is that there is a bias toward reporting the results of funds that do well. Those that close or get merged into other funds never get reported. Sometimes this bias is called *instant history bias* because the backfilled returns provide an instant history. Another term used is *incubation bias*. Mutual fund data sets should not be plagued by this type of bias because they have reporting obligations right from their beginning.

2. **Survivorship bias.** This bias arises when a database keeps track of only the live funds. The reason why you would like to keep track of all funds is that the investor, *ex ante*, does not know which funds will disappear. Dead funds often have ugly returns during their death spiral, so it's important to keep track of these funds. But other funds may disappear from the database because they have been *too successful* and have closed to new investors. A third class of fund may be closed because the managers have moved on to other opportunities. Or the managers may just choose not to report for some other reason. Because funds that disappear from the database may not be dead, we will follow other authors in calling disappearing funds defunct. It's important to determine (a) what percentage of funds in a database are defunct, and (b) how did their returns compare with those that remain in the database.

One other bias is worth noting although it's difficult to treat it empirically. This is *liquidation bias*. This bias refers to the fact that managers of hedge funds that are failing are likely to stop reporting returns to a database before the final liquidation value of the fund is realized. For example, the funds that lost their capital in the Russian debt crisis of August 1998 did not report returns of –100 percent in that month. Instead, the returns ended in July 1998.[17] Any attempts to adjust for survivorship bias will miss the liquidation bias when the fund closes down.

Quantitative estimates of backfill bias range widely from one study to another. That's because the methodology for determining the bias varies as well. Malkiel and Saha (2005) estimate backfill and survivorship bias using the TASS database from 1994 to 2003. The TASS database distinguishes between returns that have been backfilled into the TASS database from returns subsequently recorded by the same fund. And it keeps track of defunct funds as well as the funds still alive in each year. Malkiel and Saha define the backfill bias as being the gap between the backfilled and non-backfilled returns. As shown in Table 9.6, the bias is estimated to be 7.3 percent per year. This is a huge gap. The authors do not calculate what might be a more interesting statistic, the gap between the non-backfilled returns and all of the returns together.

Fung and Hsieh (2006) criticize this methodology for determining backfill bias. They point out that hedge funds typically report to several databases, and the returns that appear to be backfilled in one database may have already been reported to another database. Fung and Hsieh are particularly concerned about the TASS database because Tremont bought TASS in 2001 and then added the funds in the Tremont database to the TASS database at that time. Fung and Hsieh propose to estimate backfill bias by trying to determine the average incubation period of a fund. They do this by

TABLE 9.6 Biases in Hedge Fund Returns in TASS Database

Malkeil and Saha (2005) Estimates		Fung and Hsieh (2006) Estimates	
1994–2003		1994–2004	
Backfill Bias		Backfill Bias	
Backfilled Returns	14.6%	All Funds	12.0%
Non-Backfilled	7.3%	Exclude 1st 14 Months	10.5%
Bias	7.3%	Bias	1.5%
Survivorship Bias		Survivorship Bias	
Live Funds*	13.7%	Live Funds	14.4%
Live and Defunct*	9.3%	Live and Defunct	12.0%
Bias	4.4%	Bias	2.4%

*The returns for the live and defunct funds exclude backfilled returns. The estimates of survivorship bias are for 1996 to 2003.

examining the dropout rates for hedge funds in three databases, TASS, HFR, and CISDM. Using a data set of hedge funds over the period 1994-2004, they find that the highest dropout rate occurs at about 14 months. They then eliminate the first 14 months of returns for the hedge funds in the three databases. The resulting bias estimate of 1.5 percent for the TASS database is shown in Table 9.6. The biases for the other two databases are almost identical.

The backfill bias estimates of the two studies are so far apart that it is difficult to reconcile them. But it's natural to ask the question: If the Malkiel-Saha estimates are measuring returns that are not truly backfilled, but merely previously missing from that database, why are those returns so much lower than the non back-filled returns?

Survivorship bias is potentially quite large given the high rates of exit from the industry. Consider first how many funds survive over time. Malkiel and Saha (2005) use the TASS database to follow firms through time from the first date that they entered the database. (So no backfilled returns are used). They divide firms into the live firms that continued to exist at the end of the data set, December 2003, from the defunct firms that dropped out of the data set prior to that date. To determine the resulting survivorship bias, it's necessary to compare the returns of the live firms with the live and defunct firms together. In Table 9.6, Malkiel and Saha estimate survivorship bias to be 4.4 percent. Fung and Hsieh (2006) measure survivorship bias using their three databases from 1994 to 2004. Unlike Malkiel and Saha, Fung and Hsieh include all returns in their estimate of this bias, including backfilled returns. Table 9.6 reports a survivorship bias of 2.4 percent using the TASS database. Their estimates for the other two databases are similar, 1.8 percent for the HFR database and 2.4 percent for the CISDM database.

Even if the lower set of estimates from Fung and Hsieh (2006) are used, 1.5 percent for backfill bias and 1.8 to 2.4 percent for survivorship bias, the effects on hedge fund returns are enormous. If you reduce the returns in Table 9.4 by about 3.5 percent to 4 percent, the alphas then become much more modest in size. So taking into account biases is really important in assessing hedge fund returns. The previous discussion shows that it's difficult to assess this bias, and leading researchers can come to different quantitative conclusions. But the importance of bias is undisputed.

PERFORMANCE ACROSS MANAGERS

Managers are not created equal. That's true of any asset class where active management is pursued since managers differ in their abilities to select assets. But it's especially true of hedge funds. The performance of managers varies widely because different strategies are pursued. But the dispersion in performance across managers is much too large to be explained by whether one strategy, such as market-neutral equity, is chosen rather than another, like fixed-income arbitrage. Generating alpha is not easy, especially not the large alphas that are found for some hedge funds.

To investigate the dispersion in manager performance, it's helpful to compare hedge funds with other types of investments. That's exactly what Malkiel and Saha (2004) did in the working paper version of the study cited earlier. Using TASS data for hedge fund managers and Lipper data for mutual fund managers, they calculated the returns of the top quartile and third quartile managers for each of five asset classes. These were hedge funds and four types of mutual funds for real estate, international equity, U.S. equity, and U.S. fixed income. Figure 9.5 reports the *excess returns* of the first quartile and third quartile managers over the median manager for that asset class. Thus in the case of U.S. equity mutual funds, the top quartile manager delivered 0.9 percent more than the median manager while the third quartile manager delivered 0.5 percent less than the median manager. For hedge funds, the gap between quartile returns was much larger. The top quartile manager delivered 8.6 percent more than the median manager. And the third quartile manager delivered 8.1 percent less. Manager *selection* is everything when it comes to hedge funds. Or, perhaps since so many managers are closed to new investors, manager *access* is everything.

A second source of information about manager dispersion is provided by Bernstein Wealth Management Research (2006). Using the same set of data described earlier for hedge funds and long-only equity and bond managers,

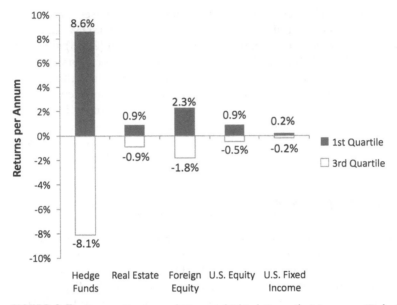

FIGURE 9.5   Excess Returns of First and Third Quartile Managers (Relative to Median Manager), 1994–2004
Source: Malkiel and Saha (2004).

Bernstein sorted managers by performance using the *alphas* of each manager net of fees. Figure 9.6 shows alphas for the top-decile manager and bottom-decile manager for each asset class. All alphas are shown relative to the median alpha for that asset class. The top decile long-only equity manager delivers an alpha that is 2.5 percent above that of the bottom-decile manager, a reasonably small range. In contrast, the gap in alphas between the top and bottom decile managers for hedge funds is more than 25 percent for directional hedge funds and more than 15 percent for market-neutral hedge funds. As with the Malkiel-Saha data set, it really matters which manager you choose (or get access to).

FUND OF FUNDS

Manager risk represents a significant problem for hedge fund investors. Not only is there great variation in performance across managers, but there is also the risk that managers might blow up. So many investors have chosen to diversify the manager risk by investing through a *fund of hedge funds*.

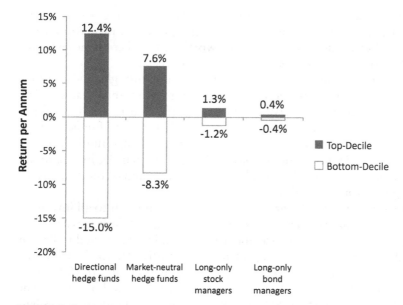

FIGURE 9.6 Alphas of Top Decile and Bottom Decile Managers, 1996–2005 *Source:* Bernstein (2006).

Figure 9.2 shows that 24 percent of the hedge funds in the TASS database are funds of hedge funds.

What advantages do fund of funds offer to the investor? There are two major advantages. First, the funds of funds offer due diligence and expertise in choosing hedge funds. With about 10,000 hedge funds to choose from, many of which have short track records, it's difficult for an investment advisor to make decisions about which funds to invest in. A fund of funds offers a group of recommended hedge funds that the fund of funds manager has investigated. And a fund of funds manager should be able to constantly monitor the hedge funds that are chosen in case there are changes in personnel or other material changes in operations. Due diligence by the managers of the funds of funds will not ensure against blow ups, but probably reduces their number.

The second advantage of the fund of funds lies in the diversification of manager risk. As with all assets, investing in 15 managers rather than two managers undoubtedly reduces risk. Just as importantly, a fund of funds can give the investor diversification across hedge fund styles. So if convertible arbitrage falls out of favor, perhaps long-short will begin outperforming. Funds of funds may have an additional advantage over direct investment in hedge funds. Investors may obtain *access* to better hedge fund managers. As shown above, there is very large dispersion in the performance of managers. If funds of funds can get an investor into superior funds, the extra cost of hiring a fund of funds manager may be worth it. But there is no evidence whether or not funds of funds provide superior access.

There must be some disadvantages to investing through fund of funds since only 24 percent of hedge fund investments follow this strategy. One obvious disadvantage is diversification. (Diversification is always a disadvantage if you are trying to strike it rich). With 15 hedge funds, there is virtually no chance to end up in the top quartile of hedge funds. It's true that some of the 15 hedge funds may be in the top quartile, but lightning only strikes so many times in one place—even if the fund of funds manager has strung lightning rods all over.

There is another disadvantage that should be important to all investors. Fund of fund managers charge an extra layer of fees, and these fees are often quite high. Consider the evidence about hedge fund fees reported in Brown et al (2004). In that study, management and incentive fee for hedge funds averaged 1.4 percent and 18.5 percent, respectively. On top of those fees, funds of funds charged a 1.5 percent management fee and a 9.1 percent incentive fee. To overcome two layers of fees, the hedge fund managers had better deliver some very high returns.

Consider the effects of fees on performance. Let's assume that hedge funds charge 1 percent management fees and 20 percent incentive fees. In order for the investor to earn an 8 percent net return, a hedge fund must earn 11 percent gross return:

$$(0.11 - 0.01) * (1 - 0.20) = 0.08$$

An investor in a fund of funds, however, must find hedge funds earning much higher gross returns in order to earn the same 8 percent net return. Let's assume that the funds of funds charge an extra 1 percent management fee and an extra 10 percent incentive fee. Then the hedge funds must earn a gross return of 13.4 percent to net the investor 8 percent:

$$[(0.134 - 0.01) * (1 - 0.20) - 0.01] * (1 - 0.10) = 0.08$$

It's probably unlikely that the expertise of the fund of funds in selecting managers is going to deliver, on average, the extra 2.4 percent required to keep net returns at 8 percent. So investing through a fund of funds is costly. Whether the extra layer of fees is worthwhile depends on how much the investor values the due diligence and diversification provided by the fund of funds.

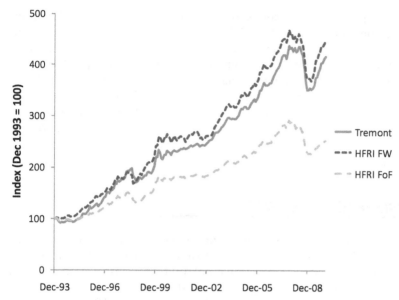

FIGURE 9.7   Hedge Fund and Fund of Fund Returns, 1994–2009
Data Sources: HFRI and Credit Suisse/Tremont.

How costly is the fund of funds approach to investing in hedge funds? One way to approach this question is to compare fund of funds returns with those on the hedge funds themselves. HFRI provides two aggregate indexes of hedge fund returns: the Fund-Weighted index previously introduced and a Fund of Funds index. Over the period from January 1990 through December 2009, the former has a compound average return of 12.2 percent compared with an 8.2 percent compound return for the latter. Of course, the mix of hedge funds in the two indexes is undoubtedly different since one consists of an equal weighted average of hedge funds while the other is a mix of whatever hedge funds the managers of the funds of funds select. But nonetheless this gap in returns of 4 percent is quite sizable. Apparently the average manager of the funds of funds in the HFRI index is not able to overcome the extra layer of fees with superior access to managers. Figure 9.7 compares the HFRI fund of funds index with two hedge funds indexes, the HFRI Fund-Weighted Index and the Credit Suisse/Tremont (total) Hedge Fund Index. The latter begins in 1994, so the figure traces out the three returns from 1994 to 2008. It is apparent from the figure that the funds of funds index lags consistently behind the two hedge fund indexes. The extra layer of fees does create quite a drag of cumulative returns.

Yet perhaps this comparison is misleading. An investor with $5 million or $10 million cannot earn the HFRI Fund-Weighted hedge fund return because there is no way for such an investor to invest in a diversified array of hedge funds. Minimum investments in hedge funds are typically in the $1 million range or more. It's true that an endowment with $500 million can choose a diversified array of funds as can an ultra-high net worth family with that much wealth. But there are few investors with sufficient wealth to get diversification on their own. Suppose an investor is forced to approach hedge funds through a fund of fund investment. Would it still pay to invest in hedge funds?

HEDGE FUNDS IN A PORTFOLIO

Table 9.7 reports on a diversification experiment where an investor shifts from an all-traditional portfolio to a portfolio that includes 10 percent investment in hedge funds. The traditional portfolio (A) consists of 25 percent in the Barclays Aggregate U.S. bond index, 50 percent in the Russell 3000, and 25 percent in the MSCI EAFE index. Portfolio B shifts 10 percent of the U.S. stock investment into the HFRI Fund-Weighted Index. Portfolio C shifts 10 percent of the U.S. stock investment into the HFRI Fund of Funds index.

The most impressive results are obtained when the HFRI Fund-Weighted index is chosen as the hedge fund vehicle. The compound return on the portfolio is lifted by 0.4 percent and the Sharpe ratio is increased from 0.35 to 0.41. That translates into an alpha* of 0.6 percent. But investment in the fund of funds index also improves performance of the portfolio. The return on the portfolio is not increased, but the Sharpe ratio is increased

TABLE 9.7 Effects of Hedge Funds on Portfolio Performance, 1990–2009

	Geometric Average	Arithmetic Average	Standard Deviation	Sharpe Ratio
Portfolio A (No hedge fund)	7.4%	7.8%	11.4%	0.35
Portfolio B (Fund Weighted)	7.8%	8.1%	10.5%	0.41
Portfolio C (Fund of Funds)	7.4%	7.7%	10.3%	0.38

Portfolio A consists of 25 percent in the Barclays Aggregate Bond Index, 50 percent in the Russell 3000 all-stock index, and 25 percent in MSCI EAFE index. Portfolio B replaces 10 percent of the Russell 3000 with the HFRI Fund-Weighted hedge fund index, while Portfolio C replaces the Russell 3000 with the HFRI Fund of Funds index.
Data Sources: HFRI, Barclays Capital, Russell®, and MSCI.

from 0.35 to 0.38. That translates into an alpha* of about 0.3 percent. This is admittedly a very small improvement. In fact, Table 9.7 shows that hedge funds are not the wonder drug that some observers claim. But, according to these results, they do add to risk-adjusted performance.

SUMMARY—KEY FEATURES OF HEDGE FUNDS

With stock and bond markets unlikely to deliver the stellar returns of the last 25 years, hedge funds have become increasingly popular among investors. The growth in this asset class in the last 15 years is nothing short of phenomenal. The hedge fund industry has developed a multitude of strategies aimed at generating much more alpha than long-only managers have been able to produce. Some of these strategies are actually hedged against market risk, while others are directional with significant market risk.

The record for returns is impressive. These returns are large whether they are measured in absolute terms or relative to market benchmarks. Alphas higher than 5 percent are found for some hedge fund strategies. Hedge fund returns do not extend back very far since most databases were only developed in the 1990s. But the biggest problem is that these returns are plagued with backfill and survivor bias. Once you adjust for these biases, the returns look much less impressive.

When investing in hedge funds, manager skill is everything. And that skill is very unevenly distributed. The gap between the top-performing and lower-performing manager is far larger than for traditional asset classes. Manager selection and manager access are absolutely crucial to successful hedge fund investing. Does that mean that an investor should choose a fund of funds? The answer must weigh the advantages of a fund of funds manager, due diligence and expertise in choosing managers, as well as diversification against the biggest disadvantage, an extra layer of fees.

Hedge funds are not just the latest passing fad for investors. In a world with moderate long-only returns, it's inevitable that investors will hunt for returns with managers who pursue more complex strategies. And investment managers will continue to be attracted to the huge fees offered by this industry.

NOTES

1. Fung and Hsieh (2006) report that between 78 percent and 86 percent of managers in three major databases charge 20 percent incentive fees. More than 70 percent of the management fees in these three databases lie between 1 percent and 1.99 percent.

2. For further details, see Hodge (2003).
3. AIMA (2008), p. 16.
4. CNNMoney.com, Hedge Funds: They're Back, March 12, 2010 using figures from Hedge Fund Research.
5. Not all directional strategies are correlated with the stock market, of course, since the hedge fund manager may be making a bet on interest rates or currencies or the direction of some other market.
6. The 6 percent premium was primarily a currency premium designed to compensate the investor if Italy failed to qualify and subsequently allowed the Lira to depreciate against the Deutschmark. Once a country has joined a currency union, differentials between interest rates such as those between Greece and Germany seen in 2010 reflect default risks rather than currency premiums.
7. Lowenstein (2000) provides a lively account of LTCM's brief history. The convergence strategy was one of LTCM's most profitable strategies, helping LTCM earn 60 percent returns in both 1996 and 1997. At the beginning of 1998, after this strategy had played out, LTCM returned half of the capital to its investors citing the lack of comparable investment opportunities. Nine months later it had to be rescued.
8. This is the breakdown of 2,771 live funds in the TASS database as reported in Getmansky, Lo, and Mei (2004b). The authors eliminate funds that give only gross returns or quarterly, not monthly, returns.
9. As discussed below, those that do, then don't cause survivorship bias. Those that don't, then backfill cause backfill bias.
10. These databases are provided by Lipper TASS, Hedge Fund Research (HFR), and the Center for International Securities and Derivative Markets (CISDM) at the University of Massachusetts. All three have more than 10 years of data collection experience.
11. This figure is based on a Venn diagram in Agarwal et al (2009) showing overlap among four databases including a newer one developed by MSCI. The four databases together have 3,924 live funds at the end of December 2002. The overlap among the three largest databases was analyzed after eliminating the funds that only appeared in MSCI. The percentages were rounded to the nearest decimal.
12. As explained in Chapter 5, the underperformance of EAFE relative to U.S. stocks is almost entirely due to Japan.
13. Recall that beta is equal to the correlation coefficient times the ratio of the standard deviation of the asset relative to the standard deviation of the benchmark. The beta is $0.36 = 0.77 * (0.071/0.152)$.
14. Since the average return on the risk-free Treasury bill is 3.8 percent and the average return on the Russell 3000 is 9.2 percent, the alpha = 11.8 percent − $[3.8\% + 0.36*(9.2\% − 3.8\%)] = 6.1\%$.
15. Over the same period, the correlation between the S&P 500 index and the Russell 1000 large-cap index is 1.00 and the correlation between the S&P 500 and the Russell 3000 all-cap index is 0.99. This is further evidence that each

hedge fund index is measuring the performance of a somewhat different set of hedge funds than another index.

16. Similar results are found for the other indexes in Table 9.5. HFRI was down 20.4 percent, Hennessee was down 21.0 percent, while MSCI was down 14.0 percent over this same 15 month period.

17. This example is due to Fung and Hsieh (2006).

CHAPTER 10

Venture Capital and Private Equity

When investors speak of *alternative investments*, they often mean hedge funds or private equity rather than other alternatives to stocks and bonds like real estate or commodities. Private equity differs from hedge fund investments in several ways. First, private equity gives the investor privileged access to ownership in an enterprise that is not publicly available. Hedge funds, in contrast, typically invest in publicly available securities. Second, private equity requires long lock-up periods for investment to give time for the enterprises to mature. Hedge funds may have lock-up periods, but these are limited usually to one or two years rather than a decade.

Private equity encompasses several different types of investment types.[1] At one extreme, there is venture capital, the investment in enterprises at early stages of their development. A typical venture capital (VC) firm takes only a minority stake in the new enterprise. At the other extreme are buyout firms that take over public companies, then refinance and reorganize them before selling them back to the public. These buyout firms, which represent the largest category of private equity, typically take majority ownership and control of the enterprise. In between VC and buyouts, there are mezzanine investments that can either be late-stage VC investments or highly leveraged buyout transactions. The key characteristic of mezzanine investments is the use of subordinated debt (junior to bank loans) and perhaps options to buy common stock. This chapter will focus on the two most important forms of private equity, venture capital and buyouts.

The first section of the chapter will discuss common features of these two forms of private equity including how the partnerships are structured and what fees are paid by investors. The second and third sections will focus on venture capital practices and analyze returns since the early 1980s. The fourth and fifth sections will examine buyout funds.

COMMON FEATURES OF VENTURE CAPITAL AND BUYOUT FUNDS

The common feature of all private equity investments is their organizational form and fee structure. Private equity firms are organized as partnerships with general partners running the show and limited partners providing the capital. The limited partners are typically pension funds or other institutional investors. The limited partners agree to commit a certain amount of capital, and the general partners draw down this amount as they invest in enterprises. The drawdown period typically takes several years, so the investors must keep the capital in liquid form in the meantime. Capital is typically committed for 10 years with limited extensions at the discretion of the general partners.

Fees generally take two forms, a management fee levied on the committed capital and an incentive fee (termed carried interest or carry) based on performance. A typical fee structure involves a 2 percent management fee and a 20 percent incentive fee. The 2 percent management fee is levied on the committed capital from the beginning of the fund regardless of how much has been drawn down. So if there is a $100 million fund with capital committed for 10 years, then the total management fee will be $20 million over the 10-year period ($2 million per year).[2] The incentive fee kicks in after the limited partners have recovered their committed capital. Note that the management fee is very different from a mutual fund fee. The latter is always calculated as a percentage of the value of the portfolio, whereas the former is calculated as a percentage of the committed capital even if none has been invested yet. The reason why private equity firms levy fees this way is that they must cover their expenses during the early years of the partnership when they are searching for new projects.

The 2 percent/20 percent fee structure does vary somewhat across funds. Metrick and Yasuda (2010) study a sizable sample of venture capital and buyout funds provided by an anonymous investor, presumably a large institutional investor with long experience in the alternative space. There are 94 VC firms in the sample and 144 buyout firms. Table 10.1 reproduces some of their statistics on fees charged by these funds. Almost half of the VC firms charge management fees in excess of 2 percent, but almost all have incentive fees at 20 percent. About half of the buyout firms have management fees less than 2 percent, but all 144 buyout funds in this sample have incentive fees at 20 percent.

The management fee is levied on the committed capital, but there are variations in how this fee is levied. In his study of VC funds, Metrick (2007) describes how some funds levy the fee on the full amount of committed capital in the early years of the fund, but then lower the fee as the capital

TABLE 10.1 Distribution of Venture Capital and Buyout Fund Fees

Number of Funds With	Venture Capital	Buyout
Management Fees		
>2%	40	11
=2%	44	59
<2%	9	74
Carry Fees		
>20%	4	0
=20%	89	144
<20%	1	0

Source: Metrick and Yasuda (2010).

is employed and returns start to accrue to the investments. Similarly, the 20 percent incentive fee follows different patterns. The incentive fee typically does not kick in until after the limited partners have recovered their capital. So if the limited partners have committed $100 million in capital, payouts from the investments must rise above $100 million before the general partners begin to receive carried interest. Thereafter, the GPs will be paid 20 percent of any returns. So if the fund eventually closes out with $200 million in exit proceeds, the GPs will earn $20 million (i.e., 20 percent of $200 million - $100 million). But some firms base their carry on the difference between the exit proceeds and the investment capital rather than committed capital. The investment capital is the committed capital less the management fee, so this variation on the carry results in a larger payout to the GPs.

To complicate matters, private equity funds often have hurdle rates that must be earned by the limited partners before carried interest is paid to the general partners. Metrick and Yasuda (2010) show that the most common hurdle rate for both VC and buyout funds is 8 percent. According to their example, suppose that a $100 million fund earns $108 million the first year, $2 million the second, and $10 million the third year. The first $108 goes to the limited partners because of the 8 percent hurdle rate. The next $2 million goes to the general partners because of a catch-up provision. The final $10 million is split 80 percent/20 percent between the limited and general partners. According to Metrick and Yasuda (2010), almost all buyout funds have hurdle rates, whereas only about half of the VC funds have hurdle rates.

Figure 10.1 gives an example of fee payment for a hypothetical $100 million fund.[3] The limited partners commit $100 million for 10 years including management fees. The committed capital is actually invested only in stages

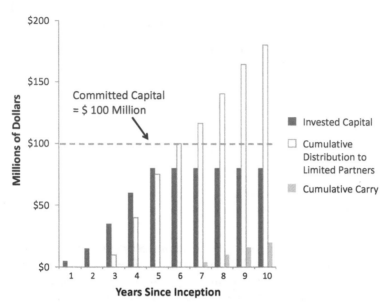

FIGURE 10.1 Invested Capital, Distribution, and Carry Fees for a
Hypothetical Fund
Source: Ayako Yasuda Lecture Notes, Wharton School.

as the general partners draw down the commitment. In the meantime, the
2 percent fee (not shown) is levied every year. After 10 years, there will
be a total of $20 million in management fees paid. Since this $20 million
is part of the commitment by the limited partners, the investment capital
available to the fund is only $80 million. The fund starts distributing cap-
ital back to the limited partners in year three, but only in year seven does
the cumulative distribution exceed the committed capital. In year seven, the
$20 million earned by the fund is divided 80/20 between the limited part-
ners and the general partners. By year 10, a total of $200 million has been
distributed, $100 million in capital returned to the limited partners and an
extra $80 million of the rest paid to the limited partners. The general partners
pocket $20 million in carried interest (20 percent of the extra $100 million)
plus $20 million in management fees (not shown).

Private equity firms are usually very small partnerships. In Metrick and
Yasuda's (2010) sample of VC and buyout firms, the median number of
partners in their 94 VC firms is five and the median number of professionals
is only 11. Among buyout firms, the corresponding numbers are six for
partners and 20 for professionals. Their study has the interesting result that
buyout funds earn lower revenue per managed dollar than VC funds, but

buyout firms earn more per partner and per professional than their VC counterparts. That's because buyout firms invest much larger sums.

VENTURE CAPITAL

Venture capital was *the* investment of the late 1990s. At the time, investors were clamoring to get into this investment class because of the storied returns earned by the VC firms that had provided startup financing for firms like AOL, Compaq, Cisco, Sun, and others. A healthy IPO market was crucial to the VC firms' successes. In 1999 alone, returns on small cap growth stocks exceeded 40 percent. So investors sought to invest in new growth companies, and investment banks eagerly brought many VC projects to market. With the collapse of the tech boom, VC firms suffered a sharp reversal of fortune, and investors turned to other hot products such as buyout investments.

What distinguishes VC investments from others? Andrew Metrick has written an insightful book about venture capital investments which he describes as a textbook, but which has some very interesting chapters for the investment professional. At the beginning of the book, Metrick lists five main characteristics of venture capital:

1. A VC is a financial intermediary, meaning that it takes the investors' capital and invests it directly in companies.
2. A VC invests only in private companies.
3. A VC takes an active role in monitoring and helping the companies in its portfolio.
4. A VC's primary goal is to maximize its financial return by exiting investments through a sale or an initial public offering (IPO).
5. A VC invests to fund the internal growth of companies.

The investments can be at different stages of the firm's development. Early stage investments may provide financing to complete development of the product and begin initial marketing efforts.[4] Mid-stage investing may provide working capital for the initial expansion of the company, or fund plant expansion, or fund further marketing efforts. Companies may still not be profitable in this mid-stage. Late stage investing may go to companies that are now generating profits, but need money for further expansion in preparation for a public offering.

VC investments are concentrated in two broad sectors, health care and information technology (IT) where the latter includes communications, semiconductor, software and hardware industries. In recent years, VC investment in health care has been concentrated in the biotech industry. Naturally, the geographical distribution of VC investment reflects the concentration of IT and biotech in certain areas of the country. According to Metrick (2007), 32 percent of VC investment in the United States is in Silicon Valley, the center of IT in the United States, while 11 percent is in New England, particularly around Boston where biotech is so important. The rest of VC investment is scattered around the country with 8 percent in New York, 6 percent in Texas, and 5 percent in DC. Worldwide, there are no separate totals for venture capital, but PricewaterhouseCoopers provides figures for private equity as a whole in the *Global Private Equity Reports*. Metrick (2007) summarizes the figures for 2004. Of the $44.4 billion invested worldwide, $22.8 billion is invested in the U.S. and Canada, $13.1 billion in Western Europe, and $8.5 billion in Asia. The United Kingdom leads European investment with $6.2 billion, while Japan dominates Asian investment with $4.3 billion.

VC investment has gone through three periods in the last 25 years. In what Metrick (2007) calls the pre-boom period, which stretched from the early 1980s through the mid-1990s, VC investment was less than $10 billion per year. As we will see below, VC returns began to rise in the early 1990s, so money flowed into VC funds. Figure 10.2 shows the rise in new

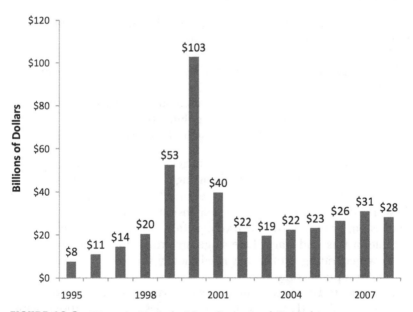

FIGURE 10.2 Venture Capital—New Committed Capital
Source: MoneyTree™ Report from PricewaterhouseCoopers LLP (PwC) and the National Venture Capital Association (NVCA), based on data provided by Thomson Reuters.

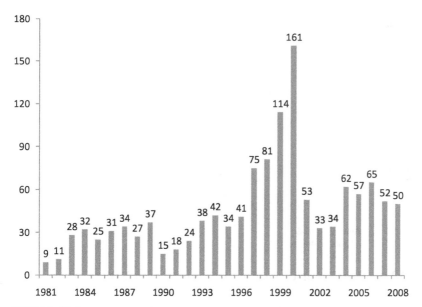

FIGURE 10.3 Number of Venture Capital Funds by Vintage Year
Source: Cambridge Associates LLC.

committed capital in the VC industry starting in 1995 as detailed in the PricewaterhouseCoopers/National Venture Capital Association MoneyTree Report for 2009.[5] In the boom period from 1995 through 2000, VC investment rose to more than $50 billion in 1999 to a peak of more than $100 billion in 2000. The post-boom period since 2000 has seen VC investment fall back in the $20 billion to $30 billion range.

The flow of funds into VC is also reflected in the number of new funds created in each vintage year. Figure 10.3 draws on data from Cambridge Associates to track the number of funds in vintage years 1981 to 2008. The peak vintage year was 2000 when 161 funds were launched. The number of new funds fell to only 50 in 2008.

Institutional investors have always dominated investments in venture capital. This is in sharp contrast to investments in hedge funds where individuals and families typically provide more than 50 percent of the investment capital. Figure 10.4 reports on the distribution of limited partners as reported by Metrick (2007) using data from the National Venture Capital Association. The largest category of limited partners is represented by pension plans with a 43 percent share. Financial and insurance firms as well as endowments and foundations provide the bulk of the remaining capital. Individuals and families provide only 10 percent of the capital.

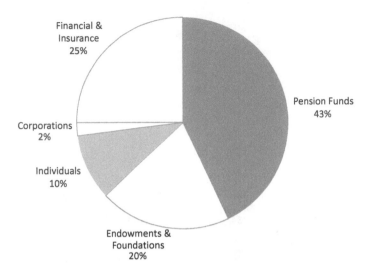

FIGURE 10.4　Venture Capital Limited Partners by Type in 2002
Source: Metrick (2007).

Perhaps that's because most wealthy families are unable or unwilling to put up with the illiquidity of this class of investment. Hedge funds sometimes have year-long or longer lock-up periods, but almost never require a decade for redemptions!

RETURNS ON VENTURE CAPITAL

By the very nature of venture capital, returns occur over an extended period of time. Investors have to commit capital for a decade or more, and the first years of the partnerships bring few if any returns. The pattern of cash flows is highly uneven, so the calculation of returns is tricky.

The returns on venture capital are best calculated using the internal rate of return (IRR) rather than time-weighted returns. To see why this is the case, consider a simple example from Metrick (2007). Suppose that an investor has committed $11 million to a fund. At the beginning of the first year, $1 million is drawn down. At the end of this year, the investor receives $2 million on this investment. At the same time, the remaining $10 million is drawn down for a second investment which returns $6 million at the end of the second year. A time-weighted return would consist of compounding the 100 percent return on the first investment with the 40 percent loss on the second investment for a cumulative return of $(1 + 1.0) * (1 - 0.4) - 1 = 20\%$. The annual equivalent is $(1 + 0.20)^{\frac{1}{2}} = 9.5\%$. Surely there is something misleading about this calculation since the investor hasn't even recovered the $11 million initially invested.

The cash flows of this investment are very uneven. At the beginning of the first year, there is a $1 million outflow. Then there is a net $8 million outflow at the beginning of the second year ($10 − $2). Finally, there is a $6 million inflow at the end of the second year. An IRR calculation for this set of cash flows would involve solving the following equation for the IRR, r.

$$\$1\,m(1+r)^2 + \$8\,m(1+r) = \$6\,m$$

The IRR is equal to −31 percent. Surely that reflects better the actual plight of the investor in this ill-fated fund!

Metrick (2007) uses two sources of returns on venture capital for his analysis, Sand Hill Econometrics (SHE) and Cambridge Associates (CA). The Sand Hill Econometrics database is a comprehensive database of returns provided by the VC funds themselves. These returns are gross of fees and expenses. Cambridge Associates, an institutional investment consulting firm, provides an index of returns net of fees as reported to the limited partners that CA has as clients. Since CA has a large share of the institutional market, its index covers upward of 80 percent of all VC funds in existence. The index begins in 1981.

Metrick (2007, Chapter 3) provides an analysis of the biases in each index. The returns on SHE are actually lower than those on CA despite the fact that the latter nets out management fees and carried interest. He uses a rough estimate of management fees and carried interest to adjust the SHE returns to a net basis. This results in a 7.5 percent gap between the CA and SHE indexes.[6] Metrick argues that the CA index has survivorship bias due to the fact that many VC firms attract institutional money only after they have had successful VC funds. He suggests treating the CA index as an upper bound for estimates of true VC returns.

All VC returns are plagued by stale pricing. In any given period, few VC projects are able to be priced reliably because few emerge in IPOs or are sold to larger companies in that period. So VC firms assign values to the projects based on stale information, often basing the valuations on conditions at the time of the last round of financing. Stale pricing also affects the standard deviations of the VC returns since the true variability of the values of projects cannot be reflected in the return series if old valuations remain in place.

This chapter will analyze venture capital returns using the Cambridge Associates index (which is publicly available).[7] Table 10.2 reports these returns from the beginning of the database in the second quarter of 1981 through the second quarter of 2009. For comparison with public equity, the table also reports the returns on the S&P 500 index as well as the

TABLE 10.2   Returns on U.S. Venture Capital and U.S. Stocks,
1981(Q2)–2009(Q2)

	Geometric Average	Arithmetic Average	Standard Deviation	Sharpe Ratio
Venture Capital	12.8%	14.1%	21.7%	0.41
S&P 500	10.0%	11.0%	16.6%	0.35
Russell 3000	9.8%	10.9%	17.2%	0.33
Russell 2000 Growth	5.7%	8.9%	25.8%	0.14
Russell 2000 Value	11.2%	12.7%	19.7%	0.38

Data Sources: Cambridge Associates LLC U.S. Venture Capital Index®, S&P, and Russell®.

all-cap Russell 3000 index and the small-cap Russell 2000 Growth and Value indexes. The growth index is included because so many of the venture capital investments eventually emerge (if they emerge at all) as small-cap growth stocks. Over this 28-year period, venture capital earns a return about 3 percent higher than the S&P 500 and Russell 3000. The standard deviation for venture capital is reported in the table, but that statistic is unreliable because of the stale pricing discussed above. For similar reasons, the Sharpe ratio is suspect.

Because venture capital typically invests in projects that are in the technology and biotech space, we should view venture capital as an alternative to investment in small-cap growth stocks. If this comparison is made, then VC comes out way ahead as Table 10.2 makes clear. Venture capital has an excess return that is about 7 percent above that of small-cap growth. If an investor is wealthy enough to qualify as a limited partner in VC and if that investor is able to put up with the illiquidity of VC investments, it may make sense to forgo public investment in technology and biotech and instead choose venture capital for that part of the portfolio.

Naturally, it's important for an investor to know whether long-term returns vary much over time. In the case of venture capital, timing is everything. A vintage year like 1981 would have provided quite different returns than vintage years in the early 1990s (which eventually benefitted from the boom of the late 1990s). Figure 10.5 compares the returns on venture capital with those for the S&P 500 over five-year intervals from 1981 on. The wide swings in excess returns are quite evident in this figure. In the 1980s, venture capital returns lagged far behind those of the stock market, whereas in the 1990s, venture capital generated enormous excess returns for investors.[8] In the five-year period from 1996 to 2000 alone, investors earned an excess return over stocks of 44 percent *per year*. No doubt the exuberant IPO

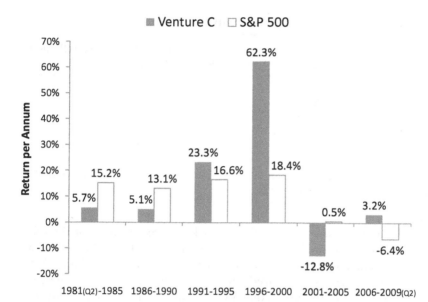

FIGURE 10.5   Venture Capital and Stock Returns over Five-Year Intervals
Data Sources: Cambridge Associates LLC U.S. Venture Capital Index® and Standard
& Poor's.

market of the late 1990s had something to do with that. Indeed, in 1999, the return on the Cambridge Associates Venture Capital Index was an astounding 279 percent. With returns this variable, it's not evident that we actually know the long-run returns on venture capital. Is the long run likely to give us the returns of the 1980s or the 1990s?

Table 10.3 reports the correlations between venture capital and private equity, on the one hand, and various stock market indexes on the other hand. Because venture capital returns reflect stale valuations for many projects, the true correlations are probably quite a bit higher, but the relative correlations with different stock market indexes are nonetheless interesting to examine. Venture capital has a correlation of 0.45 with the Russell 3000 all-market index and an even larger correlation of 0.49 with small-cap growth as measured by the Russell 2000 Growth Index. Notice that venture capital's correlation with small-cap value is much lower at 0.20. This is to be expected because so few of the investments by venture capital firms are in the value space.

It's useful to look at venture capital returns in a portfolio context since VC investments are likely to be only a marginal part of the investor's portfolio. Figure 10.6 shows the beta and alpha of VC when the market is

TABLE 10.3 Correlations, 1986 (Q2)–2009(Q2)

	Venture Capital	Russell 3000	Russell 2000 Growth	Russell 2000 Value
Venture Capital	1.00			
Russell 3000	0.45	1.00		
Russell 2000 Growth	0.49	0.92	1.00	
Russell 2000 Value	0.20	0.81	0.82	1.00
Private Equity	0.63	0.68	0.64	0.49

Data Sources: Cambridge Associates LLC U.S. Venture Capital Index® and U.S. Private Equity Index® and Russell®.

represented by the Russell 3000 all-cap market index. Because of the relatively low correlation of VC with the market, the beta for VC investments is only 0.51. The corresponding return on the security market line (SML) return is only 8.1 percent compared with the average return of 10.9 percent for the Russell 3000. Because actual VC returns average 14.1 percent, the result is an alpha of 6.0 percent for venture capital. That's truly impressive.

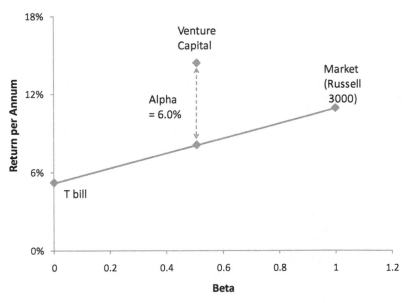

FIGURE 10.6 Beta and Alpha of Venture Capital
Data Sources: Cambridge Associates LLC U.S. Venture Capital Index® and Russell®.

How should we interpret these results? First, we must recognize that the Cambridge Associates series is upwardly biased for the reasons discussed above. The bias alone may be large enough to explain this alpha. Metrick (2007) provides a more sophisticated analysis. He introduces the Fama-French (1993) model that adds two factors to standard CAPM regressions, one to measure the value premium and one to measure the small-cap premium.[9] These two factors adjust asset returns to reflect their value (or growth) and small-cap biases. More interestingly, Metrick also introduces a liquidity factor developed by Pastor and Stambaugh (2003). Venture capital investment certainly is less liquid than investment in public equities, so presumably part of the alpha reported above should be attributed to that. Metick's regressions using the Cambridge Associates and Sand Hill indexes lead to similar results. After adjusting for the value, small-cap, and liquidity effects, the alpha that remains is less than 0.5 percent per year. The (il)liquidity factor itself is surprisingly small at 1 percent per year.

If an investor opts for venture capital, what are the chances that the average returns reported above will actually be earned by the investor? Here we encounter a serious problem with VC investments: manager performance varies widely, so manager search and manager access are very important. Figure 10.7 reports on a 20-year study of manager performance carried

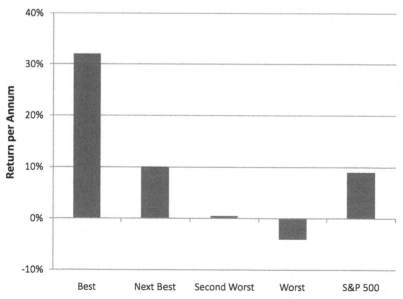

FIGURE 10.7 Average Returns on Venture Capital Funds by Quartile
Source: Wall Street Journal, May 27, 2004.

out by Venture Economics as reported in the *Wall Street Journal* (May 27, 2004). The returns on VC partnerships are divided into quartiles from the best to the worst, with 226 funds in each quartile. For comparison purposes, the S&P 500 return is reported for the same period. The top quartile earns a return in excess of 30 percent per year, no doubt pleasing the limited partners who were lucky enough to invest in these funds. The next quartile barely outperforms the S&P 500, while the last two quartiles have very disappointing returns.

Further evidence consistent with the Venture Economics findings is reported by David Swensen in the latest edition of his book, *Pioneering Portfolio Management* (2009). Swensen examines returns on funds invested in traditional asset classes as well as funds invested in alternatives such as hedge funds and private equity. According to Swensen, there is only a 0.5 percent return differential between first and third quartile fixed income managers. The return differential is larger for U.S. equity managers and larger still for small-cap and international equity managers. But the gap for private equity managers is truly astounding. Leveraged buyout managers in the first quartile make 13.3 percent per annum on average while those in the third quartile lose money. Venture capital is even worse. First quartile managers earn 28.7 percent returns, while those in the third quartile lose 14.5 percent!

If returns vary widely across funds, there are two issues that investors face. First, are the fund returns *persistent* over time? In that case the key issue is whether the investor can identify the superior funds. Second, if the fund returns are persistent, can the investor get *access* to the superior funds?

Kaplan and Schoar (2005) provide interesting evidence on manager persistence in the private equity space. They use fund level data for both VC and buyouts over the 1981–2001 period. The question they pose is whether a VC or buyout firm that has high returns in one vintage fund is likely to have high returns in a subsequent fund. They find that a 1 percent higher return on one fund is associated with 0.54 percent higher return in the next fund. This is impressive, since most evidence about mutual funds finds no such persistence.

So if VC fund returns are *persistent*, then the next question is whether an investor can obtain *access* to the better funds. In the VC space, certain firms have established long-run track records which make them particularly sought after. Metrick (2007) identifies some of the most famous such as Sequoia Capital (which invested in Apple, Cisco, Google, and Yahoo) and Kleiner, Perkins Caufield & Byers (which financed Amazon, Genentech, Google, and Sun). Which investors naturally have the best access to firms with such attractive records? The answer probably is that Yale University and others who have been committed to this space for decades probably enjoy the best access. Whether a newcomer can get the same access is a debatable question. Figure 10.7 and Swensen's evidence show how important that question is.

BUYOUT FUNDS

Unlike venture capital funds, buyout funds usually obtain a controlling interest in the firms that they invest in. As explained above, the partnership structure and fees are very similar to VC funds, but the types of firms that buyout firms invest in are quite different. Instead of technology startups, buyout firms often buy old-line industrial firms that need restructuring. The most famous buyout of the 1980s involved an old-line firm, RJR Nabisco, which was subsequently broken in two parts, Nabisco being separated from RJR. This buyout, the largest of its time at $25 billion, made Kohlberg, Kravis, and Roberts famous. It also marked the high point for buyouts until the resurgence of buyouts seen recently. Besides KKR, other top tier buyout firms include the Blackstone Group (founded by former Lehman Brothers partners in 1985), the Carlyle Group (famous for its association with former President George H.W. Bush and former British prime minister John Major), Bain Capital, and Texas Pacific (now TPG Capital). Among Blackstone's most prominent deals were its buyouts of Hilton Hotels, Equity Office Properties, and Allied Waste. Carlyle's deals have included Hertz and Dunkin Brands.

How do buyouts earn returns for their investors? There are two key elements in the success of buyouts. First, buyout funds often increase the leverage of the firms they purchase. For that reason, buyouts are often labeled leverage buyouts (or LBOs). The debt they issue is often below investment grade, so the best environment for buyout funds is a period when spreads on high-yield debt are low. The second key element of buyout success is the restructuring process itself. Buyout firms often install new management who streamline operations of the firm that is bought out. Employees often suffer in such streamlining, so buyouts are often dreaded by employees of those firms taken over.

To a limited extent, buyout funds overlap with hedge funds that invest in distressed companies. However, there is still a clear distinction between the two types of funds. Buyout funds often invest in distressed companies with the intent to gain control of the companies (and presumably turn them around). Hedge funds, in contrast, invest in these companies for short-term trading gain. The horizon must be short term because investors in hedge funds are not locked in for more than a couple of years at best. If longer lockups were adopted, the hedge funds would be morphing into private equity funds. No doubt that transformation may occur in some of the larger

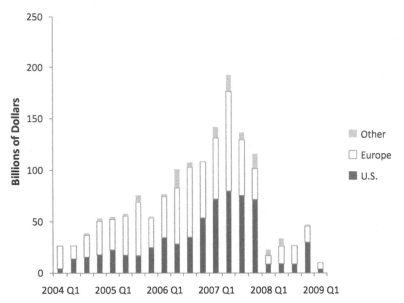

FIGURE 10.8 LBO Loan Market Size in Billions of Dollars
Data Source: Bank for International Settlements.

hedge fund companies, but it will likely be the exception rather than the rule.

The boom in buyout funds in this decade was fueled by a very favorable financing environment. Not only was this a low interest rate period, but spreads of high-yield bonds over Treasury debt fell as low as 2.5 percent. That's a far cry from the 10 percent spreads available in late 2002. Figure 10.8 shows the growth in the LBO loan market from 2004 through the first quarter of 2009. The loan market reached a peak of almost $200 billion in the second quarter of 2007 before falling as the financial crisis crippled the high-yield market.

Cambridge Associates tracks data on buyout funds and mezzanine funds in what it terms a Private Equity database. Since buyouts are 90 percent of this database, we will consider the Cambridge private equity as being primarily LBOs. Figure 10.9 tracks the number of private equity funds from 1986 through 2008. The number of funds peaks in 2000, then falls with the 2001 recession before rising again from 2004 to 2007. The number of new funds falls drastically in 2008 as the financial crisis takes hold. Figures 10.8 and 10.9 both tell the same story. The boom in buyouts reached a peak in the middle part of the decade, but then collapsed as financing came apart. The leverage in LBOs evidently makes a tremendous difference.

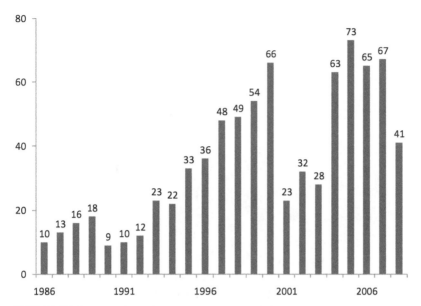

FIGURE 10.9 Number of Private Equity Funds by Vintage Year
Source: Cambridge Associates LLC.

Private equity is an international phenomena, but the United States accounts for the bulk of the cash flows. U.S. institutional investors, in particular, have embraced private equity much more than their European counterparts. Figure 10.10 presents Bank for International Settlements data on equity cash flows into private equity broken down between Europe and the United States. By private equity, the BIS means both venture capital and LBOs. Presumably the late 1990s boom included a lot of VC cash flows, while the cash flows in this decade were predominantly for LBOs.

RETURNS ON BUYOUT FUNDS

Consider now the returns on buyout funds. Cambridge Associates provides a private equity series that includes buyout funds, but also includes mezzanine funds. Buyouts, however, represent the most important component of this series. In a report on all private equity funds with vintage years from 1976 to 2004, Thompson Venture Economics shows that buyouts totaled $556 billion, while mezzanine funds totaled only $51 billion.[10] So buyouts constitute more than 90 percent of private equity (excluding venture capital). The CA series, which begins in the second quarter of 1986, covers 70 percent of

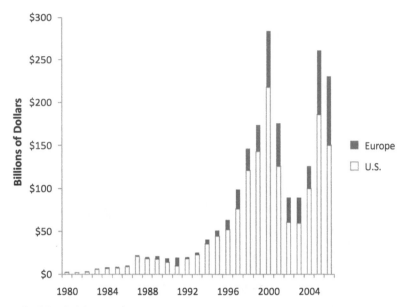

FIGURE 10.10 Private Equity Cash Flows in the United States and Europe
Data Source: Bank for International Settlements.

the total dollars raised by leveraged buyout and other private equity firms over this period.

Table 10.4 reports on private equity returns from the second quarter of 1986 when the CA series begins through the second quarter of 2009. The table also reports on the returns on the broad stock market, as represented by the S&P 500 and the Russell 3000, and returns on two small-cap indexes. The returns on private equity exceed those of the broad stock market by about 4 percent per year. It's also interesting to compare the private equity return with that of small-cap value, since presumably many of the firms targeted for buyouts are in the value space.[11] The premium of private equity over the Russell 2000 Value Index is also high at 3.7 percent.

The Cambridge Associates series for private equity has a suspiciously low standard deviation of 9.9 percent. The value of buyouts is ultimately determined by public stock market valuations (since buyout funds hope to take their buyouts public either directly or through sale to publicly traded companies). So LBO returns must be much more variable than would be suggested by this low standard deviation. We know that stale pricing biases downward the measured standard deviation, but it is surprising how little variability there is in the CA series. If the standard deviation is downward

TABLE 10.4 Returns on Private Equity Compared with U.S. Stocks, 1986 (Q2) –2009 (Q2)

	Geometric Average	Arithmetic Average	Standard Deviation	Sharpe Ratio
Private Equity	12.6%	12.5%	9.9%	0.83
S&P 500	8.5%	9.6%	16.7%	0.32
Russell 3000	8.3%	9.6%	17.1%	0.31
Russell 2000 Growth	4.8%	8.1%	25.6%	0.15
Russell 2000 Value	8.9%	10.6%	19.9%	0.32

Data Sources: Cambridge Associates LLC U.S. Private Equity Index®, S&P, and Russell®.

biased, then the Sharpe ratios reported in Table 10.4 are upwardly biased. But we do not know the magnitude of the bias.

Figure 10.11 shows the variation over time of private equity returns compared with those of the broad stock market. In the late 1980s, private equity lagged more than 3.5 percent per year behind the S&P 500. But in the late 1990s, tables were reversed as private equity earned 21.9 percent

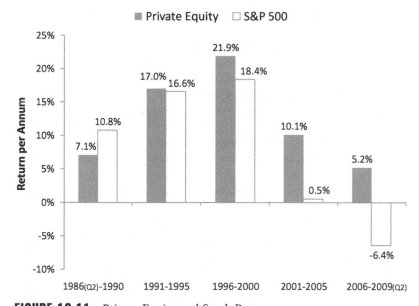

FIGURE 10.11 Private Equity and Stock Returns.
Data Sources: Cambridge Associates LLC U.S. Private Equity Index® and Standard & Poor's.

TABLE 10.5 Contribution of Venture Capital and Private Equity to a Diversified Portfolio, 1986 (Q2) –2009 (Q2)

	Geometric Average	Arithmetic Average	Standard Deviation	Sharpe Ratio
Portfolio A	8.1%	8.7%	12.6%	0.35
Portfolio B	8.7%	9.1%	11.9%	0.41

Portfolio A consists of 25 percent in the Barclays Aggregate Bond index, 50 percent in the Russell 3000 index, and 25 percent in the MSCI EAFE index. Portfolio B replaces 10 percent of the R 3000 allocation with 5 percent each in the Cambridge Associates Venture Capital and Private Equity indexes.
Data Sources: Cambridge Associates LLC U.S. Venture Capital Index® and U.S. Private Equity Index®, Barclays Capital, MSCI, and Russell®.

per annum returns. In this decade, private equity performed much better than the S&P 500. It should be noted, however, that the 2008 return of −23.3 percent (reflected in the 5.2 percent per annum return from 2006 to the second quarter of 2009) looks suspicious. How can private equity do so (relatively) well in a year when the S&P 500 was down 37 percent?[12] Perhaps private equity investors are relieved that their investments are not marked to market with current values. But surely stale pricing is evident here.

As noted above, stale pricing keeps standard deviations low. That's the key to the low beta found for the private equity series. Table 10.3 reports that the correlation between private equity and the Russell 3000 is 0.68. The standard deviation of private equity as reported in Table 10.4 is 9.9 percent compared with a standard deviation of 17.1 percent for the Russell 3000. So the beta for private equity is only 0.39.[13] That surely is an underestimate of the true beta, but it's not possible to offer a more accurate estimate.

Table 10.5 shows that both forms of private equity contribute to portfolio diversification. Portfolio A is a traditional portfolio with long-only stocks and bonds. This portfolio has 25 percent invested in the Barclays Aggregate bond index, 50 percent in the Russell 3000 stock index, and 25 percent in the MSCI EAFE index. Portfolio B replaces 10 percent of the Russell 3000 with an equal amount of private equity split evenly between the CA venture capital and private equity indexes. The results are better than for a similar experiment with hedge funds. The average portfolio return is increased by 0.4 percent, while the standard deviation is reduced by 0.7 percent. Naturally the Sharpe ratio of Portfolio B is larger, 0.41 compared with 0.35 for the traditional portfolio. That translates into an alpha* of about 0.7 percent. It should be noted that these results are affected by the stale pricing discussed above. If the true standard deviation of private equity is higher than measured and if the true correlation between private equity and public equity is also higher than measured, then the gains from diversification are correspondingly lower—how much lower is hard to determine.

KEY FEATURES OF PRIVATE EQUITY

Venture capital and buyout funds offer wealthy investors privileged access to investments that are unavailable to the general public. Presumably this privileged access brings superior returns to those institutions and families willing to put up with the illiquidity of these investments. This chapter has shown that the returns earned by these funds are on average superior to those on public equities. The measured returns are upwardly biased, but it's difficult to know the size of this bias.

Regardless of the level of average returns, they are variable over time. In the 1990s, VC funds made enormous excess returns as a booming IPO market boosted the valuations of tech firms. Since that time, returns on VC have disappointed most investors. In the meantime, buyout firms soared as credit conditions became ideal for leveraged buyouts. Now that credit conditions have tightened, buyouts will be less profitable. Investors in this space must become used to wide pendulum swings.

Both types of funds have handsome payment structures for the general partners. Evidence suggests that some of these general partners provide persistent returns for investors. If returns are persistent, then access to the superior funds is an important challenge for investors. It's probably safe to say that the investors who have been in this space for decades have preferred access over other investors.

NOTES

1. This description is based on Metrick (2007), Chapter 1.
2. Sometimes the management fee is reduced once the investment period is completed.
3. This example is from Ayako Yasuda's class notes from the Wharton MBA course on venture capital.
4. See Exhibit 1-5 of Metrick (2007) based on the 2005 National Venture Capital Association Yearbook.
5. The report is available at http://www.pwcmoneytree.com.
6. Metrick admits that the gap between the two indexes is not easily explainable.

7. The source for the data is http://www.cambridgeassociates.com. The return calculations are based on cash-on-cash returns over equal periods, modified for the residual value of the partnership's equity or portfolio company's NAV.

8. Since the Cambridge data set reports on vintages that were begun in 1981 or later, returns in the first few years of the 1980s are low probably because few of the projects begun then were mature enough to provide payoffs to the investors.

9. More specifically, the value factor is measured as the excess return of value over growth, while the small-cap factor measures the excess return of small caps over large caps.

10. See Thomas Venture Economics, 2005, *Investment Benchmarks Report: Buyouts and Other Private Equity.*

11. That characterization of private equity as targeting value stocks may not be that accurate, however, since Table 10.3 shows the correlation between private equity and small-cap value is lower than the correlation between private equity and the broad stock market.

12. The VC return for 2008 was equally suspicious at only −16.2 percent.

13. This beta can be written as the product of the correlation times the ratio of the private equity standard deviation to that of the Russell 3000, or $0.68 * (0.099/0.171) = 0.39$.

CHAPTER 11

Real Assets—Real Estate

R eal estate is probably the most widely held alternative investment. It provides equity-like returns that are relatively low in correlation with traditional equity. In his book *Unconventional Success* (2005), David Swensen of the Yale endowment recommends that ordinary investors consider real estate for as much as 20 percent of the portfolio rather than pursue the other, more exotic, types of alternatives that Yale focuses on.

By real estate, we mean investment real estate such as office buildings, shopping malls, apartment buildings, hotels, and other types of commercial real estate. Such real estate usually provides a stream of investment income based on the rents charged to tenants. There may also be capital gains when the properties are sold. So they resemble stocks in their payout structures, although real estate usually provides higher rents than the dividends offered by stocks. Residential homes are not usually considered investments, at least by investment advisors (though many home owners may disagree). When he wrote a column for the *Wall Street Journal*, Jonathan Clements would periodically devote a column to the question of whether homes constitute a good investment. His conclusion was always that the investor would be better off choosing a smaller home and investing the remainder in a conventional portfolio. The last part of this chapter will provide an analysis of residential housing that will support Clements' point of view.

The total amount invested in investment real estate can be measured by tracking the sources of capital for real estate, both debt and equity, at least the capital that can be easily measured. Figure 11.1 measures this debt and equity as of the second quarter of 2009.[1] In the second quarter of 2009, there was a total of $3.9 *trillion* invested in real estate.[2] Of that total, about three-quarters of the total represents debt, both public and private, rather than equity. That should not be surprising since real estate has always been a highly leveraged investment. The equity portfolio consists of $187.1 billion in public equity (mostly traded REITS) and $678.2 billion in private equity (including investments by institutional investors like pension funds).

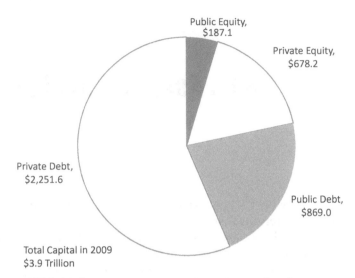

FIGURE 11.1   Real Estate Capital in Billions of Dollars, 2009
Source: Emerging Trends in Real Estate (2010).

Figure 11.2 provides a more detailed picture of real estate equity. REITS constitute 19.3 percent of equity with another 2.3 percent in untraded public equity funds (including non-traded REITS). Institutional investors such as pension plans and insurance companies account for another 18 percent, while foreign investors account for 5.3 percent of total equity. But the largest category of investor is private investors which consists of real estate partnerships (including those held by high net worth individuals), hedge funds, and other private real estate funds.

There is much better information available about the REIT sector than about the larger private sector of real estate. So this chapter will begin with an analysis of REITS.

In the following section, returns on real estate held by institutional investors will be compared with returns on REITS. In the final section, residential housing will be analyzed as an investment.

REAL ESTATE INVESTMENT TRUSTS

Real estate investment trusts, or REITS, were developed in the early 1970s as a liquid alternative to direct ownership of real estate. REITS own, and in most cases operate, income-producing real estate such as apartments, shopping centers, offices, hotels, and warehouses. REITS are corporations

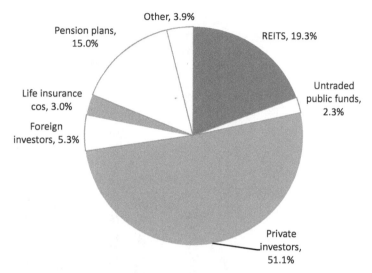

FIGURE 11.2 REITS and Other Sources of Equity Real Estate Capital in U.S., 2009
Source: Emerging Trends in Real Estate (2010).

that invest in real estate but are set up to pay little or no corporate income tax.[3] To qualify for tax exemption, the REITS must distribute 90 percent of their income each year to investors. REITS may be publicly or privately held just like other corporations. Publicly traded REITS typically trade on stock exchanges such as the NYSE and NASDAQ.

Prior to the 1990s, the total capitalization of the REIT sector was less than $10 billion. But in the early 1990s, long-established real estate operating companies began to package properties they owned into REITS. This led to an IPO boom that sharply increased the REIT sector. Figure 11.3 tracks the growth of the REIT market from 1972 to 2009 using data from the National Association of Real Estate Investment Trusts (NAREIT).[4] In 1992, REITS totaled only $11.2 billion, but that total rose to $78.3 billion four years later and to $400.7 billion in 2006.

Since REITS are stocks, it's also interesting to compare them with the stock market itself. As of 2004, REITS represented about 2 percent of the equity universe as measured by the Wilshire 5000 index.[5] Since individual REITS are usually relatively small in capitalization, they fall mostly in the small-cap and mid-cap sectors of the market. REITS make up about 7 percent of the Russell 2000 small-cap index. Most are also classified as value stocks. Indeed, REITS represent more than 12 percent of the Russell 2000 Value Index and more than 9 percent of the Russell Mid-Cap Value Index.[6]

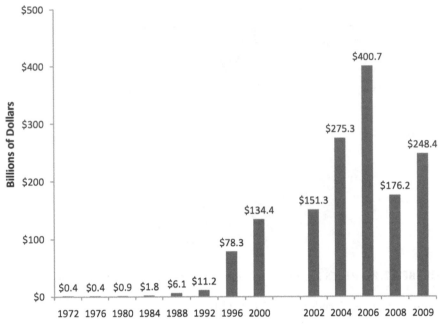

FIGURE 11.3 Growth of REIT Market, 1972–2009
Source: NAREIT.

Since the early 1970s, NAREIT has maintained indexes of REIT returns that are widely used in the investments industry. NAREIT has an index for mortgages, but this chapter will focus only on the equity REIT index. The REITS included in the index must have at least $100 million in capitalization and must have a minimum amount of turnover.[7] Figure 11.4 gives the breakdown of properties included in the equity NAREIT index in 2010. The largest sector is retail with 12.1 percent in regional malls, 10.4 percent in shopping centers, and the rest in free-standing retail real estate. The residential component representing 14.8 percent of the index consists largely of apartment buildings. Healthcare complexes and office buildings are the next two largest categories. Thus there are a variety of different types of property included in the index.

NAREIT provides monthly returns starting in 1972. Because the REIT market was so small until the early 1990s, we will present REIT returns over two periods, from the start of the series in 1972 and from 1992 on. Table 11.1 compares REIT returns with large-cap and small-cap stocks. For the period from 1972 to 2009, small caps are represented by the SBBI Small Cap Index. For the shorter period, small caps are represented by the

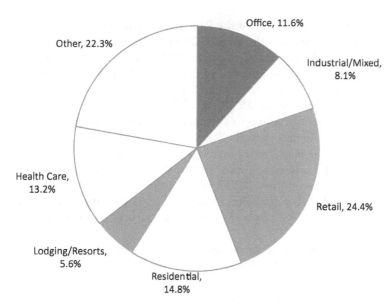

FIGURE 11.4 Property Sectors in Equity REIT Index
Source: NAREIT.

TABLE 11.1 NAREIT and Stock Returns Compared

	Geometric Average	Arithmetic Average	Standard Deviation	Sharpe Ratio
1972–2009				
FTSE NAREIT	11.6%	12.6%	17.2%	0.41
S&P 500	9.9%	10.7%	15.6%	0.33
SBBI Small-Cap	12.9%	14.6%	21.6%	0.42
1992–2009				
FTSE NAREIT	10.2%	11.8%	20.0%	0.42
S&P 500	7.8%	8.6%	14.8%	0.35
Russell 2000	8.3%	9.9%	19.2%	0.34
Russell 2000 Value	10.9%	11.8%	16.7%	0.50

For 1992 to 2009, the Russell 2000 index replaces the SBBI Small-Cap index and the Russell 2000 Value index is also included.
Data Sources: ©FTSE, ©Morningstar, Standard & Poor's, and Russell®.

Russell 2000 Index. Since so many of the REITS are small-cap value stocks, the table also reports returns on the Russell 2000 Value index.

In both time periods, REIT returns exceed those on the S&P 500, by 1.7 percent in the longer period and by 2.4 percent in the period beginning in 1992. REIT returns are a little more than 1 percent lower than small-cap returns for the period starting in 1972, and REIT returns are a little less than 1 percent lower than small-cap value stocks for the period starting in 1992 although they are higher than the Russell 2000 series as a whole. The standard deviation of the REIT series is smaller than that of the SBBI small-cap series, so the Sharpe ratios are almost identical for the longer period. It's only in comparison with the Russell 2000 value series in 1992 to 2009 that the Sharpe ratio for REITS falls behind that of any of the equity indexes. So it's safe to say that REITs provide equity-like returns with attractive risk-adjusted statistics.

Figure 11.5 traces the time series for REITS and the S&P 500 from December 1991 through 2009. Notice that in the late 1990s, stocks fueled by the tech boom surged ahead of real estate. At the end of 1999, there was relatively little excitement about real estate. Tech was the

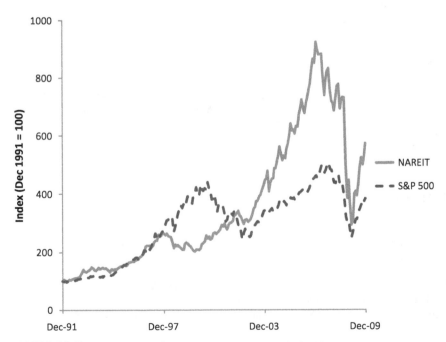

FIGURE 11.5   NAREIT and S&P 500 Returns, 1992–2009
Data Sources: ©FTSE and Standard & Poor's.

TABLE 11.2 Correlations between the NAREIT Index and Stocks

	NAREIT	S&P 500	Small caps
1972–2009			
FTSE NAREIT	1.00		
S&P 500	0.56	1.00	
SBBI Small-Cap	0.63	0.75	1.00
1992–2009			
FTSE NAREIT	1.00		
S&P 500	0.51	1.00	
Russell 2000	0.62	0.77	1.00
Russell 2000 Value	0.76	0.75	0.93

For 1992 to 2009, the Russell 2000 index replaces the SBBI Small-Cap index.
Data Sources: ©FTSE, ©Morningstar, Standard & Poor's, and Russell®.

center of attention and investors were enamored with stocks. Then with the collapse of the tech boom, attention turned to real estate. And how it soared! In the three years from 2000 through 2002, the NAREIT returns rose by 49.5 percent while S&P 500 returns dropped 37.6 percent. Investors who were diversified into real estate celebrated their wise decision. In the 2007 and 2008 crisis, of course, both assets declined sharply. In the two years from 2007 to 2008, the NAREIT return dropped 47.5 percent while the S&P 500 return dropped only 33.5 percent. Figure 11.5 traces the rise and fall of both indexes. Table 11.1 nonetheless shows that over the whole period from 1992 on, the NAREIT investment outperformed the S&P 500.

Tables 11.2 and 11.3 look more formally at the diversification gains from investing in REITS. Table 11.2 reports correlations between REITS on the one hand, and various stock indexes on the other hand. The correlations between REITS and the S&P 500 are relatively low, at 0.56 over 1972 to 2009 and 0.51 over 1992 to 2009. Notice that these correlations are lower than those between the S&P and small-cap stocks.

Table 11.3 looks more formally at the diversification gains by examining portfolios without REITS and those with a 10 percent allocation to REITS. The base portfolios consist of 25 percent invested in bonds, 50 percent in U.S. stocks, and 25 percent in foreign stocks (in the MSCI EAFE Index). For the period beginning in 1972, U.S. stocks are split 45 percent in the S&P 500 and 5 percent in the SBBI Small-Cap Index,[8] while U.S. bonds are long-term Treasuries. For the period beginning in 1992, U.S. stocks are represented by the Russell 3000 all-cap index and U.S. bonds by the Barclays Capital Aggregate Bond Index.

TABLE 11.3 Role of REITS in a Diversified Portfolio

	Geometric Average	Arithmetic Average	Standard Deviation	Sharpe Ratio
Portfolio A: 1972–2009				
Without REITS	10.3%	10.6%	11.8%	0.42
10% REITS	10.6%	10.7%	11.5%	0.45
Portfolio B: 1992–2009				
Without REITS	7.3%	7.7%	11.1%	0.38
10% REITS	7.7%	8.0%	11.0%	0.42

Portfolio A (for 1972 to 2009) consists of 25 percent in long-term Treasuries, 45 percent in the S&P 500, 5 percent in the SBBI Small-Cap index, and 25 percent in EAFE. When a 10 percent REIT position is added, the S&P is reduced by 10 percent.
Portfolio B (for 1992 to 2009) consists of 25 percent in the Barclays Aggregate, 50 percent in the Russell 3000, and 25 percent in EAFE. When a 10 percent REIT position is added, the Russell 3000 position is reduced by 10 percent.
Data Sources: ©FTSE, ©Morningstar, Standard & Poor's, Barclays Capital, Russell®, and MSCI.

The results in Table 11.3 show gains from diversification in both periods. In the longer period, including REITS in the portfolio increases returns by a modest amount (0.3 percent) and lowers standard deviations by 0.3 percent. So the Sharpe ratio rises from 0.42 to 0.45. In the period beginning in 1992, returns rise by 0.4 percent when REITS are added, while the standard deviation of the portfolio falls by 0.1 percent. The Sharpe ratio rises from 0.38 to 0.42 which is equivalent to a rise in return of 0.4 percent at the risk level of the more diversified portfolio.

On the basis of this evidence, the natural conclusion is that portfolios should include REITS along with stocks and bonds. Returns have generally been as high as those on equities, and risks (measured by standard deviations) have been lower. More importantly, REITS are low enough in correlation with stocks to provide diversification benefits. Portfolios that include REITS have higher risk-adjusted returns. No wonder David Svensen suggested that real estate should be the alternative investment in ordinary investors' portfolios.

DIRECT OWNERSHIP OF REAL ESTATE

Having examined returns from investing in REIT stocks, it's natural to ask about returns from direct ownership of real estate. In theory, direct ownership should provide higher returns than indirect ownership through REITS. That's because REITS provide much greater liquidity to the investor, so presumably a lower return is required. The returns from direct ownership, however, are more difficult to assess than REIT returns since there is no day-to-day market valuation for the real estate holdings. The income from properties can be tracked by the investor, but changes in the values of these properties depend on appraisals unless the property is sold in that particular time period. The same problems arise in measuring returns on private equity investments (as discussed in the chapter on private equity).

Since the early 1980s, the National Council of Real Estate Investment Fiduciaries (NCREIF) has collected return data on real estate owned by institutional investors (the great majority of which are pension funds).[9] The data are reported to NCREIF by the investors themselves or by institutional real estate investment managers. In 2004, there were 4,152 properties in the index with a total market value of $145 billion.[10] The properties range from apartments and hotels to industrial properties, office buildings, and retail shop structures.

The NCREIF returns are reported quarterly with data beginning in 1978. The returns consist of two elements, net operating income (gross rental income less operating expenses) and the capital gain on the property.[11] The capital gain measure is based on periodic appraisals using standard commercial real estate appraisal methodology. All of the investment returns are reported on a *non-leveraged* basis so as to make them comparable. While there are many properties in the index that have leverage, returns are reported as if there were no leverage.

Gyourko and Keim (1993) discuss the problems that arise in using appraisal-based returns on real estate. First, the smoothing inherent in the appraisal process results in an understated variation in the series. This first characteristic ensures that the standard deviations are far lower than those found for REITs. Second, the infrequency of appraisals results in the index lagging changes in actual real estate values. Gyourko and Keim show that there is correlation between the NAREIT and NCREIF series, but that it is lagged changes in the REIT index that are correlated with the appraisal-based series. Consider the recent period of falling real estate (and stock market) values. From December 2007 through March 2009, the NAREIT total return index fell 57.6 percent while the S&P 500 index fell 43.9 percent. But the NACREIF index was down only 13.3 percent. This is strong evidence that the valuations on which this series is based are stale —being based on past appraisals.

With these limitations in mind, consider Table 11.4 which compares the returns on the NCREIF index with those on the NAREIT index where the latter has been calculated on a quarterly basis.[12] As in earlier tables,

TABLE 11.4 NCREIF and NAREIT Returns Compared, 1978–2009

Indexes	Geometric Average	Arithmetic Average	Standard Deviation	Sharpe Ratio
NCREIF	8.8%	8.6%	4.6%	0.66
FTSE NAREIT	12.4%	13.6%	18.3%	0.44
S&P 500	11.3%	12.2%	16.3%	0.40

Before annualizing the returns, the arithmetic average for the NCREIF index is below the geometric average.
Data Sources: ©FTSE, NCREIF, and S&P.

the real estate returns are also compared with stock returns. The results are quite striking. The returns on the NCREIF index are 3.6 percent below those of the NAREIT index. What's more, the sluggishness of the NCREIF series has helped keep returns up in the crisis. If the period were shortened to end in December 2006 rather than December 2009, there is a 5 percent gap between the two indexes. The main reason for this gap is differences in leverage. The NCREIF index is based on *unleveraged* returns, while REITS typically employ substantial leverage. Peyton et al. (2005) cites an estimate by Green Street Advisors, a REIT research organization, that REITS average about 50 percent leverage. That could easily explain the difference in returns as shown in Table 11.4. Institutional investors are well aware of these differences. Because they still view direct holdings as superior to indirect investments through REITS, they typically allocate more of their real estate investments to direct holdings. The same study by Peyton et al cites data from Pensions & Investments and NACUBO indicating that more than 75 percent of real estate investments are direct holdings.

Table 11.4 also presents standard deviations and Sharpe ratios for these two types of real estate investments. The standard deviation of 4.6 percent for the NCREIF index is not to be taken at face value because of the smoothing properties of the appraisal system. For the same reason, the Sharpe ratio for direct holdings of real estate is upwardly biased. These statistics are presented in the table as an indication of the biases inherent in appraisal-based returns.

What conclusions can be drawn from this evidence? The main lesson has to do with the source of REIT returns. The real estate holdings themselves probably do not generate 15 percent-plus returns. It's leverage that raises the returns to these levels. That's important to keep in mind in evaluating the role of real estate within the portfolio. Of course, corporations also employ leverage, and so stock returns benefit from this leverage. It's just in comparisons between the NCREIF Index and the NAREIT Index that leverage has to be taken into account.

HOME OWNERSHIP

For many families in the United States, their home is their largest financial asset. In many cases, home ownership is leveraged with mortgage debt with the latter typically representing the largest financial liability of the family. But even taking into account mortgage debt, home ownership represents a substantial portion of net wealth for many families. So it's important to study returns on homes as part of a larger study of investment returns.

Many families believe that home ownership provides some of the highest returns that they earn in their lifetimes. One of the reasons for this belief is that families often suffer from money illusion. If your house doubles in value over time, that may or may not be a good return on investment. It all depends on how much the cost of living has risen over the same period. Too often families view the nominal appreciation of their homes as the return on their investment.

This chapter will examine the real returns on housing since the 1970s. The primary source of data will be price indexes maintained by the oversight agency for Fannie Mae and Freddie Mac, the Federal Housing Finance Agency (FHFA). The predecessor to FHFA, the Office of Federal Housing Enterprise Oversight (OFHEO), developed these indexes in the early 1990s using series that Fannie Mae and Freddie Mac had developed earlier.[13] Many of the housing series extend back to the mid-1970s. The indexes use a repeat-sales methodology developed by Case and Shiller (1989) that relies on observing sales prices of the same homes over time. The use of repeat transactions for the same house helps to control for differences in the quality or location of houses comprising the sample for any particular area.

The FHFA indexes use data for single-family detached properties that have been financed by mortgages processed by either Fannie Mae or Freddie Mac. These agencies limit their activities to moderate size conforming mortgages (up to $417,000 in 2009).[14] So the indexes underweight more expensive homes that require jumbo mortgages. This is a particularly important limitation for areas of the country, like California, where house prices are way above national levels with the result that many houses require jumbo mortgages. In addition, FHFA indexes underweight sub-prime and other lower-rated mortgages. For this reason, we will later consider another set of indexes developed by Case and Shiller. FHFA provides indexes for the country as a whole, all states, as well as most metropolitan areas. Table 11.5 presents real house appreciation for the United States as a whole

TABLE 11.5 Real House Appreciation in United States and Six Largest States

	1975 Q2–2009 Q4		2000 Q1–2009 Q4	
	Geometric Average	Cumulative Return	Geometric Average	Cumulative Return
United States	0.9%	35.9%	1.6%	17.7%
California	2.6%	146.7%	2.9%	33.6%
Texas	−0.1%	−2.0%	1.1%	11.6%
NY State	1.7%	79.0%	3.2%	37.5%
Florida	0.4%	14.8%	2.3%	25.1%
Illinois	0.5%	19.3%	0.9%	9.2%
Pennsylvania	0.7%	27.9%	2.4%	27.0%

The real rates of appreciation are calculated using the consumer price index. Housing data are from the FHFA. CPI data are from the IMF, *International Financial Statistics*.

as well as for the six largest states by population. Two periods are studied, from the second quarter of 1975 (when the series began) through the end of 2009, roughly 35 years, and the last 10 years starting in 2000. The U.S. housing market provided a real appreciation of 0.9 percent per year beginning in 1975 and 1.6 percent per year over the last 10 years. That national average hides tremendous variation across the country. California benefited from a 2.6 percent per year appreciation since 1975. The cumulative rise in California prices over 34 years is 146.7 percent. In contrast, Texas saw a slight drop in house prices (in real terms) since 1975 and a disappointing 1.1 percent appreciation over the last 10 years. Clearly, location matters.

It's interesting to examine real house appreciation by metropolitan areas as well. Table 11.6 shows the real house appreciation in the 12 largest metropolitan areas of the country.[15] Most of the metropolitan area data begins later than the state data, so the table reports returns beginning in the first quarter of 1978. New York City, Boston, and San Francisco provide the largest appreciations over the full period, while New York City, Los Angeles, and Washington lead in the 10 years ending in 2009. Dallas and Houston experienced *negative* real appreciation over the longer period. And Detroit prices have fallen 30.2 percent in real terms over the last 10 years. Consider how much location matters. Over the last 32 years, residents of New York City have seen their homes appreciate in real terms by more than 163.5 percent, while residents of Philadelphia have had to be content with a real appreciation of 56.7 percent and residents of Houston lost ground to inflation.

TABLE 11.6 Real House Appreciation in 12 Largest Cities

	1978 Q1–2009 Q4		2000 Q1–2009 Q4	
	Geometric Average	Cumulative Return	Geometric Average	Cumulative Return
New York	3.1%	163.5%	4.5%	55.8%
Los Angeles	2.1%	93.6%	4.4%	54.1%
Chicago	0.5%	17.8%	1.4%	14.4%
Dallas	−0.2%	−6.8%	0.6%	6.3%
Philadelphia	1.4%	56.7%	3.6%	41.8%
Houston	−0.7%	−21.4%	2.1%	22.5%
Miami	1.1%	42.4%	3.2%	36.6%
Washington	1.6%	68.3%	4.4%	53.4%
Atlanta	0.2%	6.3%	0.1%	0.8%
Detroit	−0.4%	−12.7%	−3.5%	−30.2%
Boston	3.1%	163.8%	3.5%	40.4%
San Francisco	2.8%	145.2%	3.9%	46.9%

Cities are ranked by size of metropolitan statistical areas. Housing data are from the FHFA.
CPI data are from the IMF, International Financial Statistics.

Why are the rates of house appreciation so varied? An interesting paper by Gyourko, Mayer, and Sinai (2006) entitled *Superstar Cities* focuses on two key factors. For house prices to rise rapidly, there must be substantial growth of population in the area, and that requires substantial job growth. But that alone is not enough, since a city like Atlanta has surely seen a lot of growth. In addition, a city (or, more accurately, metropolitan area) must impose limits on land use. Los Angeles and San Francisco certainly qualify in this regard. Scarce land combined with rapid growth lead to the bidding up of land prices.

Figure 11.6 shows the rise in house prices in California and its two largest cities since 1978. At the peak of the housing boom, the cumulative real appreciation of prices was almost 200 percent even for the state as a whole. It's interesting to note that the ascent of prices was interrupted by a substantial decline in the early 1990s. The housing boom of the late 1980s was followed by a prolonged slump with real housing prices reaching bottom in 1996 or later, nearly seven years after the peak. A less dramatic slump in prices occurred in the New York City metropolitan area. The New York City series peaked in June 1988 and reached bottom (in real terms) only in March 1997.

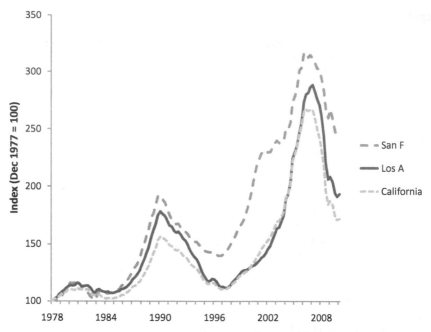

FIGURE 11.6   Real House Appreciation in California, 1978–2009
Data Source: Federal Housing Finance Agency.

As discussed above, the FHFA house price indexes are restricted to houses financed with conforming mortgages that are guaranteed by Fannie Mae or Freddie Mac, so more expensive houses are underrepresented in the indexes. Karl Case and Robert Shiller, two academic economists, developed alternative house price indexes for 20 metropolitan areas based on county records of sale transactions.[16] So these indexes include houses at all price levels, including those with sub-prime mortgages and jumbo loans. The indexes use the repeat sales technique that Case and Shiller developed, but they put more restrictions on the indexes than does FHFA. Unlike FHFA, Case and Shiller do not use appraisal values for houses (if they are refinanced). And they exclude any sales pairs that are six months or less apart (since these could be non-arms length transactions). Another difference between the two sets of indexes is that Case and Shiller use value weighting, whereas FHFA uses equal weights for its indexes.[17] The Case-Shiller indexes only begin in 1987, and no indexes are available for Philadelphia and Houston, two of the largest six cities in the United States.

Figure 11.7 compares the FHFA and Case-Shiller indexes for those cities in Table 11.6 that have Case-Shiller data beginning in 1987. In the case of all

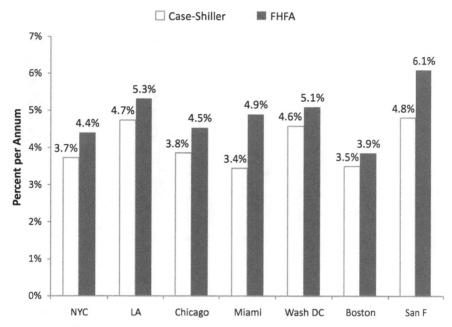

FIGURE 11.7 Nominal Rates of House Appreciation from 1987 to 2009,
Case-Shiller and FHFA Indexes
Data Sources: FHFA and S&P Case-Shiller.

seven cities examined, the nominal appreciation for the FHFA index exceeds
that of the Case-Shiller index. In the case of Los Angeles, the average rate
of appreciation is 4.7 percent for the Case-Shiller index, but it is 0.6 percent
faster for the government series. The gap between the two indexes is largely
due to price changes since the housing crisis began. If rates of appreciation
are compared over the period from 1987 to 2006 (prior to the crisis), they
are much more similar.[18]

Figure 11.8 shows the cumulative fall in prices over the 36 months
starting in January 2007. In the case of Los Angeles, for example, the
Case-Shiller index fell 36.5 percent over this period, while the FHFA index falls only 28.2 percent. The gap is even larger for San Francisco. What
accounts for this gap? One reason seems to be that jumbo and sub-prime
loans are underrepresented in the government series. Those are two types
of loans that have been most affected by the crisis. In addition, mortgage rates charged outside of the Fannie Mae/Freddie Mac umbrella have
risen a lot above those offered by the two agencies. Whatever the reason, it's clear that the FHFA indexes provide an upper bound for price
appreciation. So using the FHFA indexes will shed the best possible light

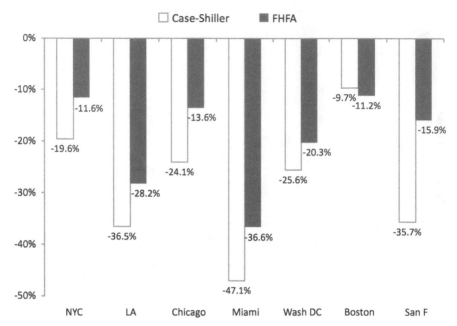

FIGURE 11.8 Nominal Rates of House Appreciation in 2007–2009, Case-Shiller and FHFA Indexes
Data Sources: FHFA and S&P Case-Shiller.

on housing *as an investment*. If housing is a poor investment when measured with FHFA data, it surely will be even worse when measured with Case-Shiller data.

Real rates of appreciation do not represent *rates of return* on housing, so they cannot be directly compared with stock returns or the returns on other assets. First of all, rates of appreciation do not take into account the leverage provided by mortgage financing. Secondly, the rates of appreciation do not take into account either the benefits of living in a house or the expenses of maintaining it. Returns on stocks and REITS, in contrast, take into account leverage as well as the dividends paid to investors.

To take into account leverage, consider a simple model of the return on housing. The return should depend on the capital gain on the house less the cost of mortgage financing. There is also the benefit of living in the house as well as the tax shelter provided by the favorable treatment of property taxes and mortgage interest in the tax code. But let's assume that those benefits are offset by the property taxes, maintenance expenses, and other expenses of living in the house.[19] In that case, the return on the house would depend only on the capital gain less the cost of the mortgage. If *h* is the percent of the purchase price of the house that is financed, then the return on the house measured in dollars is given by:

$$\text{Return} = P * [\text{capital gain} - h * \text{mortgage cost}],$$

where P is the price of the house at purchase. We are interested in the rate of return on the equity invested in the house. The equity is equal to P * (1 − h), so the rate of return is:

$$\text{Rate of return} = \text{capital gain}/(1 - h) - \text{mortgage cost} * [h/(1 - h)]$$

To see how the rate of return is affected by leverage, consider a house that is financed with a 75 percent mortgage and a 6 percent mortgage cost. If the house appreciates at 6 percent per year, the owner makes a 6 percent rate of return, but if the appreciation is 12 percent per year, the rate of return rises to 30 percent per year. That is,

$$\text{Rate of return} = 12\%/(1 - 0.75) - 6\% * [0.75/(1 - 0.75)] = 30\%$$

If the rate of appreciation is only 9 percent, the rate of return is still 18 percent per year. So leverage is terrific—at least on the way up.

To assess the effects of leverage on the rate of return on housing, let's consider the returns on U.S. housing based on historical mortgage rates. The Federal Housing Finance Agency publishes data on the cost of conventional single family house mortgages and on the loan to price ratios of those mortgages.[20] These data are used together with FHFA data on house prices to estimate rates of return which are then deflated by consumer price inflation to obtain real rates of return. The average loan to price ratio is 75.9 percent over the full sample period, so a leverage ratio of 75 percent is assumed.[21]

Table 11.7 presents the rates of return for the U.S. housing market as a whole as well as for the California market. The table reports the nominal rate of appreciation, the average mortgage cost, and the real rate of return based on a 75 percent leverage ratio. Four periods are studied:

1. A period beginning in 1975 (second quarter) through the last quarter of 2006 (i.e., ending before the housing bust)
2. A period beginning in 1975 but ending in the last quarter of 2009
3. The 10 years ending in 2006, *a boom period* for housing, and
4. Ten years following the peak of house prices in 1989, *a bust period* for housing

TABLE 11.7   Real Returns on Housing in United States and California

	1975*–2006	1975*–2009	Boom Years 1997–2006	Bust Years 1990–1999
Nominal House Appreciation				
United States	6.0%	5.2%	6.9%	3.1%
California	8.9%	7.0%	12.1%	1.0%
Mortgage Costs	9.5%	9.2%	7.0%	8.3%
Real Rate of Return				
United States	−8.7%	−10.8%	3.9%	−15.0%
California	2.6%	−3.8%	24.2%	−23.1%

Rates of return based on 75 percent mortgage. * 1975 data begin in second quarter. *Data Sources:* FHFA and Federal Housing Board. Inflation rates from IMF, *International Financial Statistics.*

Naturally housing will look attractive in a boom period like 1999 to 2006. But will it be a good investment in the long run?

Consider first the two long-run periods starting in 1975. During the 32-year period ending in 2006, U.S. housing had a *negative* 8.7 percent per annum real return while California real estate earned a *positive* 2.6 percent per annum. When three more years are added to this sample period, so that the period from 1975 to 2009 is examined, even California housing has a negative real return.

Table 11.8 compares these real returns with those on the S&P 500 stock index and the FTSE NAREIT index over these same two periods. In the period ending in 2006 before the bust begins, the positive real rate of

TABLE 11.8   Real Returns on Housing and Other Assets

	1975*–2006	1975*–2009	Boom Years 1997–2006	Bust Years 1990–1999
Housing				
United States	−8.7%	−10.8%	3.9%	−15.0%
California	2.6%	−3.8%	24.2%	−23.1%
REITS	11.2%	8.7%	11.7%	6.0%
S&P 500	8.2%	6.7%	5.8%	14.8%

*1975 data begin in second quarter.
Data Sources: Table 11.7 for housing rates of return. ©FTSE and S&P for other asset returns.

return on housing in California of 2.6 percent is totally swamped by the 11.2 percent real return on REITS and 8.2 percent real return on stocks. If the period ends in 2009 instead, all assets perform worse. But real return on housing in California is now negative at −3.8 percent and the real return for the United States as a whole is an astounding large -10.8 percent per year. This is over a period when REITS are earning 8.7 percent in real terms and stocks are earning 6.7 percent. So it's clear that Jonathan Clements knew what he was talking about when he described housing as a poor investment.

What if we look only at the boom period for housing, the 10 years ending in 2006. Guess what? If you leverage any asset during a period when it is going to boom, you will become rich! The real return on California housing is 24.2 percent per year during this period. Of course, not all of us can be lucky enough to live in California. If we invested during the boom period in the United States as a whole, we would earn a 3.9 percent real return per year. That is easily swamped by the returns on REITs and stocks. So even during the boom period, you had to live in California (or some other high flying state) to beat conventional assets.

What if you lever up in a bust period? That's a very relevant question writing in 2010 as housing remains severely depressed. Borrowing 75 percent of the purchase price leads to a 15.0 percent loss per year in the United States as a whole. And if you are lucky enough to live in California, you can build up losses of 23.1 percent per year. So much for the belief that the home is a safe long-run asset.

There is a surprising gap between perception and reality when it comes to investment in home ownership. No doubt part of the reason for this gap is that home prices are not marked to market. But it's also because home owners do not primarily regard their home as being an investment. It's a place to live. It's only after periods of appreciation of home prices that many individuals begin to regard their home as an investment. And they come to believe that the home provides higher, and more stable, returns than risky investments. So it's important to consider the strong evidence to the contrary

CONCLUDING REMARKS

There is a huge contrast between the returns on investable real estate and homes. Since their introduction in the early 1970s, REITS have delivered returns somewhat higher than those on the S&P 500 with a higher Sharpe ratio. The relative returns on REITS and stocks have varied over time, but the long-run performance of REITS has been impressive. Direct ownership of real estate has delivered lower returns than REITS, but that's only because the series used to describe returns on institutional ownership of real estate has been de-leveraged. Both sets of returns show that real estate is an attractive means to diversify an investment portfolio.

Home ownership is another story. The returns on home ownership are disappointing in most periods compared with investment in REITS or stocks. It's true that with high leverage, home ownership can deliver spectacular returns when house prices are rising (as they did in the 10 years through 2006). But that same leverage can lead to spectacular losses when home prices fall. Fortunately, when house prices fall, investors do not mark their homes to market (unless they are in the unfortunate position of having to sell). So they can ignore price trends knowing that there is no investment statement coming in the mail to jolt them back to reality. They simply sit in their houses waiting for the next boom to occur.

NOTES

1. Figure 11.1 does not capture most smaller holdings of real estate unless they are bundled into REITS or other easily measurable funds.
2. These figures are from Emerging Trends in Real Estate, 2010, an annual report produced by the Urban Land Institute and PricewaterhouseCoopers.
3. REITS must receive at least 75 percent of their gross income from real estate rents, mortgage interest, or other qualifying income and must invest at least 75 percent of assets in rental real estate, real estate mortgages, or other qualifying real estate.
4. See Historical REIT Industry Market Capitalization on www.nareit.com/library.
5. This estimate was provided by Swankoski (2005).
6. These figures are based on end-2004 capitalization as reported in Swankoski (2005).
7. The requirements are described in NAREIT and FTSE (2006). Recently, the index was renamed the FTSE NAREIT index.
8. Small caps are roughly 10 percent of the capitalization of the U.S. market. In 2009, for example, the Russell 2000 index represented 8 percent of the Russell 3000 index.
9. The pension consultant Frank Russell Company initiated efforts to develop the data set in the late 1970s.
10. NCREIF (2005).
11. The NCREIF series that is analyzed is the total return series, NPI index.
12. The monthly returns for the NAREIT index were compounded into quarterly returns for comparison with the NCREIF index.
13. The FHFA was established by legislation signed into law in July 2008. It merged two agencies, the Office of Federal Housing Enterprise Oversight and the Federal Housing Finance Board.

14. There is a higher limit of $729,750 established for higher cost areas by the Economic Stimulus Bill of 2008.
15. Metropolitan areas in some cases are substantially larger than the cities they contain. Dallas, for example, is the fourth largest metropolitan area (because it includes Fort Worth and surrounding areas), but it is the eighth largest city.
16. There are 22 Case-Shiller indexes including 20 metropolitan indexes and two composite indexes (for 10 metro areas and for 20 metro areas). These indexes have since been adopted by Standard & Poors (so they are now called the S&P/Case-Shiller® Home Price Indexes) and now form the basis of several exchange-traded products.
17. OFHEO (2008) analyzes the differences between the two indexes. The biggest differences the study cites are that OFHEO (and now FHFA) includes appraisals rather than just sale prices, does not adjust as much for long-gaps in sale prices, and includes only Fannie Mae/Freddie Mac transactions.
18. For Los Angeles, for example, the gap is only 0.1 percent.
19. A formal model of housing returns is presented in Himmelberg et al (2005). They estimate that property taxes and maintenance together add up to 4 percent of the value of the house.
20. Table 17 from www.fhfb.gov.
21. For simplicity, the leverage is kept constant over time even though homeowners normally reduce their leverage as they pay back the principal on the loan.

CHAPTER 12

Real Assets—Commodities

Precious commodities, especially gold and silver, have been cherished by investors through the ages. In wars or revolutions, these assets were portable and could be hidden so they afforded protection against seizure. And even in peacetime, these real assets protected against the corrosive effects of inflation. In this relatively stable historical period, investments in commodities ought to be evaluated in terms of returns and risks rather than any other characteristics. Gold is suitable for earrings and necklaces, but is it suitable as an investment? This chapter will focus on commodities as an asset class.

There are four distinct ways to invest in commodities:

1. Direct ownership of the commodity
2. Investing in the stocks of commodity-producing companies
3. Passive investment in commodity futures
4. Active investment in commodity futures through managed futures funds

Direct ownership of the commodity has sufficient drawbacks that few investors will elect this option. The carrying costs of direct ownership are high since there is no dividend to offset the financing of the position. There are also storage costs, including insurance, that further detract from any potential return.

Investing in the stocks of firms that produce commodities appears to be more promising. The basic drawback is that these stocks do not provide a pure play on the commodity itself. Consider an extreme example: For many years, Barrick Gold of Canada followed a hedging policy that attempted to remove the gold play from its stock.[1] Barrick wanted to be evaluated not as a gold resource, but as a management company capable of finding new reserves of gold and managing the extraction of current reserves. So it hedged its current gold reserves as soon as they were discovered. If this hedge were complete, there should be little correlation between gold prices and the price of Barrick's stock.

Most commodity producers adopt less extensive hedging policies. But their stocks are subject to many influences in addition to changes in commodity prices. Consider a study by Gorton and Rouwenhorst (2006) of the stocks of commodity firms over the period from 1962 to 2003. Gorton and Rouwenhorst compared passive investment in commodity future contracts with the stocks of commodity firms producing the same commodities. They found that the correlation between the two investments was only 0.40. At the same time, the correlation between the stocks of these firms and the S&P 500 was 0.57. So the stocks of the commodity producers were more highly correlated with stocks than the commodities that they produced.

Commodity futures provide a pure play on commodity investment. But passive investment is very different from active investment. Passive investment involves buying a futures contract at the beginning of the period, then closing the position automatically at the end of the period. Active investment involves deciding whether to buy or sell the futures contract or simply staying out of the futures market this period. Many managed futures funds also take positions in currencies in addition to commodities. As a result, the returns on managed futures are low in correlation with those of passively managed futures (as will be seen below). They are quite distinct investments. In a sense, managed futures are a form of hedge fund. You are investing in the manager's expertise. That expertise will guide the manager on when to be long or short in the commodity, whether to overweight one commodity relative to another, or whether to take positions more aggressively in currencies rather than commodities. Passive investments in commodity futures represent a much purer play on the commodities themselves. For this reason, most of the chapter will be devoted to passive investment.

SOURCES OF RETURN ON COMMODITY FUTURES

Before considering actual returns on commodity contracts, it's important to understand the sources of return on commodity futures. There are two main sources of return, risk premiums and forecast errors.

John Maynard Keynes wrote extensively about futures contracts in his *Treatise on Money* (1930). Keynes was an active investor himself both for his own account and that of King's College, Cambridge. In analyzing futures, Keynes focused on factors that might make the current futures price different from the expected spot price at the end of the futures contract. He argued that there was a systematic tendency for the *futures price to be lower than the expected future spot price*. Hedging demand by commodity producers

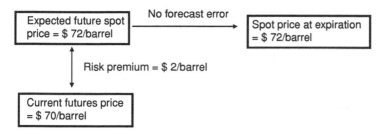

Example where futures return is due to a risk premium only.

FIGURE 12.1 Risk Premium but No Forecast Error Resulting in Normal Backwardation

(like Barrick in later years) push down the price of the futures contracts relative to the expected future spot prices. That's because the producers typically *sell* the commodity in the futures market. He called the resulting gap between the current futures price and the expected future spot price *normal backwardation.* It's a risk premium that entices investors to take the other side of the position—buying commodities in the futures market so that the producers can sell them.

Figure 12.1 illustrates the risk premium due to normal backwardation. The expected price of oil at the end of the current futures contract is $72 per barrel. Because of selling pressure by commodity producers who are hedging their positions, the current futures price is only $70 per barrel. So there is an expected profit of $2 per barrel representing the risk premium paid to buyers of the oil futures. Notice that at any given time, the spot price of a commodity may differ from the expected future price of that commodity. (The current spot price, not shown in Figure 12.1, could also be higher or lower than the current futures price).[2] In a period of inflation, for example, market participants may expect the prices of commodities to rise over time. If the current price of a futures contract were equal to the expected future price, however, there is no expected profit in taking a futures position. The rise in commodity prices is anticipated in the futures price itself. It's the gap between the current futures price and the expected future spot price that matters to the investor.

In addition to the risk premium, there is another major source of returns on futures contracts, forecast errors. In any given period, the actual spot price at the end of a contract may be higher or lower than the *expected* spot price. Consider Figure 12.2 where the actual spot price at expiration of the futures contract is $75 per barrel rather than the $72 per barrel that was expected. Then the total return from buying the futures contract will be $5 per barrel consisting of a $2 per barrel risk premium plus a $3 per barrel

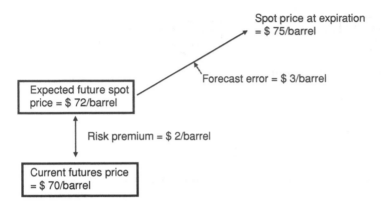

Example where there is also a forecast error.
Futures return = risk premium + forecast error

FIGURE 12.2   Risk Premium Plus Forecast Error

forecast error. If the forecast error were of opposite sign, then the total return would be reduced rather than increased. For example, a negative $3 per barrel forecast error would reduce the futures return to −$1 per barrel. In financial markets, forecast errors should have an expected value of zero. And over a long enough period of time, average forecast errors should be close to zero. Otherwise a profit machine could be set up that harvested profits just as surely as the profits gained from playing roulette on a wheel that is unbalanced. But even if expected forecast errors are equal to zero, actual forecast errors can persist in one direction for extended periods of time. In such periods, forecast errors can be the predominant source of futures returns.

The return on a commodity futures position will also be affected by the degree of leverage employed. On U.S. exchanges, futures contracts can be secured with a small margin position, so it's possible to employ high leverage in the positions. The margin itself is invested in Treasury bills, so the total return on the futures position will depend heavily on the amount of leverage employed. The major commodity indexes (to be discussed below) assume fully collateralized positions. So the return on the futures contract consists of the Treasury bill return plus the return on the futures themselves. An example may be useful. Suppose that an investor took an oil futures position at $70 per barrel, investing the collateral in 5 percent Treasury bills. And assume that the investor insists that there be no leverage, so the collateral is 100 percent of the futures position. (For convenience, assume that the futures contract is for one year). If the spot price of oil at expiration is $75 per barrel, then the total return on the futures contract is 12.1 percent consisting of the margin return of 5 percent plus the return on the futures themselves ($75/$70 – 1) = 7.1%.

RETURNS ON COMMODITY FUTURES

Interest in commodities as an asset class has surged recently because returns have been so high. Over the seven-year period from 2000 to 2006, the Goldman Sachs Commodity Index (to be described below) provided a compound return of 10.7 percent. There is nothing like high returns to generate interest among investors. But another reason that investors have begun to pay more heed to commodities is the influential paper by Gorton and Rouwenhorst (2006) that began circulating as a working paper in 2004. The returns on commodity futures contracts that Gorton and Rouwenhorst reported were so impressive that they attracted considerable attention.

Gorton and Rouwenhorst gathered futures data from the Commodity Research Bureau database from 1959 to 2004. They formed an equally weighted index of these contracts and studied returns from fully collateralized futures positions. At inception in 1959, only nine contracts were included in the study, but additional contracts were added so that by 2003 there were 36 contracts in all. The first energy contracts appeared in 1978 (heating oil) and 1983 (crude oil). So the composition of the index has changed substantially over time.

Table 12.1 compares the returns on Gorton and Rouwenhorst's commodity index with returns on U.S. stocks and bonds over the same period. The returns reported are annualized, but are based on monthly rebalancing. The assets used for comparison are large-cap stocks, corporate bonds,

TABLE 12.1 Gorton-Rouwenhorst Commodity Returns Compared with U.S. Stocks and Bonds, July 1959–December 2004

	Geometric Average	Arithmetic Average	Standard Deviation	Sharpe Ratio
Commodity Return (Gorton-Rouwenhorst)	10.0%	10.7%	12.1%	0.43
Large-Cap Stocks	10.4%	11.1%	14.8%	0.38
Corporate Bonds	7.5%	7.7%	8.6%	0.26
Long-Term Treasury Bonds	7.3%	7.5%	9.7%	0.21
Medium-Term Treasury Bonds	7.2%	7.2%	5.4%	0.33

Data Sources: Commodity returns are from Gorton and Rouwenhorst (2006), Tables 1 and 2. Stock and bond returns are from ©Morningstar.

long-term (20 year) and medium-term (five-year) Treasury bonds, all from the SBBI database. The commodity returns are almost as high as the stock returns, but with a lower standard deviation. Over this period, commodities earn much higher returns than bonds. The Sharpe ratio for the commodity positions is higher than for any other asset class. What is particularly impressive about these findings is that commodity futures deliver equity-like returns while being very low in correlation with stocks and bonds. Gorton and Rouwenhorst report monthly correlations with stocks of only 0.05 and with bonds of only −0.14. One year correlations are even lower. These results are so impressive that investors had to take heed of commodities if they had not already done so.

To see whether these results are affected by changes in the composition of the futures indexes or changes in the time period, this chapter will investigate returns on two widely used commodity indexes. The Goldman Sachs Commodity Index (GSCI) was developed in the early 1990s with returns backdated to 1970.[3] The index uses production values to weight the individual futures contracts into an index.[4] Currently there are 24 commodities in the index, including six energy, five industrial metals, eight agricultural, three livestock, and two precious metals contracts. The GSCI puts no limits on the weights of any contracts. So currently, because of the importance of energy in the world economy, the index has a 70 percent weight on the energy sector. The weights are shown in Figure 12.3. The returns are fully collateralized, so the returns reported include the interest earned on the margin invested in Treasury bills.

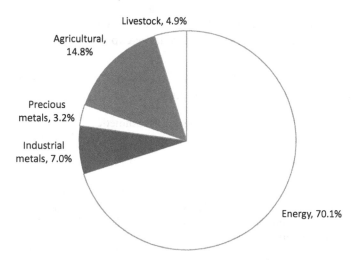

FIGURE 12.3 Goldman Sachs Commodity Index
Source: 2009 weights from www2.goldmansachs.com.

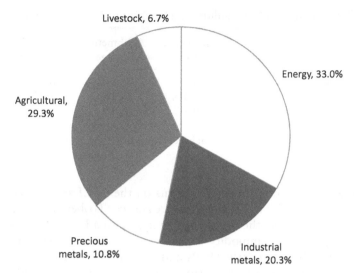

FIGURE 12.4 Dow Jones-UBS Commodity Index
Source: 2009 weights from www.djindexes.com.

The second index (DJ UBS) was developed by Dow Jones and AIG in 1998 with a backfilled history that starts in January 1991.[5] The weights, however, are based on the liquidity in trading each commodity as well as its production value, with liquidity as a dominant factor. The reason why liquidity is emphasized is that production data understates the economic importance of store-of-value assets such as gold or silver. Livestock have a short shelf life, but production is large. Gold lasts forever (just like diamonds), but current production is small. In addition, DJ UBS limits the total weight of any commodity to 33 percent of the index. So the index, shown in Figure 12.4, has a very different weighting than the GSCI.

Because the returns on the GSCI extend back so much further than those of the DJ UBS index, we will begin by studying the GSCI data set. Table 12.2 reports the returns on the GSCI over the period from January 1970 to June 2009. GSCI returns are compared with two stock indexes, those for the S&P 500 and the MSCI EAFE indexes. The GSCI returns are a little higher than those of the S&P 500 and EAFE indexes with compound returns of 10.0 percent compared with 9.4 percent and 9.8 percent for the two stock indexes. The standard deviation of the GSCI returns is also higher, so the Sharpe ratio is almost identical to those of the two stock indexes. Clearly there is justification for saying that this commodity index provides equity-like returns.

TABLE 12.2 Returns on Commodities and Stocks, Jan 1970–Jun 2009

	Geometric Average	Arithmetic Average	Standard Deviation	Sharpe Ratio
Goldman Sachs Commodity Index	10.0%	11.5%	20.1%	0.29
S&P 500	9.4%	10.3%	15.7%	0.30
MSCI EAFE	9.8%	10.8%	17.2%	0.30

Data Sources: S&P (for Goldman Sachs Commodity Index), ©Morningstar, and MSCI.

In Figure 12.5, the cumulative returns on the GSCI are compared with those on the S&P 500 and long-term Treasuries. To better assess relative performance over time, the returns are analyzed on a log scale. It is evident from this figure that commodity futures earned much higher returns than stocks and bonds in the early 1970s and that stocks caught up with commodity futures in the 1990s. After surging earlier in this decade and faltering recently, the cumulative return on the GSCI is only marginally higher than that of stocks. But this in itself is most impressive, particularly given the low

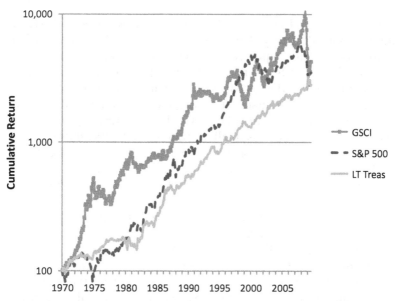

FIGURE 12.5 Cumulative Returns on GSCI and Other Assets (Log Scale), Jan 1970–Jun 2009
Data Sources: S&P and ©Morningstar.

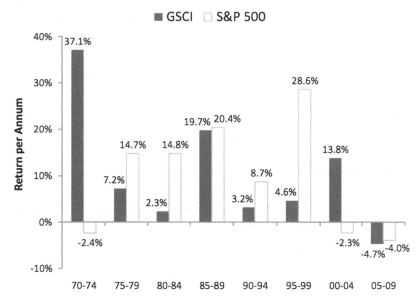

FIGURE 12.6 Five-Year Returns on GSCI and S&P 500, Jan 1970–Jun 2009
Data Sources: S&P and ©Morningstar.

correlations between stocks and commodities (as documented in the next section).

Figure 12.6 breaks up the GSCI returns into five-year intervals (except for the last period, January 2005 to June 2009). The figure reports compound returns for each five-year period expressed per annum. In the first five years of the data set, commodity futures earned 37.1 percent per annum at a time when the S&P 500 was losing 2.4 percent per year on average. There are less dramatic differences in later five-year windows, but stocks outperformed commodities by 24 percent per year in the late 1990s and commodities outperformed stocks by 16 percent per year in 2000 to 2004. The variation in relative returns is quite remarkable.

Why were commodity returns so high in the early 1970s? In 1973, for example, the GSCI futures return was 75.0 percent. One possible answer to this question is that inflation rose unexpectedly after the dollar broke free of the gold standard, and this inflation led to unanticipated increases in commodity prices. In 1973, for example, copper prices increased 114 percent while wheat prices shot up by 102 percent.[6] Some of this increase might have been anticipated by the futures market, but remember that Treasury bill yields, one measure of anticipated general price inflation, averaged 7 percent that year. If even half of the increase in commodity prices was unanticipated

TABLE 12.3 Returns on Commodities Compared with Stocks, Feb 1991–Jun 2009

	Geometric Average	Arithmetic Average	Standard Deviation	Sharpe Ratio
Goldman Sachs Commodity Index	3.6%	5.9%	21.4%	0.10
Dow-UBS Commodity Index	5.3%	6.3%	14.7%	0.18
S&P 500	7.7%	8.5%	14.9%	0.33
MSCI EAFE	5.0%	6.3%	16.6%	0.16

Data Sources: S&P, Dow-Jones-UBS Commodity Indexes©, and MSCI.

in 1973, the forecast error in the futures market would have dwarfed the normal backwardation risk premium.

It's interesting that returns for the GSCI drop sharply if measured only beginning in 1975 rather than 1970. Over the period from 1975 to 2006, the compound average return on the GSCI is only 8.0 percent. Over this same period, the S&P 500 has a 13.5 percent return and EAFE has a return of 13.2 percent. If the period is extended to 2008, all of the average returns drop sharply. The GSCI return is 6.4 percent, but the S&P 500 return is more than 5 percent higher at 11.3 percent and the EAFE return is 10.9 percent. So, according to one interpretation of the historical record, the equity-like returns on commodities are *due to the surprise inflation of the early 1970s and little else.* If that interpretation were accepted, we would have to justify commodity allocations in terms of their portfolio performance. This will not be hard to do, as will be seen in the next section, but such an interpretation puts a damper on investor beliefs that commodities are a wonder asset.

As discussed above, the Dow Jones UBS (formerly DJ AIG) Commodity Index is available only beginning in 1991. Table 12.3 reports the returns on both commodity indexes, GSCI and DJ AIG from February 2001 until June 2009. The table compares these returns with those on the same S&P 500 and MSCI EAFE indexes. There are several notable features of this table. First, the commodity index returns are much lower than those reported in Table 12.2. Few investors would get excited about an alternative investment that earns 3.6 percent per annum or even 5.3 percent per annum over an 18-year period. Second, these returns are much lower than the S&P 500 returns, so we can no longer say that the returns rival those of the U.S. equity market. It's true that the DJ UBS return is higher than the EAFE return, but recall from Chapter 5 that the EAFE return ex Japan would have been much higher than that reported in Table 12.3.

Figure 12.7 compares the cumulative returns on the two commodity indexes with those of the S&P 500. Notice how closely the two commodity

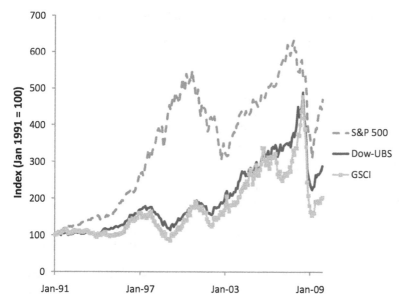

FIGURE 12.7 GSCI and Dow Jones-UBS Commodity Indexes Compared with S&P 500, Feb 1991–Jun 2009
Data Sources: S&P and Dow-Jones-UBS Commodity Indexes©.

indexes track one another. Only in the last few years has the GSCI cumulative return dropped below that of the DJ UBS Index. The monthly correlation between these two indexes is 0.89. Figure 12.7 shows the remarkable performance of the S&P 500 over this period. It's only after the S&P 500 hit the bear market in 2000 that commodities started to roar back into contention. It's that contrariness that attracts investors.

PERFORMANCE IN A PORTFOLIO

Commodities are a true alternative investment. Not only do they offer returns varying widely over time relative to stocks, but their correlations with stocks and bonds are low. Consider the correlations reported in Table 12.4 between the Goldman Sachs and Dow Jones-UBS commodity indexes on the one hand, and stock and bond indexes on the other hand. The table gives correlations for two periods, one beginning in 1970 and the second beginning in 1991 (when the DJ UBS commodity index begins). Commodities have low correlation with stocks and bonds, particularly in the longer period. From 1970 to 2009, the correlation between the Goldman Sachs index

TABLE 12.4 Correlations between Commodities and Other Assets

	DJ UBS	GSCI	S&P 500	EAFE	MT Treasury
Jan 1970–Jun 2009					
GSCI		1.00			
S&P 500		0.05	1.00		
EAFE		0.11	0.60	1.00	
MT Treasury		−0.06	0.13	0.06	1.00
CPI Inflation		0.18	−0.09	−0.08	−0.12
Feb 1991–Jun 2009					
DJ UBS	1.00				
GSCI	0.90	1.00			
S&P 500	0.23	0.16	1.00		
EAFE	0.37	0.29	0.73	1.00	
MT Treasury	−0.02	−0.02	−0.09	−0.09	1.00
CPI Inflation	0.29	0.34	0.01	0.04	−0.17

Data Sources: S&P, Dow-Jones-UBS Commodity Indexes©, ©Morningstar, MSCI, and IMF.

and the S&P 500 is only 0.05 and the correlation with the EAFE index is only 0.11.[7] For the shorter period beginning in 1991, the correlations are a little higher between commodities and stocks. For example, the correlation between the DJ UBS index and the S&P 500 is 0.23, and the correlation between the Goldman Sachs index and the S&P 500 is 0.16. The correlation between commodities and bonds is low in both periods.

One other correlation is of particular interest, the correlation between commodity futures and inflation. To be a good hedge against inflation, commodities must be highly correlated with inflation. For the period beginning in 1970, the correlation between the GSCI and CPI inflation is only 0.18.[8] For the shorter period beginning in 1991, the correlation between CPI inflation and the two commodity indexes range from 0.29 to 0.34. Correlations that low suggest that commodity futures provide only moderate protection against inflation.

One way to view the advantages of commodity futures in an investment portfolio is to examine its performance relative to the security market line. Figure 12.8 does this for 1991 to 2009 using the Russell 3000 all-cap index as the market benchmark. Since the Dow Jones UBS commodity index has a correlation with the Russell 3000 of 0.24, the beta with respect to this benchmark is also small at 0.24. To be on the security market line, the commodity return would have to be at least 4.9 percent. Since the return on the DJ UBS index is actually 6.3 percent, the alpha is equal to 1.4 percent.

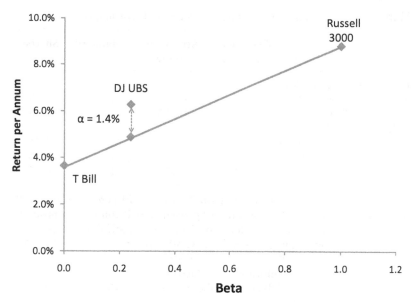

FIGURE 12.8 Dow Jones-UBS Commodity Index Relative to Security Market Line, Feb 1991–Jun 2009
Data Sources: Russell® and Dow-Jones-UBS Commodity Indexes©.

So the low return since 1991 doesn't look that unattractive if you take into account the very low beta of this investment. With its low beta, commodities are a true alternative investment.

The alpha for investment in commodity futures for the longer sample period is much larger. Recall that the return on the GSCI for the period beginning in 1970 was actually a little higher than for stocks. Yet the beta is still very low (0.03) over the longer sample period. For the period beginning in 1970, the alpha is an astoundingly large 5.6 percent. Not bad for a passive investment. What if we were to shorten the data set to exclude the period shortly after the peg to gold was abandoned, 1970 to 74? Then the alpha for period 1975 to 2008 declines to 2.2 percent.[9] With a beta close to zero, it is relatively easy to make a case for investment in commodities—even if commodity returns don't match equity returns. But the case is nowhere near as strong if we omit the period in the early 1970s.

A second way to examine the advantages of diversifying into commodities is to compare portfolios with and without a commodity position. Table 12.5 reports the results of two diversification experiments. In the first experiment, the effects of investing in the GSCI over its full sample period are investigated. Over the period from 1970 to June of 2009, a portfolio

TABLE 12.5 Impact of Commodity Futures on Portfolio Performance

	Geometric Average	Arithmetic Average	Standard Deviation	Sharpe Ratio
Portfolio A: Jan 1970–Jun 2009				
Portfolio without commodities	9.8%	10.1%	11.8%	0.38
Portfolio with 10% GSCI	10.1%	10.2%	10.6%	0.43
Portfolio B: Feb 1991–Jun 2009				
Portfolio without commodities	7.2%	7.6%	11.2%	0.35
Portfolio with 10% DJ UBS	7.1%	7.4%	10.3%	0.36
Portfolio with 10% GSCI	7.1%	7.5%	10.4%	0.37

Portfolio A consists of 25 percent in long-term Treasuries, 50 percent in the S&P 500, and 25 percent in MSCI EAFE. When a 10 percent (GSCI) commodity position is added, the S&P 500 allocation is reduced by 10 percent. **Portfolio B** consists of 25 percent in the Barclays Aggregate bond index, 50 percent in the Russell 3000, and 25 percent in MSCI EAFE. When a 10 percent commodity position (GSCI or DJ UBS) is added, the Russell 3000 allocation is reduced by 10 percent.
Data Sources: S&P, Dow-Jones-UBS Commodity Indexes©, ©Morningstar, MSCI, Barclays Capital, and Russell®.

without commodities consisting of 25 percent invested in long-term Treasuries, 50 percent invested in the S&P 500, and 25 percent in the MSCI EAFE index delivers a 9.8 percent compound return with an 11.8 percent standard deviation. If a 10 percent position in the GSCI is added with the funds being withdrawn from the S&P 500, the return on the portfolio rises from 9.8 percent to 10.1 percent, while the standard deviation falls from 11.8 percent to 10.6 percent. Naturally, the Sharpe ratio of the portfolio that includes commodities is higher (0.43 versus 0.38). That's equivalent to an increase in return on a risk-adjusted basis (α^*) of about 0.5 percent.

Table 12.5 also reports on a portfolio experiment involving the DJ UBS index or GSCI over the shorter sample period beginning in February 1991 when the DJ UBS index is available. Over this shorter sample period, more diversified stock and bond indexes are available than over the longer sample period. So the non-commodity portfolio consists of 25 percent in the Barclays Capital Aggregate bond index, 50 percent in the Russell 3000 all-cap index, and 25 percent in the EAFE index. When a 10 percent allocation to the DJ UBS index is added to the portfolio, the return falls by 0.2 percent, and the standard deviation is reduced from 10.7 percent to 9.8 percent. As a result, the Sharpe ratio rises from 0.35 to 0.36, a negligible change. Similar results are found if the GSCI replaces the DJ UBS index.

Thus in the recent period, in particular, there is only a weak case for diversifying a portfolio with a passive investment in commodities. Despite having a very low beta, it's not a miracle drug for the portfolio.

DOES GOLD BELONG IN THE PORTFOLIO?

For millennia, gold has been considered the ultimate store of value. So does it deserve a place in a modern portfolio? To answer that question, consider the return on the GSCI Gold index, a sub-component of the Goldman Sachs commodity futures index. Like the overall GSCI index, the return on the GSCI Gold index is derived from passive investment in futures contracts, in this case the futures contract tied to the London gold price (which is quoted in dollars).[10] This gold index is available beginning in 1979.

Table 12.6 reports returns on the GSCI Gold Index as well as other assets. From 1979 to June of 2009, gold earned a compound return of 4.6 percent compared with a return of 7.2 percent on the GSCI index as a whole. The gold index is as volatile as the GSCI, so the Sharpe ratio for the gold index is much smaller at 0.04. Neither commodity index, moreover, can compare with stocks over this sample period. The compound return on the S&P is 6.3 percent *above* the gold return and with a lower volatility.

The GSCI Gold index is the return on futures contracts. Could an investor do better holding the metal itself? Table 12.6 also reports the capital gain on gold holdings using the London gold price (in dollars) reported by the International Monetary Fund in its International Financial Statistics database. The capital gain that is reported in the table ignores the storage and insurance costs of holding the metal, so it is an overestimate of the true return.[11] The capital gain on gold is roughly comparable to the return from the GSCI Gold futures contracts and the Sharpe ratio is also comparable.

TABLE 12.6 Returns on Gold and Other Assets, Jan 1979–Jun 2009

Index	Geometric Average	Arithmetic Average	Standard Deviation	Sharpe Ratio
GSCI Gold Index	4.6%	6.3%	19.1%	0.04
GSCI Commodity Index	7.2%	8.9%	19.5%	0.17
Capital Gain on Gold Price	5.1%	6.5%	17.9%	0.05
S&P 500	10.9%	11.6%	15.5%	0.39
MSCI EAFE	9.5%	10.7%	17.5%	0.29

Data Sources: S&P and MSCI for commodity indexes and stock returns. The gold price (from London) is from the IMF, International Financial Statistics.

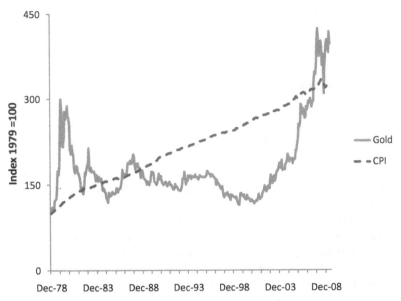

FIGURE 12.9 Total Return Index for Gold (GSCI Gold Index) and Consumer Price Index, Jan 1979–Jun 2009
Data Sources: S&P and IMF (inflation rate).

So that approach to investing in gold is at least as unattractive as investing in gold futures contracts.

The 30-year return on gold futures hides tremendous variation over time. The return on gold futures is even more episodic than the return on commodities in general. Figure 12.9 shows the total return on the GSCI Gold index along with the CPI index. Gold had a terrific run in the late 1970s, then collapsed for 20 or more years. At the end of 2001, the gold index was only 26.4 percent above its level at the end of 1978! Then in the seven years from 2002 to 2009, the gold index rose 200 percent or 17 percent per year on average. No wonder gold bugs emerged!

At least gold is a great hedge against inflation, say the gold bugs. Using monthly data from 1979 to 2009, the GSCI gold index has a correlation with the CPI of only 0.10 (compared with a correlation between the GSCI (overall) index and the CPI of 0.23). Only in annual data do we see a higher correlation of 0.41 between GSCI gold and the CPI. When corporations use futures contracts to hedge risks (like oil risks for an airline), they don't accept hedges with only a 0.41 correlation with their exposures. So it's hard to justify an investment in gold as an inflation hedge.

The historical evidence stretching back 30 years fails to provide support for treating gold as a special asset. There is a case for including commodities in a portfolio, but it makes sense to diversify the commodity investment rather than to concentrate holdings in one precious metal.

ACTIVE INVESTMENT IN COMMODITIES—MANAGED FUTURES

Managed futures are on investors' minds. In the 2008 downturn, this asset class gave investors an 18.3 percent return in a year when the DJ UBS index was *down* 35.7 percent and the Goldman Sachs commodity index was *down* 46.5 percent. Commodity prices turned down at mid-year and the active managers in the managed futures space obviously played this turning point well.

Investment in managed futures could have been analyzed in the chapter on hedge funds. But it's useful to compare the performance of these investments with their passive counterparts. In Chapter 9, returns on the Credit Suisse/Tremont hedge fund index were analyzed over the period 1994 to 2009. A subset of this overall index is the Credit Suisse/Tremont Managed Futures index tracking the returns of Commodity Trading Advisors (CTA) who take positions in bond, currency, and equity as well as commodity futures markets.[12] Since 1980, the Barclay CTA index has provided another source of managed futures returns. The index was begun in 1985 with backdating of returns to January 1980.[13]

Table 12.7 reports the returns on these two active indexes and compares them with returns on the two passive indexes described earlier. Over the period from 1994 to June of 2009, the Credit Suisse/Tremont Managed Futures and Barclay CTA indexes have compound returns similar to the return on the DJ-UBS index but above that of the GSCI index. This is a relatively short period of time, so not too much should be made of this difference. In fact, when the four indexes are compared over the period from 1994 to 2007, the two passive indexes have compound returns that are more than 3 percent higher on average than the active indexes. One year, 2008, makes that much difference! The two managed futures indexes do have lower Sharpe ratios than either passive index. That's because the standard deviations are so much lower than those of the passive indexes. Active management does hold down risk.

What is far more interesting is the lack of similarity between the two styles of investing. In fact, passive and active futures indexes should be regarded as distinct investments. This is shown clearly in Table 12.8 where the correlations among the four passive and active indexes are displayed.

TABLE 12.7 Managed Futures Funds Compared with Passive Commodity Futures Indexes, Jan 1994–Jun 2009

Index	Geometric Average	Arithmetic Average	Standard Deviation	Sharpe Ratio
Credit Suisse/Tremont Managed Futures Index	6.4%	6.9%	11.8%	0.27
Barclay CTA Index	6.2%	6.3%	7.8%	0.33
Goldman Sachs Commodity Index	4.7%	7.2%	22.9%	0.15
Dow Jones UBS Commodity Index	6.2%	7.3%	15.7%	0.23

Indexes for Managed Futures Funds: Credit Suisse/Tremont Managed Futures Hedge Fund Index and Barclay CTA Index. Indexes for passive commodity futures funds: Goldman Sachs Commodity Index and Dow Jones UBS commodity Index.
Data Sources: Credit Suisse/Tremont and ©BarclayHedge, LLC for managed futures indexes. S&P and Dow-Jones-UBS Commodity Indexes© for passive commodity indexes.

The two active indexes have high correlation with one another. Credit Suisse/Tremont Managed Futures and Barclay CTA have a correlation of 0.84. The two passive indexes also have a high correlation of 0.91. But the correlation between the active and passive indexes ranges from 0.17 to 0.26. These are two totally different investments.

Perhaps the best way to view commodity investments is as follows: Decide whether to invest in passive commodity futures indexes depending on the evidence presented in this chapter. Then decide whether to invest in actively managed futures funds only after comparing them with other hedge fund investments. After all, an investor in managed futures funds does not

TABLE 12.8 Correlations Among Managed Futures and Commodity Futures Indexes, Jan 1994–Jun 2009

	Credit Suisse/ Tremont	Barclays CTA	GSCI
Credit Suisse/Tremont Managed Futures Index	1.00		
Barclay CTA Index	0.84	1.00	
Goldman Sachs Commodity Index	0.17	0.19	1.00
Dow Jones UBS Commodity Index	0.22	0.26	0.91

Data Sources: see Table 12.7.

TABLE 12.9 Managed Futures Funds Compared with Other Hedge Funds, Jan 1994–Jun 2009

Index	Geometric Average	Arithmetic Average	Standard Deviation	Sharpe Ratio
Credit Suisse/Tremont Managed Futures Index	6.4%	6.9%	11.8%	0.27
Barclay CTA Index	6.2%	6.3%	7.8%	0.33
Credit Suisse/Tremont Hedge Fund Index	8.9%	8.9%	7.9%	0.65
HFRI Fund Weighted Hedge Fund Index	9.5%	9.4%	7.4%	0.77

Data Sources: Credit Suisse/Tremont, ©BarclayHedge, LLC, and HFRI.

even know whether he or she is long in commodities. Managers of managed futures funds should be evaluated on their skill in generating alpha, not on their ability to tie the investor to commodity futures contracts.

If managed futures are judged as hedge fund investments, how do they fare? The answer to this question is given in Table 12.9 where the two actively managed futures indexes are compared with two (overall) hedge fund indexes, the Credit Suisse/Tremont Hedge Fund index and the HFRI Fund-Weighted Hedge Fund Index. Since 1994, the two active indexes have given returns that are 2.5 percent or more below those of the (overall) hedge fund indexes with equal or higher volatility. The Sharpe ratios of these two managed futures indexes, moreover, are half the size of those of the hedge fund indexes.

It's only in terms of systematic risk that managed futures hold their own relative to hedge funds in general. The betas of the managed futures indexes are negative (relative to the Russell 3000), so their returns are high enough to generate attractive alphas. The Credit Suisse/Tremont Managed Futures index has an alpha of 3.8 percent while the Barclay CTA index has an alpha of 2.9 percent. That performance is comparable to the overall hedge fund indexes which have alphas of 4.2 percent and 4.4 percent. So there is no doubt that managed futures should be considered as a possible strategy in a hedge fund portfolio.

SUMMARY—KEY FEATURES OF COMMODITY INVESTMENTS

Although there are four distinct ways to invest in commodities, this chapter has focused primarily on the method that gives the most direct exposure to commodity risk, passively managed futures contracts. The returns on futures contracts stem from two main sources, a risk premium due to the gap between futures prices and future expected prices and any forecast error in predicting these futures prices. The risk premium, termed normal backwardation by Keynes, is due to the one-sided demand of producers to hedge their production by selling the commodity in the futures market. Forecast errors can be either positive or negative. In the long run, average forecast errors should be close to zero. But at times forecast errors can totally dominate futures returns, as in years following the abandonment of the dollar's peg to gold.

Returns on futures contracts vary widely over time. The early 1970s saw huge returns on commodities, but since that time commodity returns have been more similar to those for bonds than for stocks. The main advantage of commodity futures lies in their diversification properties. Correlations with bonds and stocks are zero or negative, so excess returns relative to CAPM are impressively large. If added to portfolios, commodities reduce risk and enhance risk-adjusted returns. They are a true alternative asset.

One type of commodity that has been singled out for separate study is gold. That's because gold has always attracted a lot of attention from at least some investors. Recently, returns on gold have been very high. But the long-run record of gold as an investment is not as favorable. Gold delivers very low returns with high risk. On the other hand, gold makes great jewelry.

Passive investment in commodities is altogether different from active investment in managed futures funds. Correlations between the two types of investment are very low, and their relative returns vary widely over time. They should be treated as separate investments. Since managed futures funds are a form of hedge fund, they should be compared with other types of hedge funds. Evidence suggests that they should be included in a well-diversified portfolio of hedge fund strategies.

NOTES

1. When gold prices rose in 2003, Barrick abandoned its gold hedge policy in hopes of boosting its share price (Forbes.com, Dec. 3, 2003).
2. Futures traders term this gap between the current spot price and the current futures price backwardation as opposed to the normal backwardation that Keynes described.
3. Gorton and Rouwenhorst (2006) argue that the survivorship bias from using backdated commodity futures returns is not clearly in one direction or another. Stocks fail because of bankruptcy while commodity futures may be delisted simply because there is little trading volume.

4. The weights are based on rolling five-year averages of production values. The index included only five commodities in 1970, but today that index has been expanded to 24 commodities.
5. In May 2009, AIG sold its rights to this index to UBS, so it is now known as the Dow Jones-UBS commodity index.
6. The copper price is a London exchange price quoted in dollars, while the wheat price is the U.S. price of wheat at Gulf ports. Both price series are from the IMF, International Financial Statistics.
7. These correlations between commodities and stocks in the period beginning in 1970 are as low as the correlations reported by Gorton and Rouwenhorst (2006) for a period beginning in 1959.
8. If annual data are used, the correlation between the GSCI and CPI inflation rises to 0.36.
9. The beta is 0.06 over this shorter period, while the (arithmetic) average return is 8.1 percent.
10. Like the GSCI index as a whole, the return on the gold index includes the return on the collateral that is invested in Treasury bills.
11. If the investor chose to own gold coins, there would also be transactions costs from buying and selling that are far in excess of those in the futures market.
12. The description of the Credit Suisse/Tremont managed futures index is found on www.hedgeindex.com.
13. According to www.barclaygrp.com, there were 897 CTAs in the database in mid-2007.

CHAPTER 13

Asset Allocation with Alternative Investments

Alternative investments have captured the fancy of investors, both individuals and institutions. Many of these investors have become convinced that the bull market in equities experienced in the 1980s and 1990s is over, and that the secular downturn in inflation that led to unusually high bond returns is also drawing to a close. Many of those same investors have heard of the incredible returns earned by institutional investors like Yale University who have shifted from conventional stock and bond investments to alternative investments like real estate, hedge funds, and private equity. In Chapters 9 to 12, we have examined the chief alternative investments one by one. These investments have many attractive features as well as some important drawbacks. Now it is time to consider how well they perform in a portfolio. The first section of the chapter considers what we might term alternative investments for the ordinary investor as recommended by a leading institutional investor. The second section then introduces what we might term more exotic alternative investments, namely hedge funds, commodity futures, and private equity. The investments are evaluated in portfolios designed for high net worth and ultra-high net worth investors, respectively. The third section then examines the extraordinary record of one institutional investor, the Yale University Endowment, over the period since 1985 when David Swensen took over its direction. The analysis of the Yale endowment will be designed to disentangle the effects of asset allocation from the superior access to managers provided by the Yale Endowment. The final section examines how alternative investments performed in the financial crisis.

DIVERSIFYING INTO REAL ESTATE—ALTERNATIVES FOR ORDINARY INVESTORS

In 2005 David Swensen, the director of the Yale Endowment since 1985, published a book on investment designed for the ordinary investor. The book, entitled *Unconventional Success: A Fundamental Approach to personal Investment* presented a model portfolio for investors not wealthy enough (or perhaps too risk averse) to invest in exotic alternative investments. Swensen recommended that such investors consider two somewhat unconventional investments, real estate and Treasury inflation-protected bonds.

Let's consider the diversifying power of real estate first. As Chapter 11 explained, there are many ways to invest in real estate. Most investors own a residence, but here we are discussing investable real estate including apartment buildings, office buildings, retail office space, and factory buildings. Many wealthy investors own such real estate directly rather than through funds. For these investors, the common feature of their real estate holdings is their lack of diversification. The real estate is typically in a single area of the country and often in the same type of real estate. For example, an investor may own apartment buildings or office buildings in the Los Angeles area, but not elsewhere in the country. Or an investor may own rental real estate in a vacation area, but little else.

As explained in Chapter 11, REITS offer diversification to an investor, both geographic diversification and diversification in the types of real estate. For that reason, we will study real estate by focusing on the REIT market. The series we will use is the same one discussed in the earlier chapter, the FTSE NAREIT index of REIT equity returns provided by the National Association of Real Estate Investment Trusts. Returns from the REIT index begin in 1972. Over the period since then, REITS have earned a premium over the S&P 500 of 1.6 percent. The correlation between REITS and the S&P 500 is only 0.56. No wonder Swensen believes that real estate could help to improve the performance of a portfolio.

To see the potential for diversification into real estate, consider Figure 13.1 where two portfolios are compared. There is a stock and bond portfolio consisting of the Russell 3000 all-cap U.S. stock index, the MSCI EAFE index, and the Barclays Capital Aggregate bond index. As explained in Chapter 8 on strategic asset allocation, this three-asset portfolio provides diversification across the entire U.S. stock market, international diversification, and diversification across different types of U.S. investment grade bonds. The three asset, stock and bond portfolio is compared with a portfolio that also includes REITS. The sample period used to measure standard

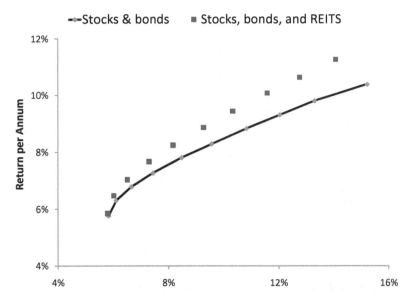

FIGURE 13.1 REITS Added to Stock and Bond Portfolios
Sources for returns: Tables 8.3 and 13.2.

errors and correlations is 1979 to 2009 (truncated because the Russell series begins in 1979). The returns are measured through 2009 using the premium method described in Chapter 8 (and in Table 13.2 below). The addition of REITS to the portfolio shifts the frontier in a northwesterly direction. The shift is not dramatic, but it's at no cost to the investor.

It should be noted that the optimization is done without imposing constraints on the portfolio allocation. As discussed in Chapter 8, the optimizer often chooses portfolios that might appear strange to the investor. For example, the portfolio with bonds at 30 percent of the allocation has 36.7 percent in REITS, 21.5 percent in EAFE, and only 11.8 percent in U.S. stocks. This allocation shows the diversifying power of real estate, but it is not one that most investors would choose.

For that reason, we will consider constrained portfolios. For guidance in how to constrain the portfolio, let's consult David Swensen's book, *Unconventional Success* (2005). The portfolio he recommends to ordinary investors is displayed in Figure 13.2. He recommends that investors diversify a conventional stock and bond portfolio by adding two assets: (a) real estate and (b) Treasury inflation-protected securities (TIPS). The latter were introduced in 1997 by the Clinton Administration, so the historical series of returns is rather short. Swensen recommends TIPS as a hedge against unexpected

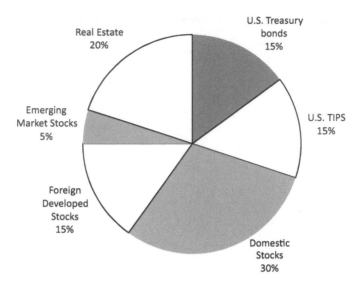

FIGURE 13.2 David Swensen's Portfolio for Individual Investors
Source: Swensen, *Unconventional Success* (2005).

inflation much like an endowment might look to commodities or timberland for such protection. Swensen allocates half of the 30 percent bond portion of the portfolio to TIPS. The other half is allocated to conventional Treasury bonds since Swensen is skeptical about the advantages of incurring credit risk by investing in non-Treasury bonds. Swensen also allocates 20 percent of the portfolio to real estate. This is truly an unconventional portfolio. But given Swensen's extraordinary success in investing Yale's endowment, his views ought to be considered seriously.

To evaluate the Swensen portfolio, we again employ the premium method for estimating returns. As explained in Chapter 8 on asset allocation, the premium method builds on the fundamental capital market assets, U.S. Treasury bonds and the S&P 500. Those returns were estimated to be 4.9 percent and 9.4 percent, respectively.[1] Since REITS earned a premium over the S&P 500 of 1.6 percent from 1972 to 2009, the REIT return is estimated to be 11.2 percent.[2] TIPS were introduced in 1997, so the data set extends only from March 1997 through December 2009. Over this period, TIPS earned a 0.5 percent premium over the medium-term Treasury bond, so the TIPS return is estimated to be 5.4 percent. As an alternative to the portfolio recommended by Swensen, a conventional portfolio is chosen with ordinary Treasury bonds replacing the TIPS allocation and stocks replacing the REIT allocation (with the foreign/domestic proportions for equities

TABLE 13.1 Comparison between Swensen's *Unconventional Success* Portfolio and Conventional Portfolio

| Portfolio Shares | Unconventional Success Portfolios | | Conventional Portfolio |
	With Real Estate and TIPS	With no TIPS	
U.S. Treasury Bonds (SBBI MT)	15%	30%	30%
U.S. TIPS (Barclays TIPS)	15%		
Domestic Equity (Russell 3000)	30%	30%	42%
Foreign Developed Equity (EAFE)	15%	15%	21%
Emerging Market Equity (MSCI EM)	5%	5%	7%
Real Estate (FTSE NAREIT)	20%	20%	
Average Return	9.3%	9.3%	9.0%
Standard Deviation	10.5%	10.3%	10.5%
Sharpe Ratio	0.56	0.57	0.53
Alpha*	0.3%	0.4%	

The *Unconventional Success* portfolio refers to the portfolio recommended for ordinary investors by David Swensen (2005). Expected returns are from Tables 8.3 and 13.2. Standard deviations are calculated using Zephyr AllocationADVISOR for sample period from 1990 to 2009 except for the TIPS series which begins in March 1997.
Data Sources: ©Morningstar, Barclays Capital, Russell®, MSCI, and ©FTSE.

remaining the same). The two portfolios were evaluated using Zephyr AllocationADVISOR. The standard deviations and correlation coefficients for both portfolios were based on the same sample period beginning in 1990 (when the MSCI Emerging Markets Index begins) except that the TIPS returns begin only in March 1997.[3]

The results of this comparison are reported in Table 13.1. Swensen's recommended portfolio with REITS and TIPS earned 0.3 percent more than the conventional portfolio (9.3 percent versus 9.0 percent). Since the standard deviations of the two portfolios are identical, the Sharpe ratio of Swensen's recommended portfolio is higher than that of the conventional portfolio, 0.56 versus 0.53. That translates into an excess return, or alpha*, of 0.3 percent for Swensen's portfolio.[4] That's certainly not much of an improvement in performance, but it's achieved while staying with quite conventional alternative investments. Swensen designed the portfolio for the ordinary investor, and there is nothing about this portfolio that should alarm such an investor.

How much of that outperformance is due to the addition of real estate and how much to the addition of TIPS? The answer is provided in Table 13.1 in the middle column of the table where the allocation to TIPS is replaced by conventional Treasury securities. The portfolio without TIPS actually performs a little better than Swensen's recommended portfolio. The modified Swensen portfolio outperforms the conventional portfolio by 0.4 percent in risk-adjusted terms. So it's the real estate investment that delivers the improvement in performance in Swensen's portfolio. A 20 percent allocation to real estate gives the investor an extra boost in terms of risk-adjusted returns.

The statistics in Table 13.1 may not do true justice to Swensen's argument for diversification into TIPS. The main reason that Swensen adds TIPS to a conventional portfolio is to guard against unexpected inflation. In an endowment portfolio like Yale's there are several types of investments, like timberland and oil and gas properties, that will help protect the portfolio against inflation. The value of these assets is never fully appreciated unless inflation rises unexpectedly. Since 1997 when TIPS were introduced, it's been deflation rather than inflation that has preoccupied many minds.

Swensen's portfolio suggests that there are advantages to diversifying the portfolio beyond conventional stocks and bonds. Institutional investors as well as high net worth investors, however, often consider alternative investments more exotic than those in this portfolio designed by Swensen for ordinary investors. The next section of this chapter will consider how investments like hedge funds, commodities, and private equity can help to diversify the portfolio. Then in the following section, the Yale endowment portfolio will be analyzed. Yale's portfolio combines many of these alternative investments in a very unconventional way.

EXPANDING THE MENU OF ALTERNATIVE ASSETS

In earlier chapters, several different types of alternative investments were discussed in detail, among them hedge funds, commodities, and private equity, along with real estate. This section will analyze how these alternative assets help to diversify the portfolio. Several portfolios containing conventional and alternative assets will be examined.

In addition to the FTSE NAREIT index discussed in the last section, the indexes chosen are as follows:

Hedge funds: the HFRI Fund of Funds Index and Credit Suisse/Tremont Hedge Fund Index. The HFRI index begins in 1990 while the Credit Suisse/Tremont index begins in 1994.[5]

Commodity futures: the Dow Jones UBS Commodity Index. As discussed in Chapter 12, this index limits the weight of any individual commodity to 33 percent of the index, so it is a more representative index than the Goldman Sachs Commodity Index (which is dominated by energy). The DJ UBS index begins in February 1991.

Venture capital: the Cambridge Associates LLC U.S. Venture Capital Index®. This index begins in the second quarter of 1981.

Private equity: the Cambridge Associates LLC U.S. Private Equity Index®. This index, which begins in the second quarter of 1986, consists primarily of buyout funds.

It should be noted that some of these indexes for alternative investments are quite different from the stock and bond indexes used in a conventional indexed portfolio. First, unlike the DJ AIG commodity futures index, which measures the returns on a passive investment in commodity futures contracts, the indexes for REITs, hedge funds, and private equity all measure the performance of *active managers*. For example, the FTSE NAREIT real estate index measures the returns of REIT managers who actively manage portfolios of real estate assets. Similarly, hedge fund and private equity managers actively manage their portfolios of assets, so indexes for hedge funds and private equity measure some average of the managers' performance. Second, some of these indexes, notably the hedge fund indexes, have *significant biases* in measuring the set of active managers. So they should be regarded as asset benchmarks rather than genuine indexes.

To obtain measures of the expected returns on these alternative investments, we use the premium method introduced in Chapter 8. Table 13.2 reports the premiums for these alternative assets. The table reports the index used for each alternative asset, the premium over the S&P 500, the period of measurement, and the resulting estimated return. For example, as discussed in the first section of this chapter, the FTSE NAREIT Index of REITs has a premium of 1.6 percent above the S&P 500 over the period starting in 1972 (when the FTSE NAREIT series begins). If the expected return on the S&P 500 in the long run is 9.4 percent, this results in an expected return on the REIT index of 11.2 percent. In contrast, the Dow Jones AIG Index of commodity futures returns has a negative premium of −2.5 percent over the period from February 1991 to December 2009. So the estimated return is 6.7 percent.[6]

Portfolios containing alternative investments will be compared with a conventional portfolio of stocks and bonds. The conventional portfolio to be used as a benchmark in all of the comparisons consists of the same four indexes used in earlier experiments: the Barclays Capital Aggregate index of investable U.S. bonds, the Russell 3000 all-cap U.S. stock index, the MSCI EAFE Index of foreign developed country stocks, and the MSCI Emerging Market Index. The benchmark portfolio consists of 25 percent in bonds

TABLE 13.2 Premiums of Alternative Investment Returns over S&P 500

Alternative Asset Index	Premium over S&P 500	Estimated Return	Period of Measurement
FTSE NAREIT	+1.6%	11.2%	1972–2009
HRFI Fund of Funds	+0.0%	9.4%	1990–2009
Credit Suisse/Tremont Hedge Fund	+1.6%	11.2%	1994–2009
DJ UBS Commodity	−2.5%	6.7%	Feb 1991–Dec 2009
Venture Capital	+2.1%	11.7%	1981 Q2–2009 Q3
Private Equity	+3.4%	13.1%	1986 Q2–2009 Q3

The alternative indexes are the FTSE NAREIT Index for REITS, the HFRI Fund of Funds and Credit Suisse/Tremont Hedge Fund indexes, the Dow Jones UBS commodity futures index, and the Cambridge Associates LLC U.S. indexes for venture capital and private equity. The premiums are measured relative to the S&P 500 over the periods indicated and applied to the long-run S&P 500 (geometric average) estimated return of 9.4 percent.
Data Sources: S&P, ©FTSE, HFRI, Credit Suisse/Tremont, Dow-Jones-UBS Commodity Indexes©, Cambridge Associates LLC U.S. Venture Capital Index®, and U.S. Private Equity Index®.

and 75 percent in stocks. Forty percent of the stocks (or 30 percent of the portfolio) is invested overseas with one-third of the foreign stocks invested in emerging markets. This portfolio is illustrated on the left side of Figure 13.3. When alternative assets are added to the portfolio, domestic and foreign stocks remain in the same proportion as in the benchmark portfolio.

HIGH NET WORTH (HNW) PORTFOLIOS

Several portfolios with alternative investments are examined. The first two portfolios are designed for high net worth investors who are willing to invest in hedge funds and commodity futures as well as in real estate, stocks, and bonds. Both HNW portfolios have 25 percent invested in bonds, 50 percent in stocks, and 25 percent in alternative investments (including real estate). The first of these portfolios has 10 percent in hedge funds, 5 percent in commodity futures, and 10 percent in REITS. This portfolio is illustrated on the right side of Figure 13.3. The second HNW portfolio excludes commodity futures with the REIT allocation increased to 15 percent from 10 percent. The other portfolios are designed for ultra-high net worth investors who can cope with the illiquidity of venture capital and private equity investments. These portfolios will be discussed below.

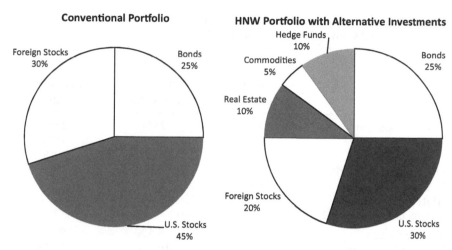

FIGURE 13.3 Conventional Portfolio with Traditional Investments and HNW Portfolio with Alternative Investments

The two HNW portfolios are examined in Table 13.3. The hedge fund index used for these portfolios is the HFRI Fund of Funds index since high net worth investors usually cannot diversify manager risk adequately by investing directly in hedge funds.[7] The expected returns of each portfolio are calculated using Zephyr AllocationADVISOR, but only after the individual asset returns are replaced by the estimated returns obtained using the premium method (as in Table 13.2).[8] The standard deviations and correlations for each portfolio are measured by Zephyr from February 1991 (when the DJ UBS index begins) until December 2009.

Consider the first HNW portfolio that includes 10 percent in hedge funds, 5 percent in commodities, and 10 percent in REITS. This portfolio is shown in the second column of Table 13.3. The addition of three alternative investments—real estate, hedge funds, and commodities—lowers risk by 1.8 percent while lowering the average return by 0.2 percent. The Sharpe ratio for this HNW portfolio is 0.59 compared with the Sharpe ratio of 0.52 for the conventional portfolio measured over the same period. In Figure 13.4, this portfolio is compared with the conventional portfolio. After adjusting the risk of the conventional portfolio down to that of the HNW portfolio, the return on the latter exceeds that of the conventional portfolio by 0.7 percent. So the shift of 25 percent of the portfolio from stocks to the three alternative assets raises the risk-adjusted return 70 basis points.

Table 13.3 also shows the performance of a second HNW portfolio that replaces the 5 percent allocation to commodity futures with an additional 5 percent in REITS. So this portfolio has 10 percent in hedge funds and

TABLE 13.3 Comparison between HNW Portfolios (with Alternative Investments) and Conventional Portfolio (no Alternatives)

| | HNW Portfolios | | |
	With Commodities	Without Commodities	Conventional Portfolio
Portfolio Shares			
Barclays Aggregate	25%	25%	25%
Russell 3000	30%	30%	45%
MSCI EAFE	13.3%	13.3%	20%
MSCI Emerging Markets	6.7%	6.7%	10%
FTSE NAREIT	10%	15%	
HFRI Fund of Funds	10%	10%	
DJ UBS Commodity Index	5%		
Average Return	9.2%	9.5%	9.4%
Standard Deviation	9.7%	10.1%	11.5%
Sharpe Ratio	0.59	0.59	0.52
Alpha*	0.7%	0.7%	

The returns for individual assets are based on the premium method as reported in Tables 13.2 and 8.3. Standard deviations are measured starting in February 1991. *Data Sources:* Barclays Capital, Russell®, MSCI, ©FTSE, HFRI, Dow-Jones-UBS Commodity Indexes©.

15 percent in REITS. The results are very similar to those for the first HNW portfolio. This portfolio has a higher return than the first HNW portfolio because REITS have earned a higher return than commodities, but the Sharpe ratios of the two HNW portfolios are identical.

So does a HNW investor with access to alternative investments do much better than an ordinary investor confined to conventional assets? The answer is provided by the alpha* calculations. Yes, the HNW investor does earn an extra 0.7 percent adjusted for risk. It should be noted, though, that an excess return of that size could easily be swamped by excessive investment expenses or taxes, or other sources of investment expense. And remember that the hedge fund returns are upwardly biased. So the alpha* calculation may overstate the actual advantage of the alternative strategy.

ULTRA HNW PORTFOLIOS

Ultra HNW investors are in a somewhat different investment world than the rest of us. Those investors are able to tie up capital for extended periods of time, so the world of venture capital and private equity is open to them.

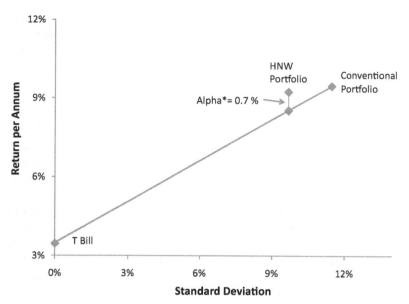

FIGURE 13.4   HNW Portfolio Compared with Portfolio Without Alternative Investments
Data Sources: Barclays Capital, Russell®, MSCI, ©FTSE, HFRI, Dow-Jones-UBS Commodity Indexes©.

At what wealth level do such investments become possible? Some brokerage firms define ultra HNW investors as having as little as $20 million or $30 million in wealth.[9] But it's not clear that an investor with $20 or $30 million could afford to tie up 10 percent of the portfolio in an investment that would be illiquid for 10 years or more. Certainly such an investor could not obtain much diversification within the private equity portion of the portfolio, since the minimums for investment in venture capital or buyouts would preclude more than one or two investments (if the total amount to be invested was $2 or $3 million). In any case, our definition of the ultra HNW investor will be made in terms of eligible investments rather than in terms of wealth. *An ultra HNW investor is any investor who can devote 10 percent or more of the portfolio to private equity or other illiquid investments.* This definition is useful because we are primarily interested in portfolio performance rather than levels of wealth per se.

Since many ultra-HNW investors can obtain sufficient diversification of hedge fund investments by directly investing in hedge funds, the Credit Suisse/Tremont Hedge Fund index will be used to measure hedge fund performance rather than the HFRI Fund of Funds index. The Tremont index begins in 1994, so standard deviations and correlations will be measured over the period from 1994 through the third quarter of 2009. To measure private equity returns, the two Cambridge Associates series described in Chapter 10 are used. These series are for venture capital and private equity.[10] The portfolios described below will allocate equal proportions to each type of investment. The CA series are available only quarterly, so the correlations and standard deviations had to be loaded manually into the Zephyr program (since all other series are available monthly). As discussed in Chapter 10, the volatility of these investments is probably seriously underestimated because the returns are smoothed by infrequent valuations. So the standard deviations of the resulting portfolios are downwardly biased. The measured correlations are also probably lower than in reality.

Table 13.4 compares portfolios for the ultra HNW investor with the conventional portfolio previously described. The table examines two ultra HNW portfolios. In the second column, Portfolio A assigns 25 percent to alternative investments overall with 5 percent allocated to venture capital and another 5 percent to private equity. In the third column, Portfolio B doubles the allocation to alternatives to 50 percent of the portfolio.

TABLE 13.4 Comparison between Portfolios for Ultra-HNW Investors and Conventional Portfolio

| | Ultra-HNW Portfolios | | Conventional Portfolio |
Portfolio Shares	Portfolio A	Portfolio B	
Barclays Aggregate	25%	25%	25%
Russell 3000	30%	15%	45%
MSCI EAFE	13.3%	6.7%	20%
MSCI Emerging Markets	6.7%	3.3%	10%
FTSE NAREIT	5%	10%	
Credit Suisse/Tremont Hedge Fund	10%	20%	
Venture Capital	5%	10%	
Private Equity	5%	10%	
Average Return	9.7%	10.0%	9.4%
Standard Deviation	10.4%	9.4%	11.8%
Sharpe Ratio	0.60	0.70	0.50
Alpha*	1.0%	1.9%	

The returns for individual assets are based on the premium method as reported in Tables 13.2 and 8.3. Standard deviations are measured from 1994 to 2009 Q3.
Data Sources: Barclays Capital, Russell®, MSCI, ©FTSE, Credit Suisse/Tremont, Cambridge Associates LLC U.S. Venture Capital Index®, and Private Equity Index®.

Consider first Portfolio A with 25 percent invested in alternatives. The return on this portfolio is 0.3 percent higher than that of the conventional portfolio and the standard deviation is 1.4 percent lower. So the Sharpe ratio of the ultra HNW portfolio is higher. Translated into an excess return, this higher Sharpe ratio results in an alpha* of 1.0 percent. That's a little higher than achieved by the HNW investor who is confined to real estate and hedge funds. But the addition of venture capital and private equity to the portfolio does not matter that much.

Portfolio B doubles the allocation to alternative investments to 50 percent of the portfolio. That has the predictable effect of increasing the relative performance of the ultra HNW portfolio. The return of Portfolio B is 0.6 percent above that of the conventional portfolio while the risk is 2.4 percent lower. The Sharpe ratio is high enough to result in an alpha* of 1.9 percent relative to that of the conventional portfolio. These results in Table 13.4 are notable, but they are not as impressive as we might expect. Remember that these returns are obtained only after tying up part of the portfolio in very illiquid investments. Surely an extra 0.3 percent return (comparing the alpha* of 1.0 percent for Portfolio A with the alpha* of 0.7 percent for the HNW portfolio in Table 13.3) is not much compensation for investing 10 percent of the portfolio in illiquid VC and PE investments.

The results developed in this section must puzzle some readers. It's well known that some wealthy institutions have made huge returns by investing in alternative investments. The Yale Endowment is perhaps the best example, but other institutions such as Harvard University and the Rockefeller Foundation have also achieved superior returns by investing in alternatives. How we reconcile their results with those analyzed above is the subject of the next section of this chapter.

LESSONS ABOUT ALTERNATIVES FROM THE YALE ENDOWMENT

Interest in alternative investments has been enhanced dramatically by the remarkable performance of the Yale Endowment under its long-term director, David Swensen. Since he took over direction of the Endowment in 1985, the Endowment has compiled one of the most impressive records of any investment organization. As will be shown in this section, Yale beats all normal benchmarks including those of peer institutions. What is more impressive perhaps is that it has led the way in revolutionizing the investment practices of educational institutions nationwide. Under David Swensen, Yale has embraced alternative investments and they have been the key to its

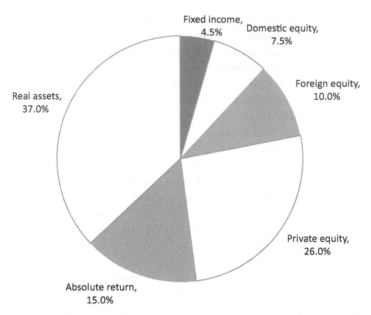

FIGURE 13.5 Target Portfolio of Yale Endowment, 2009
Sources: 2009, The Yale Endowment.

success. Whether other investors should emulate Yale is a question that will be addressed in this section.

Consider the strategic asset allocation reported in the 2009 Yale Endowment report as illustrated in Figure 13.5. Only 22 percent of the portfolio is in traditional stock and bond investments. It's interesting that Yale has more invested in foreign equity (10 percent) than in U.S. equity (7.5 percent). All of the rest of the portfolio is in three alternative asset classes:

Private equity (26 percent of portfolio), primarily in *venture capital* and *buyouts*

Absolute return (15 percent), split between *event-driven strategies* (tied to mergers, bankruptcy restructurings, or other corporate events) and *value-driven strategies*

Real assets (37 percent), primarily *real estate, oil and gas properties,* and *timberland*

A small investment staff led by Swensen and Dean Takahashi, Swensen's deputy, chooses the management firms that in turn invest in all of these alternative asset classes.

With such a large allocation to alternative investments, the Yale endowment has lowered risk to much lower levels than would normally be associated with a portfolio allocation with so little in fixed income.[11] In fact, over the period from 1986 to 2009, a period that covers Swensen's tenure to date at Yale, the standard deviation of the portfolio has been only 13.3 percent compared with a standard deviation for the Russell 3000 of 16.3 percent. The fact that Yale has averaged a return of 14.2 percent is quite impressive given that the Russell 3000 return was only 9.2 percent over the same period and the S&P 500 return only 9.3 percent.[12] Lower risk and much higher returns—that's an impressive record. Adjusting the Russell 3000 (all-equity) return down to the risk level of the Yale endowment, the excess return of that endowment is an impressive 5.7 percent per annum. In other words, Yale has outperformed the U.S. stock market *adjusted for risk* by almost 6 percent per year on average since 1986.

In 1986 when Swensen took over the portfolio, Yale invested only 3.2 percent in private equity, 8.5 percent in real assets (mostly real estate) and nothing in absolute return assets.[13] Between 1985 and 2009, the Yale Endowment increased its commitment to alternative investments from 11.7 percent of the portfolio to 78 percent. Figure 13.6 compares Yale's

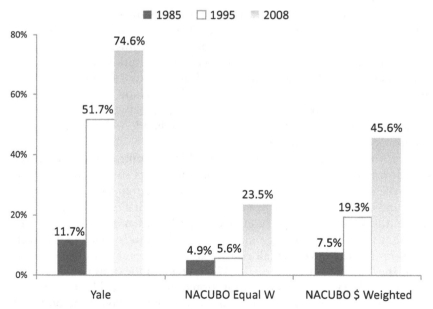

FIGURE 13.6 Allocation to Alternative Investments: Yale Endowment and University Endowments (NACUBO Survey)
Sources: Yale Endowment (various reports) and NACUBO.

allocation to alternatives with those of other university endowments as reported by NACUBO, the National Association of College and University Business Officers. Each year NACUBO conducts a survey of its members to determine the asset allocations that their endowments are following. NACUBO reports two sets of figures, those that equally weight all colleges and universities and a dollar-weighted average. The massive size of the endowments of the richest institutions ensures that the dollar-weighted average is heavily influenced by the asset allocation decisions of the biggest endowments. In 2008, the top 10 institutions had 36 percent of the endowment monies of the 791 institutions in the survey. The dollar-weighted average, therefore, better reflects the asset allocations of Yale's peers.

Figure 13.6 shows the asset allocations over more than three decades. In 1985 when Swensen took over the Yale Endowment, Yale's allocation to alternatives was still only 11.7 percent compared with NACUBO's equal-weighted average of 4.9 percent.[14] By 2008, NACUBO's average allocation to alternatives had increased to 23.5 percent while Yale's had risen to 74.6 percent. Interestingly enough, the NACUBO dollar-weighted average allocation had increased from 7.5 percent in 1985 to 45.6 percent in 2008. So Yale's shift toward alternatives is part of a larger trend in the endowments of many universities.[15]

To what extent is the shift toward alternatives by Yale part of a larger shift by all institutional investors? Some evidence about this issue is provided by the 2009 Greenwich Associate survey of pension plans, endowments, and foundations. The average asset allocation of the institutions in this survey is given in Figure 13.7.[16] These institutions devoted only 14.8 percent of their portfolios to alternative investments (defined to include real estate, private equity, and hedge funds). So there is a large gap between the allocations to alternatives by Yale and its peers on the one hand, and non-educational institutions on the other hand.

Investments in hedge funds provide the biggest contrast between university endowments and the other institutional investors studied in the Greenwich surveys. In 1999, the Greenwich survey did not even have a category for hedge funds. Between 2001 (when hedge funds were first reported) and 2009, average allocations to hedge funds increased from 0.6 percent to 4.0 percent. That's a large percentage increase in hedge funds, but the 4 percent allocation in 2009 is very small relative to the 15 percent strategic allocation of the Yale Endowment or the 12.9 percent allocation of the average university endowment.[17] So the institutional investor world has started to embrace hedge funds, but the university endowments have gone on to full courtship.

Yale's push into alternative investments has evidently been a key reason for its investment success. One way to see how well the Yale endowment has performed is to compare it with the conventional portfolio discussed

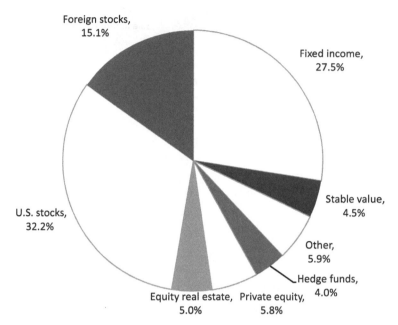

FIGURE 13.7 Investments of Pension Plans, Endowments, and Foundations
Source: Greenwich Investment Report, 2009.

earlier that is made up of traditional stock and bond investments. This is the portfolio shown on the left side of Figure 13.3. Figure 13.8 compares the Yale and conventional portfolios for the period since Swensen's tenure began. Since the conventional portfolio has a slightly higher risk standard deviation than the Yale portfolio (13.5 percent versus 13.3 percent), its risk is reduced to that of the Yale portfolio in order to make a proper comparison. The alpha* of the Yale portfolio relative to this benchmark portfolio is an impressive 4.3 percent.

It's important to try to disentangle the sources of Yale's success. Is the extraordinary return due to Yale's devotion to alternative investments? Or is it due to Yale's selection of (and access to) superior managers? We can try to extract an answer to these questions by constructing an experiment. Let's set up a portfolio with the same asset allocation that Yale followed each year over the period from 1986 to 2009, but with each asset invested in an index rather than in the managers that Yale selected. As previously noted, the indexed portfolio will reflect active management in some of the alternative asset classes such as hedge funds, venture capital, and private equity. So the returns on what we call the indexed portfolio will reflect the asset allocation chosen by Yale together with the performance of the average fund managers in the alternative investment indexes. And recall that

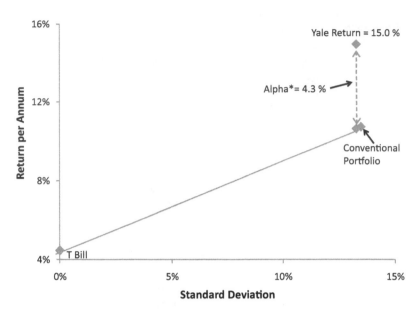

FIGURE 13.8 Alpha* of Yale Endowment Returns Relative to Conventional Portfolio, 1985–2009
Sources: Yale Endowment (various reports), ©Morningstar, Russell®, and MSCI.

some of these alternative investment indexes, particularly those for hedge funds, are upwardly biased. Comparing the return on this indexed portfolio with Yale's actual return gives us a measure of how much value added has come from Yale's manager selection and access to superior managers. This is an important issue because ordinary investors may not have the same access to managers that Yale does and because ordinary investors may not have the resources to find the best managers in the first place. But because of the biases in the indexes used, we will *underestimate the value added provided by Yale's superior manager selection and manager access*.

To apply this methodology, we must identify an index or indexes for each asset class. For some alternative asset classes, this is a difficult task since the range of alternatives chosen by Yale is difficult to capture in indexes. The following is a list of indexes chosen to represent each asset class:[18]

Cash: one month Treasury bill return from SBBI

Bonds: medium-term Treasury bond from SBBI (since Yale's bond portfolio is made up primarily of Treasuries)

Domestic equity: Russell 3000 all-cap stock index

Foreign equity: MSCI EAFE and MSCI Emerging Market indexes (with two thirds weight on MSCI EAFE)

Private equity: Cambridge Associates indexes for private equity and venture capital (one half weight for each)[19]

Absolute return: HFRI fund-weighted composite hedge fund index through 1993 and Credit Suisse/Tremont thereafter[20]

Real assets: NCREIF institutional real estate index and Goldman Sachs Commodity Futures Index (one half weight to each)

The real asset category in Yale's portfolio consists mainly of real estate, timberland, and oil and gas properties. For real estate, the NCREIF institutional real estate index is used instead of the FTSE NAREIT index because Yale uses it as its real estate benchmark. Since there are no good indexes for timberland and oil and gas properties, the GS commodity futures index, with its heavy weight on energy, is used instead.[21]

If Yale had invested in all of these indexes during Swensen's tenure, the endowment would have earned a return of 13.0 percent with a standard deviation of 13.4 percent (compared with Yale's 13.3 percent). An alpha* calculation can compare the relative returns on a risk-adjusted basis. Figure 13.9 shows the calculation. If an investor chose the Yale allocation each year, but invested in indexes, that investor would have earned *on a risk-adjusted basis* 2.3 percent more than an investment in the benchmark (traditional) portfolio. Yale's choice of managers then added *an extra 2.0 percent* to its performance. So *Yale's performance was based on its manager selection and access as well as on its reliance on alternative investments.* That's exactly what David Swensen told investors in his book *Unconventional Success (2005)*. It's important to reiterate that the return calculated using indexes is probably upwardly biased because some of the indexes for alternative investments, particularly the hedge fund indexes, are upwardly biased. So the estimate of what Yale earned due to manager selection and access is probably larger than indicated above. It's impressive enough as it is.

If Yale has led the charge into alternative investments, how well has it done relative to other universities? In Table 13.5, the returns of the Yale Endowment are compared with the average returns reported in the NACUBO studies. Over the period from 1986 to 2009, Yale has achieved a compound return of 14.2 percent compared with a return of 8.8 percent for the NACUBO equal-weighted return.[22] The NACUBO returns have less risk than Yale's, so it's important to compare the returns adjusted for risk. The Sharpe ratio for the Yale endowment is 0.79 compared with a Sharpe ratio

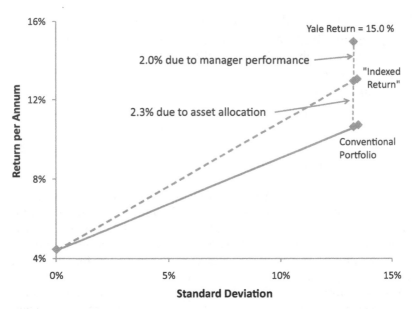

FIGURE 13.9 Alpha* of Yale Endowment Returns Relative to Indexed Portfolio and Conventional Portfolio
Sources: Yale Endowment (various reports) ©Morningstar, Russell®, MSCI, NCREIF, S&P, Cambridge Associates LLC U.S. Venture Capital Index® and Private Equity Index®, HFRI, and Credit Suisse/Tremont.

for the NACUBO index of 0.48. The risk-adjusted excess return, or alpha*, for the Yale endowment is an impressive 4.2 percent per annum. This excess return implies that Yale's endowment has delivered a cumulative excess return over the 24-year period of more than 160 percent. Not bad for a handful of staff in a New Haven office far from Wall Street!

TABLE 13.5 Performance of Yale Endowment Compared with University Endowments, 1986–2009

	Geometric Average	Arithmetic Average	Standard Deviation	Sharpe Ratio	Alpha*
Yale Endowment	14.2%	15.0%	13.3%	0.79	4.2%
NACUBO	8.8%	9.2%	10.0%	0.48	

Sources: Yale Endowment (various reports) and NACUBO.

LESSONS ABOUT ALTERNATIVE INVESTMENTS
LEARNED IN THE FINANCIAL CRISIS

Yale and other institutional investors suffered along with the rest of us when the financial crisis hit in 2007 to 2009. Yale's portfolio suffered a loss of 24.6 percent in the fiscal year 2009 (from July 2008 to June 2009). Harvard's portfolio was down 27.3 percent. The average return of NACUBO members was −18.7 percent. How do we explain these results? This section will examine how different types of alternatives fared during the crisis. Then it will examine Yale's performance.

One important feature of investments during the crisis was that they varied widely in how accurately they reflected true economic values. Stocks are priced on organized exchanges—marked to market at every point in time. The same is true of REITS and the commodity futures contracts measured by the GSCI or DJ UBS commodity indexes. The same cannot be said of private equity or the NCREIF valuation-based index of real estate returns.

Consider first the damage inflicted on publicly traded equities during the crisis. The S&P 500 index reached a peak for this cycle on October 9, 2007. For the next 17 months it fell 56.8 percent until reaching a trough on March 9, 2009. Using monthly data for total returns on the S&P 500 (including dividends), the cumulative return on the S&P 500 was −46.7 percent from October 2007 through March 2009. Over the same 17 months, the return on the EAFE index was −53.6 percent and the return on the MSCI Emerging Markets index was −55.9 percent.

Over the same period, private equity suffered, but their returns were far better than those of public equity. Table 13.6 compares returns on the S&P 500 with those on venture capital and private equity from Cambridge Associates. In contrast to the −46.7 percent return on the S&P 500, venture capital returned −15.6 percent and private equity −22.6 percent. Recall from Chapter 10 that the returns on VC and PE are based on valuations, which often reflect stale prices for the projects being evaluated. During the crisis, these valuations must have lagged far behind the public equity's pricing of similar companies. After all, private equity firms are trying to prepare their investments for eventual sale to the public equity markets. When the latter are down more than 40 percent, how can the private equity valuations be down less than half as much?[23]

A similar pattern is seen in real estate returns. Over this same period, the FTSE NAREIT return on publicly traded REITS was down 63.4 percent. But the NCREIF index reflecting the real estate holdings of institutional investors was down only 10.5 percent. Surely there cannot be that large a difference in the commercial real estate properties held in REITS on the one hand, and those held in institutional portfolios on the other hand. As explained

TABLE 13.6 Returns on Stocks and Alternative Investments during Financial Crisis

Index	October 2007–March 2009*	Fiscal 2009**
S&P 500	−46.7%	−26.2%
Venture Capital	−15.6%	−17.3%
Private Equity	−22.6%	−22.0%
FTSE NAREIT	−63.4%	−43.3%
NCREIF	−10.5%	−19.6%
GSCI	−51.3%	−59.7%
Credit Suisse/Tremont Hedge Fund	−19.0%	−13.7%

Notes: *S&P 500 peaked in October 2007 and fell until March 2009. Venture capital, private equity, and NCREIF returns are quarterly from 2007 Q4 through 2009 Q1. **Fiscal year is the 12 months ending in June 2009.
Data Sources: S&P, Cambridge Associates LLC U.S. Venture Capital Index® and Private Equity Index®, ©FTSE, NCREIF, and Credit Suisse/Tremont.

in Chapter 9 on real estate, the NCREIF index is based on appraisals, not market prices. Illiquid investments have stale valuations which are slow to reflect falling market values. Those stale valuations seem to shield investors from market downturns. But surely this is misleading.

Not all alternative investments are illiquid. Nor do all of them fail to reflect current pricing. The Dow Jones UBS Commodity Index and the Goldman Sachs Commodity Index are made up of commodity futures contracts which are constantly marked to market. So these indexes reflect current values. Nonetheless, commodities failed to protect investors from the crisis. The world recession that crushed equity valuations also leveled commodity markets. The GSCI fell 51.3 percent from October 2007 through March 2009, while the Dow Jones UBS Commodity Index fell 38.9 percent. Hedge funds, in contrast to commodities, did help to cushion investors from market turmoil during this period even though they are also marked to market.[24] The Credit Suisse/Tremont Hedge Fund Index was down only 19.0 percent over the 17- month period beginning in October 2007. It's true that some individual hedge fund strategies were down much more. Indeed, the Tremont market-neutral hedge fund index had a return of −41.8 percent over this same period. And it's also true that many hedge funds shut their gates, preventing investors from cashing out. In such cases, it was not very reassuring that your hedge fund investments were only down 19.0 percent if you had no access to them in the crisis period.

This crisis provided almost no place to hide from losses even if losses on some asset classes were smaller than on others. Almost every investment yielded negative returns. The most important exception was Treasury bonds. As the financial world came close to crumbling, investors fled to the safety of U.S. Treasury bonds and the dollar. The return on Barclays Capital Long-Term Treasury Index was a positive 22.5 percent over this same 17-month period! In contrast, bonds with credit risk fell in the crisis. The Barclays (investment-grade) Corporate Bond Index returned −6.1 percent and the Barclays High Yield Index returned −23.2 percent.

So for investors who only invested in stocks and bonds, Treasury bonds alone shielded the investor from losses. For investors who also had alternative investments, some but not all alternative investments helped to limit losses in the portfolio. First, there were hedge funds which fell much less than stocks. The cushion to portfolios was provided not by non-market pricing but because hedge fund betas are relatively low. Then there were the illiquid assets where the *reported* returns, at least, were less negative than those of publicly traded equities or publicly traded REITS. So a portfolio with alternatives declined less than a comparable portfolio with only publicly traded assets (both equity and real estate).

Consider the ultra HNW Portfolio A described in Table 13.4. Recall that this portfolio had 25 percent in bonds, 50 percent in stocks, and 25 percent in alternatives. This portfolio fell 30.0 percent from October 2007 through March 2009.[25] The conventional portfolio in Table 13.4 with 75 percent in stocks and no alternatives had a −35.5 percent return. So holding private equity and hedge funds did help to cushion the returns reported during the crisis. But as discussed above, some of that cushioning was more apparent than real.

With this discussion of asset returns during the crisis as background, we can now consider Yale's performance during the crisis. As stated earlier, for the fiscal year ended June 2009 Yale had a return of −24.6 percent. How much of that is due to Yale's asset allocation and how much is due to manager performance? Table 13.7 attempts to estimate the return Yale would have earned just based on index performance. The table uses Yale's *actual* asset allocation in *June 2008*, just before the beginning of the 2009 fiscal year. The indexes used for each asset class are the same ones used for the indexed portfolio in Figure 13.9. As Table 13.7 reports, Yale's portfolio should have earned −26.0 percent in the 2009 fiscal year if it had just invested in the indexes themselves. Instead Yale actually earned −24.6 percent.[26] That's a relatively small difference given the large losses suffered in almost every asset class. So at least according to this (admittedly imperfect) measure of the indexed return, Yale's losses are due to its asset allocation and not due to the failure of its managers to perform relative to their benchmarks. Indeed, the

TABLE 13.7 Performance of Yale Endowment Compared with Indexes in Fiscal Year 2009 (July 2008 to June 2009)

Asset	Index	Weight	2009 Return
Bonds	MT Treasury	4.0%	5.5%
Cash	Treasury Bill	−3.9%	0.6%
Domestic Equity	Russell 3000	10.1%	−26.6%
Foreign Equity	2/3 EAFE, 1/3 EM	15.2%	−29.9%
Real Assets	1/2 NCREIF, 1/2 GSCI	29.3%	−39.6%
Private Equity	1/2 VC, 1/2 PE	20.2%	−19.6%
Absolute Return	Credit Suisse/Tremont Hedge Fund	25.1%	−13.7%
Weighted Average			−26.0%
Yale Return			−24.6%

Notes: Weights represent Yale's actual asset allocation in June 2008 (before the 2009 fiscal year began). The foreign equity return is based on the EAFE return of −31.0 percent and MSCI EM return of −27.8 percent. Other returns are in Table 13.6.
Data Sources: Yale (2009), ©Morningstar, Russell®, MSCI, NCREIF, S&P, Cambridge Associates LLC U.S. Venture Capital Index® and Private Equity Index®, and Credit Suisse/Tremont.

managers on balance seem to have added marginally to Yale's performance even in the crisis.

So does Yale's loss in 2009 undermine its earlier performance? As David Swensen said in February 2009, *Propublica* (February 18, 2009).

> *For the period during which we're in crisis, the hoped-for benefits of diversification disappear. But once the crisis passes, then the fact that these different asset classes are driven by fundamentally different factors will reassert itself, and you'll get the benefits of diversification. It would be nice if we could always have the benefit of diversification, but life doesn't work that way.*

VERDICT ON ALTERNATIVE INVESTMENTS

No doubt asset allocation is improved with the addition of alternative investments. The adoption of alternatives will not guarantee Yale-size returns because other investors do not have the advantages of the Yale Endowment. But alternatives do shift the efficient frontier in a northwesterly direction. This chapter has documented this shift by examining the alpha* of portfolios with and without alternatives. Investors can improve their risk-adjusted performance with alternatives. They can reduce risk for a given return or increase return for a given risk. So alternatives are clearly desirable.

David Swensen expressed the view that ordinary investors could achieve a lot of this gain from diversification by sticking with conventional alternatives, real estate, and TIPS. In Swensen's portfolio for the ordinary investor, 20 percent of the allocation is given to real estate. The analysis above showed real estate investments do raise risk-adjusted returns, but the gain is small.

Diversifying beyond real estate to hedge funds and other alternatives is desirable, at least for those investors who are wealthy enough. But alternatives are no panacea for high net worth investors. Unless investors have access to the best managers, hedge funds or other alternatives are going to provide only modest improvement to the portfolio. The shift to the northwest is limited, or if excess returns are measured at a given level of risk, the alpha* is positive but relatively small. For HNW investors, that should still be enough of a recommendation.

NOTES

1. Estimated returns for these two assets are based on the real geometric average returns earned since 1951 of 2.4 percent and 6.7 percent, respectively. If long-term expected inflation is 2.5 percent a year, then the nominal compound returns are 4.9 percent and 9.4 percent per annum. These compound averages translate into the arithmetic averages needed for optimization of 5.0 percent and 10.0 percent, respectively.
2. Since the premium is measured using geometric returns, the estimated return on REITS is calculated as $(1.094)*(1.016) - 1 = 11.2\%$.
3. The standard deviations and correlations for the Barclays Capital TIPS Index were calculated beginning in March 1997 and entered manually in the Zephyr software.
4. Since the two portfolios have identical standard deviations, alpha* is just the difference between the two returns.
5. The Credit Suisse/Tremont index is a value-weighted index. The HFRI Fund Weighted index starts earlier in 1990, but it is an equally-weighted index so it seems preferable to use the Tremont index whenever possible.
6. So the estimated return is 2.7 percent below the S&P 500 return because the return is calculated using the compound formula $1.094 * (1 - 0.025) - 1 = 6.7\%$.
7. This would certainly be true of an investor with $5 million in wealth since many hedge funds have a minimum investment of at least $1 million. In the analysis of ultra HNW portfolios that follows, we will consider the returns from direct investment in hedge funds using the Credit Suisse/Tremont index because diversification of manager risk should be possible for those investors.

8. The returns required by the Zephyr optimizer are arithmetic averages, so as explained in Chapter 8 the geometric averages must be converted to arithmetic averages.

9. In the Merrill Lynch-Cap Gemini World Wealth Report (2008), for example, ultra HNW investors are those who have at least $30 million in financial assets excluding collectibles, consumer durables, and primary residences.

10. Recall that the private equity return measures buyout investments primarily.

11. Yale's allocation to fixed income was as much as 22 percent in the early 1990s, but that is still below the allocation to fixed income in most institutional portfolios.

12. The figures quoted are compound (geometric) averages. The arithmetic average returns were 15.0 percent for the Yale Endowment, 10.4 percent for the Russell 3000, and 10.7 percent for the S&P 500, the latter two indexes measured like the Endowment for the 12 months ending in June of each year.

13. The Yale Endowment (various years).

14. The chief real estate holding in 1985 was a single Manhattan office building at 717 Fifth Avenue. By the time Yale sold it in 2002, it had earned a 19.5 percent per annum return on its investment over a 24-year period! (Lerner, 2007)

15. Perhaps Yale has had influence on the allocations of other university endowments, particularly the larger endowments. Some of Swensen's colleagues have moved on to lead the endowments of other institutions, so Yale's influence may be both direct and indirect.

16. Percentages are U.S. dollar-weighted. Excludes U.S. assets held by public funds in defined contribution accounts. U.S. assets are projected to the 2009 Greenwich Associates universe of 2,040 institutional investors with $ 250 million or more in total assets based on responses from 1,009 institutions.

17. The NACUBO figure is for 2008. In 2008, Yale's actual allocation to absolute return investments was 25.1 percent. In 2009, that allocation had fallen to 24.3 percent, but it's notable that the target portfolio allocation illustrated in Figure 13.5 includes only 15 percent in absolute return. So Yale evidently intends to cut back sharply on its absolute return investments in the future.

18. These benchmarks are not identical to those used by Yale itself. For example, Yale uses the Wilshire 5000 as its benchmark for U.S. equity investments. The correlation between this index and the Russell 3000 is 0.998, so this study will continue to use the Russell 3000 as the equity benchmark. For real assets, Yale uses the NCREIF real estate index as well as a Cambridge Associates composite. This study instead uses NCREIF plus a commodity index.

19. The private equity index begins in the second quarter of 1986, so only the venture capital index is used for 1985 and 1986.

20. The HFRI index begins only in 1990, but Yale added absolute return assets to its portfolio only in 1991. The Credit Suisse/Tremont value-weighted index is used as soon as it becomes available in 1994.

21. The Goldman Sachs index is preferable to the Dow Jones AIG index because the latter puts a limit on energy at 33 percent of the index.

22. NACUBO did not provide a dollar-weighted return for 2009. Through 2008, the dollar-weighted return was 3.8 percent below that of the Yale Endowment.

23. Harvard's experience with private equity supports this view. In late 2008, Harvard was reported to have tried selling some of its private equity stake only to have to withdraw the sale because of low bids. In its 2009 endowment report, Harvard estimates that its private equity investments returned –31.6 percent in fiscal 2009 (Harvard 2009). That return includes realized capital losses of $439 million reported by *Forbes* (2009).

24. It should be noted that many hedge funds invest in illiquid securities, and marking to market involves estimation of the value of these securities, but on the whole hedge funds' returns rely much more on market pricing than private equity or direct real estate investments.

25. The crisis return of 30.0 percent is based on a 5 percent allocation to REITs (as in Table 13.4). If instead, the NCREIF valuation-based return is used for the real estate investment, then the portfolio return is −27.4 percent.

26. If the FTSE NAREIT index (instead of the NCREIF index) is used in the calculation of the real asset return, the benchmark return is −29.5 percent, so the difference between Yale's performance and the benchmark widens considerably.

CHAPTER 14

Investing and Spending by Foundations

Foundations and other charitable institutions come in a variety of forms with a multitude of missions. But most of them have one thing in common: They hope to keep carrying out their missions over a long horizon. Their endowments are not infinite, so they must husband their resources by investing wisely and spending at a rate that is sustainable in the long run. They face three tough questions, the outcome of which will determine whether their programs can continue to be funded:

1. How much can the foundation afford to spend per year?
2. What type of investment portfolio will sustain that spending plan?
3. What risks might undermine these investment and spending plans?

This chapter will attempt to answer these three questions.

The spending policy of a foundation is related to its asset allocation. After all, a foundation that prefers to invest in very safe assets must realize that its spending policy has to be equally conservative. And a foundation that diversifies its portfolio may decide that it is able to sustain a higher spending rate than a foundation that sticks with very conservative investments. That's the focus of this chapter. To what extent does the investment allocation determine spending policies, and to what extent do spending policies necessitate more or less aggressive allocations?

The spending plans of foundations are simpler to analyze than those of individual investors. That's because in most cases foundations are long-lived, while individuals have finite lives. Individuals have to factor in mortality risk along with investment risks. In the next chapter we will consider just how complicated investing can be for an individual facing a life cycle of work and retirement. Investing and spending for foundations will be complicated enough so we start with foundations.

In the 1980s and 1990s, foundations didn't have to spend much time thinking about these issues. With both bond and stock markets delivering double-digit returns, it was natural to focus on the expansion of programs rather than the husbanding of finite resources. It was an ideal time to be running any investment portfolio. And foundations drawing from such portfolios could reap the benefits of high investment returns.

With the end of the bull market in bonds as well as stocks, foundations have been forced to return to reality. Investment returns in the next 20 years are unlikely to match those of the 1980s and 1990s. In those decades, there was a bull market for bonds because we started the 1980s with very high inflation and interest rates, and ended the 1990s with much lower inflation and even lower interest rates. The capital gains from falling interest rates led to outsized returns on bond portfolios. In those decades, there was also a bull market for stocks because the U.S. economy performed so much better in those decades than in the 1970s, and because stock market valuations rose even faster than the earnings that the economy generated.

Because investment returns are likely to be more modest in the future, foundation boards have to think carefully about the sustainability of their operations. That will require dispassionate appraisal of likely investment returns, and belt-tightening in budgeting that reflects today's investment realities. This reappraisal is needed not because there is something wrong with the American economy, but because markets in the future are much more likely to resemble those found in the long history of markets prior to the 1980s.

SPENDING RULES

If a foundation wants to keep its programs running for an indefinite period, it should consider adopting a *spending rule*, a rate of spending that can be sustained through time. Sometimes foundations base their spending on the income from their bonds and stocks. They choose their portfolios so as to maximize the coupons from their bond portfolios and dividends from their stock portfolios. This strategy may or may not be ideal as an investment strategy, but it should not be the basis of a spending rule. Foundations should be willing to use both income and principal from their portfolios if the spending can be sustained.

To see why bond coupons or stock dividends may be the wrong basis for spending out of a portfolio, consider a simple example. Suppose that the foundation with a $10 million endowment puts the entire portfolio in long-term government bonds. Would it be safe to spend the coupons on these bonds? In answering this question, we will establish an important principal:

the spending rule must be based on the real, or inflation-adjusted, return on the portfolio.

Let's examine the spending rule for an all-bond portfolio under a simplifying assumption: *There is no inflation risk.* We know for certain that inflation will be only 2.5 percent per year for the next 30 years. This is a totally unrealistic assumption, but it will help us to analyze the bond portfolio. Suppose that the foundation invests its entire $10 million portfolio in 30-year Treasury bonds that have a coupon of 4.9 percent. What spending rule can be sustained? Some foundations might assume that the spending rate could be 4.9 percent, but that would be much too high. Even with a rate of inflation as low as 2.5 percent, the cost of living rises by 28 percent in 10 years and by almost 64 percent in 20 years. So the $490,000 would buy fewer and fewer goods and services as time goes by. That is, the foundation would see its *real* spending decline significantly over time.

If the foundation wanted to keep spending in line with the cost of living, then the spending rule would have to be based on the real, or inflation-adjusted, return on the bonds. Since 1951, the real return on Treasury bonds has been 2.4 percent (through 2009). The average real return is about the same for the 80+ years extending all the way back to 1926.[1] To keep spending in line with inflation, the spending rule would have to be equal to this real return.

Reality is actually worse than described above because we are not sure what future inflation will be. Because inflation could potentially rise significantly above 2.5 percent, as it did in the 1970s, a foundation would have to lower its spending rule *below* the expected real return on bonds. How low spending must be depends on assumptions regarding the volatility of inflation as well as the expected real return on bonds during retirement.

Most foundations, however, would find it hard to get along with a spending rule as low as 2.4 percent. To sustain a higher spending rule, it's important to invest in assets that, historically at least, have outperformed bonds. Foundations, however, face a problem in assessing the returns that might be earned in the future. The decades of the 1980s and 1990s saw unusually high stock and bond returns. In the 20-year period from 1981 to 2000, the real return on the S&P 500 was an incredible 11.7 percent per year on average, while the real return on the medium-term Treasury bond was 6.2 percent.[2] These returns help to explain why foundations and other institutions did not have to pay much attention to portfolios in the 1980s and 1990s. If you are earning between 6.2 percent and 11.7 percent on your portfolio in real terms, there seems to be no need to focus on whether a particular spending rule is sustainable. In the longer period stretching from 1951 to 2009, however, the real return on the S&P 500 averaged only 6.7 percent and the real return on the Treasury bond averaged only

2.4 percent. If returns revert to these long-run averages, foundations will have to pay a lot of attention to their spending rates.

ESTIMATING FUTURE BOND AND STOCK RETURNS

Spending rules have to be based on estimates of future bond and stock returns. As explained above, it's the estimates of the real returns that matter for spending rules. In Chapter 2, we discussed how to formulate estimates using long-run historical data. In that chapter, we developed estimates of the real returns on Treasury bonds and the S&P 500 using data beginning in the 1950s. There we discussed returns on both the medium-term (five-year) Treasury bond and the long-term (20-year) Treasury bond, but here we will focus just on the medium-term bond.[3] Since 1951, the medium-term bond has earned a real compound return of 2.4 percent.

In the case of the S&P 500, we developed two different estimates of the long-run real return. The first was based on the actual real returns earned from 1951 to 2009. According to Table 2.2, the real compound return has averaged 6.7 percent since 1951. That estimate reflects the actual capital gain experienced during the period. Fama and French (2002) developed alternative estimates of stock returns based on the rate of growth of earnings rather than the actual capital gain. Table 2.4 updated their estimates to obtain an average (real) compound return for the S&P 500 based on earnings growth of 5.3 percent.[4]

The first row of Table 14.1 lists these estimates of the real compound returns. Because we will need nominal arithmetic averages later in this chapter, the table also shows the nominal compound average calculated by assuming a 2.5 percent future inflation rate. For example, the nominal compound average for the S&P 500 is calculated as $(1 + 0.067) * (1 + 0.025) - 1 = 9.4\%$. The third row of the table then calculates the implied nominal arithmetic average. This is obtained by using a common approximation involving the standard deviation of the series involved.[5]

VOLATILITY AND UNCERTAINTY

The returns just cited are average real returns. It's important to assess the impact of the volatility of these returns. You can drown in a pond with an average depth of three feet. Consider the case of the S&P 500 from 1951 to 2009. The standard deviation of the S&P 500 expressed in annual terms was 14.6 percent, while the real compound return was 6.7 percent. Suppose that a foundation sets spending at the expected real return of 6.7 percent.

TABLE 14.1 Long-run Bond and Stock Returns

	Medium-Term Bond	S&P 500	
		Based on Capital Gain	Based on Earnings Growth
Real Compound Average	2.4%	6.7%	5.3%
Nominal Compound Average	4.9%	9.4%	7.9%
Arithmetic Average	5.0%	10.1%	8.7%

Sources: The real compound averages are obtained from Tables 2.2 and 2.4. The nominal compound averages are based on an assumed 2.5% inflation rate. The arithmetic averages are obtained from the compound averages using the standard deviation of each series (and an approximation formula).

Figure 14.1 shows how a $10 million portfolio grows over 20 years if invested in the S&P's real return and if spending is maintained at that same real return. The cases shown are those where actual returns are equal to 6.7 percent and where actual returns are one standard deviation above or below 6.7 percent. If average real returns are equal to the spending rate, the

FIGURE 14.1 Portfolio Values Diverge with Returns (Real Returns 1 Standard Deviation Above and Below)

foundation keeps the original portfolio intact in real terms over the 20-year period studied. The portfolio has grown in nominal terms with the cost of living, but the real value of the portfolio remains at $10 million. If average real returns are one standard deviation below 6.7 percent, the $10 million portfolio shrinks almost to $1 million over 20 years.

The situation may be even worse than pictured because the timing of the returns matters. Bad returns may occur early in the investment horizon. A bear market like that experienced in 2001 and 2002 or 2008 and 2009 can cripple a foundation's spending plan. To take into account such bad scenarios, we use simulation methods where a large range of different outcomes can be examined. By considering many trials drawn from a sample with given average returns and volatilities, we can try to model the investment uncertainties facing a foundation. Each trial will consist of at least 1000 simulations drawn randomly from a statistical distribution. It's the random nature of the drawing that gives the simulation method its Monte Carlo name.[6]

PORTFOLIOS OF STOCKS AND BONDS

Because risk is central to the success or failure of spending rules, we will try to reduce risk by diversifying the portfolio. Instead of being based on the Treasury bond alone, the bond returns are based on the Barclays Capital Aggregate Index. In the case of stocks, both foreign and domestic stocks are included in the portfolio, with foreign stocks set at one-third of the total stock allocation. Foreign stocks are represented by the Morgan Stanley EAFE index, while U.S. stocks are represented by the Russell 3000 index rather than the narrower S&P 500 index. A portfolio consisting of these three assets provides additional (admittedly modest) diversification relative to a portfolio with Treasury bonds and the S&P 500 index alone. With foreign stocks representing one-third of the stock portion of the portfolio, a 75/25 stock/bond portfolio consists of 25 percent in the Barclays Aggregate index, 50 percent in the Russell 3000 index, and 25 percent in the EAFE index.

There is one drawback to choosing such a diversified mixture of stocks and bonds. As explained in Chapter 8 on asset allocation, the three indexes chosen begin in the 1970s, not in 1951. If the returns on these indexes were used without modification, the series would be measured beginning in 1979, the first year when the shortest index, the Russell 3000 index, is available. That would mean that the simulations would be based on the high real returns of the 1980s and 1990s bull market. Instead of truncating the data set by starting in 1979, we choose to use a premium method to estimate returns. The average return on each stock index is measured relative to the

TABLE 14.2 Premium-based Estimates for Bond and Stock Returns

	Period of Estimation	Premium	Estimate
Medium-Term Treasury	1951–2009		4.9%
Barclays Aggregate	1976–2009	0.3%	5.2%
S&P 500 (Actual Capital Gain)	1951–2009		9.4%
Russell 3000	1979–2009	0.0%	9.4%
MSCI EAFE	1970–2009	0.3%	9.7%

Source: The premiums are obtained from Table 8.3. The S&P 500 estimate is based on the actual capital gain.

S&P 500 over the common period for which both series are available. Then that same discount or premium is used to estimate what the index would have earned over the 1951 to 2009 period.

Table 14.2 reports the premiums for the three series involved. In the case of the Russell 3000, for example, the premium was zero from 1979 to 2009. In the case of the EAFE index, the returns could be measured beginning in 1970. The premium + 0.3 percent over this 40-year period results in a nominal return of 9.7 percent. In the case of the Barclays Aggregate, the benchmark is the medium-term Treasury bond, and the premium of 0.3 percent leaves the bond return at 5.2 percent.

Standard deviations and correlations were handled differently. In order to reflect the benefits of diversification in the simulations, we measured standard deviations and correlations using the three assets over the common period for which they were available, 1979 to 2009. There is no particular reason to believe that volatility statistics drawn from this 30-year period won't be good estimates of the volatility of the portfolio in the future.

DESCRIPTION OF THE SPENDING PLAN

Once the portfolio is chosen and the returns are estimated, the foundation must determine the objective of its spending plan. One natural objective is to set a spending rule that can be sustained *in real terms* indefinitely. But there are two alternative types of spending rules: (1) *absolute* rule where spending is set in dollar terms as a percent of today's endowment, then adjusted each year for inflation, or (2) *proportional rule* where spending is set as a percent of each year's endowment.[7] If the latter choice is made, then spending could rise or fall depending on the returns experienced.

As will be demonstrated below, making spending rise or fall with the size of the endowment allows higher spending rates than when spending is fixed in dollar terms. The reason is that bad returns generate cutbacks in spending, and this flexibility reduces the chance that the foundation will have to cut back its spending more drastically in the future.

Returns could be bad enough to force the foundation to abandon its spending plan. This would certainly occur if the portfolio were wiped out entirely. Most foundations, however, would abandon the spending plan far short of that threshold. It seems sensible for the foundation to set an upper limit for losses on the portfolio or, equivalently, set a lower bound for the size of the endowment. In the simulations below, we will assume that if the endowment sinks more than *35 percent* in real terms, then the foundation abandons its plan.[8] In this circumstance, the spending plan is said to have failed. The aim of the simulations is to determine the probability of such failures.

USING HISTORICAL RETURNS SINCE 1951 TO SET SPENDING RULES

The first set of simulations will be based on actual historical returns on stocks and bonds since 1951. That is, the returns will be based on the 2.4 percent real return on medium-term bonds and the 6.7 percent real return on the S&P 500. Because the portfolio consists of three assets with shorter historical series, the premium method discussed above will be used to determine the returns on these three assets using the 2.4 percent and 6.7 percent real returns on the longer historical series. The expected nominal compound return on the three asset portfolio is 8.8 percent. The simulations will be done using the simulation software Zephyr AllocationADVISOR.[9]

The results of these simulations are shown in Figure 14.2. The spending rate of the foundation is set at rates between 3 percent and 6 percent. After a thousand simulations, the software calculates the percentage of times in which the portfolio falls below its minimum threshold of 65 percent of the initial portfolio value. This gives the failure rate for the spending rule. The lower curve in Figure 14.2 represents simulations in which the spending rule is kept proportional to the level of wealth. So a 4 percent spending rule represents $400,000 spent out of a $10 million dollar portfolio in the first year of operation. If nominal returns are 10 percent the first year, then the 4 percent spending rule will allow the foundation to spend $440,000 the second year. If nominal returns are –10 percent the first year, then the foundation's spending will have to fall by $40,000. The upper curve representing the alternative spending rule sets spending at a given dollar amount which is then adjusted only for inflation. So a 4 percent spending rule would

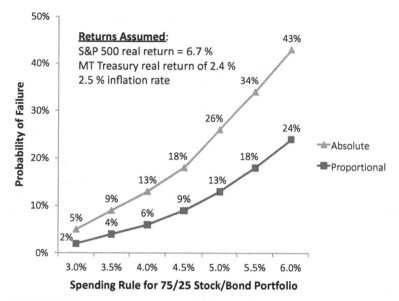

FIGURE 14.2 Spending Rules and Failure Rates: Absolute and Proportional Rules Compared

start out with $400,000 in the first year, then rise by the inflation rate of 2.5 percent the second year (or $10,000).

Consider first the set of simulations based on a proportional spending rule. A 5 percent spending rate results in a 13 percent failure rate. That is, in 13 percent of the simulations, the foundation's spending rule has to be abandoned as the endowment slips more than 35 percent. The 5 percent spending rate has special significance for American foundations because IRS rules require that many charitable foundations spend at least 5 percent of their endowments. The failure rate can be reduced significantly if spending is reduced. A spending rate of 4 percent reduces the failure rate to 6 percent.

Switching to an absolute dollar spending rule rather than a proportional spending rate leads to worse results. Without the flexibility of reducing spending when the portfolio falls in value, the failure rate rises from 13 percent to 26 percent in the case where spending is maintained at a 5 percent rate. To understand why there is such a large difference between the two rules, consider what happens to the foundation if the portfolio falls sharply in a downturn like that experienced recently. With the proportional rule, spending is cut sharply as well, but with the absolute rule spending is maintained at its original rate. No wonder the absolute rule has so many more failures. It's clear that the foundation needs some flexibility in its spending as its investment returns rise and fall. Even with a 4 percent spending rule, the failure rate is 13 percent.

Flexibility in spending, of course, has its costs. In the downturn beginning in October 2007, returns plummeted by almost 35 percent over the next 17 months through March 2009. Foundations following proportional spending rules were required to cut their programs drastically. Fortunately, many foundations followed modified proportional rules which required that they base spending on an average portfolio level over the past few years rather than portfolio values in one year alone. Yale's endowment, for example, follows a weighted average rule based on portfolio values over three years.[10] Such a smoothing rule cushions the pain of spending cutbacks, but the pain is real nonetheless. Note that a three-year rule requires that spending stay depressed for one or two years even if a portfolio regains its original value.

EFFECT OF LOWER STOCK RETURNS ON SPENDING RULES

Basing spending rules on the returns since 1951 may be a little optimistic because historical returns on stocks may be unsustainable in the future (for the reasons discussed above). It makes sense to study the sensitivity of spending rules to alternative sets of stock market returns. The simulations will continue to be based on the 2.4 percent real return on Treasury bonds and 5.2 percent nominal return on the Barclays Aggregate index. But in place of the 6.7 percent historical return on the S&P index, we will consider the estimate of real returns based on S&P 500 earnings growth. As reported in Table 14.1, this alternative estimate is that the S&P 500 will give average real returns of 5.3 percent rather than 6.7 percent. The equivalent compound nominal return based on 2.5 percent inflation is 7.9 percent. Some market observers would consider stock return estimates in the 8 percent range as being more realistic than the 9.4 percent returns implied by historical averages.

The returns for the Russell 3000 and EAFE indexes used in the simulations are reduced along with the return on the S&P index. With a 75/25 stock/bond allocation, the nominal expected (compound) return for the portfolio as a whole falls to 7.7 percent from 8.8 percent for the simulations based on historical data. With such a fall in expected returns, there is a correspondingly large increase in the failure rates for each spending rule.

Figure 14.3 reports failure rates for the two cases including the simulations based on historical averages previously reported. Both sets of simulations assume a proportional spending rule, so spending rises and falls with the size of the endowment. Let's focus first on a 5 percent spending rule.

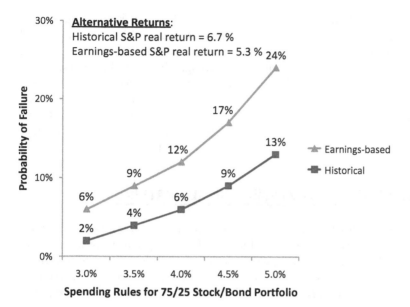

FIGURE 14.3 Spending Rules for Alternative Return Assumptions (Historical and Earnings-Based)

The historical data results in a failure rate of 13 percent. Using the estimate of stock returns based on earnings growth raises the failure rate to 24 percent. A spending rate of 5 percent already looks problematical under historical return assumptions unless the foundation's board is willing to contemplate a 13 percent failure rate. If stocks earn the lower level of returns based on earnings growth, however, a 5 percent spending rule looks reckless. If the spending rate is lowered to 4 percent, the failure rates range from 6 percent to 12 percent. So it matters a lot what return assumptions are adopted by the foundation in setting a spending rule.

What if we were to ask how high a spending rate it is reasonable for the foundation to adopt? The answer would partly depend on how high a failure rate the foundation is willing to tolerate. If a 10 percent failure rate is the upper limit, then it seems that spending must stay within the 3 percent to 3.5 percent range. If the foundation adopts historical returns as a guideline for future returns, it can stay at the higher end of this range with a 4 percent or even 4.5 percent spending rate. If the foundation adopts the lower estimate of future stock returns, then a 3.5 percent spending rule leaves them with a 9 percent failure rate. There is no doubt that this set of expected returns will involve considerable belt tightening.

Before considering other asset allocations, let's ask how a foundation can reconcile a mandated 5 percent spending rate with a recommended spending rate of from 3 percent to 3.5 percent (assuming that there is such a mandate). If the foundation wants to hold its spending out of the endowment to 3-3.5 percent, then its only recourse is to raise additional funds to meet the mandated spending rate of 5 percent. In other words, the gap between the 5 percent mandate and a prudent spending rate becomes a guide to the fundraising that the foundation's board has to accomplish.[11] Confronting the new investment reality will be a real challenge for such boards.

EFFECTS OF DIFFERENT STOCK/BOND ALLOCATIONS

Low spending rules are required because of the risk of investment shortfalls. Is it possible to reduce the probability of failure by choosing a less risky portfolio? The answer to this question is counterintuitive. You would think that reducing the proportion of stocks in the portfolio from 75 percent to (say) 20 percent would reduce the risk of failure. In fact, it has the opposite effect.

To study the effects of different stock-bond allocations, consider a set of simulations based on the lower real stock return of 5.3 percent. The spending rate is set at the rate of 5 percent (that IRS rules require for many foundations). Figure 14.4 presents the failure rates for stock allocations ranging from 0 percent to 80 percent. Consider first the failure rate of 44 percent for a 20 percent stock allocation. The reason it is so much higher than that associated with a 75 percent stock allocation is that the 20 percent allocation has much too low an expected real return. The foundation is spending 5 percent even though most of its portfolio is invested in an asset with a 2.4 percent expected real return. The expected real return on bonds is simply too low to support such a spending rate.

Figure 14.4 suggests that there is a tradeoff between the stock allocation and the spending rule that foundations should be aware of. The lower the allocation to stocks, the lower the spending rule has to be (at least over the range of asset returns and spending rules being considered). In fact, it makes sense for the foundation's board to make the asset allocation decision in conjunction with its decision regarding spending policy. The two are intertwined.

It's important to recognize how the concept of risk changes when a foundation considers asset allocation along with its spending rule. Many investors focus on the downside risk of next year's returns. Stocks are undoubtedly more risky than bonds when viewed in this context. A foundation, however, has to think about the long-run viability of its portfolio strategy.

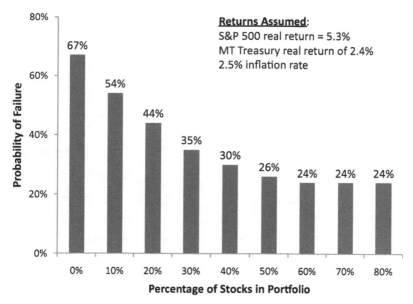

FIGURE 14.4 Effects of Stock-Bond Allocation on Failure Rates

More importantly, it has to think of the portfolio's expected return relative to the foundation's spending policy. It is the consistency of that spending plan with the portfolio strategy that matters. Adopting a bond portfolio may allow board members to sleep better at night, at least in the short run. But bond investments may be inconsistent with a reasonable spending rule. Over long historical periods, bonds have earned too little in real terms to sustain spending plans. The risk that *should* keep the foundation's board awake at night is the longer-run risk that its spending is going to collapse in the future because its portfolio has run out of money. It's that longer-run risk arising from the inconsistency of spending plans and investment allocations that should really matter.

There is a subtle feature of the asset allocation decision that is worth pointing out. There is a range of asset allocations in Figure 14.4 over which the failure rate varies very little. If the foundation were to set its stock allocation at 50 percent rather than 70 percent or 75 percent, there is remarkably little increase in the failure rate for its spending rule (from 24 percent to 26 percent). Suppose that the foundation's board was very risk averse. Then moving the stock allocation from 75 percent to 50 percent raises the failure rate only marginally. Moving from 50 percent to 10 percent, on the other hand, has a dramatic effect on the failure rate, raising it from 26 percent to 54 percent.

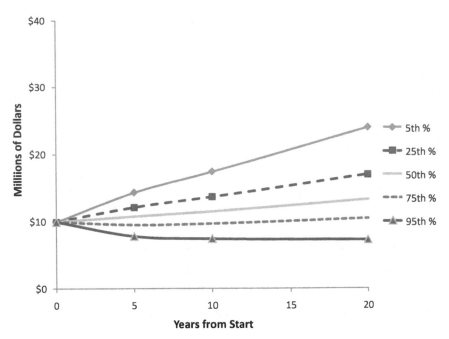

FIGURE 14.5 Range of Outcomes for 50/50 Stock/Bond Portfolio

Figure 14.4 seems to suggest that there is little cost for such a move to a lower 50 percent stock allocation. But there is a cost in terms of giving up *upside potential* for the portfolio. Figure 14.5 studies a range of outcomes for a 50/50 stock/bond portfolio. Starting at $10 million, the portfolio rises to $13.2 million (unadjusted for inflation) over the next 20 years if returns are in the fiftieth percentile. If returns are in the lowest 5 percent of the statistical distribution, however, the portfolio falls to $7.3 million. At the other extreme, if returns are in the highest 5 percent of the distribution, then the portfolio rises to $23.9 million over 20 years.

Now consider the effects of a higher stock allocation. Figure 14.6 reports the range of outcomes for a portfolio with 75 percent in stocks. If actual returns are equal to expected returns, the portfolio rises in 20 years from $10 million to $15.3 million. If returns are in the lowest 5 percent of the distribution, the portfolio falls to $6.7 million in 20 years, so choosing a higher allocation of stocks has relatively little effect on the downside risk of the portfolio. That's for the same reason why the failure rates in Figure 14.4 vary little as stock allocations fall from 75 percent to 50 percent. Moving to a higher stock allocation raises the expected real return, and this offsets the higher volatility of the portfolio. The advantage of a higher stock

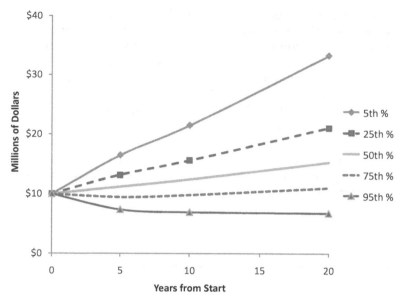

FIGURE 14.6 Range of Outcomes for 75/25 Stock/Bond Portfolio

allocation is found in the upside potential of the portfolio. If returns are in the highest 5 percent of the distribution, in 20 years the portfolio rises to $33.2 million rather than $23.9 million for the lower stock allocation. Similarly, the twenty-fifth percentile of the distribution has the portfolio rising from $10 million to $21.1 million rather than to $17.0 million.

What asset allocation is typically chosen by foundations and other tax-exempt institutions? The latest Greenwich Associates survey of more than 2000 pension plans, endowments, and foundations reports that the average institution had 27.5 percent of its assets in fixed income and most of the rest of the portfolio in public equities.[12] So most institutions recognize the need to invest a substantial part of the portfolio in stocks, and they appear to prefer some upside to the portfolio.

CONCLUDING COMMENTS

Foundations must recognize the new reality of investment returns. They cannot count on the bull markets of the 1980s and 1990s returning when spending seemed to have no limits. The new reality may be one where bonds and stocks provide the same level of real returns as they have over long stretches of the past. If so, foundations need to rethink their spending plans.

No set of simulations can give to the foundation a spending rule that is the correct one. So let's summarize the key issues that the foundation must address. First, the foundation needs to focus on the risk that really matters, the risk of running out of money rather than market volatility this year or next. Second, the foundation needs to base its spending rate on the returns it expects to earn on its portfolio *after inflation has been taken out*. Third, the higher the proportion of bonds in the portfolio, the lower has to be the spending rate. Fourth, the spending rate has to be lower than the expected real, or inflation-adjusted, return because otherwise its risk of failure will be too high. Fifth, the foundation has to recognize that we are not sure about what average real returns will be in the future, so we may have to be even more conservative about return assumptions than past returns would indicate.

NOTES

1. As reported in Table 2.2, the average real return from 1926 to 2009 is 2.3 percent.
2. See Table 2.2.
3. In Chapter 7 on bonds, we showed that the medium-term bond is a better benchmark for fixed income returns than the long-term bond. The latter has substantially lower risk-adjusted returns.
4. This estimate based on earnings growth was measured over the 1951 to 2007 period because (as explained in Chapter 2) earnings were so volatile in 2008 and 2009. Table 2.4 also presents an estimate based on actual capital gains of 7.3 percent for 1951 to 2007. In this chapter we will use the lower estimate of 6.7 percent measured over the full 1951–2009 period, as reported in Table 2.2, since the rest of the book uses data through 2009.
5. The approximation is that the arithmetic average, $R(A) = R(G) + 0.5 * (\text{stdev})^2$, where $R(G)$ is the geometric average. Note that this formula is applied using a monthly standard deviation for the S&P of 4.21 percent.
6. Monte Carlo methods are widely used in the physical and social sciences to simulate random outcomes.
7. There are other possible spending rules that could be adopted. Some foundations, for example, have a spending rule proportional to a weighted average of portfolio values over the preceding few years as a means of smoothing outlays.
8. The collapse of stocks beginning in October 2007 would have just barely escaped triggering this threshold. Between October 2007 and March 2009, the 25/50/25 portfolio described above earned a −35.0 percent return. But this involved the Russell 3000 return falling almost 47 percent and the EAFE return almost 54 percent, an unusual collapse in equity markets.
9. Zephyr AllocationADVISOR requires an arithmetic nominal return for each asset in the portfolio, not a compound (or geometric) real return. So the

simulations are performed using a 9.14 percent arithmetic average return for the portfolio.

10. Yale's smoothing rule is based on 80 percent of the previous year's spending and 20 percent of the targeted long-term spending rate applied to the market values of the two years prior. See Yale (2009), p. 19.

11. Since universities have the ability to raise additional funds, their spending rules tend to be closer to 5 percent. According to the 2008 NACUBO Endowment Study, the average spending rate for colleges and universities in 2008 was 4.6 percent.

12. Greenwich Investment Report (2009). 47.3 percent of the average portfolio was in stocks with another 5.0 percent in equity real estate.

CHAPTER 15

Investing and Spending
in Retirement

After a foundation chooses its asset allocation, it should be able to leave that allocation unchanged for the indefinite future. As the last chapter showed, a foundation can set up a spending plan and choose a long-run strategic asset allocation to support it. Unless there is major distress in the markets, the foundation should be able to carry out its plans without making changes to its allocation. It will hire and fire managers, but the overall investment plan should remain unchanged. Some foundations, of course, will pursue *tactical* asset allocation in an attempt to take advantage of short-term opportunities to overweight or underweight specific asset classes. But usually the tactical asset shifts are relative to a *strategic* (i.e., long-run) asset allocation that remains unchanged.

Individual investors are different. Most individual investors have one major investment goal—to save enough for retirement. Spending out of their portfolio is usually minimal in the years when they are working. Then spending becomes essential at the time of retirement. For this reason, there is a *life-cycle* to investing. In the years when wealth is being accumulated, asset allocation is much more aggressive than when the investor nears retirement.

In the last few years, investment firms have begun to formalize this process by which asset allocation changes over time. These firms have created *target retirement funds* which change continuously as the investor gets closer to retirement. The funds are usually defined relative to the year of retirement. So in 2010 a 52 year old might invest in a 2025 retirement fund because that investor intends to retire at 67 years of age (for full Social Security benefits).[1] Consider the 2025 target retirement fund offered by Vanguard as shown in Figure 15.1. The 52 year old is initially invested in a 75/25 stock/bond portfolio (diversified between domestic and foreign stocks). By the time of retirement 15 years later, this investor will have only 50 percent invested

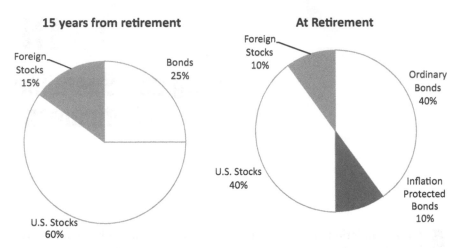

FIGURE 15.1   Portfolios for Investors 15 years Prior to and at Retirement
(Vanguard 2025 Target Retirement Fund)
Source: www.vanguard.com.

in stocks and 50 percent invested in bonds with a 10 percent allocation in
inflation-protected bonds (to help protect against inflation in retirement).

Target retirement funds are designed to model the life cycle of investing
beginning with the early years of working when very aggressive allocations
are called for. Figure 15.2 shows the evolution over time of the Vanguard
allocations in their 2035 target retirement fund. Until the investor reaches
25 years before retirement, Vanguard chooses a 90/10 stock/bond allocation. Then the fund begins to increase its allocation to bonds until the investor finally reaches the retirement age (denoted R in the figure). Even after
retirement, the allocation continues to shift. Five years after retirement, the
stock/bond allocation is at 36/64. Experts can debate whether these specific
allocations are optimal, but the figure shows clearly how the proportion of
riskier assets depends on the distance from the age of retirement.

Vanguard is only one of the firms that offer such target retirement
funds. Figure 15.3 shows the allocation chosen by four major firms for an
investor in 2010 planning to retire in 2025.[2] The stock/bond ratio varies
from 68/32 in the Fidelity program to 79/21 in the T Rowe Price program.
And the percent of stocks invested in foreign markets varies from 30 percent
in the Schwab program to 20 percent in the Vanguard program. Figure 15.3
shows that experts can disagree about the specific asset allocation. But it's
clear that for all such programs, the asset allocation is governed by savings
and spending decisions for retirement. This is the reason why a book on
asset allocation has a separate chapter for retirement.

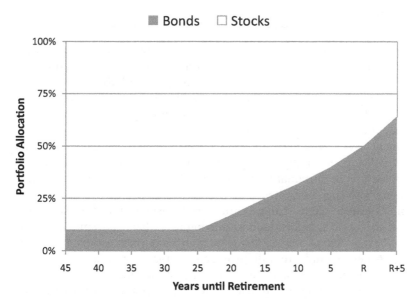

FIGURE 15.2 Vanguard's Target Portfolio Allocations Determined by Years until Retirement
Source: www.vanguard.com.

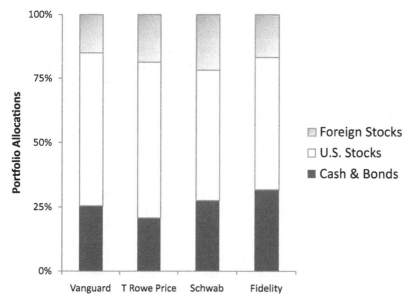

FIGURE 15.3 2010 Asset Allocations for Four Target 2025 Funds
Sources: web sites of firms—see text.

LONGEVITY

Many Americans don't really understand how long their retirement may be. Life expectancy has increased steadily over the last 50 years at the same time that the age of retirement has fallen. According to the Labor Department, the median age of retirement for both men and women is about 62 years of age.[3] That's down from an average age between 66 and 67 in the 1950s. Americans at 62 can often look forward to 20 or even 30 more years of life in retirement. Yet few Americans have a coherent plan to make sure their resources will last that long. Savings are often inadequate and spending is often too high to be sustainable. Investment decisions, moreover, are often inconsistent with spending rates.

Some Americans are fortunate enough to have guaranteed pensions that provide them with a steady income throughout their retirements. These are the old-style *defined benefit pensions* that were once quite common in corporate America (and are still provided by many state and local governments). The pensions provide a guaranteed income to the employee and often to the employee's spouse in the event of the death of the employee. Sometimes the income is indexed to inflation, rising with the cost of living during retirement. Today, the balance has shifted away from defined benefit pension plans to *defined contribution* pension plans, like the 401(k) plan, where workers contribute part of their salaries to the plan, with firms often matching or supplementing the employee contributions. According to a Department of Labor study summarized in Figure 15.4, in 2003 only 24 percent of Americans in the private sector still had defined benefit pensions compared with 48 percent that had defined contribution plans.[4] Employees with the latter type of pension plan are, in a sense, responsible for their own retirement. If they save enough during their careers and invest wisely, they can enjoy a comfortable retirement.

How much is enough? That depends on how much they hope to spend in retirement and how much income they can derive from their portfolios. This chapter will explore both investing and spending in retirement. Decisions that Americans make about investing and spending can make a big difference in determining how financially secure they are in retirement.

In considering these issues, it will be helpful to know just how long our savings must last. Figure 15.5 presents some estimates of how long current 62 year olds are likely to live.[5] For a 62-year-old man today, the median age of death is estimated to be 85 years, with 25 percent of his cohort likely to live to be 92 years old. For a 62-year-old woman, the median age is 88 and the 25 percent point is reached at 94 years. For a married couple at 62 years old, the relevant statistic is the life expectancy of the *surviving* spouse.

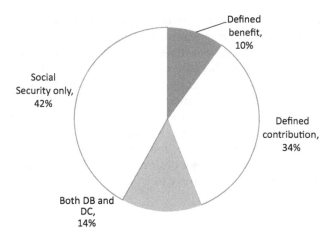

FIGURE 15.4 Pensions of Full-Time Employees in Private Industry in 2003
Source: U.S. Department of Labor (Wiatrowski, 2004).

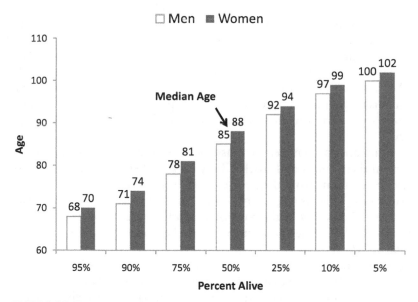

FIGURE 15.5 Life Expectancies of Today's 62 Year Olds
Source: Financeware®.

The median age of death for the surviving spouse is 92 years of age! So the nest egg accumulated for retirement must last a long time.

With lifetimes this long, investment horizons must be just as long. In fact, they need to be longer because you may live longer than the average person your age. Yet Americans entering retirement often choose portfolios appropriate for retirees of their grandparents' generation who typically lived only a few years after they retired. Retirees of that generation used to invest in bonds during retirement. Investing in bonds surely seems the safe thing to do. It helps us to sleep at night if we avoid stocks and other volatile investments. That's all well and good for emotional wellbeing, but does the average American realize how little can be spent if a portfolio is weighted heavily toward bonds?

SPENDING RULES FOR RETIREMENT

There is a key concept in retirement planning that most Americans have not even heard of. That is the concept of a *spending rule*, a rate of spending in retirement that can be sustained through time. As explained in the last chapter, foundations have spending rules that guide their activities through time. So must retirees, since they also must live off of their endowment—the wealth they have accumulated for retirement. If the retiree has a *defined benefit* retirement plan, spending can be tied to the income from that plan (plus Social Security). Most of us are not fortunate enough to have such a plan. For the many Americans with only *defined contribution* retirement plans, there is no guaranteed income from those plans, and retirement spending must depend on returns from accumulated wealth. So a spending plan is necessary.

Like foundations, some retirees base their spending in retirement on the *income* from their bonds and stocks. They choose their portfolios so as to maximize the coupons from their bond portfolios and dividends from their stock portfolios. This strategy may or may not be ideal as an investment strategy, but it should not be the basis of a spending rule. Retirees should be willing to use both income and principal from their portfolio *if the spending can be sustained.*

Like foundations, retirees have to worry about the volatility of their portfolio returns. We can measure that volatility using standard deviations, but somehow that doesn't fully capture investment risk as perceived by retirees. After all, a foundation can go out of business if it draws bad returns. A retiree must struggle on. The timing of returns certainly matter. Bad returns may occur early in retirement. A bear market like that experienced in 2001 or 2008 can cripple a retirement. To take into account such bad scenarios, we use simulation methods where a large range of different outcomes can be examined. By considering many trials drawn from a sample with given average returns and volatilities, we can try to model the investment uncertainties facing retirees. Each trial will consist of at least 1000 simulations drawn randomly from a statistical distribution.

Returns are not the only source of uncertainty for the retiree. Central to investing and spending in retirement is *longevity risk*. If we knew for certain when we were to die, we could have a strategy for using up our capital before death. This is the principal behind annuities that guarantee income up until death (see discussion that follows). To properly model spending rules, it's important to incorporate longevity risk directly into the simulation. The simulation software we will use, *Financeware®*, does just that. Whenever a simulation is run, it draws from the mortality distributions developed by the Society of Actuaries. So in any given simulation, the man or woman may die early in retirement or live long past the median age of death for that cohort.

PORTFOLIOS OF STOCKS AND BONDS

By the time of retirement, the investor should have reduced the proportion of stocks in the portfolio way below that chosen during earlier working years. As discussed above, the Vanguard Target Retirement Fund shifts the investor from a 90 percent stock portfolio when the investor is 25 years from retirement to a 50/50 portfolio at retirement. The 50/50 retirement portfolio is a common one chosen, at least early in retirement.

Because risk is central to the success or failure of spending rules, we will try to reduce risk by diversifying the portfolio just as in the previous chapter on foundations. In the case of bonds, the bond returns are based on the Barclays Aggregate index. In the case of stocks, both foreign and domestic stocks are included, with foreign stocks being one-fifth of the total stock allocation (as in the Vanguard Fund). Foreign stocks are represented by the Morgan Stanley EAFE index, while U.S. stocks are represented by the Russell 3000 index. So a 50/50 bond/stock portfolio consists of 50 percent in the Barclays Aggregate index, 40 percent in the Russell 3000, and 10 percent in the MSCI EAFE indexes.

As in Chapter 8, the returns on these three indexes are obtained using the premium method. The premiums are then applied to the historical returns on the basic capital market assets, the S&P 500 and medium-term Treasury bond measured over the period since 1951. The compound *real* returns on these assets were 2.4 percent for the Treasury bond and 6.7 percent for the S&P 500.[6] The premiums are the same as in the previous chapter: 0.3 percent for the Barclays Aggregate and MSCI EAFE indexes and 0 percent for the Russell 3000 index. Standard deviations and correlations were calculated over the 1979 to 2009 sample period just as in the last chapter.

BASELINE CASE: CAN TWO LIVE MORE CHEAPLY THAN ONE?

We begin with two sets of simulations that will investigate differences between spending rules for single individuals and married couples. The first simulation will be for a 62 year-old man who has just retired. The second simulation will be for a 62 year-old married couple also newly retired.

At retirement, the 62 year-old man is assumed to choose a spending rule that is to rise with inflation. For example, a 5 percent spending rule for a retiree with $1 million will permit the retiree to spend $50,000 (before tax) the first year. With a 2.5 percent inflation rate, spending will rise to $51,250 the second year, and so on. Later simulations will allow part of the spending to fluctuate with the size of the portfolio rather than being a set dollar amount (adjusted for inflation).

The 62 year old is assumed to want to use his wealth to support his retirement. That is, he has no plans to leave a bequest, so his wealth can be used up during his lifetime. This will allow him to raise his rate of spending higher than in the case where his aim is to keep a given wealth level intact. Later simulations will allow for a specific bequest. Of course, he does not know his age of death ahead of time, so the challenge will be to adopt a spending rule that will keep his wealth positive throughout the remainder of his life.

The retiree must choose a spending rule low enough so that he does not *run out of money before death*. In the presence of uncertainty, however, it is difficult to eliminate all possibility of running out of money. So the aim is to choose a spending rule low enough so that the probability of running out of money (failure) is low. So we will be asking the following question: What is the probability of failure if a specific spending rule is adopted?

Simulations are run for spending rules ranging from 4 percent to 6 percent of initial wealth. The results for a single man at 62 are moderately encouraging. A spending rule of 4.5 percent has only a 4 percent probability of failure. That is, in 4 percent of the simulations, the 62 year-old man runs out of money before his death. A 5 percent spending rule raises the failure rate only to 10 percent.

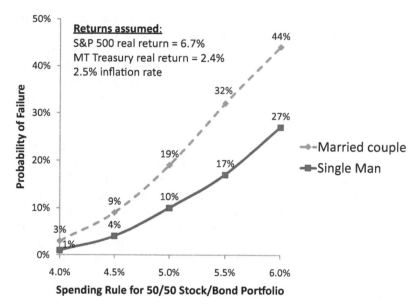

FIGURE 15.6 Spending Rules and Failure Rates for Single Man and Married Couple

Consider how these results are changed if the family consists of a married couple rather than a single man. The results will be different for two reasons. First, there are two lives to worry about rather than one, so the median age of death of the surviving retiree will generally be later than that of a single retiree. Second, the second person involved is a woman with a longer life expectancy. The results of both sets of simulations are reported in Figure 15.6.

Consider first a 5 percent spending rule. The probability of failure for the couple is 19 percent rather than the 10 percent found for a single man. If the spending rule is lowered to 4.5 percent, the probability of failure becomes 9 percent rather than 4 percent. The moral of the story seems to be: *reduce your spending in order to enjoy marital bliss.* Isn't it true that two can live more cheaply than one?

EFFECTS OF BEQUESTS AND VARIABLE SPENDING RULES

There are two features of the simulations discussed above that need to be investigated. First, the simulations assume the retirees are willing to use up wealth during their lifetimes. Some retirees may want to leave a bequest to charity or to their heirs. By introducing a planned bequest, the retiree also provides a cutoff point for the spending plan before wealth is more seriously depleted by market events. After all, not many retirees will adhere to a spending plan that completely impoverishes them. Second, the simulations assume that the retirees will keep spending at a given rate regardless of how high or low their investment returns are. We will investigate changing both features.

Consider first the bequest motive. The simulations might be designed so that the *target* level of wealth at death is some fraction of the original wealth level (adjusted for inflation). The retirees may choose this target for two different reasons. As stated above, the higher target will provide a bequest after death. But the higher target may also be chosen because retirees regard a decline in the portfolio anywhere near 100 percent as a disaster. Instead of a target level of zero wealth at death, suppose we assume that the retirees have a target level equal to 50 percent of the initial wealth.

Raising the target level of wealth will raise the probability of failure, since now failure is defined as having initial wealth fall below 50 percent of the initial wealth. So it's important to find some other way to mitigate the effects of a bad sequence of returns. Realistically, retirees are not going to keep spending the same amount if their wealth has fallen drastically. And they are not likely to keep their spending constant if they have had a whole string of good returns. So the second modification we will make is to have spending vary with current wealth.

It may not make sense for all spending to vary with wealth. (A proportional spending rule of 5 percent would cut the dollar amount spent in half, adjusted for inflation, if wealth falls by 50 percent). Perhaps a reasonable plan is to make half of the spending vary with wealth and to make half of it fixed (in real terms) over time. We will consider a plan where wealth is allowed to drop to 50 percent of its initial level and where half of the spending is tied to current wealth. So, for example, a 5 percent spending rule for retirees with $1 million will be split into $25,000 that is held fixed over time (adjusted for inflation) and 2.5 percent that will vary with the level of wealth. (The fixed allocation might be designed to cover fixed expenses). This flexibility in the spending rule will make it easier to keep wealth above the target level.

Figure 15.7 shows the results of these simulations. These simulations are once again for 62 year-old married couples who are newly retired. For comparison purposes, the simulations based on no bequest are shown again. The results are quite distressing. Spending rules of 5 percent are downright dangerous with a 31 percent failure rate. (Would you want a nearly one-third

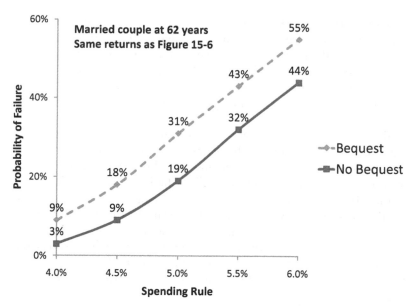

FIGURE 15.7 Effects of Bequest and Flexible Spending

chance of dropping 50 percent below your initial wealth?) Spending rules of 4.5 percent result in an 18 percent failure rate (compared with 9 percent when no bequest is made). The bottom line is that spending rates as low as 4.5 percent appear to be problematic if the retirees want to make sure that the portfolio stays at least 50 percent intact.

Do retirees have portfolios large enough to live on less than 4.5 percent of wealth? Some do, of course. But for many American families, retirement in this new age of defined contribution plans may be bleak.

HOW CAN I TURN A DEFINED CONTRIBUTION PLAN INTO A DEFINED BENEFIT PLAN?

Many retirees relying on their savings to finance a retirement envy the financial security of those with defined benefit plans. Such plans guarantee an income flow for the rest of the retiree's life. In some cases, the income flows are indexed to inflation. The great advantage of such plans is that they insure against the most important risk in retirement—longevity risk.

Retirees relying on defined contribution plans can try to create a defined benefit plan *ex post*. This income stream is obtained by investing a portion of the initial wealth in an *immediate fixed annuity*. The annuity works by pooling a large group of retirees of the same age in the same pool. Some will die early and will end up not capturing as much income as the average member of the pool. Others will die much later and will capture much more than the average member of the pool. By joining a pool of other retirees of the same age, retirees can guarantee that they never run out of money.

Why does that increase income in retirement? The reason is that the wealth invested in the annuity can be deliberately exhausted before death. It's always possible to increase the income on a bond portfolio if we are willing to use up the capital in that portfolio. The immediate fixed annuity does just that. Individual retirees cannot take the chance of using up all of their capital unless they know the date of their death in advance! But a pool of retirees can jointly use up their capital since actuaries can predict fairly accurately the longevity of a large pool of retirees. To further protect the individual retiree, an insurance company not only organizes the pool but guarantees annuity payments in the event that the actuaries underestimate annuity commitments.[7]

There is one big drawback of many annuities offered to retirees. They do not protect against inflation. For the same reason that we base spending rules on real returns so that nominal spending can rise with inflation, we should want to invest in annuities that are indexed to inflation. The income from these inflation-indexed annuities will naturally be lower than in the case of a nominal annuity. But investing in an inflation-indexed annuity will protect against two major risks in retirement—longevity risk and inflation risk. This is exactly what the current social security system does. It provides us lifetime income that is indexed to the CPI.

It's not really necessary to run new simulations to illustrate outcomes if such annuities are purchased. Consider a retiree who decides to invest a third of the portfolio in immediate annuities indexed to inflation. That annuity will provide a floor on retirement income very much like Social Security does. Given that floor, the retiree can consider simulations like those already analyzed, but where disaster leaves the retiree with some floor level of income.

CONCLUDING COMMENTS—POSTPONE RETIREMENT?

Americans are retiring in their early 60s and living long lives in retirement. Many of these Americans lack the luxury of a defined benefit plan providing them income in retirement. They might have accumulated wealth to carry them through the retirement years, but many do not understand how to invest that wealth and how to make sure that it lasts a lifetime. That's why it is so important to address the issue of spending rules in retirement.

No set of simulations can give you a spending rule that is the correct one. So let's summarize the key issues that those contemplating retirement must address. First, you need to focus on the risk that really matters in retirement, the risk of running out of money. Second, you need to base your spending rate on the returns you expect to earn on your portfolio *after inflation has been taken out*. Third, the spending rate has to be lower than the expected real, or inflation-adjusted, return because otherwise your risk of failure will be too high. Fourth, you have to recognize that we are not sure about what average real returns will be in the future, so we may have to be even more conservative than past returns would indicate.

If investors want to raise spending in retirement beyond the spending rules analyzed above, then it makes sense to annuitize some of the retirement portfolio. But there is one other suggestion that may make sense to investors—postpone retirement. The benefits of working a few more years are multiple. First, Social Security benefits increase each year that retirement is postponed. A 62 year old gains an extra 7 percent or more per year in benefits by delaying retirement until 66 (the normal retirement age for those nearing retirement). Second, the investor has a few more years to save for retirement. Third, the investor can allow the portfolio to grow further before beginning to draw it down with retirement spending. Fourth, when the investor finally does retire, annuities will provide even better returns than before. That's because the annuity tables work in favor of older investors.

With all of these reasons to postpone retirement, more Americans are deciding to work longer. In fact, the fastest growing part of the labor force is the cohort aged 65 years or older which the U.S. Department of Labor projects will grow by more than 80 percent between 2006 and 2016.[8] That percentage is applied to only 4.4 million Americans in 2006, but that's still an extra 3.5 million or so to be added to the labor force by 2016. (This projection was made before the financial crisis and the loss of more than eight million jobs. But the portfolio losses associated with this crisis have put even more pressure on those nearing retirement to work longer). As Figure 15.8 shows, the only other segment of the labor force likely to grow substantially over this 10-year period is the cohort aged 55 to 64 years of age. So much for early retirement and endless days of golf!

No spending rule and investment plan can eliminate the financial uncertainties of retirement, but sensible planning can help to stretch wealth through the retirement years. For this to happen, retirees must be much

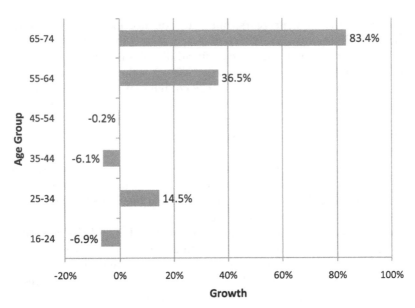

FIGURE 15.8 U.S. Labor Force by Age Percent Change from 2006 to 2016
Source: U.S. Dept. of Labor, (Toossi, 2007).

more deliberate in their financial decision-making in retirement. And that starts with sensible spending rules and investment allocations.

NOTES

1. The full retirement age for a 52 year old in 2010 is actually 66 years and 8 months. See http://ssa.gov/pubs/ageincrease.htm.
2. Each firm maintains web sites with specific allocations for a 2025 target date fund. Fidelity's web site, for example, is found at www.fidelity.com. The data was drawn from the four web sites in July 2010, so the investor at that point was about 15 years from retirement.
3. According to the U.S. Bureau of Labor Statistics, the median age of retirement for the years 1995 to 2000 was 62.0 for men and 61.4 for women (see Gendell, 2001).
4. Fourteen percent of these had both types of pensions, so 34 percent of them had only defined contribution plans. See Wiatrowski (Department of Labor, August 2004).
5. The estimates are from Financeware® based on mortality tables from the Society of Actuaries.

6. This chapter will not investigate the effects of even lower stock returns based on earnings growth rather than capital gains. Though the results that follow are depressing enough, the alternative stock return estimates considered in the last chapter would lower spending rules even further.

7. The financial crisis reminded us that annuities carry the risk of an insurance company default. So a prudent investor should try to diversify that risk by arranging annuities with several insurance firms.

8. See Toosi (Department of Labor, November 2007).

CHAPTER 16

The Discipline of Asset Allocation—Rebalancing

Investing is not easy. It takes a lot of discipline for an investor to choose an appropriate asset allocation and then stick to it. How many investors abandoned their stock allocations after the NASDAQ collapsed in 2000 or after the financial crisis drove down stocks in 2008?

Many investors believe that they can *time the market*. It's not just the aggressive investors who have an investment philosophy built around entry and exit from the market. A much larger group of investors are willing to adopt a long-run asset allocation strategy *as long as markets behave themselves*. But when the stock market swoons, as it periodically does, these investors will abandon that strategy. And having done that, it will be very difficult for them to wade back into the market. After a sharp downturn like we experienced recently, it's seldom clear when to reenter the market. And by the time the rally is in full swing, the investor has missed most of the rebound. Chapter 1 discussed investor experience during the nine recessions since 1951. On all but one occasion, the market reached bottom before the end of the recession. And in all nine recessions, the rise in the market was very rapid once it reached bottom. Few investors react quickly enough if they time the market.

Investors also abandon asset allocation in boom times. When unusual investment opportunities present themselves, as in the case of the NASDAQ bubble in the late 1990s or the real estate bubble earlier this decade, investors will often jump into the bubble blindly. If they do it soon enough, they will make some money and perhaps feel confident enough to double up again. But investors are often late to the party. In the NASDAQ boom of the late 1990s, many investors piled into tech stocks or into venture capital partnerships only after substantial gains had already been made. And in the recent real estate boom, investor enthusiasm peaked shortly before prices started to turn down.

REBALANCING DEFINED

Rebalancing is the term used to describe the periodic adjustment of a portfolio to restore a strategic asset allocation. Rebalancing sounds so sensible in theory. You rebalance in order to keep investments in line with your original allocation. In practice it is very difficult to carry out. Consider the experience of investors in 1999 as shown in Figure 16.1. In 1999 growth stocks had soared, while value stocks just lumbered on. The Russell 1000 Growth Index registered a 33.2 percent return while the Russell 2000 Growth Index gave a return 10 percent higher than its large cap counterpart. An investor who believed in asset allocation should have rebalanced away from these growth investments into the value sector even though the Russell 1000 Value Index had returned only 7.3 percent in 1999. But given the splendid performance of the growth sector, how many investors were willing to *sell their winners and buy their losers*? It takes an awful lot of discipline to rebalance when one type of investment is doing so well. Besides, the investor assured himself that *this time it is different*. The world had changed and growth stocks, tech stocks in particular, no longer had to follow ordinary rules.

Little did the investor know that the tide was about to change. In the following year, growth stocks plunged. The large-cap and small-cap growth

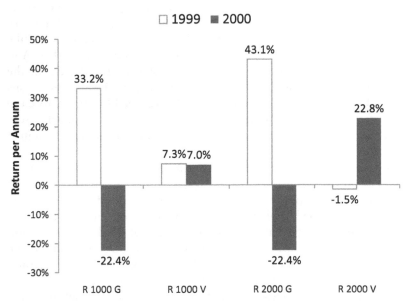

FIGURE 16.1 Russell Growth and Value Returns in 1999 and 2000
Data Source: Russell®.

indexes both lost more than 22 percent in that year. In the meantime, large-cap value earned another 7 percent return. This turnaround in fortune for growth stocks is admittedly unusual. But it should nonetheless not be surprising.

Notice how challenging it was to evaluate investment managers during this two-year period. Unless the investor used a benchmark to evaluate each manager, it would be difficult for a value manager to survive in 1999. After all, why would you keep a manager with a 7 percent return when you could shift money to a manager earning a 30 percent-plus return?

The experience of investors in 1999 and 2000 suggests how difficult it is to stick to an asset allocation in practice. The failure to do so, however, will undermine investment strategy.

REBALANCING WHEN TIMES ARE GOOD

Rebalancing is difficult when times are good or bad. Consider the experience of investors in the five-year period from October 2002 (the trough of the market) through October 2007.[1] Normally, stock markets bottom out prior to the end of a recession. But in the recession following the NASDAQ collapse, stock markets were still falling when the recession ended in November 2001. It was only in October 2002 that markets finally reached bottom.

Suppose that in October 2002, an investor chose a portfolio with 30 percent invested in bonds and 70 percent in stocks. Let's diversify the stock market investments so that we have 40 percent in U.S. stocks (represented by the Russell 3000 Index), 15 percent in the MSCI EAFE Index, 5 percent in MSCI Emerging Markets, and 10 percent in REITS. The bond investment is tracked using the Barclays Capital Aggregate Index. Figure 16.2 summarizes the allocation.

Over the next five years, stock markets boomed. EAFE rose 189.8 percent while the MSCI EM index rose 443.9 percent and the FTSE NAREIT index rose 181.3 percent. Bonds, in contrast, limped along with a 24.1 percent total return over five years. An investor who never rebalanced would find that the portfolio had drifted to a much riskier allocation. Figure 16.3 shows the drift of this portfolio. Even though the investor left the portfolio alone, the bond allocation drifts down from 30 percent in bonds to 17.2 percent by October 2007. Where did the money go? The rise in stock markets lifted the emerging market allocation from 5 percent to 12.6 percent, lifted the foreign stock allocation from 15 percent to 20.1 percent, and lifted the REIT allocation from 10 percent to 13 percent. Investors ended up with a lot more risk than they bargained for.

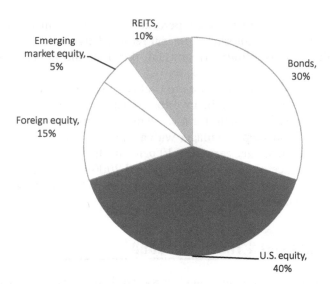

FIGURE 16.2 Diversified Portfolio in October 2002

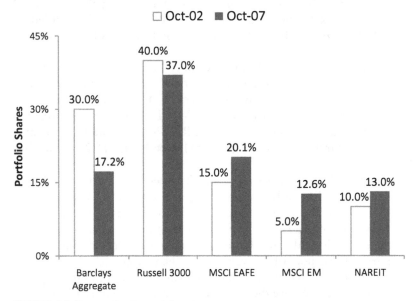

FIGURE 16.3 Drift of Portfolio Shares in Boom
Data Sources: Barclays Capital, Russell®, MSCI, and ©FTSE.

In the case of a booming market, the failure to rebalance increases the risk profile of the asset allocation unnecessarily. Some investors like to ride a good wave. That may be really enjoyable for a while.

REBALANCING WHEN TIMES ARE BAD

If it seems difficult to rebalance when markets are soaring, it is even more difficult to do so when markets are tumbling. Consider the experience of investors during the bust from October 2007 through March 2009.[2] During that period, the S&P 500 fell by almost 47 percent as did the Russell 3000. Foreign stocks fell even more, EAFE by 53.6 percent and MSCI Emerging Markets by 55.9 percent. REITS topped them all by falling 63.4 percent.

Figure 16.4 shows how these sharp losses distorted the asset allocation. The bond allocation drifted upward from 30 percent of the portfolio to 48.7 percent. The U.S. stock allocation plummeted by 8 percent, foreign stocks by 4.5 percent. REITS fell from 10 percent of the portfolio to 5.5 percent.

What should the investor have done in that bleak winter of 2008 and 2009? If the investor followed a disciplined approach to asset allocation,

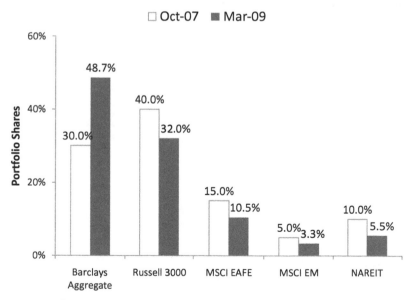

FIGURE 16.4 Drift of Portfolio Shares in Bust
Data Sources: Barclays Capital, Russell®, MSCI, and ©FTSE.

the portfolio should have been rebalanced at the trough or, perhaps more realistically, early in 2009 when annual returns were reported for 2008. But what tremendous discipline would have been required! The United States and the world as a whole had just gone through the worst financial crisis since the 1930s depression. Several major financial institutions had failed or had been saved by mergers and government bailouts. The economy was already in one of the deepest recessions since the Second World War. It takes a hardy soul to rebalance in such circumstances.

Yet consider the cost of not rebalancing. An investor who had meant to have 70 percent allocated to stocks has a little more than 50 percent in stocks as the market starts to rebound. And the shortfall is due to inaction, not to deliberate investment policy. This just illustrates how hard it is to follow a consistent asset allocation strategy. And that is why, at the end of the day, an investor has to really believe in asset allocation to match the long-term returns that have been reported in this book.

NOTES

1. The trough for the S&P 500 occurred on October 9, 2002. It reached a peak five years later on October 9, 2007.
2. The S&P 500 peaked on October 9, 2007 and reached bottom on March 9, 2009.

References

Agarwal, Vikas, Naveen D. Daniel, and Narayan Y. Naik, 2009, "Role of Managerial Incentives and Discretion in Hedge Fund Performance," *Journal of Finance* (October), 2221–2256.

Alternative Investment Management Association, 2008, *AIMA's Roadmap to Hedge Funds*, November.

Altman, Edward I., and Brenda J. Karlin, 2008, *"Defaults and Returns in the High-Yield Bond Market: the Year 2007 in Review and Outlook"*, New York University Salomon Center.

Arnott, Robert D., and Peter L. Bernstein, 2002. "What Risk Premium Is 'Normal'?", *Financial Analyst Journal* (March-April).

Banz, Rolf W., 1981, "The Relation between Return and Market Value of Common Stocks, "*Journal of Financial Economics* (March), pp. 3–18.

Basu, Sanjoy, 1977, "Investment Performance of Common Stocks in Relation to Their Price-Earnings Ratios: A Test of the Efficient Market Hypothesis," *Journal of Finance* (June), pp. 663–682.

Bernstein Wealth Management Research, 2006, *Hedge Funds: Too Much of a Good Thing?*, Bernstein Global Wealth Management (June).

Black, Fischer, and Robert Litterman, 1992, "Global Portfolio Optimization," *Financial Analysts Journal* (September-October), pp. 28–43.

Bodnar, Gordon, Bernard Dumas, and Richard Marston, 2004, "Cross-Border Valuation: The International Cost of Equity Capital," in Hubert Gatignon and John Kimberly, eds., Globalizing: Drivers, Consequences and Implications, INSEAD-Wharton Alliance.

Brown, Stephen J., William N. Goetzmann, and Bing Liang, 2004, "Fees on Fees in Funds of Funds," *Journal of Investment Management* (4th Quarter), 39–56.

Cambridge Associates, 2009, U.S. Private Equity Index® and Selected Benchmark Statistics, December 31.

Cambridge Associates, 2009, U.S. Venture Capital Index® and Selected Benchmark Statistics, December 31.

Campbell, John Y., and Tuomo Vuolteenaho, 2004, "Bad Beta, Good Beta," *American Economic Review* (December), pp. 1249–1275.

Case, Karl E., and Robert J. Shiller, 1989, "The Efficiency of the Market for Single-Family Houses," *American Economic Review* (March), 125–137.

Citigroup, 2006, "Citigroup Global Fixed-Income Index Catalog—2006 Edition, August 31.

Dimson, Elroy, Paul Marsh, and Mike Staunton, 2002. *Triumph of the Optimists: 101 Years of Global Investment Returns*, Princeton: Princeton University Press.

Fama, Eugene F., and Kenneth R. French, 1992, "The Cross-Section of Expected Stock Returns," *Journal of Finance* (June), pp. 427–465.

Fama, Eugene F., and Kenneth R. French, 2002. "The Equity Premium," *The Journal of Finance* (April), pp. 637–659.

Fama, Eugene, and Kenneth French, 1993. "Common Risk Factors in the Returns on Stocks and Bonds," *Journal of Financial Economics* (February), 3–56.

Forbes, 2009, "Did Harvard Sell at the Bottom," October 26, 2009.

Fung, K.H., and David A. Hsieh, 2006, "Hedge Funds: An Industry in Its Adolescence," *Federal Reserve Bank of Atlanta Economic Review* (Fourth Quarter), 1–33.

Gendell, Murray, 2001. "Retirement Age Declines Again in 1990s," *Monthly Labor Review* (Department of Labor), October.

Getmansky, Mila, Andrew W. Lo, and Igor Makorov, 2004, "An Econometric Model of Serial Correlation and Liquidity in Hedge Fund Returns, *Journal of Financial Economics* (December), pp. 529–609.

Getmansky, Mila, Andrew W. Lo, and Shauna X. Mei, 2004, "Sifting through the Wreckage: Lessons from Recent Hedge-Fund Liquidations," *Journal of Investment Management* (4th Quarter), 6–38.

Goetzmann, William N., and Philippe Jorion, 1999, "Re-Emerging Markets," *Journal of Financial and Quantitative Analysis* (March) pp. 1–32.

Goetzmann, William N., Andrey D. Ukhov, and Ning Zhu, 2007, "China and the World Financial Markets 1870-1939: Modern Lessons from Historical Globalization," *Economic History Review* (May), pp. 267–312.

Gorton, Gary, and K. Geert Rouwenhorst, 2006, "Facts and Fantasies about Commodity Futures," *Financial Analyst Journal* (March/April), pp. 47–68.

Greenwich Associates, 2009, Greenwich Investment Report.

Gyourko, Joseph, and Donald B. Keim, 1993, "Risk and Return in Real Estate: Evidence from a Real Estate Stock Index," *Financial Analyst Journal* (September/October), pp. 39–46.

Gyourko, Joseph, Christopher Mayer, and Todd Sinai, 2006, "Superstar Cities," working paper.

Harvard Management Company Endowment Report, 2009, "Message from the CEO", September.

He, Guangliang, and Robert Litterman, 1999, "The Intuition Behind Black-Litterman Model Portfolios," Goldman Sachs Investment Management Division.

Hennessee Group LLC, 2007, "Sources of Hedge Fund Capital," *The 2007 Manager Survey*.

Himmelberg, Charles, Christopher Mayer, and Todd Sinai, 2005, "Assessing High House Prices: Bubbles, Fundamentals and Misperceptions," *Journal of Economic Perspectives* (Fall), 67–92.

Hodge, Nicholas, 2003, "Marketing alternative investments: law and regulation in the United States," Chapter 41 in *Evaluating and Implementing Hedge Fund Strategies: The Experience of Managers and Investors*, edited by Ronald A. Lake, Euromoney Institutional Investor, 3rd edition.

Ibbotson® SBBI® 2008 Classic Yearbook, ©2008 Morningstar.

Ibbotson® SBBI® 2010 Classic Yearbook, ©2010 Morningstar.

Kaplan, Steven N., and Antoinette Schoar, 2005. "Private Equity Performance: Returns, Persistence, and Capital Flows," *Journal of Finance* (August), 1791–1823.

Keim, Donald B., 1983, "Size Related Anomalies and Stock Return Seasonality," *Journal of Financial Economics* (June), 13–22.

Keynes, John M., 1930, *A Treatise on Money*. London: Macmillan.

Kocherlakota, Narayana R., 1996, "The Equity Premium: It's Still a Puzzle," *Journal of Economic Literature* (March) pp. 42–47.

Kravis, Irving B., Z. Kenessey, Allan Heston, and Robert Summers, 1975, *A System of International Comparisons of Gross Product and Purchasing Power*. Baltimore: Johns Hopkins Press.

Lerner, Josh, 2007, "Yale University Investments Office: August 2006," *HBS Case Study 9-807-073*, revised May 8, 2007.

Lowenstein, Roger, 2000, *When Genius Failed: the Rise and Fall of Long-term Capital Management*, Random House.

Malkiel, Burton G., and Atanu Saha, 2004, "Hedge Funds: Risk and Return," *working paper*.

Malkiel, Burton G., and Atanu Saha, 2005, "Hedge Funds: Risk and Return," *Financial Analyst Journal*, (November/December), 80–88.

Markowitz, Harry, 1952, "Portfolio Selection," *Journal of Finance* (March), pp. 77–91.

Marston, Richard, 2004, "Risk-Adjusted Performance of Portfolios," *Journal of Investment Consulting*, Vol. 7, No. 1, (Summer): pp. 46–54.

Mehra, Rajnish, and Edward C. Prescott, 1985, "The Equity Premium: A Puzzle," *Journal of Monetary Economics* 15 (March): 145–161.

Merrill Lynch-Capgemini, 2008, *World Wealth Report*.

Metrick, Andrew, 2007, *Venture Capital and the Finance of Innovation*. Hoboken: John Wiley & Sons.

Metrick, Andrew, and Ayako Yasuda, 2010, "The Economics of Private Equity Funds," *Review of Financial Studies* (June), 2303–2341.

Modigliani, Franco, and Leah Modigliani, 1997, "Risk-Adjusted Performance," *Journal of Portfolio Management*, (Winter): 45–54.

MSCI/Barra, 2008, MSCI Barra Emerging Markets: A 20-Year Perspective, www.mscibarra.com/products/indices/em_20/EM_20_Anniversary.pdf.

MSCI/Barra, 2009, MSCI Market Classification Framework (June).

National Association of College and University Business Officers and Commonfund Institute, *2009 NACUBO-Commonfund Study of Endowments*.

National Association of Real Estate Investment Trusts and FTSE, 2006, "FTSE NAREIT U.S. Real Estate Index Series: Frequently Asked Questions," www.nareit.com.

National Council of Real Estate Fiduciaries, 2005, "Frequently Asked Quesitons About NCREIF and the NCREIF Property Index (NPI), www.ncreif. com.

OFHEO, 2008, "Revisiting the Differences between the OFHEO and S&P/Case-Shiller House Price Indexes," (January), www.fhfa.gov/webfiles.

Pastor, Lubos, and Robert Stambaugh, 2003. "Liquidity Risk and Expected Stock Returns," *Journal of Political Economy* (June), 642–685.

Peyton, Martha S., Thomas Park, and Fabiana Badillo, 2005, "REITS and Directly Owned Real Estate: A Perfect Pair," *TIAA-CREF Asset Management* (Summer).

PricewaterhouseCoopers/National Venture Capital Association, 2010, *MoneyTree^{TM} Report*. www.ncva.org

Reinganum, Marc R., 1981, "Misspecification of Capital Asset Pricing: Empirical Anomolies Based on Earnings Yields and Market Values," *Journal of Financial Economics* (March), pp. 19–46.

Reinganum, Marc R., 1983, "The Anomalous Stock Market Behavior of Small Firms in January: Empirical Tests for Tax-Loss Selling Effects, *Journal of Financial Economics* (June), pp. 89–104.

Rosenberg, Barr, Kenneth Reid, and Ronald Lanstein, 1985, "Persuasive Evidence of Market Inefficiency," *Journal of Portfolio Management*, 11 (3), pp. 9–16.

Sharpe, William F., 1974, "Imputing Expected Security Returns from Portfolio Composition," *Journal of Financial and Quantitative Analysis*, (June), 463–472.

Shiller, Robert J., 2000, *Irrational Exuberance*, Princeton: Princeton University Press.

Siegel, Jeremy J., 1998, *Stocks for the Long Run*, 2nd Edition. New York: McGraw Hill.

Siegel, Jeremy J., 2002, *Stocks for the Long Run*, 3rd Edition. New York: McGraw-Hill.

Solnik, Bruno, and Dennis McLeavey, 2004. *International Investments*, Boston: Pearson Addison Wesley, 5th edition.

Standard and Poor's, 2008, *S&P Global Stock Markets Factbook*.

Standard and Poor's, 2009, *S&P Global Stock Markets Factbook*.

Swankoski, Mark, 2005, "Asset Allocation: REITS—An Additional Source of Portfolio Diversification," *Smith Barney Consulting Group Research Publication* (June).

Swensen, David F., 2005, *Unconventional Success: A Fundamental Approach to Personal Investment*, New York: Free Press.

Swensen, David F., 2009, *Pioneering Portfolio Management, Second Edition: An Unconventional Approach to Institutional Investment*, New York: Free Press.

Thomas Venture Economics, 2005, *Investment Benchmarks Report: Buyouts and Other Private Equity*.

Toossi, Mitra, 2007, "Labor Force Projections to 2016: More Workers in Their Golden Years," *Monthly Labor Review* (U.S. Department of Labor), November.

Urban Land Institute and PricewaterhouseCoopers, 2010, *Emerging Trends in Real Estate, 2010.*

Wiatrowski, William J., 2004. "Medical and Retirement Plan Coverage: Exploring the Decline in Recent Years," *Monthly Labor Review* (U.S. Department of Labor), August.

Yale Endowment, 2009, *2009 The Yale Endowment.*

Index